United States Edition

20

Workbook for Lectors, Gospel Readers, and Proclaimers of the Word®

Mary A. Ehle, PHD

and Margaret Nutting Ralph, PHD

LTP
LITURGY
TRAINING
PUBLICATIONS

WORKBOOK FOR LECTORS, GOSPEL READERS, AND PROCLAIMERS OF THE WORD® 2013, United States Edition © 2012 Archdiocese of Chicago. All rights reserved.

Liturgy Training Publications, 3949 South Racine Avenue, Chicago IL 60609, 1-800-933-1800, fax 1-800-933-7094, orders@ltp.org, www.LTP.org.

As a publisher, LTP works toward responsible stewardship of the environment. We printed the text of *Workbook for Lectors, Gospel Readers, and Proclaimers of the Word*® with soy-based ink on paper that contains 50% less wood fiber than traditional paper in its category. This reduced quantity of wood pulp content benefits the environment by using fewer trees. The wood pulp that was required in the making of this paper was sourced from certified forests (managed and re-planted forests). Additionally, this paper was processed using ECF (Elementally Chlorine Free) technologies in order to reduce the release of elemental chlorine (Cl) into the environment.

The printing process used to manufacture this book uses a non-heatset process that significantly reduces emission of volatile organic compounds (VOCs) into the atmosphere.

Printed in the United States of America.

ISBN: 978-1-61671-028-6
WL13

CONTENTS

The Authors

Mary A. Ehle, PhD holds a doctorate in Religious Studies from Marquette University in Milwaukee, Wisconsin, as well as degrees from St. John's University in Collegeville, Minnesota, and St. Norbert College in De Pere, Wisconsin. She is an experienced liturgist, pastoral musician, and director of faith formation. Mary is the author of the 2009 and 2011 editions of *Workbook for Lectors, Gospel Readers, and Proclaimers of the Word*. She resides in Albuquerque, New Mexico. Mary has written the commentaries for Ordinary Time and the Christmas season.

Margaret Nutting Ralph, PhD has taught grade school, college, graduate school, and adult education througout the country. She currently directs the Master of Arts in Pastoral Studies program for Catholics at Lexington Theological Seminary. Margaret is the author of ten books on Scripture, including *And God Said What?* and the *Breaking Open the Lectionary* series published by Paulist Press. She has written the commentaries for Advent, Lent, and Easter Time.

In accordance with c. 827, permission to publish was granted on May 9, 2012, by Reverend Monsignor John F. Canary, Vicar General of the Archdiocese of Chicago. Permission to publish is an official declaration of ecclesiastical authority that the material is free from doctrinal and moral error. No legal responsibility is assumed by the grant of this permission.

INTRODUCTION

The liturgy is the public prayer of the Church. Prayer itself involves a relationship—a relationship between God and you, the person praying. In public prayer such as the liturgy, the relationship also includes members of the assembly, those present and those not present. The *Catechism of the Catholic Church* says the liturgy is "a participation in Christ's own prayer addressed to the Father in the Holy Spirit. In the liturgy, all Christian prayer finds its source and goal" (1073).

As a proclaimer of the Word, your ministry helps facilitate the public prayer of the Church in the Liturgy of the Word. This is a tremendous responsibility, but one which you need not take on by yourself. Other proclaimers of the Word, along with the ordained ministers and lay ecclesial ministers in your parish community, are present to help form you so that you will be able to carry out your ministry of proclamation and prayer. You also belong to a church community that has called you forth and recognized that you have gifts that suit you for this ministry. Through your continued participation in the Church's liturgy, your involvement in workshops for proclaimers of the Word, your own preparation, and above all, your willingness to grow in your relationship with God, you will hone your proclamation skills and gifts. And in this day and age, when people are often more comfortable interacting through e-mail or cell phones, you will make possible genuine human interaction through the sharing of God's Word as you proclaim it to the best of your ability.

The Liturgy of the Word as Prayer

The Second Vatican Council's Dogmatic Constitution on Divine Revelation, or *Dei Verbum* (DV), teaches us that the Liturgy of the Word and the Liturgy of the Eucharist are to be regarded with the same reverence: "The Church has always venerated the divine Scriptures as she venerated the Body of the Lord, in so far as she never ceases, particularly in the sacred liturgy, to partake of the bread of life and to offer it to the faithful from the one table of the Word of God and the Body of Christ" (DV, 21). In imparting the Word of the Lord to the assembly, you feed them with the Bread of Life, and provide nourishment for them to continue their life of prayer and to develop further their relationship with the Lord.

The way in which the Liturgy of the Word is celebrated can foster a deepening of peoples' relationship with God. You have an important role to play in this. But first, as a proclaimer of the Word, you yourself always need to be mindful that the Liturgy of the Word is prayer, a dialogue between God and his people. Aware of this, your presence and your proclamation of the Word will nurture the assembly's prayer. In the Introduction to the Lectionary (#28) we read of the Liturgy of the Word as meditation, a form of prayer:

> The liturgy of the word must be celebrated in a way that fosters meditation; clearly, any sort of haste that hinders recollection must be avoided. The dialogue between God and his people taking place through the Holy Spirit demands short intervals of silence, suited to the assembled congregation, as an opportunity to take the word of God to heart and to prepare a response to it in prayer.

The General Instruction of the Roman Missal (#29) also reflects on the dialogue of prayer that occurs in the Liturgy of the Word:

> When the Sacred Scriptures are read in the Church, God himself speaks to his people, and Christ, present in his own word, proclaims the Gospel.

The Holy Spirit works through the words you proclaim and in the hearts of believers who are recalling the saving works of God in history (CCC, 1103). Your presence, the variations in tone and volume you use, and the different paces and rhythms you employ, all serve to provide room for the Spirit to work in people's hearts, leading them to prayer.

In the beginning was the Word, and the Word was with God, and the Word was God.

Depending on the time in the liturgical year, the events of a person's life, and world events, this prayer might be one of praise, thanksgiving, desire, forgiveness, pleading, or joyful expectation. Your aim is to support that prayer of the assembly and not to distract from it by drawing attention to yourself. You do not want to place any barriers between the assembly and the Holy Spirit, who is making present God's marvelous deeds through your proclamation.

You have been called forth to serve as a proclaimer of God's Word. The Council Fathers said that those who serve in the ministry of the Word should immerse themselves in the Scriptures through study and reflection, and during the proclamation at liturgy, and they also remind us that "prayer should accompany the reading of sacred Scripture, so that a dialogue takes place between God and man" (DV, 25). Your communication of God's Word during the public prayer of the Church is proclamation. Yet it is also proclamation in the context of prayer. This sometimes is forgotten. One way to be attentive to your proclamation as prayer is to center your preparation on prayer—on your conversation with God.

Preparation as Prayer

Saint Augustine in one of his sermons spoke of the necessity of coming to the ministry of the Word from one's personal prayer. Although he was referring to clergy, his thought applies today to all who proclaim the Word of God. He asserted that one is "an empty preacher of the Word of God to others, not being a hearer of the Word in his own heart" (*Sermon*, 179). In other words, you have to listen to God through the prayer of your heart if you want to be a sincere and truthful proclaimer of the Word. You might want to ask yourself, "How can I be more attentive to the Word of God in my own heart so I can communicate the Word to the assembly gathered before me to pray?"

Spiritual preparation as a proclaimer of the Word is essential. Because of the weightiness of the ministry you perform, the preparation required is twofold: spiritual and technical. The Introduction to the Lectionary describes the lector's preparation as "above all" spiritual. This spiritual preparation "presupposes at least a biblical and liturgical formation." According to paragraph 55 of the Introduction,

> The biblical formation is to give readers the ability to understand the readings in context

God so loved the world that he gave his only Son, so that everyone who believes in him might not perish but might have eternal life.

and to perceive by the light of faith the central point of the revealed message. The liturgical formation ought to equip the readers to have some grasp of the meaning and structure of the liturgy of the word and of the significance of its connection with the liturgy of the Eucharist.

If you are an experienced proclaimer of the Word, you might have already developed a method of spiritual preparation that works well for you. Newcomers to the ministry might want to experiment with different methods of preparation. Whatever the method you choose, it is important to have a regular method of spiritual preparation. Center this preparation on prayer. Converse with God about how best you can be the conduit in proclaiming his presence to the assembly. Some parishes provide opportunities for their ministers of the Word, or all their liturgical ministers for a given Sunday, to come together during the week prior to the Sunday to pray and reflect on the Scripture readings for the Sunday on which they will be serving. If group preparation is not feasible, you might prepare by praying with reflection questions based on the readings. Very often, parishes print reflection questions for the next week in the current week's bulletin or publish them on the parish website. If you don't know where to find reflection questions on the readings, you might ask a member of the parish staff.

The preparation you as a proclaimer of the Word need to do before a liturgical celebration is more involved than the preparation of your other liturgical minister colleagues. While it would be good for all liturgical ministers to prepare spiritually for the liturgy at which they will serve, your spiritual preparation goes beyond simple reflection on the readings. As the last quote from the Introduction to the Lectionary mentioned, spiritual preparation also involves biblical and liturgical formation. The biblical preparation entails developing an understanding of the readings in their context. For this, some tools of the lector's ministry are essential. Try preparing with the Bible and *Workbook* by your side. With the Bible you will be able to read the readings in the context of the entire chapter or book in which they are contained. Sometimes the introductions at the beginning of each book of the Bible provide beneficial information. Frequently, the footnotes are useful in developing a better understanding of the meaning of a passage.

The commentaries located beneath the Scripture readings in *Workbook* aid in both your biblical and liturgical formation. They provide historical and critical background to assist you in understanding the reading in its original context. They also draw connections between the readings and the time in the liturgical year, so that as a proclaimer of the Word, you are better able to appreciate why particular readings are proclaimed on the days they are. Furthermore, the commentaries offer pastoral suggestions for helping you make connections between the reading and our world and Church today. By understanding the original intention of the author in writing the inspired words of Scripture and by relating them to the contemporary context, you will communicate God's presence in the Word to the assembly. Your ministry will then effectively deepen your own prayer and that of those present in your community.

One way of looking at the goal of the spiritual preparation of the proclaimer of the Word is in relation to the early church fathers and mothers of the desert. These men and women of prayer were so devoted to cultivating their relationship with God through the Scriptures that they simply wanted to "become

This is my commandment: love one another as I love you.

prayer."[1] They wanted their entire life—their presence and their actions to show forth the presence of God. But, what does this mean for a minister of the Word to "become prayer" in the twenty-first century? First, it entails openness to the Spirit of the Lord working in your own life. In your preparation time, as well as in the ordinary events of your life, cultivate an awareness of the presence of God in yourself and in others you meet. The direction with which you live your life is both inward and outward toward God—open to the Spirit of God within you and in others. Second, immerse yourself in the practice of your faith. Participate consistently in the Sunday Eucharistic liturgy of the Church. Pray as a conversation with God, but also with the traditional prayers of the Church. Third, let the Scriptures be your guide in talking with God. God never stops inviting us to closer union with him through his Word.

As you prepare the readings, perhaps you will want to start out several days before the Sunday you are scheduled to proclaim the Word simply by reading over the passages, and getting a sense of their themes or main points. As you go through your life during the week, perhaps there is a phrase that you will want to remember and draw on. Let this phrase be your prayer every time it comes to mind. Use it as the direction for living your life during the week—at home, at work, in the community, and in the parish. The Word of God is living and active—it's not meant to remain on the written page.

If proclaimers truly work at "becoming prayer," they will always be welcoming and generous—to their fellow ministers, to those seeking to enter the ministry, and to the entire parish. In a way, every liturgical minister is a minister of hospitality. Ministers of the

Word must be willing to greet those they meet before and after the liturgy, welcoming those they know, and reaching out to those who are newcomers or who clearly need their assistance. Consonance between the Word of God proclaimed and the Word of God lived out is, in the end, what it means to "become prayer."

When we are able to witness to the Word of God in our words and actions, we are closer to "becoming prayer" in our day and age. Then, your proclamation of the Word of God in the context of the Church's public prayer, the liturgy, will be a proclamation filled with integrity. The assembly gathered to worship with you will sense the genuineness of your proclamation. They will know you have prepared both spiritually and technically.

Prayerfulness and Practical Matters

The spirit of prayerfulness in the Liturgy of the Word is reflected both in the way ministers of the Word present themselves and in the manner in which they proclaim the Word of God. There are many practical matters in relation to the minister of the Word that affect the celebration of the Liturgy of the Word. Even for the seasoned proclaimer, a reminder every so often about some of these matters is helpful. As you read through these comments, be aware that some details are specific to the parish in which you serve, particularly matters concerning the sound system and microphones. In order to address issues such as these, many parishes already have implemented yearly or semi-annual formational gatherings with all the ministers of the Word.

When you are scheduled to be a minister of the Word, make sure to arrive at least twenty minutes before the liturgy is scheduled to begin. You do not want to be rushing out the door and arriving at the church at the last minute. This creates unnecessary anxiety both for you, and for those who are expecting you to be present. You do not want to leave anyone wondering whether or not you are coming. Arriving early also provides you with time to check the Lectionary, making sure your reading is marked correctly so that you do not spend time needlessly flipping pages trying to locate the reading after you approach the ambo. Before the liturgy begins, you will also want to find out if there are any additional rites taking place during the Mass that would affect the time when you need to approach the ambo, for

example, dismissal for Children's Liturgy of the Word, Rite of Acceptance, Baptism, and so forth. Being aware of such changes will help you do your part to maintain the flow of the liturgy and leave no one waiting for you to move into place.

Some ministers of the Word will want to sit in silence and prayer either in the sacristy or in the church before the celebration of the liturgy begins. Others will want to greet members of the assembly or welcome other liturgical ministers. For some, this interaction with the community enables them to sense the presence of God and to remember that the faith we profess and the God we worship in the liturgy is present among us, in each other. Find a method of immediate preparation that works best for you and which lets you center yourself in God before the liturgy. No matter the method of immediate preparation you choose, you will want to be focused as the liturgy begins.

Your posture, both when you are proclaiming the Word of God and during the rest of the liturgy when you are not carrying out your specific ministry, is very important. As you approach the ambo, make sure you are standing tall and erect. You want to exude confidence, but not arrogance. The manner in which you comport yourself lets the assembly know you have something important to tell them. When you are seated in the assembly or the sanctuary area, sit upright, actively listening and responding, involving yourself in the prayer of the liturgy.

As a minister of the Word, you are also a role model for the rest of the community. People will recognize you before, during, and after the liturgy. How you present yourself at times other than when you are proclaiming the Word is as important as how you appear in front of the assembly when it is your turn to perform your ministry. So sing, pray, and listen attentively throughout the liturgy as part of the

Magnify the LORD with me; let us exalt his name together.

Blessed are the poor in spirit, for theirs is the kingdom of heaven.

assembly. Through your Baptism you are first a part of the assembly; then, you are called forth from the assembly because you have a specific gift the Church recognizes and you are willing to share. But you always remain part of the assembly. Anything that would set you apart as "better than" others or not in unity with those in the assembly will detract from your ministry. Conversely, your full, conscious, and active participation will help lead others to do the same. So, even though your gift might be in public speaking and not public singing, still participate in the sung prayer of the community!

After you arrive at the ambo, take a brief moment to focus yourself. Many ministers of the Word are nervous when they read. This energy, when channeled correctly, can help convey the message of the reading. One way that works for some proclaimers of the Word is to discreetly take a deep breath after arriving at the ambo. While taking that breath, you might want to say a short prayer offering your proclamation of the reading to God. Doing so reminds you that the reading is not about you, but about God. When you are focused, begin with the announcement of the reading in a confident, strong tone of voice. Both the announcement before and the acclamation after the reading are important liturgically, so deliver them with care. Make eye contact with the assembly and speak in a strong, deliberate way to engage your listeners.

If you make a mistake during the proclamation, keep your composure. You do not want to look frustrated, laugh, or draw attention to yourself and the mistake. Depending on the mistake, you might want to return to the beginning of the sentence. The assembly's comprehension of the reading will be aided with this method. If you clearly mispronounce or stumble over a word, simply restate it and proceed. Do not attempt to work out the correct pronunciation by saying it over and over again. This makes it obvious to everyone that you have not prepared. More than that, however, it results in a lack of reverence for the Word and disrupts people's train of thought as they attempt to understand the meaning of the reading. Because we are human beings, we all make mistakes. Your ability to maintain your composure in itself reverences the Word of God.

Our natural human anxiety causes us to read faster when we are in front of people. Indeed, most ministers of the Word tend to speak too fast; some even race, wanting to finish the reading quickly. Many whose pace is rapid are not even aware that this is the case. A good reminder for most proclaimers, then, is slow down, slow down, slow down. A slower pace will help the assembly to understand the meaning of the reading. In a culture that has so much visual stimulation, we are becoming less proficient at processing auditory information. This challenges you to always be aware of your pace, to take your time communicating the Word to the assembly.

Your appearance also reflects the reverence you have for the Word of God and for God's presence in the Eucharist and the assembly. Although different parishes have different guidelines for dress, your appearance needs to speak of the importance of the liturgy itself and your particular ministry. Choose attire that is neither flashy nor shabby so as not to make yourself the center of attention. In addition, choose attire that is practical—especially shoes. It is not wise to carry out your ministry in big winter boots or shoes with high or noisy heels. People in the assembly will be looking at what you are wearing, rather than listening to what you are proclaiming. Take a quick look in the mirror before the liturgy to correct anything that is amiss. This is particularly important for those ministers of the Word who serve at the very early morning Masses and sometimes have to trudge through inclement weather to do so, as well as for those who are called on to proclaim at the last minute!

In addition to its role in spiritual formation—liturgical and biblical formation, *Workbook* is also meant to assist you in the correct and expressive delivery of the reading. The bolded text of the readings suggests words to emphasize, although all need not be given the same degree of emphasis. The margin notes on the left side of the readings provide pronunciations for difficult or uncommon words and names, explanations of certain words or phrases from the reading, and suggestions for how to proclaim the reading (such as when to take pauses and what tone of voice to use). Use *Workbook* as a guide, not as a

The LORD's word is true; all his works are trustworthy.

manual with definitive pronouncements on how to proclaim the readings. Your own technical preparation and the feedback you receive from the assembly and parish staff can also assist you in becoming a better minister of the Word.

Once you have addressed the practical matters, you can concentrate on praying with the community. You will be able to remember that your proclamation of the Word is part of the Church's liturgy. It deepens your relationship with God and moves those in the assembly to grow in theirs as well. Through your ministry, then, you will offer praise to God and draw others to that same praise in the liturgy and in the ordinary events of their lives. You will have helped to lead the assembly to the full, active, and conscious participation the Church desires. You and the assembly will have "become prayer" and God will have been glorified because of the ministry you do.

Prepared to Proclaim

As the liturgy approaches, ask yourself, "Am I prepared to proclaim the Word well?" Think about the following questions: Do I understand the main points in the reading? How would I express the meaning of the passage in my own words? How do I understand the relationship between this reading and the season of the liturgical year, the feast, or solemnity on which it will be proclaimed? Am I able to pronounce all the words

in the reading without hesitating? Can I articulate the difficult words clearly and with confidence? If I were to proclaim the reading to others, would they be able to tell me the message of the reading? Would they have difficulty understanding any section of the reading? What are one or two ways I could live the message of the Scriptures in my own life this week? What will be my prayer to God as I approach the ambo to carry out the ministry of the Word?

Perhaps time got away from you this week, and you didn't prepare as thoroughly as you would have liked. If this is the case, resolve to plan more time to prepare the next time you are scheduled. In fact, consider setting aside some regular time each week, whether or not you are scheduled, to prepare "as if" you were the scheduled proclaimer. This is one of the best ways to grow in your skills, confidence, and spirituality—and to be sure that you are well prepared to listen or to proclaim at Sunday's liturgy.

For now, as the liturgy approaches, offer a prayer to God expressing that you will do the best you can in your ministry. Draw on your experience from the other occasions on which you have proclaimed the Word to give yourself confidence. Communicate calm to the assembly as you undertake your ministry.

Proclaiming the reading well is very important, but sometimes, in spite of the best intentions, mistakes are made and preparation is lacking. Yet all is not lost. The presence of God is still ours to communicate, in word and in the dignity with which we carry out our ministry.

After the liturgy, evaluate your own proclamation and solicit feedback from a few people whose opinion you trust. Ask questions such as: What is your initial reaction to my proclamation of the Word? How was my pacing, the volume, and so on? Did I emphasize words appropriately and in a way that helped communicate the meaning of the passage? Did my enunciation help express the meaning of the reading? Was my body language reverent? Did I in any way distract from the reading? Express your gratitude for any feedback, positive or negative, that you receive. Assure yourself and others that you are always working to improve your proclamation skills, to better understand the reading you proclaim, and to help others in the assembly do the same. Go forth from the liturgy knowing that you are a child of God, created in his image and likeness. You have offered yourself as prayer to your parish community and you go into the world to do the same.

A New Opportunity

The third edition of *The Roman Missal* encourages ministers of the Word to chant the introduction and conclusion to the readings ("A reading from . . . "; "The word of the Lord."). For those parishes wishing to use these chants, they are demonstrated in audio files that may be accessed either through the QR codes given here (with a smart phone) or through the URL indicated beneath the code. (This URL is case sensitive, and be careful to distinguish between the letter l (lower case L) and the numeral 1.)

The first QR code contains the tones for the First Reading in both a male and a female voice.

http://bit.ly/l2mjeG

The second QR code contains the tones for the Second Reading in both a male and a female voice.

http://bit.ly/krwEYy

The third QR code contains the simple tone for the Gospel.

http://bit.ly/iZZvSg

The fourth QR code contains the solemn tone for the Gospel.

http://bit.ly/lwf6Hh

A fuller explanation of this new practice, along with musical notation for the chants, is provided in a downloadable PDF file found at http://www.ltp.org/ t-productsupplements.aspx. Once you arrive at this webpage, scroll until you find the image of the cover of *Workbook*, click on it, and the PDF file will appear.

Pronunciation Key

bait = bayt	thin = thin
cat = kat	vision = VIZH*n
sang = sang	ship = ship
father = FAH-ther	sir = ser
care = kair	gloat = gloht
paw = paw	cot = kot
jar = jahr	noise = noyz
easy = EE-zee	poison = POY-z*n
her =her	plow = plow
let = let	although = ahl-THOH
queen = kween	church = cherch
delude = deh-LOOD	fun = fun
when = hwen	fur = fer
ice = īs	flute = floot
if = if	foot = foot
finesse = fih-NES	

Recommended Works

Find this list of recommended reading in a downloadable PDF file at http://www.ltp.org/t-productsupplements.aspx.

Notes

1. *The Roots of Christian Mysticism: Texts from the Patristic Era with Commentary*. Translated by Theodore Berkeley, ocso, and Jeremy Hummerston. Hyde Park, New York: New City Press, 1993.

1st SUNDAY OF ADVENT

Lectionary #3

READING I   Jeremiah 33:14–16

Jeremiah = jayr-uh-MĪ-uh

ABegin with a tone of excitement, but drop your voice for "says the LORD."

Emphasize "promise." Jeremiah is referring to God's covenant promises to the Israelites.

Israel = IZ-ree-uhl; IZ-ray-uhl

Judah = JOO-duh

A reading from the Book of the Prophet Jeremiah

The days are **coming**, says the LORD,
    when I will fulfill the **promise**
    I made to the house of **Israel** and **Judah**.
In **those days**, in **that time**,
    I will **raise up** for **David** a **just shoot**;
    he shall do what is **right** and **just** in the land.
In **those days Judah** shall be **safe**
    and **Jerusalem** shall dwell **secure**;
    this is what they shall **call** her:
    "The LORD our justice."

READING I   Jeremiah was a prophet in the southern kingdom, Judah, from 627–587 BC, a terribly turbulent time in the life of the Israelites. The northern kingdom had already been conquered by the Assyrians, and now the Babylonians were threatening the southern kingdom. The words we read today are words of hope that Jeremiah offered his fellow Israelites when everything that they held dear seemed to be falling apart.

The Israelites understood that God had made promises to their ancestors, covenant promises that God would protect them and their nation. God, through the prophet Nathan, had promised their ancestor, King David, that his nation would be secure forever (see 2 Samuel 7). Their present king, Zedekiah, was not faithful to covenant love. He relied on political alliances with the Babylonians, not on fidelity to God, for his safety. Now the nation, Judah, was at risk.

When Jeremiah says that God will raise up a "just shoot" for David, he is contrasting a future good king with the present unfaithful king. But even if the present king is not faithful to covenant love, God is and will be faithful. Jeremiah assures the beleaguered Israelites that this future king will act justly. When that day comes, Judah and her capital city, Jerusalem, will be safe.

We read Jeremiah's prophecy about the fulfillment of God's promise on the first Sunday of Advent because there, in Jeremiah's words, a foreshadowing of the coming of the truly just king, Jesus Christ. As you proclaim the reading, speak with confidence and hope. God will keep this promise.

Thessalonians = thes-uh-LOH-nee-uhnz

Paul is encouraging the Thessalonians.

Say this with excitement. This is the basis for their hope. Emphasize "with all his holy ones." ("with all his saints"). Now, drop your voice. Paul is exhorting, not blaming.

Say this with certainty.

READING II   1 Thessalonians 3:12—4:2

A reading from the first Letter of Saint Paul to the Thessalonians

Brothers and sisters:
May the Lord make you **increase** and **abound** in **love**
    for one **another and** for **all**,
    just as **we** have for **you**,
    so as to **strengthen** your **hearts**,
    to be **blameless** in **holiness** before our **God** and **Father**
    at the coming of our **Lord Jesus** with **all** his **holy** ones. Amen.

Finally, brothers and sisters,
    we earnestly **ask** and **exhort** you in the **Lord Jesus** that,
    as you received from **us**
    how you should **conduct** yourselves to **please God**
    —and as you **are** conducting yourselves—
    you do so **even more**.
For you **know** what **instructions** we **gave** you
        through the **Lord Jesus**.

READING II   Just as Jeremiah was offering hope to the Israelites during difficult times, so is Paul offering hope to the Thessalonians. Paul wants to "strengthen" the Thessalonians' hearts. Why do their hearts need strengthening?

Paul is writing to the Thessalonians about AD 51 after Paul has been to Thessalonica and taught them about Jesus Christ (see Acts 17:19). The Thessalonians are now expectantly waiting for the second coming. However, some in their number have died. The Thessalonians want to

know if those who have died have missed out on rising with Jesus or not. Paul assures them that they have not (1 Thessalonians 4:13–18). Paul teaches this same welcome news in today's reading when he refers to the coming of our Lord "with all his holy ones." The Thessalonians should have no fear about their dearly departed. Their loved ones will rise with Christ

Paul encourages the Thessalonians, as they continue to wait for the Lord's coming, to persevere in living so as to please God. Paul reminds them that he has already

taught them how to do this: they are to continue to grow in love for one another and for all. The tone of the reading is one of both reassurance and confidence. The Thessalonians "know" what Paul has taught them about Jesus Christ.

GOSPEL   In today's reading, Jesus is describing the coming of the "Son of Man . . . with power and great glory" who will redeem the disciples at a time when they are being persecuted.

GOSPEL° Luke 21:25–28, 34–36

A reading from the holy Gospel according to Luke

As you begin, speak in a soft voice. While this is frightening news for some, it is not meant to be frightening to the disciples.

Jesus said to his disciples:
"There will be **signs** in the **sun**, the **moon**, and the **stars**,
 and on **earth nations** will be in **dismay**,
 perplexed by the **roaring** of the sea and the waves.
People will **die** of **fright**
 in **anticipation** of what is **coming** upon the **world**,
 for the **powers** of the **heavens** will be **shaken**.

Say this with awe.

And then they will see the **Son of Man**
 coming in a **cloud** with **power** and **great glory**.

Speak firmly and confidently. This is good news.

But when these signs **begin** to happen,
 stand erect and **raise** your heads
 because your **redemption** is at **hand**.

There is a tone of warning here.

"**Beware** that your **hearts** do not become **drowsy**
 from **carousing** and **drunkenness**
 and the **anxieties** of daily life,
 and that day catch you by **surprise** like a **trap**.
For that day will assault **everyone**
 who lives on the face of the earth.

Increase your volume slightly and end with a tone of authority.

Be **vigilant** at **all** times
 and **pray** that you have the **strength**
 to **escape** the tribulations that are **imminent**
 and to **stand** before the **Son of Man**."

imminent = IM-ih-nuhnt

When he speaks of the "Son of Man," Jesus is using an image from the Book of Daniel (see Daniel 7:13–14). The Book of Daniel is an example of a kind of writing called apocalyptic literature. Apocalyptic literature was written to people who were suffering persecution; it offered them hope. In Daniel, the Son of Man is a messianic figure who receives authority from God over other nations. In today's reading we hear Jesus apply this messianic title to himself.

 This passage from Luke is part of a larger conversation. After Jesus warns his disciples that persecution lay in their

future, they ask him when this will happen and what will be the signs (see Luke 21:7). Jesus uses the cosmic imagery common in apocalyptic literature, imagery involving the sun, moon, and stars, to describe the cataclysmic, earth-shaking events. When the disciples witness all this they are not to lose hope; rather, they are to "stand erect and raise [their] heads" because they know that "redemption is at hand."

 By the time Luke is writing (around AD 85), persecution has happened and the Temple has been destroyed (AD 70). However, the expected second coming of

the Son of Man on the clouds of heaven has not yet taken place. Because no one knows exactly when the Son of Man will come, Jesus' disciples should be ready always. We read this passage during Advent because we, too, are preparing for the coming of the Son of Man—his first and his second coming. As you proclaim the reading, make eye contact with those who are listening to you. The Church is reminding all of us that we, too, are to be ready always.

THE IMMACULATE CONCEPTION

Lectionary #689

READING I   Genesis 3:9–15, 20

Genesis = JEN-uh-sis

The narrator's voice is simply setting the stage.

God doesn't yet know that anything is wrong.

The man, as he says, is afraid and hiding.
God is, at first, puzzled.
Now God begins to understand the awful truth.

The man is blaming.
God is gentle and inquiring.

The woman, too, is blaming.

A reading from the Book of Genesis

After the **man**, **Adam**, had **eaten** of the **tree**,
    the LORD God **called** to the man and **asked** him,
        "**Where are you**?"
He answered, "I **heard** you in the garden;
    but I was **afraid**, because I was **naked**,
    so I **hid** myself."
Then he asked, "**Who told you** that you were naked?
You have **eaten**, then,
    from the **tree** of which I had **forbidden** you to eat!"
The man replied, "The **woman** whom you put here with me—
    she gave **me** fruit from the tree, and so **I ate it**."
The LORD God then asked the woman,
    "**Why** did you **do such** a **thing**?"
The woman answered, "The **serpent tricked me** into it,
    so I **ate** it."

Then the LORD **God** said to the **serpent**:
    "**Because you have done this**, **you** shall be **banned**
        from **all** the **animals**
        and from **all** the **wild creatures**;
    on your **belly** shall you **crawl**,
        and **dirt** shall you **eat**
        all the days of your **life**.

READING I In the First Reading we enter this well-known story of the man and woman in the garden after they have disobeyed God's instructions and eaten fruit from the tree of knowledge of good and evil (see Genesis 2:4—3:24). Notice that the author does not picture God as all-knowing. God is portrayed anthropomorphically; that is, like a human being. This God walks and talks in the garden (see Genesis 3:8). This God comes for his usual evening walk and talk without realizing anything is wrong. That is where we enter into the story.

When God arrives in the garden, Adam is hiding. This takes God completely by surprise. God asks, "Where are you?" When Adam says he is hiding, God asks why. Adam explains that he is hiding because he is naked. This is a very strange answer because Adam has always been naked, and he has never hidden before. God realizes that Adam is ashamed of himself, and that he must have eaten from the forbidden tree.

Adam, in Hebrew, is a collective neuter noun, not a masculine singular noun. Adam stands for each of us. Adam's attempt

to hide his nakedness is a symbol for the shame each of us feels when we sin. The story of Adam and Eve is teaching a profound truth through symbols: that sin causes suffering because it changes who we are and makes us less able to respond in love to God, to others, and even to ourselves.

In today's reading, Adam has already responded less lovingly to God and himself. Because of his shame, he has hidden rather than gone out to meet God. Next, Adam responds less lovingly to Eve: instead of taking responsibility for his own actions, he blames her. Eve does the same: instead

I will put **enmity** between **you** and the **woman**,
　　and between **your offspring** and **hers**;
he will **strike** at **your** head,
　　while **you strike** at **his** heel."

The man called his wife **Eve**,
　　because she became the **mother** of **all** the **living**.

Here God is firm and compassionate. God is explaining the ramifications of what the serpent has done.
The narrator concludes the story.

READING II　Ephesians 1:3–6, 11–12

A reading from the Letter of Saint Paul to the Ephesians

Brothers and sisters:
Blessed be the **God** and **Father** of our **Lord Jesus Christ**,
　　who has **blessed** us in **Christ**
　　with **every spiritual blessing** in the heavens,
　　as he **chose** us **in him**, **before** the **foundation** of the **world**,
　　to be **holy** and **without blemish** before him.
In **love** he **destined us** for **adoption** to himself
　　　　through Jesus **Christ**,
　　in accord with the **favor** of his **will**,
　　for the **praise** of the **glory** of his **grace**
　　that he **granted us** in the **beloved**.

In him we were **also chosen**,
　　destined in accord with the purpose of the One
　　who accomplishes **all things** according to the **intention**
　　　　of his **will**,
　　so that we might exist for the **praise** of **his glory**,
　　we who **first hoped** in **Christ**.

Ephesians = ee-FEE-zhuhnz

This is said with great gratitude.

Read slowly, with pauses.

Increase your volume as you proclaim this line.

Now back to an explanatory tone.

Again, emphasize "praise of his glory" by increasing your volume.

---

of taking responsibility for her actions, she blames the serpent. All the loving relationships that allowed the man and woman to live in the garden without suffering are now destroyed. Sin causes suffering.

God then explains the suffering caused by sin to the man, the woman, and the serpent. Today's reading includes only the explanation to the serpent. The serpent is told that God "will put enmity between you and the woman,/ and between your offspring and hers;/ he will strike at your head,/ while you strike at his heel." It is because of this passage that we read this

story on the Solemnity of the Immaculate Conception.

On this solemnity, we celebrate the truth that Mary was conceived without original sin. The story of Adam and Eve is a story about the suffering that sin causes. The serpent, who represents evil, is told that there will be enmity between the serpent and the woman. After Mary became the Mother of Jesus Christ, she was understood to be the woman with whom the serpent has enmity. That is why Mary is so often pictured standing on a snake. Mary

is the Church's new Eve, the woman who, unlike Eve, was without sin.

When you proclaim this story, try to identify with each character: First, God is puzzled. Adam is ashamed and then blaming. Eve is blaming, too. Finally God is explaining consequences. Try to make the drama come alive for the listeners.

READING II　When we think of someone chosen "before the foundation of the world,/ to be holy and without blemish," we probably think of Mary, not ourselves. However, in today's Second

The narrator's voice sets the stage.
Gabriel = GAY-bree-uhl
Galilee= GAL-ih-lee
Nazareth = NAZ-uh-reth

The angel speaks with authority, but gently.

The angel is both calming and encouraging Mary.

Here increase your volume for a proclamation.

Mary is truly puzzled.

GOSPEL   Luke 1:26–38

A reading from the holy Gospel according to Luke

The angel **Gabriel** was sent from **God**
 to a town of **Galilee** called **Nazareth**,
 to a **virgin** betrothed to a man named **Joseph**,
 of the house of **David**,
 and the virgin's **name** was **Mary**.
And coming to her, he said,
 "**Hail**, **full of grace**! The **Lord** is **with you**."
But she was greatly **troubled** at what was said
 and **pondered** what sort of **greeting** this might be.
Then the angel **said** to her,
 "Do **not** be **afraid**, Mary,
 for **you** have found **favor** with **God**.
Behold, you will **conceive in your womb** and **bear a son**,
 and you shall **name** him **Jesus**.
He will be **great** and will be called **Son of the Most High**,
 and the **Lord God** will give him the throne of **David** his **father**,
 and he will **rule** over the house of **Jacob forever**,
 and of his **Kingdom** there will **be no end**."
But **Mary** said to the angel,
 "**How can this be**,
 since I have **no relations** with a **man**?"

Reading, Paul is telling the Ephesians and us that we, too, have been chosen. We, too, have been blessed in Christ with "every spiritual blessing." We have not been chosen because we earned it; rather, we have been chosen because God loves us. We are adopted through Jesus Christ to be God's own sons and daughters. We now "exist for the praise of his glory." God's saving power is evident not only in Mary, but in us. As you proclaim this reading, try to fill your voice with joy, with awe, and with gratitude. To God be the glory!

GOSPEL   If we did not have the Gospel according to Luke we would never have heard the story of the Annunciation to Mary. We would never have heard Mary's response to the angel's announcement. Because we have Luke's account of the Gospel we, the Church, know Mary as our model for discipleship.

As Luke begins the story he stresses Mary's virginity by mentioning it twice in the introduction. Gabriel is sent to a "virgin betrothed to a man named Joseph," and "the virgin's name was Mary."

Gabriel greets this holy young woman with the words: "Hail, full of grace! The Lord is with you." These words embody the belief we celebrate today under the title, the Immaculate Conception. The angel's words to Mary, that she is full of grace, did not become true at the moment the angel spoke them; they had always been true. Mary, from the moment of her conception, was full of grace.

Mary is very puzzled by the angel's words because she has had "no relations with a man." The angel explains that this

Again, the angel is calming but speaks with authority.

And the angel said to her in **reply**,
    "The **Holy Spirit** will come **upon you**,
        and the **power** of the **Most High** will **overshadow you**.
Therefore the **child** to be **born**
    will be called **holy**, the **Son of God**.
And **behold**, **Elizabeth**, your relative,
    has **also conceived** a **son** in her **old age**,
        and this is the **sixth month** for her who was called **barren**;
    for **nothing** will be **impossible** for God."

Read Mary's response slowly and emphasize each word.

The narrator makes a concluding remark.

Mary said, "Behold, **I am the handmaid of the Lord**.
May it be done to **me** according to **your** word."
Then the angel departed from her.

child will be conceived through the Holy Spirit. Mary accepts the angel's words and responds with a wholehearted yes: "Behold I am the handmaid of the Lord. May it be done to me according to your word." It is this yes, often called Mary's *fiat* (Latin for "let it be done") that makes her a model disciple.

While Luke brings Mary on stage and lets us meet her, the story of the Annunciation is primarily a Christological story that teaches the divinity of Jesus

Christ. Mary's child will be named Jesus, which means "savior." He will be called "Son of the Most High," and he will have an everlasting kingdom. The child will be "holy" and will also be called "Son of God." Stories like the Annunciation teach what was understood about Jesus after the Resurrection: Jesus is divine.

Mary also learns that her cousin, Elizabeth, has conceived a child after years of being barren. In every gospel account, Elizabeth's son, John the Baptist, announces the coming of Jesus. However,

only in Luke does John do so while still in the womb (see Luke 1:41).

When proclaiming this Gospel, read the words of Mary's fiat slowly and with perfect trust. On the Solemnity of the Immaculate Conception, when we focus on Mary's holiness and our call to holiness, we want Mary's words to be our words, too: "May it be done to [us] according to your word."

2ND SUNDAY OF ADVENT

Lectionary #6

READING I   Baruch 5:1–9

A reading from the Book of the Prophet Baruch

> **Jerusalem, take off** your robe of **mourning** and **misery**;
>   **put on** the **splendor** of **glory** from **God forever**:
> **Wrapped** in the cloak of **justice** from God,
>   **bear** on your head the **mitre**
>   that **displays** the **glory** of the **eternal name**.
> For God will show **all the earth** your **splendor**:
>   **you** will be **named** by **God forever**
>   the **peace** of **justice**, the **glory** of God's **worship**.
>
> **Up, Jerusalem! stand** upon the **heights**;
>   **look** to the **east** and **see** your **children**
> gathered from the **east** and the **west**
>   at the **word** of the **Holy One**,
>   **rejoicing** that **they** are **remembered by God**.
> Led away on **foot** by their **enemies** they **left** you:
>   but **God** will bring them **back** to you
>   borne **aloft** in **glory** as on **royal thrones**.
> For God has **commanded**
>   that **every lofty mountain** be made **low**,
> and that the **age-old depths** and **gorges**
>   be **filled** to **level ground**,
>   that **Israel** may advance **secure** in the **glory** of **God**.

Baruch = buh-ROOK

The prophet is crying out to the people. Proclaim the first two lines in a loud voice.

Jerusalem = juh-ROO-suh-lem; juh-ROO-zuh-lem

Use slightly less volume, but still speak with authority.

mitre = MĪ-ter

This is the reason for hope. God is doing something wonderful but not yet visible.

Again, call out as for the first two lines. Lower your voice slightly.

This is a sad memory.

Say this triumphantly.

gorges = GOHR-juhz

READING I   The Baruch to whom this book is attributed is the prophet Jeremiah's scribe. The setting for the book is the Babylonian exile. Notice that the author speaks of Jerusalem being in "mourning and misery" and recalls the reason: Jerusalem's children have been "Led away on foot by their enemies" In today's passage, Baruch is offering the exiles hope.

One hope offered is that the exiles will be brought back to Jerusalem. "Mountains" will be made "low" and

"gorges . . . filled to level ground" so that the Israelites may return. A second hope offered is that the people's suffering has not been in vain. "All the earth" will see the glory that God plans to give Jerusalem. All nations will come to know peace and will see God's glory.

The greatest cause for hope is that the people will once more be secure in their covenant relationship with God. Because the Israelites had understood that God would protect them and their nation from their enemies, their experience of the Babylonian exile caused them a crisis of

faith. Had Israel misunderstood? Was God their God? Were they God's people? Baruch assures the people that when Jerusalem sees her children returning from exile she will rejoice "that they are remembered by God." Because God is Israel's God, and the Israelites are God's people, they have every reason to live in hope. As you proclaim the reading, fill your voice with joyful expectation. God will save God's people.

The **forests** and every **fragrant** kind of tree
    have **overshadowed Israel** at God's **command**;
for **God** is **leading Israel** in **joy**
    by the **light** of his **glory**,
      with his **mercy** and **justice** for company.

Say this with great certitude.

Israel = IZ-ree-uhl; IZ-ray-uhl

READING II   Philippians 1:4–6, 8–11

Philippians = fih-LIP-ee-uhnz

The tone of this reading is joyful.

A reading from the Letter of Saint Paul to the Philippians

Brothers and sisters:
I pray always with **joy** in my **every prayer** for **all** of you,
    because of your **partnership** for the **gospel**
    from the **first day** until **now**.
I am **confident** of this,

Now confidence is added to joy.
Speak with certitude.

    that the one who **began** a **good work** in you
    will **continue** to **complete** it
    until the day of **Christ Jesus**.
God is my **witness**,

Now Paul is expressing his love for the Philippians.

    how I **long** for **all** of you with the **affection** of **Christ Jesus**.
And **this** is my **prayer**:

Drop your voice here. Paul is describing his prayer.

    that your **love** may **increase** ever **more** and **more**
    in **knowledge** and **every kind** of perception,
    to **discern** what is of **value**,
    so that you may be **pure** and **blameless** for the day of **Christ**,

Read slowly as you conclude.

    filled with the fruit of **righteousness**
    that **comes** through **Jesus Christ**
    for the **glory** and **praise** of **God**.

READING II **Paul, too, lived in hope. Paul wrote the Letter to the Philippians while he was in prison (Philippians 1:12–13). Despite his own suffering, Paul's letter is full of joy. Why? Because he loves the Philippians, and despite his own situation, he remains full of confidence that God, "who began a good work in [them] will continue to complete it until the day of Christ Jesus." Like Baruch, Paul has not let present suffering lessen his confidence that God is, and will remain, faithful.**

Even though God is accomplishing the good work in them, the Philippians must still cooperate with God. Paul exhorts the Philippians to continue to grow in love so that they can "discern what is of value." They should live "pure" and "blameless" lives so that they can receive the "righteousness that comes through Jesus Christ." The tone of Paul's letter moves from joy to confidence to love. Try to project those same tones as you exhort today's Christians to live in fidelity and hope.

GOSPEL **Luke begins the story of Jesus' public ministry by placing Jesus within the political and religious setting of his day. As the story of Jesus will unfold, many of these powerful political and religious leaders will play some role in trying to thwart him. For instance, Herod will kill John the Baptist and will want to kill Jesus. The high priest, Caiaphas, will be head of the Sanhedrin that condemns Jesus. However, none of them will be able to prevent Jesus from accomplishing what he came to accomplish.**

This is all background information. Luke is setting the stage.

Tiberius Caesar = tī-BEER-ee-uhs SEE-zer

Pontius Pilate = PON-shuhs PĪ-luht

Herod = HAYR-uhd; tetrarch = TET-rahrk

Galilee = GAL-ih-lee; Ituraea = ih-too-REE-ah; Trachonitis = trak-uh-NĪ-tis

Lysanias = lī-SAY-nee-uhs; Abilene = ab-uh-LEE-nee; Annas = AN-uhs

Caiaphas = KAY-uh-fuhs; KĪ-uh-fuhs

Here, raise your voice and speak slowly.

Zechariah = zek-uh-RĪ-uh

Now resume your previous tone and pace.

This is a proclamation. Raise your volume and speak with authority.

Jordan = JOHR-d*n

Isaiah = ī-ZAY-uh

This is good news indeed!

GOSPEL Luke 3:1–6

A reading from the holy Gospel according to Luke

In the fifteenth year of the reign **of Tiberius Caesar**,
when **Pontius Pilate** was **governor of Judea**,
and **Herod** was **tetrarch** of **Galilee**,
and his brother **Philip tetrarch** of the region
of **Ituraea** and **Trachonitis**,
and **Lysanias** was **tetrarch** of **Abilene**,
during the high **priesthood** of **Annas** and **Caiaphas**,
the **word** of **God** came to **John** the son of **Zechariah**
in the **desert**.
John went throughout the **whole region** of the **Jordan**,
proclaiming a **baptism** of **repentance** for the **forgiveness**
of **sins**,
as it is **written** in the book of the words of the prophet **Isaiah**:
*A **voice** of one **crying out** in the **desert**:*
*"**Prepare** the **way** of the **Lord**,*
*   **make straight** his **paths**.*
*Every **valley** shall be **filled***
*   and **every mountain** and **hill** shall be made **low**.*
*The **winding roads** shall be made **straight**,*
*   and the **rough ways** made **smooth**,*
*and **all flesh** shall **see** the **salvation** of **God**."*

Next, Luke introduces John the Baptist. John will prepare the way for Jesus by calling the people to a baptism of repentance and testifying on Jesus' behalf. To describe John's role, Luke quotes the prophet, Isaiah. Notice that the words from Isaiah are similar to the ones we read in Baruch: "Every valley shall be filled/ and every mountain and hill shall be made low."

These words in Isaiah are part of the call story of a prophet known as Second Isaiah. Like Baruch, he lived at the time of the Babylonian exile and was called to assure the Israelites that God would save them and bring them home. Like Baruch, he assured the exiles that all the world, "all flesh shall see the salvation of God." The "Lord" for whom Second Isaiah is preparing the way is God. The "Lord" for whom John is preparing the way is Jesus. By

using the words of Second Isaiah in this way, by placing them on the lips of John the Baptist, Luke is teaching that Jesus is God. As you proclaim this great good news, you, too, are preparing the way of the Lord, Jesus, who is God. Do so with both confidence and joy.

3RD SUNDAY OF ADVENT

Lectionary #9

READING I   Zephaniah 3:14–18a

Zephaniah = zef-uh-NĪ-uh

The reading itself tells you the tone. Speak loudly and joyfully.

Zion = ZĪ-uhn; ZĪ-ahn

Israel = IZ-ree-uhl; IZ-ray-uhl

Drop your voice here. These lines explain why the people should be joyful.

Jerusalem = juh-ROO-suh-lem; juh-ROO-zuh-lem

Now the tone is one of hope and excitement. Start with a lowered volume so that you can gradually raise it.

Now speak with joy and certitude. God does love his people.

A reading from the Book of the Prophet Zephaniah

> **Shout** for **joy**, O daughter Zion!
>> Sing **joyfully**, **O** Israel!
> Be **glad** and **exult** with **all** your **heart**,
>> O **daughter Jerusalem**!
> The LORD has **removed** the **judgment against** you,
>> he has **turned away** your **enemies**;
> the **King of Israel**, the LORD, is in your **midst**,
>> you have no further **misfortune** to fear.
> On **that day**, it shall be said to **Jerusalem**:
>> **Fear not**, O Zion, **be not discouraged**!
> The LORD, your **God**, is in your **midst**,
>> a **mighty savior**;
> he will **rejoice** over you with **gladness**,
>> and **renew** you in his **love**,
> he will **sing joyfully** because of **you**,
>> as one **sings** at **festivals**.

READING I   At first reading, you might assume that today's passage from Zephaniah is one more message of hope that was originally addressed to the exiles in Babylon (587–537 BC). However, Zephaniah's words are earlier, addressed to the people of the southern kingdom during a time of both fear and eventual reform (640–609 BC).

When David was king, the nation, Israel, consisted of all twelve tribes. However, the nation split in 922 BC. The northern kingdom, also called Israel, which consisted of ten tribes, was defeated by the Assyrians in 721 BC. The southern nation, called Judah, still existed, but was threatened by the Assyrians. For some years her kings accommodated Assyria. However, a great reformer, Josiah, along with the prophet, Zephaniah, called the people back to fidelity, to covenant love.

Today's reading is in that context: Zephaniah is assuring those in Judah that once they reform and live in fidelity to God, they will no longer have any reason to fear their enemies: "The Lord has removed the judgment against you,/ he has turned away your enemies." The Israelites should live in fidelity and security, knowing that God is in their midst. When the Israelites repent and turn back to God, he, who has never stopped loving them, will "renew [Israel] in his love." This is reason to "shout for joy." Proclaim this good news with joy and confidence.

READING II   Paul, like Zephaniah, is urging the people to rejoice, knowing that God is with them: "Rejoice in the Lord always./ I shall say it again: rejoice!" To rejoice in the Lord always is to

Philippians = fil-LIP-ee-uhnz

This is a command. Say this line joyfully, but with authority.

Drop your voice for "I shall say it again . . ."

Paul is reassuring the Philippians. Say these lines in a comforting tone.

Say the concluding lines with gentle confidence.

READING II   Philippians 4:4–7

A reading from the Letter of Saint Paul to the Philippians

Brothers and sisters:
Rejoice in the **Lord always**.
I shall say it **again**: **rejoice**!
Your **kindness** should be known to **all**.
The **Lord** is **near**.
Have **no anxiety** at **all**, but in **everything**,
    by **prayer** and **petition**, with **thanksgiving**,
    make your **requests known** to **God**.
Then the **peace** of God that surpasses **all understanding**
    will **guard your hearts** and **minds** in **Christ Jesus**.

GOSPEL   Luke 3:10–18

A reading from the holy Gospel according to Luke

The **crowds** asked John the **Baptist**,
    "**What** should we **do**?"
He said to them in **reply**,
    "Whoever has **two** cloaks
    should **share** with the person who has **none**.
And whoever has **food** should do **likewise**."
Even tax collectors came to be baptized and **they** said to him,
    "**Teacher**, **what** should **we do**?"

The question is asked with some urgency.

John speaks with authority.

Drop your voice when the narrator speaks.

Again, the question is asked with urgency.

---

rejoice not only when things are going well, but when they are not. Why should the Philippians rejoice always? Because God is with his people in every circumstance: "The Lord is near."

If the Philippians recognize the Lord's presence and rejoice always, their inner conviction will affect both how they act and how they feel. Their "kindness" will be known to all. In addition, they will have peace of mind and heart. They will have no anxiety about anything.

Knowing that God is near and that God loves them, the Philippians are reminded

always to turn to God in prayer, to make their needs known. Their prayers should be offered not just with "petition" but with "thanksgiving." To be able to thank God, even before prayer is answered, is to live in certainty that God hears prayer and will act for the petitioner's good. As with the First Reading, the tone is one of joy and confidence. As Paul is urging the Philippians, so are you urging those who have gathered for worship to rejoice because the Lord is near.

GOSPEL In last week's Gospel, we learned that John the Baptist proclaimed a baptism of repentance for the forgiveness of sins. In today's Gospel, we read that a number of people have taken John's message very seriously. They want to know what they should do to repent and bear good fruit.

The first people who pose the question are members of the crowd. John instructs them to share their food and clothing with the poor. Next, tax collectors and soldiers ask what they should do. Both tax collectors and soldiers would have been looked

Again, the answer is given with authority.

Urgency.

Authority.

The narrator is speaking. Drop your voice.

Begin with authority.

Now add urgency.

chaff = chaf

This is the narrator's voice concluding the story.

He answered them,
    "**Stop** collecting **more** than what is **prescribed**."
Soldiers also asked him,
    "And **what** is it that **we** should **do**?"
He told them,
    "**Do not** practice **extortion**,
    do not falsely accuse anyone,
    and be **satisfied** with your **wages**."

Now the **people** were filled with **expectation**,
    and **all** were asking in their **hearts**
    whether **John might** be the **Christ**.
John answered them **all**, saying,
    "**I** am **baptizing** you with **water**,
    but one **mightier than I** is **coming**.
I am **not worthy** to **loosen** the **thongs** of his **sandals**.
He will **baptize** you with the **Holy Spirit** and **fire**.
His **winnowing fan** is in his **hand** to **clear** his **threshing** floor
    and to **gather** the **wheat** into his **barn**,
    but the **chaff** he will **burn** with **unquenchable fire**."
Exhorting them in **many other ways**,
    he preached **good news** to the people.

down on by most of the Jews because they were agents of Rome, imposing Roman rule in an occupied country. John tells the tax collectors not to collect more than is due. He tells the soldiers not to use their authority dishonestly by extorting or falsely accusing anyone.

John makes such a deep impression on those who hear him that some begin to ask if John might be the messiah. John does not encourage this kind of speculation at all. He says that while he baptizes

with water, the one who is to come will baptize the people with the Holy Spirit and with fire. John claims that he is not worthy even to loosen the thongs on the sandals of the one who is to come.

When John describes the ministry of the one who is to come, he uses imagery of judgment. The expected one will "gather the wheat into his barn,/ but the chaff he will burn with unquenchable fire." When Jesus comes, he, like John, preaches repentance, but he does not place his greatest emphasis on judgment. Jesus

invites everyone, especially the marginalized, into the Kingdom.

Today's Gospel includes many different voices: the questioners speak with urgency, John the Baptist speaks with authority, and the narrator fills in necessary information. Try to represent the tone of each speaker as you proclaim today's Good News.

4TH SUNDAY OF ADVENT

Lectionary #12

READING I   Micah 5:1–4a

Micah = MĪ-kuh

Speak with authority. This is a proclamation.

Bethlehem-Ephrathah = BETH-luh-hem EF-ruh-thuh
Judah = JOO-duh
Say "ruler in Israel" slowly, with emphasis.
Israel = IZ-ree-uhl; IZ-ray-uhl

Say "she who is to give birth has borne" slowly, with emphasis.

Let your voice crescendo in this line.
This is very good news. Proclaim it with joy and awe.
Lower your volume and say this with solemn authority.

A reading from the Book of the Prophet Micah

Thus says the LORD:
You, **Bethlehem-Ephrathah**
   too small to be among the **clans** of **Judah**,
from **you** shall come **forth** for **me**
   one who is to be **ruler** in **Israel**;
whose **origin** is from of **old**,
   from **ancient times**.
Therefore the Lord will give them **up**, until the time
   when **she** who is to give **birth** has **borne**,
and the **rest** of his **kindred** shall **return**
   to the **children** of **Israel**.
He shall **stand firm** and **shepherd** his **flock**
   by the **strength** of the LORD,
   in the **majestic name** of the LORD, his **God**;
and they shall **remain**, for **now his greatness**
   shall reach to the **ends** of the **earth**;
   he shall be **peace**.

READING I   Once more we read words of hope offered to the exiles in Babylon (see Micah 4:10). The Babylonian exile (587–537 BC) caused many of the Israelites to lose hope. After all, God had promised that David's kingdom and his throne would be secure forever (see 2 Samuel 7:16). Now the kingdom had been defeated by the Babylonians, and the king, along with all of the upper class residents of Jerusalem, had been lead away to exile in Babylon.

The prophet is reminding the exiles of God's promise to their ancestor David when he says that the king's "origin is from of old,/ from ancient times." The prophet is also referring to David when he says that a future great king will come from Bethlehem. David not only came from Bethlehem (see 1 Samuel 17:12), but was anointed king there (1 Samuel 16:1, 13).

This future king will be faithful to God; he will "stand firm and shepherd his flock/ by the strength of the Lord." Because this king will be faithful, he will bring about a new day for the exiles. In the future, the people will not only return, but will "remain" in Israel. The greatness of this faithful future king will be recognized "to the ends of the earth." He will not only establish peace; "he shall be peace."

As we read this description, we might think that the prophet has given an idealized picture of a future king. However, in the light of Christ, we know that the future king's greatness did indeed reach "to the ends of the earth" and that the future king is "peace." He reconciled the world to God. Proclaim this great Good News with joy and awe.

Hebrews = HEE-brooz

Emphasize "not." God wants obedience, not offerings.

Emphasize "no delight."

holocausts = HOL-uh-kawsts; HOH-luh-kawsts

Read this line slowly. This is the main point of the contrast.

Now the narrator's voice is explaining the point he just made.

Emphasize "desired" and "delighted." The point is being made again.

Emphasize "your will."

Here the narrator is drawing his conclusion.

READING II Hebrews 10:5–10

A reading from the Letter to the Hebrews

Brothers and sisters:
When **Christ** came into the **world**, he said:
 "**Sacrifice** and **offering** you did **not** desire,
  but a **body** you **prepared** for me;
 in **holocausts** and **sin** offerings you took **no delight**.
 Then I said, 'As is **written** of me in the **scroll**,
 behold, I come to do **your will**, O **God**.'"

First he says, "**Sacrifices** and **offerings**,
 holocausts and **sin offerings**,
 you neither **desired** nor **delighted** in."
These are offered according to the **law**.
Then he says, "**Behold**, I come to do **your will**."
He takes away the **first** to establish the **second**.
By this **"will,"** **we** have been **consecrated**
 through the offering of the **body** of **Jesus Christ once** for **all**.

READING II As the selection from Hebrews begins, the author pictures Christ, as he came into the world, praying Psalm 40: "Sacrifice and offering you did not desire;/ but a body you prepared for me;/ in holocausts and sin offerings you took no delight./ . . . 'I come to do your will, O God.'"

After picturing Christ praying the psalm, the author explains why Christ's sacrifice is far superior to the sacrifices and offerings that the Lord did not desire. Those sacrifices were "offered according to the law." They had to be offered every year; they had to be repeated.

However, Jesus' sacrifice has replaced sacrifices offered according to the Law. Jesus offered the perfect sacrifice because he perfectly conformed his will to the will of the Father. This perfect sacrifice need never be repeated. It has been offered "once for all," and through it we have been "consecrated."

The Letter to the Hebrews is often difficult to understand. Read today's passage several times to yourself and make sure you understand it before you proclaim it to the gathered assembly. Try to make clear the author's main point: the contrast between holocausts offered according to the Law and Jesus' perfect sacrifice.

GOSPEL Today's scene from Luke's gospel account, called the Visitation, like the account of the Annunciation that we read on the Solemnity of the Immaculate Conception, is part of a birth narrative, that is, the story of a great person's beginnings, written after the end of the person's life to emphasize the person's greatness. The primary purpose of

GOSPEL · Luke 1:39–45

A reading from the holy Gospel according to Luke

This is the narrator's voice setting the scene.
Judah = JOO-duh
Zechariah = zek-uh-RĪ-uh

Say this with awe.

Elizabeth speaks with great excitement.

Drop your voice. Elizabeth is puzzled.
Emphasize "mother of my Lord,"
Elizabeth is in awe.

Emphasize this sentence. Speak with sincerity and conviction.

Mary set out
   and **traveled** to the **hill** country in **haste**
   to a town of **Judah**,
   where she entered the house of **Zechariah**
   and greeted **Elizabeth**.
When **Elizabeth heard** Mary's greeting,
   the infant **leaped** in her womb,
   and Elizabeth, **filled** with the **Holy Spirit**,
   cried out in a **loud voice** and said,
   "**Blessed** are you among **women**,
   and **blessed** is the **fruit** of **your womb**.
And **how** does this **happen** to me,
   that the **mother** of my **Lord** should **come** to **me**?
For at the moment the sound of your greeting reached my **ears**,
   the **infant** in my **womb leaped** for **joy**.
Blessed are **you** who **believed**
   that what was spoken to you by the **Lord**
   would be **fulfilled**."

this story is to teach what was understood about Jesus Christ after the Resurrection: Jesus is divine.

The teaching becomes all the more clear when we realize that Elizabeth's words to Mary are an allusion to a famous story in 2 Samuel. Elizabeth says: "And how does this happen to me,/ that the mother of my Lord should come to me?" Elizabeth's words recall the words of David when David was bringing the ark of the Lord, the place where God was understood to dwell, to Jerusalem. David says,

"How can the ark of the Lord come to me?" (2 Samuel 6:9). Mary becomes the new ark of the covenant, carrying the Lord so that he may dwell with his people.

It is not only Elizabeth who recognizes the presence of the Lord. The child in her womb, John the Baptist, leaps for joy in the presence of Mary's child. John prepares the way of the Lord in all four gospel accounts. In the Gospel according to Luke, John recognizes Christ while still an infant in the womb. He will continue to prepare the way of the Lord as Jesus' public ministry begins.

Finally, today's reading teaches us something important about Mary. As Elizabeth says, Mary "believed that what was spoken . . . by the Lord/ would be fulfilled." This, in addition to Mary's obedience, is what makes her our model for discipleship. As you proclaim this reading, emphasize the lines that teach Jesus' divinity and the line that teaches Mary's faith. We, too, are to believe that the words spoken by the Lord will be fulfilled.

THE NATIVITY OF THE LORD (CHRISTMAS): VIGIL

Lectionary #13

READING I   Isaiah 62:1–5

Isaiah = ī-ZAY-uh

As the prophet will be neither silent nor quiet, let your voice, too, be neither silent nor quiet; let it come across with confidence and strength. Speak loudly and clearly as you begin this passage. Be careful not to distort the sound coming through the microphone.

Zion = ZĪ-uhn; ZĪ-ahn

diadem = DĪ-uh-dem

Create a clear contrast between the names "Forsaken" and "Desolate" and "My Delight" and "Espoused" by lightening your voice on the new names to convey happiness at being chosen by the Lord.

Make eye contact with the assembly as you proclaim the final line with joy.

A reading from the Book of the Prophet Isaiah

For **Zion's** sake I will **not be** silent,
    for **Jerusalem's** sake I will **not** be quiet,
until her **vindication** shines forth like the **dawn**
    and her **victory** like a burning **torch.**

Nations shall **behold your vindication**,
    and **all** the **kings** your **glory;**
you shall be called by a **new** name
    pronounced by the mouth of the LORD.
You shall be a **glorious crown** in the hand of the LORD,
    a **royal diadem held** by your **God.**
No **more** shall people call you **"Forsaken,"**
    or your land **"Desolate,"**
but you shall be called **"My Delight,"**
    and your land **"Espoused."**
For the LORD **delights** in you
    and makes your land his **spouse.**
As a **young man marries** a **virgin**,
    your **Builder** shall **marry you;**
and as a **bridegroom** rejoices in his **bride**
    so shall **your** God **rejoice** in **you.**

READING I Isaiah tells us that Jerusalem's restoration and the return of the Hebrew people from exile shall be a sign for all to see; their exoneration and return to glory will be so beautiful and wondrous that everyone will witness it. Our own path to glory begins with Christmas and the birth of Jesus, the one we call "Messiah." For Christians, Christmas is the beginning of an intimate relationship with God in Jesus through the Church.

The contrast between the old and new names testifies to the significance and depth of what is transpiring in the relationship between God, Jerusalem, and its people. In the past, the people had been unfaithful to the covenant; they had associated with fertility cults. The name "Espoused" recognizes that the Lord has forgiven Israel for those associations. These are not minor changes taking place in the relationship between God and Israel: they are life altering.

The entire song from which the five verses of this reading come is found in

Isaiah 62:1–12. The last two verses (11–12) are the reading for the Mass at Dawn on Christmas (see that commentary for more insights into the passage), and include the climax of the song: "your savior comes!" Since this conclusion is not in your reading, the assembly will not hear it. However, the joy and confidence of your proclamation will help lead them to this conclusion on their own.

This Christmas Eve, celebrate the continuation of the restored relationship between God and his people with your

READING II Acts 13:16–17, 22–25

A reading from the Acts of the Apostles

When **Paul** reached **Antioch** in **Pisidia** and entered
 the **synagogue**,
 he **stood** up, **motioned** with his hand, and **said**,
 "Fellow **Israelites** and you **others** who are **God-fearing**, **listen**.
The **God** of **this** people **Israel** chose our ancestors
 and **exalted** the people during their sojourn
  in the land of **Egypt**.
With **uplifted arm** he **led** them out of it.
Then he **removed Saul** and **raised** up **David** as king;
 of him he **testified**,
 'I have found **David**, **son of Jesse**, **a man** after my own **heart**;
 he will **carry** out my **every wish**.'
From **this man's descendants God**, according to his **promise**,
 has **brought** to Israel a **savior**, **Jesus**.
John heralded his coming by proclaiming a **baptism** of **repentance**
 to **all** the people of **Israel**;
 and as **John** was completing his course, he would say,
 '**What** do you **suppose** that **I am**? **I am not** he.
Behold, **one** is coming **after** me;
 I am **not worthy** to **unfasten** the **sandals** of his **feet**.'"

Antioch = AN-tee-ahk

Pisidia = pih-SID-ee-uh

Pause noticeably after "said," so as to make it obvious that what follows is Paul's speech. Deliver the speech making eye contact with the assembly as much as possible.

sojourn = SOH-jern

Saul = sawl

Jesse = JES-ee

Speak Jesus' name clearly and with reverence on this evening when we celebrate the Vigil of Christmas.

Pause noticeably after "I am not he." Then, with humility in your voice, proclaim John's announcement of Jesus' coming.

---

proclamation of the prophet's words. We who participate in the life of the Church are forever united with Christ in the covenant the Lord inaugurated with the Israelites; God in Christ will never cease to care for the Church, his spouse. This relationship of love we celebrate with joy and delight on Christmas.

READING II It seems strange to proclaim a passage from the Acts of the Apostles at the Christmas Vigil liturgy. It is usually during Easter Time that

we hear from Acts, the book that describes the spread of the Gospel and the development of early Christian communities. Yet this reading in particular focuses on the Jewish background of our Christian belief in Jesus as the Savior. The reading is a few verses away from Paul's sermon in the Jewish synagogue at Antioch, in the section of Acts that describes how Paul extends his mission beyond the Jerusalem community.

As you ponder these verses, look at Paul's entire speech (Acts 13:16–41). The verses you proclaim detail what God has done for the Chosen People of Israel. This is Paul's first oration on his first mission described in Acts. It was meant to persuade his Jewish audience that God has sent Israel a savior in the person of Jesus. Masterfully crafted, the discourse shows Paul respecting the Jews as "fellow Israelites," a title that shows his oneness with them (Paul is a Jew), and also honors

GOSPEL Matthew 1:1–25

A reading from the holy Gospel according to Matthew

The book of the **genealogy** of **Jesus Christ**,
    the son of **David**, the son of **Abraham**.

Abraham became the father **of Isaac**,
    Isaac the father of **Jacob**,
    Jacob the father **of Judah** and his **brothers**.
Judah became the father of **Perez** and **Zerah**,
    whose mother was **Tamar**.
Perez became the father of **Hezron**,
    Hezron the father of **Ram**,
    Ram the father of **Amminadab**.
Amminadab became the father of **Nahshon**,
    Nahshon the father of **Salmon**,
    Salmon the father of **Boaz**,
    whose mother was **Rahab**.
Boaz became the father of **Obed**,
    whose mother was **Ruth**.
Obed became the father of **Jesse**,
    Jesse the father of **David** the **king**.

David became the father of **Solomon**,
    whose **mother** had been the **wife** of **Uriah**.
Solomon became the father of **Rehoboam**,
    Rehoboam the father of **Abijah**,
    Abijah the father of **Asaph**.
Asaph became the father of **Jehoshaphat**,
    Jehoshaphat the father of **Joram**,
    Joram the father of **Uzziah**.

Practice the names in the genealogy so your proclamation flows smoothly on this important solemnity. Read with care, as if these were names of your own family or of your fellow parishioners. Pace yourself, not rushing, but not reading too slowly either.

Perez = PAYR-ez

Zerah = ZEE-rah

Tamar = TAY-mahr

Hezron = HEZ-ruhn

Ram = ram

Amminadab = uh-MIN-uh-dab

Nahshon = NAH-shuhn

Salmon = SAL-muhn

Boaz = BOH-az

Rahab = RAY-hab

Obed = OH-bed

Uriah = yoo-RĪ-uh

Rehoboam = ree-huh-BOH-uhm

Abijah = uh-BĪ-juh

Asaph = AY-saf

Jehoshaphat = jeh-HOH-shuh-fat

Joram = JOHR-uhm

Uzziah = uh-ZĪ-uh

---

the history of salvation already begun in the Chosen People. For the evangelist Luke, the author of the Acts of the Apostles, one period of salvation history came to an end with John the Baptist ("as John was completing his course") and a new period began. The section of the speech after the verses in today's reading show how Jesus is the fulfillment of God's promise to the Hebrew people. The conclusion, which recounts all that God has done through the Death and Resurrection of Jesus, calls people in the synagogue to faith.

For Christians, salvation history can only be understood in relation to the history of the Chosen People of Israel and the birth, life, Death, and Resurrection of Jesus. This passage gives Christians the opportunity to reflect on the intimate faith connection we have with the Jewish people. God was active in history and the lives of people before the birth of the Messiah and God is still active in the lives of those who do not yet profess Jesus as the Messiah.

We Christians have an obligation, like Paul, to evangelize, to spread the Good

News of salvation to those who have not yet heard and believed. We do this though, like Paul, in a way that recognizes God already present in their lives. Some in the assembly this evening will not yet have heard the Good News. Announce the Good News to them with humility and with respect for the presence of God already at work in them.

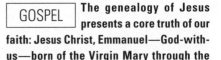

GOSPEL The genealogy of Jesus presents a core truth of our faith: Jesus Christ, Emmanuel—God-with-us—born of the Virgin Mary through the

Jotham = JOH-thuhm
Ahaz = AY-haz
Hezekiah = hez-eh-KĪ-uh
Manasseh = muh-NAS-uh
Amos = AY-m*s
Josiah = joh-SĪ-uh
Jechoniah = jek-oh-NĪ-uh

Shealtiel = shee-AL-tee-uhl
Zerubbabel = zuh-ROOB-uh-b*l
Abiud = uh-BĪ-uhd
Eliakim = ee-LĪ-uh-kim
Azor = AY-zohr
Zadok = ZAY-dok
Achim = AH-kim
Eliud = ee-LĪ-uhd
Eleazar = el-ee-AY-zer
Matthan = MATH-uhm

You have made it through the difficult names in the genealogy! Take a discreet breath before the announcement of the birth of Jesus. Read the announcement slowly and with solemnity.

Take another breath after the concluding phrase "fourteen generations." You have completed the genealogy. The pause will also make apparent the beginning of a new section of the Gospel.

Uzziah became the father of **Jotham**,
 Jotham the father of **Ahaz**,
 Ahaz the father of **Hezekiah**.
Hezekiah became the father of **Manasseh**,
 Manasseh the father of **Amos**,
 Amos the father of **Josiah**.
Josiah became the father of **Jechoniah** and his **brothers**
 at the time of the **Babylonian exile**.

After the **Babylonian exile**,
 Jechoniah became the father of **Shealtiel**,
 Shealtiel the father of **Zerubbabel**,
 Zerubbabel the father of **Abiud**.
Abiud became the father of **Eliakim**,
 Eliakim the father of **Azor**,
 Azor the father of **Zadok**.
Zadok became the father of **Achim**,
 Achim the father of **Eliud**,
 Eliud the father of **Eleazar**.
Eleazar became the father of **Matthan**,
 Matthan the father of **Jacob**,
 Jacob the father of **Joseph**, the **husband** of **Mary**.
Of **her** was born **Jesus** who is called the **Christ**.

Thus the **total** number of **generations**
 from **Abraham** to **David**
 is **fourteen generations**;
 from **David** to the **Babylonian exile**,
 fourteen generations;
 from the **Babylonian exile** to the **Christ**,
 fourteen generations.

creative act of God, enters into human history, indeed, into the history of the world. Jesus is fully human and fully divine. In this passage, Matthew offers us a theological truth similar to the one found in this evening's Second Reading: God also works through human persons, men and women who sometimes have faith and sometimes do not yet believe.

Jesus is sent from God-in-history, into the ordinariness of human life. Matthew intentionally composes the genealogy with three sections of 14 names, delineating three historical periods: from Abraham to David; David to the Babylonian captivity; and the exile to Jesus, named the Christ, the Messiah. He includes both men and women (Tamar, Rahab, Ruth, Bathsheba, and Mary) and the names of people responsible for both good and evil. Most of us are familiar with the stories of Abraham, Isaac, and Jacob, but perhaps not with the stories of Tamar, who manipulated her father-in-law into an incestuous relationship in order to obtain justice, and Bathsheba, the wife of Uriah, who committed adultery with David. The upright and the sinful, together with the simplicity and messiness of human nature all find a place in Matthew's genealogy. Moreover, the inclusion of Ruth shows that the ancestry of Jesus is not exclusively Jewish: Ruth was a Moabite who joined the Israelite community. By crafting Jesus' genealogy is this way, Matthew affirms that Jesus came to save God's people, Jews and Gentiles alike, from their sins. Those saved through Jesus are from every race, nation, culture, gender, age, and background. For Matthew, Jesus is the Messiah-King of Israel, the

Express the care and concern of Joseph for Mary as you read about his unwillingness to expose her to shame. Use a gentle tone of voice.

Emphasize the name "Jesus" and its meaning by taking your time proclaiming the line "She will bear a son." This is what Christmas is all about.

Utter these words describing Joseph's act of will with the peace he must have felt when he, like Mary, opened himself to doing the Lord's will.

Now **this** is how the **birth** of **Jesus Christ** came about.
When his mother **Mary** was betrothed to **Joseph**,
    but **before** they lived together,
    she was **found** with **child** through the **Holy Spirit**.
Joseph her **husband**, since he was a **righteous** man,
    yet unwilling to expose her to **shame**,
    decided to divorce her quietly.
Such was his **intention** when, **behold**,
    the **angel** of the **Lord** appeared to him in a **dream** and said,
    "**Joseph**, son of **David**,
    do **not** be afraid to take **Mary** your **wife** into your **home**.
For it is through the **Holy Spirit**
    that this child has been **conceived** in her.
She will bear a **son** and you are to name him **Jesus**,
    because he will **save** his people from their **sins**."
All this took place to **fulfill**
    what the Lord had said through the **prophet**:
    *Behold, the **virgin** shall **conceive** and bear a **son**,*
    *and they shall name him **Emmanuel**,*
    which means "**God** *is* **with** *us*."
When Joseph **awoke**,
    he **did** as the angel of the Lord had **commanded** him
    and took his **wife** into his **home**.
He had no **relations** with her until she bore a **son**,
    and he **named** him **Jesus**.

[Shorter: Matthew 1:18–25]

Son of David, the son of Abraham, and the son of Mary.

After the genealogy, the reading shifts to the beloved story of the angel appearing to Joseph in a dream and announcing that Mary will bear a child whom they are to name "Jesus." Matthew's focus in this story is clearly on Joseph. Joseph provides a model of trust in uncertain and threatening circumstances. Joseph, like Mary in the Gospel according to Luke, listened to the voice of God in the angel and was obedient to God's will. Joseph trusted that God would be with him as he joined himself to Mary for the birth of Jesus. In the world of Joseph and Mary, Jewish Law dictated that a betrothed Jewish woman who was seemingly unfaithful would be stoned. But Joseph, despite thinking that Mary had not been loyal to him, chose to listen to God's will rather than bring shame upon her. In doing so, Joseph welcomed the presence of the Savior in Mary. This was his fiat, his act of openness to God's will in his life.

Offer your proclamation as a reminder that we are to live Christmas as Joseph did, reverencing the presence of Emmanuel in all those with whom we come in contact, both intimates and acquaintances. Mary and Joseph provide us with examples of what it means to trust that God is always present at turning points in life's journey. This Christmas, many in the assembly will be at such crossroads in their own life journeys. Allow your own faith and trust in God to ring in your proclamation. This will lead others to hear the trust of Mary and Joseph that God is with us as we live Christmas in the ordinariness, messiness, and beauty of human life.

THE NATIVITY OF THE LORD (CHRISTMAS): MIDNIGHT

Lectionary #14

READING I   Isaiah 9:1–6

Isaiah = ī-ZAY-uh

Express the lines in the first section with contentment. Relief from darkness has come!

A reading from the Book of the Prophet Isaiah

The people who walked in **darkness**
  have seen a **great light**;
upon those who **dwelt** in the **land** of **gloom**
  a **light** has **shone**.
You have brought them **abundant joy**
  and **great rejoicing**,
as they **rejoice** before you as at the **harvest**,
  as people **make merry** when **dividing spoils**.
For the **yoke** that **burdened** them,
  the **pole** on their **shoulder**,
and the **rod** of their **taskmaster**
  you have **smashed**, as on the day of **Midian**.
For every **boot** that tramped in **battle**,
  every **cloak** rolled in **blood**,
  will be **burned** as fuel for **flames**.
For a **child** is **born** to **us**, a **son** is **given us**;
  upon **his** shoulder **dominion** rests.
They name him **Wonder-Counselor**, **God-Hero**,
  Father-Forever, **Prince of Peace**.
His dominion is **vast**
  and forever **peaceful**,

Pause before the section that begins "For the yoke . . . ." Proclaim this section with confidence. God has overcome the oppression his people faced.

Deliver each of the titles with different expression: 1) Wonder-Counselor with awe, 2) God-Hero with strength, 3) Father-Forever with confidence and assurance, and 4) Prince of Peace with gentleness. Pause after the last title.

Convey the characteristics of the royal Messiah's dominion in the same way that you spoke the titles (although the structure is not exactly parallel).

READING I An "oracle" is a statement by a prophet claiming to speak for a deity. It may announce a judgment or predict the future, and it is sometimes preceded by the words "Thus says the Lord." Today's First Reading is a messianic oracle (a prediction that a messiah will come to save the people) in which light will triumph over darkness and gloom. The Israelites faced much darkness and gloom in their history. In this selection from Isaiah, the yoke, pole, and rod evoke their oppression by the Assyrians. But for Isaiah, a prophet of hope, their oppression

will be overcome. Even in their darkest moments, God will never abandon his people. The prophet's message of hope is that a child will be born from the line of David and will continue the Davidic monarchy. He will be named "Wonder-Counselor, God-Hero, Father-Forever, Prince of Peace."

Biblical scholars discuss whether this passage represents an account of the coronation of a king or the actual birth of a child. Whichever interpretation one holds, for the Israelites, the passage gives hope that through the zeal of the "LORD of hosts,"

a new leader will bring peace and justice. Jews today still hope for the messiah described in this passage. And though our Christian belief that Jesus fulfills that messianic hope distinguishes us from our Jewish brothers and sisters, still we rejoice together when we see God overcoming darkness and gloom in the hearts of individuals and in the world. Let joy reign in your heart, be seen in your eyes, and heard in your voice as you proclaim this reading to the assembly. Let those who come to church only on Christmas sense how extraordinary is the Light coming into

from **David's throne**, and over his **kingdom**,
  which he **confirms** and **sustains**
by **judgment** and **justice**,
  both **now** and **forever**.
The **zeal** of the LORD of **hosts** will **do** this!

Zeal is strong and impassioned desire. Proclaim the concluding line with eagerness and certainty.

READING II   Titus 2:11–14

A reading from the Letter of Saint Paul to Titus

Titus = TĪ-tus

Beloved:
The **grace** of **God** has **appeared**, saving **all**
  and training us to reject **godless ways** and **worldly desires**
  and to live **temperately**, **justly**, and **devoutly** in this age,
as we **await** the **blessed hope**,
  the **appearance** of the **glory** of our great **God**
  and savior **Jesus Christ**,
  who **gave himself** for **us** to **deliver us** from **all lawlessness**
  and to **cleanse** for **himself** a people as his **own**,
  eager to do what is **good**.

Proclaiming a one-sentence reading is challenging. Thinking about the meaning of the sentence is terms of the past, present, and future will be more helpful than precisely following the punctuation.

GOSPEL   Luke 2:1–14

A reading from the holy Gospel according to Luke

Take your time with this familiar story.

Caesar Augustus = SEE-zer aw-GUHS-tuhs

In those days a **decree** went out from **Caesar Augustus**
  that the **whole world** should be **enrolled**.
This was the **first** enrollment,
  when **Quirinius** was governor of **Syria**.

Quirinius = kwih-RIN-ee-uhs
Syria = SEER-ee-uh

the darkness which you proclaim during this late-night liturgy!

READING II One sentence! At first glance this is all that this short reading from Titus seems to be! (Titus is one of the three pastoral letters—1 Timothy and 2 Timothy are the others.) But it is so much more. In this one sentence, the author of this letter discloses the grace of God active in the past, present, and future. On Christmas, we not only remember Jesus' first coming in history, his birth in Bethlehem (the past), but we

also affirm how he is God-with-us today (the present), and we look forward in blessed hope to his appearance again as the glory of God (the future).

According to the author of Titus, when we celebrate Jesus' coming as the grace of God in history, then Jesus' saving work accomplished through his life, Death, and Resurrection must be as near to our minds as his birth as an infant. The "grace of God" is the "savior Jesus Christ" who in his first coming showed us how to live, gave himself for us through his Death to deliver us from sin, washed us clean in his

Death and Resurrection, and took us as his own people.

We, who accept as true the Savior's first coming in history, have ethical responsibilities, for Christ now lives in us. Often the Christmas season is the time of year when we take these responsibilities seriously. However, the author of Titus does not specify in what times Christians are to fulfill their responsibilities. Rather his concern is that Christians always be ready and eager to do what is good. This is what Jesus Christ trained us to do through his own life.

Galilee = GAL-ih-lee

Judea = joo-DEE-uh

So **all** went to be enrolled, **each** to his **own** town.
And **Joseph** too went up from **Galilee** from the town of **Nazareth**
    to **Judea**, to the city of **David** that is called **Bethlehem**,
    because he was of the house and family of **David**,
    to be enrolled with **Mary**, his **betrothed**, who was with **child**.
While they were there,
    the **time** came for her to have her **child**,
    and she gave **birth** to her **firstborn son**.
She **wrapped** him in **swaddling clothes** and **laid** him in a **manger**,
    because there was **no room** for them in the **inn**.

Now there were **shepherds** in that region living in the **fields**
    and keeping the **night watch** over their **flock**.
The **angel of the Lord** appeared to them
    and the **glory of the Lord shone** around them,
    and they were struck with **great fear**.
The **angel** said to them,
    "**Do not be afraid**;
    for **behold**, I proclaim to you **good news** of **great joy**
    that will be for **all the people**.
For **today** in the city of **David**
    a **savior** has been born for you who is **Christ** and **Lord**.
And **this** will be a **sign** for **you**:
    you will find an **infant** wrapped in **swaddling clothes**
    and lying in a **manger**."
And **suddenly** there was a **multitude** of the **heavenly host**
    with the **angel**,
    praising **God** and **saying**:
    "**Glory to God in the highest**
        and on earth **peace** to those **on whom his favor rests**."

Emphasize the word "today." Look up and convey this line to your assembly as a solemn proclamation. While Jesus was born in Bethlehem some two thousand years ago, he is present today in the assembly, in the Word, in the Eucharist, and in the celebrant.

End on a joyful note as you proclaim the praises of the heavenly host with the angel. We have already sung the Gloria, so proclaim the praises with the same exuberance with which the Gloria was sung. A look of joy on your face is more than appropriate!

As a result of your well-prepared and skillfully delivered proclamation of this one sentence reading, others will be led a stronger belief in Jesus Christ as the Messiah, to a blessed hope in his second coming, and to an eagerness to do good.

GOSPEL Luke's account of the birth of Jesus shows us that we share in a graced humanity. For years people have been moved by the many details in Luke's narrative. Many have passed on the Lucan story to their children. Christmas pageants often dramatize this narrative. Why? The details, whether historically true or not, convey a profound truth of faith: God graced humanity with divinity.

While Luke emphasizes God's coming to all of humanity, he gives particular attention to the poor. The details in Luke's story—swaddling clothes and manger—and his emphasis on the shepherds who are the first to hear the news of Jesus' birth, show God's special concern for the poor. The circumstances of Jesus' birth attest to a power very different from the Roman ruler, Caesar Augustus, and affirm the intimate relationship between humanity and divinity.

Your task is to present this Christmas Gospel with awe at the momentous change the course of human history took some two thousand years ago. Mindful that Christ comes to save all, including those outside of social boundaries, proclaim with the confident belief expressed in the refrain of the Responsorial Psalm: "Today is born our Savior, Christ the Lord" (adapted from Luke 2:11).

THE NATIVITY OF THE LORD (CHRISTMAS): DAWN

Lectionary #15

Isaiah = ī-ZAY-uh

Look up as you proclaim the opening words. "To the ends of the earth" includes all sides of the assembly, even the back rows and those standing!

Zion = ZĪ-uhn; ZĪ-ahn

recompense = REK-uhm-pens

Soften your voice on the name "holy people." Speak the title "redeemed of the Lord" with confidence. State the name "Frequented" with reassurance, for Zion (Jerusalem)—and we—will not be forsaken.

READING I   Isaiah 62:11–12

A reading from the Book of the Prophet Isaiah

See, the LORD proclaims
    to the **ends** of the **earth**:
say to daughter **Zion**,
    your **savior** comes!
Here is his **reward** with him,
    his **recompense** before him.
They shall be called the **holy people**,
    the **redeemed** of the LORD,
and **you** shall be called "**Frequented**,"
    a **city** that is **not forsaken**.

READING I This passage from the Book of Isaiah was written at the end of the Babylonian exile to evoke the joyful return of the Israelites to Jerusalem. The city was restored and its people delivered back to their home. While the Israelites had not always been faithful to God, he was always committed to them. Imagine the elation of the people processing back to Jerusalem! In later times the joy expressed in this reading could also be seen in the procession on the first day of major pilgrimage feasts, such as the feast of Tabernacles.

The prophet's announcement of salvation extends beyond Jerusalem and its people—"to the ends of the earth." As dawn breaks on Christmas morning, we once again proclaim with conviction that the fullness of salvation has come through Jesus Christ. Just as the members of the community at Jerusalem could now be called "the holy people" and the "redeemed of the Lord," and Jerusalem called "Sought Out," we also claim these titles, but in a new way. Jesus Christ has come to redeem us.

Proclaim the announcement, "your salvation comes" so that it resounds throughout the church and beyond, as if the doors were open wide for the whole neighborhood to hear the joyful news! Try to memorize this line so that you can make eye contact with the assembly.

READING II Christmas and Easter come together! In this brief passage, we hear that from his birth to his Resurrection, Jesus Christ saves. These four verses from the Letter to Titus deal directly with what has been a central

Titus = TĪ-tus

The opening phrase refers to Jesus Christ. Emphasize this as the first point of the reading by proclaiming it more slowly than what follows.

The second point is "he saved us through the bath of rebirth." Read a little more slowly through "Holy Spirit."

Speak the words "so that we might be justified" with warmth as they refer to the gifts of justification and eternal life in Jesus—gifts your assembly receives.

READING II   Titus 3:4–7

A reading from the Letter of Saint Paul to Titus

Beloved:
When the **kindness** and **generous love**
　　of **God our savior** appeared,
not because of any **righteous deeds we** had done
　　but because of **his mercy**,
he saved us through the **bath** of **rebirth**
　　and **renewal** by the **Holy Spirit**,
whom he **richly** poured out on us
　　through **Jesus Christ** our **savior**,
so that **we** might be **justified** by his **grace**
　　and become **heirs** in **hope** of eternal **life**.

issue for Christians from the beginning: salvation.

Some in the community on Crete, for which Titus was responsible, believed they could earn their salvation by the good deeds they performed. From the authentic Pauline letters through the later pastoral epistles (1 and 2 Timothy and Titus) and up to the present day, the Christian tradition has been clear that salvation is a gift from God. God freely chose to send his Son Jesus Christ as the Savior because God loved humanity unconditionally. No deeds

or actions on our part could ever merit the gift of salvation.

Yet we are called to respond to the gift of salvation by living our lives in a particular way. In the two verses that precede this selection from Titus, we hear Christians called to perform honest work, live in gentle obedience, respect authority, speak no evil, and be kind to all. The actions of Christians are a reflection of the salvation we receive.

During this time of year, which has its own built-in stress, we might find it difficult to respond in love to others, especially

family members and close friends. As you prepare to proclaim this reading, reflect on how God's self-giving in Jesus Christ provides an example for you in living out your faith. Prepare well, but when you proclaim, let go of the need for a perfect proclamation. Allow the Holy Spirit to work through you so the assembly can be led to see anew the unmerited gift of salvation that is theirs.

 The Gospel this Christmas morning begins where the Gospel for the Mass during the Night concluded. At the end of last night's Gospel,

GOSPEL Luke 2:15–20

A reading from the holy Gospel according to Luke

When the **angels** went away from them to **heaven**,
   the **shepherds** said to one another,
   "Let us go, then, to **Bethlehem**
   to **see** this thing that has taken place,
   which the **Lord** has **made** known to **us."**
So they went in **haste** and found **Mary** and **Joseph**,
   and the **infant** lying in the **manger**.
When they **saw** this,
   they **made known** the **message**
   that had been **told** them about **this** child.
All who heard it were **amazed**
   by what had been **told** them by the **shepherds**.
And **Mary** kept **all** these things,
   reflecting on them **in her heart**.
Then the **shepherds** returned,
   glorifying and **praising God**
   for **all** they had **heard** and **seen**,
   just as it had been **told** to them.

Let eagerness be heard in your voice as you speak the shepherds' words.

Pause after "Mary and Joseph." They are not lying in the manger with the infant!

Lower your voice and speak gently and slowly about Mary. Pause after describing Mary's response. Then, raise your voice and speak joyfully and excitedly as you deliver the narrative lines of the shepherds' response.

---

the heavenly hosts and angel praise God saying, "Glory to God . . . ." At the end of today's passage, the shepherds, after listening to the angel's message about the birth of a Savior, praise God for what they had seen in the manger, while Mary reflects in her heart about what has taken place. Both the shepherds and Mary are on their own distinct faith journeys, as we are today. In their own ways, the shepherds and Mary respond to the amazing news that a Savior is born who is Christ and Lord. They simply express their amazement differently.

Some in the assembly will be natural evangelizers like the shepherds and want to go out into the world announcing the Good News of the Savior's birth. Others, like Mary, will take the Good News into their hearts, and ponder what it means for them and the world. Strive in your proclamation to emphasize equally the exuberance of the shepherds and the reflective response of Mary. A balanced proclamation, but one which also contrasts the two responses, will have the effect of affirming the genuineness of both responses in Christians today.

Luke packed this passage with meaning, so take your time communicating it. Fill your voice with the reverence, eagerness, and joy that permeate the Lucan account of the Savior's birth. Doing so will assist many in hearing this familiar Gospel anew and lead them to express joy for the Savior's birth through their own unique, God-given personalities and gifts.

THE NATIVITY OF THE LORD (CHRISTMAS): DAY

Lectionary #16

READING I   Isaiah 52:7–10

Isaiah = ī-ZAY-uh

Speak the opening lines slowly and serenely as if painting a picture. Strengthen your voice incrementally as you come to the announcement of the King. Pause significantly after the announcement.

Even the ruins are singing about what God is doing! Speak so that enthusiasm, energy, and excitement are palpable. Moderate your voice as you describe why the ruins are singing.

Memorize this last line if you can do so with ease.

A reading from the Book of the Prophet Isaiah

How **beautiful** upon the **mountains**
    are the **feet** of him who brings **glad tidings**,
announcing **peace**, bearing **good news**,
    announcing **salvation**, and saying to **Zion**,
    "Your God is King!"

Hark! Your **sentinels** raise **a cry**,
    together they **shout** for **joy**,
for they **see directly**, before their **eyes**,
    the LORD restoring Zion.
Break out together in **song**,
    O **ruins** of **Jerusalem**!
For the LORD **comforts** his people,
    he **redeems Jerusalem**.
The LORD has **bared** his **holy** arm
    in the **sight** of **all** the **nations**;
all the **ends** of the **earth** will **behold**
    the **salvation** of our **God**.

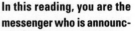 **READING I** In this reading, you are the messenger who is announcing peace and salvation. To the Hebrew people who sometimes forgot God and failed to live up to their part of the covenant, it must have seemed that God had also forgotten them, especially during the long days of the Babylonian exile. The messenger told otherwise. The traditional role of the messenger was to announce the advent (coming) of the king. The role of the messenger in this passage is no different. He had news: "God is king!" The Babylonians had been defeated by the Persians, and a new day was dawning. God was taking action again, restoring the people to Jerusalem.

In this reading, Second Isaiah (the author of chapters 40 through 55 of the Book of Isaiah) paints an arresting picture for us. We, along with the sentinels see "the LORD restoring Zion." Second Isaiah's description of the Lord is especially vivid: "The LORD has bared his holy arm/ in the sight of all the nations." The author's lyrical and poetic style, along with his use of vivid images and active verbs, all serve his purpose.

On Christmas Day, we are mindful of God's divine initiative in sending Jesus Christ to be King, the bringer of peace and salvation. Just as the author of this passage draws attention to the Lord, your challenge is to do the same. Let your proclamation exude praise for the salvation of our God—so that you leave the assembly eager to sing the refrain of the Responsorial Psalm: "All the ends of the earth have seen the saving power of God" (Psalm 98:3c).

READING II Why do we proclaim this passage on Christmas

READING II   Hebrews 1:1–6

Hebrews = HEE-brooz

In the opening line, make sure and observe the commas to differentiate between how God spoke in the two different time periods.

heir = ayr

refulgence = rih-FUHL-j*nts

A reading from the Letter to the Hebrews

Brothers and sisters:
In times past, God spoke in **partial** and **various** ways
    to our **ancestors** through the **prophets**;
    in these last days, he has spoken to **us** through **the Son**,
    whom he made **heir** of **all things**
    and **through whom** he **created** the **universe**,
        who is the **refulgence** of his **glory**, the very **imprint**
            of his **being**,
        and who **sustains all things** by his **mighty word**.
    When he had accomplished **purification** from **sins**,
        he took his **seat** at the **right hand** of the **Majesty** on **high**,
        as **far superior** to the **angels**
        as the **name** he has **inherited** is **more excellent** than **theirs**.

Pause after the colons to set off the quotations from scripture. The quotations are from Psalm 2:7, 2 Samuel 7:14, and Deuteronomy 32:43. The first two the author writes in the form of a question; the third as a strong affirmation of the Son's identity. Change the inflection in your voice appropriately.

For to **which** of the **angels** did **God ever say**:
    You are my **son**; **this** *day I have* **begotten** *you?*
Or again:
    I will be a **father** *to him, and* **he** *shall be a* **son** *to me?*
And again, when he leads the **firstborn** into the world, he says:
    Let all the **angels** *of God* **worship** *him.*

Day? The short answer is that on Christmas we assert with utmost conviction what we believe about Jesus Christ, the Son of the Father: that he is fully divine and fully human. The two statements together describe the Incarnation of God in Jesus Christ and are equally important to celebrate in word and sacrament on Christmas.

The entire Letter to the Hebrews, including the introduction we read today, is a defense of who Christians believe the Son to be. While the letter itself does not provide specific information as to its author, the date of its composition, or its addressees, its content suggests it was written for Christians who were attracted to the values of the Jewish cult. These Christians struggled with remaining faithful when challenged by those who denied the fullness of Jesus' divinity.

To persuade readers of the Christian belief in the Son's divinity, the author of Hebrews develops the theme of Jesus' high priesthood: the Son is different from and superior to past prophets because God spoke completely through him (1:1-2); the Son is superior to the angels because he sacrificed himself for the purification of sins (1:4-5); and the Son is the "refulgence of God's glory"—he is the only begotten Son of God (1:3). On the basis of these arguments, the author of Hebrews concludes that the new covenant established through Jesus offers a new priesthood superior to the old covenant Levitical priesthood.

Early Christians needed to defend their belief in the pre-existence and divinity of Jesus Christ because they were challenged by Jews and others in the Greco-Roman world who did not believe that God could actually become human while retaining the fullness of divinity. But

A reading from the holy Gospel according to John

In the **beginning** was the **Word**,
    and the **Word** was **with God**,
    and the **Word was God**.
He **was** in the **beginning with God**.
All things came to be **through him**,
    and **without him nothing came to be**.
What **came to be** through him was **life**,
    and this **life** was the **light** of the human **race**;
    the **light** shines in the **darkness**,
    and the **darkness** has **not** overcome it.
A man named **John** was **sent** from **God**.
He **came** for **testimony**, to **testify** to the **light**,
    so that **all** might **believe** through him.
He was **not** the **light**,
    but came to **testify** to the **light**.
The **true light**, which enlightens **everyone**,
        was **coming** into the **world**.
    He was **in** the world,
        and **the world** came to **be** through **him**,
        but the world **did not know** him.
    He came to what was his **own**,
        but his **own people did not accept** him.

Communicate the opening section as if you were telling a story and not teaching philosophy.

Accentuate the contrasting images by putting lightness in your voice with "life" and "light" and heaviness with "darkness."

Pause before "A man named John" to mark the Gospel's change in focus.

Pause before "The true light." Another transition begins here. Convey both the sadness and hope in this section by varying your tone of voice.

the truth for Christians is that God did do this in his Son. The later articulation of our theological beliefs about the Son's relationship to God would find many of its roots in the Letter to the Hebrews.

We worship the Son as God. Let the last line of this reading be filled with your own conviction that Jesus Christ is the Son of God, the very reflection of God's glory—indeed, fully divine. Only because Jesus Christ is both fully human and fully divine are we purified from our sins. Through the Eucharist, we share in Jesus' high priesthood of the new covenant. On

Christmas we celebrate Jesus' priesthood and our participation in it.

GOSPEL   John's prologue is replete with complicated theology and philosophy. But we needn't fully grasp all of its theological and philosophical complexity in order to communicate the prologue's fundamental meaning. In an age when some were denying the humanity of Jesus and others were rejecting his divinity, John begins his account of the Gospel with this incarnational hymn which

describes the divine becoming human in the Word made flesh.

John wrote in a time when most believed that the material world was evil and the spiritual world (the world of the divine) was good. The deep chasm that existed between the two worlds could never be bridged, lest the divine be contaminated with the vices of nature. While we are separated from John's time by thousands of years, many today still speak of the wickedness of the flesh and the evilness of human nature. Some even teach that to know God we must leave behind

This is Christmas: "And the Word became flesh"! Express the joy and wonder of Christmas in your voice.

Pause again before "John testified" This is the second time the author deviates to narrate John's story. Use the same tone as in the first section about John.

This, too, is Christmas: no one has seen God until the Son revealed God. State the concluding lines with faith and conviction. Read them slowly.

But to those who **did** accept him
  he gave **power** to become **children of God**,
  to those who **believe** in his **name**,
  who were **born not** by **natural** generation
  nor by **human** choice **nor** by **a man's** decision
  but of **God**.
    And the **Word** became **flesh**
      and made his **dwelling** among **us**,
      and **we saw** his **glory**,
      the **glory** as of the **Father's** only **Son**,
      full of **grace** and **truth**.
John **testified** to him and cried out, saying,
  "**This** was he of whom I said,
  'The one who is coming **after** me **ranks ahead** of **me**
  because he existed **before** me.'"
From his **fullness** we have all received,
  grace in place of **grace**,
  because while the **law** was **given** through **Moses**,
  grace and **truth came** through **Jesus Christ**.
No **one** has ever **seen God**.
The **only Son**, God, who is **at** the **Father's side**,
  has **revealed** him.

[Shorter: John 1:1–5, 9–14]

the flesh. How contrary to the truth of John's prologue and the truth of Christmas for Christians!

In the Word made flesh who was with God and was God from the very beginning, and through whom the world was created, God chose to bridge any chasm between the material and spiritual worlds that existed. As John tells us, God chose to give out of his own grace, the fullness of himself—the Son, the Word. No longer would the physical world, of which we

human persons are a part, be separated from the true face of God.

The Word unites humanity and divinity in a new way different from the grace given through the Law of Moses. This new way allows for a relationship between all Creation and its Creator that never before was possible. While it builds on the relationship God had with his people as recounted in the Old Testament, it also changes that relationship. All flesh has now seen the glory of God. The early church father, Saint Athanasius, puts it this way: "God became human so that we could

become divine." (*On the Incarnation*, 54). The beauty of the Incarnation and the possibilities it holds for us are what this passage from John discloses. The passage gives us the reasons we come together on Christmas to express our eternal gratitude. Your careful and solemn proclamation will lead the assembly to understand the gratitude due to God for the gift of the Word made flesh.

THE HOLY FAMILY OF JESUS, MARY, AND JOSEPH

Lectionary #17

READING I   1 Samuel 1:20–22, 24–28

A reading from the first Book of Samuel

Hannah = HAN-uh

In those days **Hannah conceived**, and at the end of her **term**
   bore a **son**
   whom she called **Samuel**, since she had **asked** the LORD
      for him.

Elkanah = el-KAY-nah

The next time her husband **Elkanah** was going up
   with the rest of his **household**
   to offer the **customary sacrifice** to the LORD and to **fulfill**
      his **vows**,
   Hannah did **not** go, explaining to her husband,
   "Once the child is **weaned**,

Use an explanatory, but not too emphatic, tone of voice. Hannah knows what she is going to do when the time comes.

   I will **take** him to **appear** before the LORD
   and to **remain** there **forever**;
   I will **offer** him as a **perpetual nazirite**."

perpetual nazirite = per-PECH-oo-uhl NAZ-uh-rīt

Hannah does what she said she would. Communicate the fulfillment of her promise with confidence.

Once Samuel was **weaned**, Hannah **brought him up** with her,
   along with a three-year-old **bull**,
   an **ephah** of flour, and a skin of **wine**,
   and **presented** him at the **temple** of the LORD in **Shiloh**.

ephah = EE-fuh

Shiloh = SHĪ-loh

After the boy's **father** had **sacrificed** the young **bull**,
   Hannah, his mother, approached **Eli** and said:
   "**Pardon, my lord**!

Eli = EE-lī

As you **live**, my lord,
   I am the **woman** who stood **near** you here, **praying** to the LORD.

An interruption of Eli by Hannah. Differentiate in your proclamation between Hannah's address of Eli as "lord" and the "LORD" to whom she prayed.

Today options are given for the readings. Contact your parish staff to learn which readings will be used.

READING I   **I SAMUEL.** Samuel's mother, Hannah, takes center stage in this reading. She had requested that the Lord grant her a son and the Lord fulfilled this request, albeit in a manner that would exceed her wildest expectations. The son she bore would be a great prophet and king of Israel. The historical books of 1 and 2 Samuel detail the rise of Samuel and the

shift of kingly power from David to Solomon.

Hannah is a strong woman who knows what she wants to do. The Lord gifted her with a child and she, desiring to be faithful, knows the correct time to bring him to the Lord. Her desire to offer Samuel as a perpetual nazirite means she will dedicate him to the Lord. He will live an ascetic life of simplicity and prayer, speaking the Word of the Lord to the Lord's people as need be.

Hannah, accompanied by her husband, brings the traditional gifts of sacrifice to the temple when she presents her son. The words she speaks remind Eli of her identity. She then offers her son to the Lord with a simple prayer of dedication.

The last line of the reading narrates Hannah's ultimate act of trust in the Lord. In freedom, she returns her son as gift to the Lord. Her act of self-giving, like Mary's "yes" to God, set God's people on a road to freedom and new life. Leave the assembly with a sense of the magnanimity of Hannah's act by proclaiming the final four

Reflect Hannah's gift of Samuel back to the Lord and his people by using a light and solemn tone of voice.

"**I prayed** for this **child**, and **the LORD granted** my request.
Now **I**, in turn, **give him** to the **LORD**;
  as **long** as he **lives**, **he** shall be **dedicated** to the **LORD**."
Hannah **left** Samuel **there**.

Or:

READING I   Sirach 3:2–6, 12–14

Sirach = SEER-ak

Deliver the first section in a teacher-like tone of voice.

A reading from the Book of Sirach

God sets a **father** in **honor** over his **children**;
  a **mother's authority** he **confirms** over her **sons**.
Whoever **honors** his father **atones** for sins,
  and **preserves** himself from them.
When he **prays**, he is **heard**;
  he **stores up** riches who **reveres** his mother.
Whoever **honors** his **father** is **gladdened** by children,
  and, when **he prays**, is **heard**.
Whoever **reveres** his father will live a **long life**;
  he who **obeys** his father brings **comfort** to his mother.

Pause noticeably before the new section begins with the words "My son." Use a gentle, personable tone of voice for the instructions that follow.

My son, **take care** of your father when he is **old**;
  grieve him not as long as he **lives**.
Even if his **mind fail**, be **considerate** of him;
  revile him not all the days of his life;
kindness to a **father** will **not** be **forgotten**,
  firmly planted against the **debt** of your **sins**
  —a house **raised** in **justice** to you.

Make eye contact with the assembly on the words "a house raised in justice to you." Proclaim with confidence in God's forgiveness.

words from memory, slowly and deliberately. Parents, especially mothers, in the assembly will understand the courage Hannah had to let go of her son. Proclaiming the final line in this manner will also give the assembly a chance to ponder Samuel's future impact. Hannah's act sets the stage for a new period in Israel's life.

Sirach. The Book of Sirach was written by Ben Sira, a scholar in the Jewish way of life, in the late third and early second centuries BC. Today's reading falls between the end of chapter 2 (which details a faithful person's duties toward God) and

before the second half of chapter 3 (which gives instructions on how to live with humility). In context, then, the fundamental principle of family life that this passage reveals is that love of God and love of one's parents cannot be separated. Fidelity to God involves children fulfilling their responsibilities toward their parents.

Three times this reading refers to honoring one's father and once to revering one's mother. The final paragraph is solely about caring for one's father, although by extension, we today would include caring

for all those who are a part of our family or community of friends.

In your proclamation, try not to over-emphasize the patriarchal dimension of the reading. Rather, draw out the consequences of caring for our parents and others in old age. The children who take care of those who have nurtured them will receive forgiveness of sins, riches, the blessings of children, answered prayers, and a long life—they will be a comfort to their mothers.

As you proclaim the final section, be cognizant that many in the assembly have

Sincerely address the assembly as "Beloved."

Make eye contact with the assembly and state the words "And so we are" with certainty.

A repetition of the address "Beloved." Use the same sincere tone as before.

The third time the address "Beloved" occurs.

Pause before delivering God's commandment. Emphasize "believe" and "love" by using two different tones of voice that reflect the meaning of the words. Pause after the commandment before the concluding verse.

READING II   1 John 3:1–2, 21–24

A reading from the first Letter of Saint John

Beloved:
See what **love** the **Father** has **bestowed** on us
   that we may be called the **children of God**.
And **so we are**.
The reason the **world does not know us**
   is that **it did not know him**.
Beloved, we are God's children now;
   what we **shall** be has **not yet** been **revealed**.
We **do know** that when it **is revealed** we shall be **like** him,
   for **we** shall **see** him **as he is**.

Beloved, if our **hearts do not condemn** us,
   we have **confidence** in **God** and **receive** from him
      whatever we **ask**,
   because we **keep** his **commandments** and **do** what **pleases** him.
And his **commandment** is **this**:
   we should **believe** in the **name** of his **Son**, Jesus **Christ**,
   and **love** one another just as he **commanded** us.
Those who **keep** his **commandments remain** in him,
   and **he** in **them**,
   and the way we **know** that he **remains** in us
   is from the **Spirit** he **gave** us.

Or:

experience caring for elderly parents or relatives. Healthcare providers who have honored the dignity of Alzheimer's and other dementia patients will also be present. Let them know that the love they have shown has taken root and they can look forward to God's love returned in justice to them.

READING II | **1 JOHN 3:1–2, 21–24.** This reading, verses of which we also hear on two Sundays in Year B of Easter Time, has two parallel sections. Both begin with the intimate address

"beloved." In the first, the author reasons about the identity of Christian believers in two different time periods, the present and future. Because of the gift of God's Son, we are God's children now. In the future, we do not know what we will be. Even though we have not received a revelation about this, because we believe, we can still say something about our future being. We will be like Christ. When the future comes, we will know what Christ is like because we will be so close to him that we will see him as he is, God's Son, the risen one.

The second section reflects the primary intention of the author of this late first century Catholic epistle. In earnest, he wants to convey the importance of connecting right belief with right living to a community who had to contend with the infiltration of false ideas about Jesus. Some suggested that Jesus wasn't really human, while others claimed Jesus wasn't the Christ. These incorrect beliefs about Jesus' identity led people to disregard their own behavior and its implications in the community. Disregard for Christ led to

READING II   Colossians 3:12–21

A reading from the Letter of Saint Paul to the Colossians

Brothers and **sisters**:
Put on, as God's **chosen** ones, **holy** and **beloved**,
    heartfelt **compassion**, **kindness**, **humility**, **gentleness**,
      and **patience**,
    bearing with one another and **forgiving** one another,
    if one has a **grievance** against another;
    as the **Lord** has forgiven **you**, **so must you also do.**
and over **all** these put on **love**,
    that is, the **bond** of **perfection.**
And let the **peace** of **Christ control** your **hearts**,
    the **peace** into which you were also **called** in **one body.**
And be **thankful.**
Let the **word** of Christ **dwell** in you **richly**,
    as in all **wisdom** you **teach** and **admonish** one another,
    singing **psalms**, **hymns**, and **spiritual songs**
    with **gratitude** in your **hearts** to **God.**
And whatever you do, in **word** or in **deed**,
    do **everything** in the **name** of the **Lord Jesus**,
    giving **thanks** to **God** the **Father** through **him.**

Wives, be subordinate to your **husbands**,
    as is **proper** in the **Lord.**
Husbands, love your **wives**,
    and avoid **any bitterness** toward them.

Colossians = kuh-LOSH-uhnz

Look up at the assembly for the greeting "Brothers and sisters." Pause noticeably after it, making sure you have their attention.

Read the list of virtues slowly, clearly enunciating each one. Reflect the meaning of each virtue in the tone and volume of your voice.

Build to the line "giving thanks to God the Father through him" and pause significantly after it.

Proclaim the household code with love and humility, not authority and arrogance.

---

a disregard for one another. Changing this was no small task.

The author takes a step toward the necessary change by citing the twofold divine commandment. The commandment calls God's children to believe in his Son and to embody the love he has for us in our love for each other. If we do this, our present and future will be clear: we will remain with God and God will remain in us. The Spirit will provide us with certainty about this.

On the Feast of the Holy Family, you present to the families in the assembly the task the author of 1 John sets before his community. Reflecting beforehand on the challenges families face to believe and live as God's children in the world today will give your proclamation integrity.

COLOSSIANS 3:12–21. On the Feast of the Holy Family, the Second Reading provides a prescription for ideal family relations. The passage itself comes from the section of Colossians which urges the members of the body of Christ, the Church, to live according to the values of the community (3:5—4:6).

Lists of virtues and vices, as well as household codes, were common in Greek philosophical works of the first century. The author of Colossians strongly urges the members of the Church to practice the virtues as the Lord intends them to (3:13). Christian families are to perform works of compassion, kindness, humility, gentleness, and patience, not for themselves, but in Christ's name (verse 17). When they do,

Children, obey your **parents** in **everything**,
for this is **pleasing** to the **Lord**.
Fathers, do **not** provoke your **children**,
so they may not become **discouraged**.

[Shorter: Colossians 3:12–17]

GOSPEL Luke 2:41–52

A reading from the holy Gospel according to Luke

Use a narrative tone to convey
the setting.

Each **year** Jesus' **parents** went to **Jerusalem** for the feast
of **Passover**,
and when he was **twelve** years **old**,
they went **up** according to festival **custom**.
After they had **completed** its days, as they were **returning**,
the boy **Jesus** remained **behind** in **Jerusalem**,
but his **parents** did not **know** it.

caravan = KAYR-uh-van

Thinking that he was in the **caravan**,
they **journeyed** for a **day**
and **looked** for him among their **relatives** and **acquaintances**,

Increase the anxiety in your voice as you
speak of Jesus' parents looking for and
not finding him.

but **not finding** him,
they **returned** to **Jerusalem** to **look** for him.
After three days they **found** him in the **temple**,
sitting in the **midst** of the **teachers**,

Emphasize "three days" to help the
assembly make the connection to Jesus'
Death and Resurrection. Release the
anxiety in your voice and replace it with
calm and relief.

listening to them and **asking** them **questions**,
and **all** who **heard** him were **astounded**
at his **understanding** and his **answers**.

the peace of Christ will lead them to gratitude and praise for all God has done.

The final four verses of the reading present the order of a Christian household. The advice has its roots in the same social or household codes of the first century which held that slaves were subject to their masters. While this part of the reading might be difficult for you to proclaim, focusing on the dimensions of love and care among family members should help. Showing affection and paying attention to the feelings and desires of family members

is the responsibility of each person in the family who seeks to live his or her life in Christ.

For Catholics, the household or family is the basic unit of the Church. It is the "domestic Church" (*Lumen Gentium, Dogmatic Constitution of the Church,* 11). In this Church, the love between parents and children identifies the family as a household of faith that gives thanks to God.

In your proclamation, use a gentle and peaceful tone of voice throughout, rather than switching to a didactic and authoritative tone for the household code. This will

help keep the unity of the passage and will assist the assembly in understanding the code in relation to the Christian virtue of love.

GOSPEL At its heart, the Gospel today is an ordinary story about a family road trip. The journey of the Holy Family is a pilgrimage that faithful Jewish families took to Jerusalem for the Passover. Their journey parallels Hannah's in the First Reading. As you begin the proclamation of the Gospel, your voice should

Mary is a little exasperated, but seeks to understand her son.

Jesus' question seeks understanding as well.

Emphasize the word "must." A reversal of roles: the child is teaching his parents.

Mutual understanding does not occur. Emphasize the word "not."

Communicate the conclusion of the narrative in a straightforward manner. Things are again as they should be: the child Jesus is obedient.

When his **parents saw** him,
they were **astonished**,
and his **mother** said to him,
"**Son**, **why** have you **done** this to **us**?
Your father and I have been **looking** for you with **great anxiety**."
And **he** said to **them**,
"**Why** were you looking for **me**?
Did you not **know** that I **must** be in **my Father's house**?"
But they did not **understand** what he said to them.
He went **down** with them and came to **Nazareth**,
and was **obedient** to them;
and his **mother kept all these things** in her **heart**.
And **Jesus advanced** in **wisdom** and **age** and **favor**
before **God** and **man**.

convey that everything seems to be going according to plan. As the story progresses, however, your voice should reflect Mary and Joseph's increasing anxiety.

Nothing is more disconcerting to a parent than a lost child. In this case, Luke tells us it took three days before they found Jesus. The "three days" anticipates the time between Jesus' Death and Resurrection.

In the dialogue between Mary and Jesus, both ask "why" questions, trying to understand what the other is doing. Jesus' question to his mother is twofold. The twelve-year-old apparently does not allow his mother time to respond, but rather offers words of explanation for what he was doing as part of his follow-up question. His answer reveals his identity as the Father's divine Son. Although Jesus' parents did not understand what he was trying to tell them, the anxiety that marked the search for the lost youth is now gone. Their life together becomes ordinary again, as the summary in the final section of the Gospel narrates. The journey toward Jerusalem will take place again in a different context.

SOLEMNITY OF MARY, THE HOLY MOTHER OF GOD

Lectionary #18

READING I Numbers 6:22–27

A reading from the Book of Numbers

Clearly identify the Lord as the speaker.
Moses = MOH-ziz
Aaron = AYR-uhn

The LORD said to **Moses**:
"**Speak** to **Aaron** and his **sons** and **tell** them:
   This is how you shall **bless** the Israelites.
Say to them:
   The LORD **bless** you and **keep** you!
   The LORD **let** his **face shine** upon you,
      and be **gracious** to you!
   The LORD **look** upon you **kindly**
      and **give** you **peace**!
So shall they **invoke** my **name** upon the Israelites,
   and I will **bless** them."

Pray the blessing slowly and with care.
Read line by line as if you were blessing
the assembly.

Pause at the end of the blessing before
the Lord's words which are not a part of
the actual blessing.

READING I Today's solemnity focuses on the Incarnation from the perspective of Mary, the Mother of God. The brief passage from the Book of Numbers comes at the end of a section on laws and regulations that the Hebrew people were to follow. One of the reasons this passage is proclaimed today is that it helps us see Mary as deeply rooted in the ancient traditions of the Hebrew people. Mary was a faithful Jew. The words of blessing in these verses were probably not far from her heart, just as many Jews and Christians continue to hold them dear.

The three lines of the blessing ask God to take care of his people, to reveal himself to them, and grant them peace. In Hebrew, the expression "let his face shine" corresponds to our word "smile." To ask the Lord to let his face shine upon us means to see God happy. God's divine pleasure and contentment come because God is in relationship with us. Even though God does not need our companionship, God is happy to freely choose a relationship with us.

The Hebrew word for "peace" (*shalom*) includes not only a sense of serenity, but also happiness and prosperity. The peace that comes from God reaches into all areas of our life and leads us to experience the contentment that comes from living our life in God.

Offer this blessing as a prayer for the assembly. In your preparation, think about the ways in which the Lord blesses you and gives you peace. This will help you to achieve a tone of prayerfulness as you impart the blessing to the assembly.

READING II   Galatians 4:4–7

Galatians = guh-LAY-shuhnz

Paul captures the entire Paschal Mystery in the single sentence: "When the fullness . . . adoption as sons." Use the commas as a guide to your proclamation. "God sent his Son" is the main clause.

Abba = AH-bah

"Abba, Father!" are the same words that Jesus used while praying in Gethsemane (Mark 14:36). "Abba" is an Aramaic term that connotes intimacy between a father and his child. Express this intimacy by using a gentle, but audible, voice. Do not shout the words.

A reading from the Letter of Saint Paul to the Galatians

Brothers and sisters:
When the **fullness** of time had **come**, **God** sent his **Son**,
    born of a **woman**, **born** under the **law**,
    to **ransom** those **under** the **law**,
    so that **we** might **receive adoption** as **sons**.
As **proof** that **you** are **sons**,
    God sent the **Spirit** of his **Son** into our **hearts**,
    crying out, **"Abba, Father!"**
So you are **no longer** a **slave** but a **son**,
    and **if** a **son then** also an **heir**, through **God**.

READING II This reading expresses the joy that comes from a life-giving transition. Paul wrote in a society in which slavery was a reality, so he used that image in making his point about the new position of Christians in relation to God. Prior to the Son's coming, the Galatians were slaves to sin. Paul often characterized this slavery as being bound by a shallow understanding of the details of Jewish Law. When Jesus Christ came, everything changed. Faith—not superficial adherence to the Law—led to the inheritance of Abraham's promises.

Christ took on our humanity, being born of a woman and under the Law. It was necessary that he take upon himself our human condition in order that we might call ourselves adopted sons and daughters of God. Because the Son redeemed humanity and its attachment to the Law, we, like the Galatians, have the possibility of a new, intimate relationship with God. We can use the Son's words "Abba, Father!" in our prayer to God. We no longer have to follow the letter of the Law in order to be in right relationship with God.

In your proclamation, convey the dynamic movement from constraint to freedom that is behind Paul's words. As you prepare, reflect on a time in your life when you experienced a change from an old way of life to a new way. How did it feel for you to be set free from the old to embrace the new? Consider this change as living life more deeply in the Spirit of the Son whom God sent. Through your own growth, you are realizing more of your identity as an adopted son or daughter of God; this is what you are calling the assembly to realize as well.

GOSPEL   Luke 2:16–21

A reading from the holy Gospel according to Luke

The **shepherds** went **in haste** to **Bethlehem**
    and found **Mary** and **Joseph**,
  and the **infant** lying in the **manger**.
When they saw this,
  they **made known** the message
  that had been **told** them about **this** child.
All who **heard** it were **amazed**
  by what had been **told** them by the **shepherds**.
And **Mary** kept **all these things**,
  reflecting on them in her **heart**.
Then the shepherds **returned**,
  glorifying and **praising** God
  for all they had **heard** and **seen**,
  just as it had been told to them.

When **eight days** were **completed** for his **circumcision**,
  he was named **Jesus**, the name given him by the **angel**
  before he was **conceived** in the **womb**.

Pause at the comma after "Mary and Joseph." They are not lying in the manger with the infant!

Let amazement be heard in your voice for "All who heard it were amazed."

Speak unhurriedly and with care as you describe Mary's actions. Mary is a focal point today and her response is well-known to many. Speaking these words in a considered fashion allows people to hear her response as if for the first time.

Pause before the final verse, then take your time with it to highlight the important point: Jesus is the fulfillment of Jewish Law.

GOSPEL This is the same Gospel proclaimed during the Christmas Mass at Dawn, except it begins a verse later and ends with an additional verse. Today, we read the Gospel from the perspective of the Solemnity of Mary, Mother of God.

Early church leaders intensely debated the identity of Mary and how Christians should refer to her. Should Mary be called the "Mother of Christ" (Christotokos) or the "Mother of God" (Theotokos)? Calling Mary the "Mother of Christ" emphasizes the human nature of Jesus, her child. On the other hand, the title "Mother of God" stresses his divine nature. The Council of Ephesus in 431 declared "Mother of God" the suitable title for Mary. At its core, this title affirms the truth about who Jesus Christ is for Christians: God incarnate.

The addition of the verse at the end of the reading shows us the significance of the Jewish Law for Jesus' parents. Jesus was born at a particular time in history and into a particular religious tradition. Mary and Joseph raised him to be faithful to Jewish laws and customs. For Luke, Jesus is the fulfillment of the hopes of the Chosen People for a messiah. He is the fulfillment of the Law.

In your preparation, reflect in your heart about who Jesus is for you and for the world. Knowing, then, that Mary gave birth to the Savior of the world, your proclamation will lead the assembly to a deeper faith in him through the intercession of Mary, the Mother of God.

THE EPIPHANY OF THE LORD

Lectionary #20

READING I   Isaiah 60:1–6

A reading from the Book of the Prophet Isaiah

Let the ups and downs of this first section be heard in your voice. Raise your voice at first, lower it as you speak of darkness, and then raise it again as you state with joy that the Lord shines over Jerusalem.

> **Rise up** in splendor, **Jerusalem**! Your **light** has come,
>   the **glory** of the **Lord shines** upon you.
> **See**, **darkness** covers the **earth**,
>   and **thick clouds** cover the **peoples**;
> but upon **you** the LORD **shines**,
>   and over **you appears** his **glory**.
> **Nations** shall **walk** by your **light**,
>   and **kings** by your **shining radiance**.
> Raise your **eyes** and **look about**;
>   they all **gather** and **come** to **you**:
> your **sons** come from **afar**,
>   and your **daughters** in the arms of their **nurses**.

Raise your eyes and look to different sides of the assembly as you proclaim, "Raise your eyes and look about." When you turn to make eye contact with different sections of the assembly, be careful not to move away from the microphone.

> **Then** you shall be **radiant** at what you **see**,
>   your **heart** shall **throb** and **overflow**,
> for the **riches** of the **sea** shall be **emptied out** before **you**,
>   the **wealth** of **nations** shall be **brought** to **you**.
> **Caravans** of **camels** shall **fill** you,
>   **dromedaries** from **Midian** and **Ephah**;
> **all** from **Sheba** shall come
>   bearing **gold** and **frankincense**,
>   and proclaiming the **praises** of the LORD.

Midian = MID-ee-uhn
Ephah = EE-fah
Sheba = SHEE-buh
The last phrase, "proclaiming the praises of the Lord," captures the main point of the passage. It is also the reason why both Jews and Christians continue to gather in prayer.

The Solemnities of the Nativity and Epiphany, together with the Feast of the Baptism of the Lord, are the three "manifestation" feasts. Epiphany was the original celebration of God's manifestation, and included both Jesus' birth and baptism. The celebration of Christmas as a manifestation feast came later, and in the West, eventually became the principal observance of Jesus' birth.

The words of the prophet Isaiah and the example of the magi in the Gospel teach us that those who see the glory of the Lord are accountable for what they see. Just as the prophet called Jerusalem to "rise up" and be a light for other nations, we are called to proclaim God's glory beyond our church buildings, in the streets and neighborhoods of our cities and towns.

READING I   This passage from Second Isaiah, the author of chapters 40 through 55 of the Book of Isaiah, provides us with a description of the new Jerusalem. The Israelites return from exile with the Lord's light shining on them and their city. The Lord's glory is so impressive that others want to join in singing God's praises.

Proclaim this reading with joy and excitement, praising God for the many ways in which he is present in your life, your parish community, the universal Church, and the world. Your own joy, like the prophet's words to Jerusalem, will encourage the assembly to reflect the Lord's shining glory in all they say and do. As a result of your ministry, many will want to stream to God.

Ephesians = ee-FEE-zhunz

Address the phrase "You have heard" directly to the assembly by looking up and making eye contact with them.

Pause significantly after the colon in the line "to his holy apostles and prophets by the Spirit."

Gentiles = JEN-tils

coheirs = co-ayrs Notice the "h" is not pronounced.

READING II Ephesians 3:2–3a,5–6

A reading from the Letter of Saint Paul to the Ephesians

Brothers and sisters:
You have **heard** of the **stewardship** of **God's grace**
    that was given to **me** for your **benefit**,
        namely, that the **mystery** was **made known** to me
            by **revelation**.
It was **not made known to people in other generations**
    as it has **now** been revealed
    to his **holy apostles** and **prophets** by the **Spirit**:
    that the **Gentiles** are **coheirs**, members of the **same body**,
    and **copartners** in the **promise** in **Christ Jesus**
        through the **gospel**.

Bethlehem = BETH-luh-hem
Judea = joo-DEE-uh
Herod = HAYR-ud

GOSPEL Matthew 2:1–12

A reading from the holy Gospel according to Matthew

When **Jesus** was born in **Bethlehem** of **Judea**,
    in the days of King **Herod**,
        behold, **magi** from the **east** arrived in **Jerusalem**, saying,
        "**Where** is the **newborn king** of the **Jews**?
We **saw** his **star** at its **rising**
    and **have come** to do him **homage**."

READING II Saint Augustine, in an early fifth-century sermon, said "Recently we celebrated the day on which Christ was born among the Jews; today we celebrate the day on which He was adored by the Gentiles" (Sermon 199, 1). When Saint Paul speaks of the "stewardship of God's grace," he is referring to the realization of God's plan in Christ Jesus, a plan for unity.

Through Christ, God manifested himself to all. Paul understood that the primary purpose of his ministry was to bring Jews and Gentiles together in adoration of Christ Jesus. Both are heirs to his promise. Both are members of the same body, the body of Christ.

In early Christian communities, Jews and Gentiles did not always accept each other fully into the body of Christ. In Christ, we are to work through our differences, trying to see each other as God sees us. As Paul found out, working to bring people together as the body of Christ is a lifelong endeavor. We are able to undertake this endeavor because God is faithful—the Spirit of Christ remains with us in the work we do.

This same Spirit is present in your proclamation of the Word. Be conscious that your proclamation unites people around the Word. Achieve this by not favoring one row or side of the assembly when you make eye contact. Include everyone— young and old, male and female, fashionable and shabby, every race and ethnicity— in the sweep of your gaze. Let everyone feel that they are "copartners in the promise."

GOSPEL Christians love the gospel story of the magi! They easily associate it with the Solemnity of

As you proclaim the section that begins "When King Herod heard this," express the cunning nature of the King in your tone of voice.

When **King Herod heard** this,
    he was **greatly troubled**,
    and **all Jerusalem** with him.
Assembling all the chief priests and the scribes of the people,
    he **inquired** of them **where the Christ** was to **be born**.
They said to him, "In **Bethlehem** of **Judea**,
    for **thus** it has been **written** through the **prophet**:

Observing the punctuation around the word "Bethlehem" will highlight the repetition of the place of Christ's birth.

        And **you**, **Bethlehem**, land of Judah,
            are by no means **least** among the rulers of **Judah**;
        since **from** you shall come a ruler,
            who is to **shepherd** my people **Israel**."
Then Herod **called** the **magi secretly**
    and ascertained from them the **time** of the star's **appearance**.
He **sent** them to **Bethlehem** and said,

King Herod really does not want to offer the child homage, despite his words to the contrary. Try adding a little sarcasm to your voice so that Herod's deceptive and fraudulent character comes through.

    "**Go** and **search diligently** for the **child**.
When you have **found** him, **bring** me **word**,
    that I too may go and do him **homage**."
After their audience with the king they set **out**.
And **behold**, the **star** that they had **seen** at its **rising**
        preceded them,
    until it **came** and **stopped** over the **place** where the **child was**.
They were **overjoyed** at **seeing** the **star**,

Impart the joy and relief of the magi. Their journey was successful!

    and on **entering** the **house**
    they **saw** the **child** with **Mary** his **mother**.
They **prostrated** themselves and did him **homage**.
Then they **opened** their **treasures**

Take your time with the lines that tell us how the magi offered homage to the Christ child. Read them with reverence.

frankincense = FRAYNK-in-sens

myrrh = mer

    and **offered** him **gifts** of **gold**, **frankincense**, and **myrrh**.
And having been **warned** in **a dream not** to **return** to Herod,
    they **departed** for their country by **another way**.

Epiphany. Over-emphasizing the details of the number of wise men and the names of their gifts can diminish the importance of the profound truth that the evangelist Matthew sought to convey.

In Matthew, the magi (who are Gentiles from a foreign land) are the first to adore Jesus. However, when some Jews, including King Herod, learned from the magi of the child's star rising, they remained unmoved, even caught up in the political import of the birth. Matthew's main point in framing his narrative in this way is that Jesus manifests God to the whole world. God does

not reserve his promise of salvation for a select few. God makes his promise available to all, to be accepted in faith just as the Gentile magi did.

At the end of today's Gospel is a line often glossed over. It tells us that the magi went back to their home country. They did not bask in excitement from their adoration of Christ. Rather, their mission began in earnest as they journeyed home to share their joy of seeing the Christ child.

In their explanation of the relationship between Christmas and Epiphany, liturgists sometimes refer to Guerric of Igny,

a twelfth-century French abbot, who said, "That which we have celebrated up to today is the birth of Christ, that which we celebrate today is our own birth" (Sermon 14.1). The magi's own birth, as followers of Jesus, occurred as they offered homage to the Child and went forth to proclaim him to the world. We, too, are born as Christians in our act of giving homage to Christ and in bringing his presence to the world. By your proclamation of the last line of this Gospel, the assembly will know that the praise of God includes spreading his Word in our cities, towns, and villages.

THE BAPTISM OF THE LORD

Lectionary #21

READING I   Isaiah 40:1–5, 9–11

Isaiah = ī-ZAY-uh

Begin with a slow, comforting pace. Let your tone reflect the meaning of the words "comfort" and "tenderly."

A reading from the Book of the Prophet Isaiah

Comfort, give **comfort** to my **people**,
   says your God.
Speak **tenderly** to Jerusalem, and **proclaim** to her
   that her **service** is at an **end**,
   her **guilt** is **expiated**;
indeed, she has **received** from the **hand** of the LORD
   double for all her **sins**.

"A voice cries out" signifies a switch in the voice speaking.

   A **voice** cries out:
In the desert **prepare** the **way** of the LORD!
   Make **straight** in the wasteland a **highway** for our **God**!
Every valley shall be **filled** in,
   every mountain and **hill** shall be **made low**;
the **rugged land** shall be made a **plain**,
   the **rough country**, a **broad valley**.
Then the **glory** of the LORD shall be **revealed**,
   and **all people** shall see it **together**;
for the **mouth** of the LORD has **spoken**.

The voice switches back to God on the words "Go up on to a high mountain."

Go **up** on to a **high** mountain,
   Zion, **herald** of glad **tidings**;
cry out at the **top** of your **voice**,
   Jerusalem, **herald** of good **news**!

Today options are given for the readings. Contact your parish staff to learn which readings will be used.

READING I   **ISAIAH 40.** Today's passage comes from the part of the Book of Isaiah known as the Book of Consolation (40:1—55:13). We hear this reading also on the Second Sunday of Advent in Year B. Today it is paired with the Gospel describing Jesus' baptism.

When this passage was written, Israel was in need of consolation. She had endured a lengthy exile and did not know how much longer it would go on. The good news in this prophecy, however, is that Israel's exile is almost at an end. The Lord's coming will bring redemption and the forgiveness of sins; God's justice will triumph. This indeed is good news! Prior to the Lord's coming, the people must prepare the way in the desert, and this preparation is not an easy task. Yet the Lord for whom they prepare the way is powerful. He will care for the people who announce his arrival as tenderly and as intimately as a shepherd tends his flock.

For the proclaimer of the Word, this passage poses many challenges. The speaker alternates between God and the voice crying out. The tone shifts from comfort and tenderness to command and power. It then moves to joy with Jerusalem's call to herald the good news of the Lord's coming. In the final section, the tone shifts from power and might to care and concern of the shepherd for his flock. Practice the reading often, trying different tones and emphases to get across the multiple shifts in both that occur.

Keep strength, though not the loudness, evident in your voice as you speak of the Lord's power.

Fear not to cry out
  and **say** to the cities of **Judah**:
  Here is your **God**!
Here comes with **power**
  the Lord **GOD**,
  who **rules** by his **strong arm**;
here is his **reward** with him,
  his **recompense** before him.
Like a **shepherd** he **feeds** his **flock**;
  in his **arms** he **gathers** the **lambs**,
carrying them in his **bosom**,
  and **leading** the ewes with **care**.

Lighten and soften your voice as you speak of the Lord as a shepherd. Try slowing your pace slightly as you approach the end of the sentence.

Or:

READING I Isaiah 42:1–4, 6–7

Isaiah = ī-ZAY-uh

A reading from the Book of the Prophet Isaiah

Proclaim the first section of the reading as if you are making an announcement. You are telling the assembly of the servant's presence in their midst.

Thus says the **LORD**:
Here is my **servant** whom I **uphold**,
  my **chosen one** with whom I am **pleased**,
upon whom I have put my **spirit**;
  he shall bring forth **justice** to the **nations**,
not **crying out**, not **shouting**,
  not making his **voice heard** in the street.
A **bruised reed** he shall not **break**,
  and a **smoldering wick** he shall **not quench**,
until he establishes **justice** on the **earth**;
  the **coastlands** will wait for his **teaching**.

Isaiah 42. This reading is one of four servant songs in Isaiah. Written by Second Isaiah in the sixth century BC, this song offers encouragement for the disheartened Israelites who thought their exile would never end.

The first section is written in the third person and provides a description of the servant's identity and mission. The servant, like Abraham, Moses, David, Israel, and all her leaders, is the Lord's chosen one. The Lord's spirit fills him as it filled kings and other leaders. Yet, his mission contrasts starkly with that of political and

military leaders. The servant would bring forth justice that is a reflection of God's love for his people and the earth.

The second section is written with the personal pronoun "you." The identity of the servant is unclear. The servant could be an individual, the prophet, or Israel herself. Regardless of the servant's identity, the Lord's words here are a direct address, the Lord's personal call of the servant, and a declaration of the messianic task set before the servant. There are similarities between the description of the servant's mission in the two sections of the reading.

Note the repetition of the word "justice" and the references to images of light in both sections.

In your proclamation, accentuate the difference in the addressees of the two sections by delivering the first in a narrative style. In the second section, address the assembly directly, making more eye contact with them. This will convey that through Baptism, God personally calls each of us to participate in the servant's mission of covenant, light, and freedom.

Proclaim the second section, which begins with "I, the LORD, have called you" in a personal tone. Make eye contact with the assembly, for the Lord calls its members.

I, the LORD, have called **you** for the victory **of justice,**
I have grasped **you** by the **hand;**
I **formed you,** and **set you**
as a **covenant** of the **people,**
a **light** for the **nations,**
to **open** the **eyes** of the **blind,**
to **bring out prisoners** from **confinement,**
and from the **dungeon,** those who live in **darkness.**

READING II   Titus 2:11–14; 3:4–7

Titus = TĪ-tuhs

A reading from the Letter of Saint Paul to Titus

The opening section is one sentence. The punctuation is a good guide to your proclamation. Also, try pausing after "saving all" to add emphasis.

Beloved:
The **grace** of **God** has **appeared, saving all**
and **training** us to reject **godless** ways
and **worldly** desires
and to live **temperately, justly** and **devoutly** in **this** age,
as we **await** the **blessed hope,**
the **appearance** of the **glory** of our great **God**
and **savior Jesus Christ,**
who **gave himself** for **us** to **deliver us** from **all lawlessness**
and to **cleanse** for **himself** a **people** as his **own,**
eager to do what is **good.**

The second section is also one sentence. Let your enunciation of the words "kindness," "generous love," and "mercy" reflect their meaning.

When the **kindness** and **generous love**
of **God** our **savior appeared,**
not because of any **righteous deeds** we had done
but because of his **mercy,**

READING II   **TITUS.** The first half of this reading is the Second Reading for the Christmas Mass during the Night. It is only one sentence. In this section of the pastoral letter, the author discloses the grace of God active in the past, present, and future. When we celebrate Jesus' coming as the grace of God in history, we also remember that he delivered us from sin and cleansed us as his people. As a result, we are eager to do what is good.

The second half of the reading beginning with "When the kindness," which is also one sentence, makes the obvious connection with today's feast. The bath of rebirth through which Jesus Christ saved us is Baptism. In Baptism, God pours the Holy Spirit on us through his Son in order to justify us. This justification results in our becoming heirs of eternal life. We live in hope now that we indeed will share in this life after our earthly life is complete.

Titus struggled to protect his community on the island of Crete from false teaching. Many had been led to disregard Christian virtues, and this resulted in an unkind community whose members did not take care of each other. In contrast, Jesus Christ lives out to the fullest the divine attributes of kindness and generous love mentioned at the beginning of the second section. His own baptism marks his commission as the Son of God sent to be kindness and generous love through his life, Death, and Resurrection.

ACTS. Christmas and Easter come together again on today's feast. Today's Second Reading from the Acts of the Apostles includes three verses that are a part of the First Reading proclaimed on Easter Sunday all three years of the Lectionary cycle.

he **saved us** through the **bath** of **rebirth**
and **renewal** by the **Holy Spirit**,
whom he **richly poured out** on us
through **Jesus Christ** our **savior**,
so that **we** might be **justified** by his **grace**
and become **heirs** in **hope** of **eternal life**.

Or:

Fill your voice with hope and optimism because of our justification and the gift of eternal life.

heirs = ayrz

Use a narrative tone of voice for the introductory line, pausing after the comma to make sure you have the assembly's attention for Peter's words.

Cornelius = kohr-NEEL-yuhs

Judea = joo-DEE-uh; joo-DAY-uh

As the comma indicates, pause after "by the devil." Proclaim the words "for God was with him" slowly and make eye contact with the assembly. You are trying to help the assembly understand the presence of God in Jesus that we celebrate on the Feast of the Baptism of the Lord.

READING II Acts 10:34–38

A reading from the Acts of the Apostles

Peter proceeded to **speak** to those gathered
in the house of **Cornelius**, **saying**:
"In **truth**, I see that **God** shows **no partiality**.
Rather, in **every** nation whoever **fears** him and **acts uprightly**
is **acceptable** to him.
You know the word that he **sent** to the **Israelites**
as he proclaimed **peace** through **Jesus Christ**, who is **Lord** of **all**,
what has **happened all over Judea**,
beginning in **Galilee** after the **baptism**
that John **preached**,
how God **anointed Jesus** of **Nazareth**
with the **Holy Spirit** and **power**.
He went about doing **good**
and **healing all** those **oppressed** by the **devil**,
for **God** was **with him**."

The reading is from Peter's speech to Cornelius's household prior to their conversion and baptism. After the opening statements about God's impartiality, the words "You know" suggest that Peter intends his teaching primarily for those who are already Christian. What follows presents the continuity between the Word God spoke to the Israelites and its fulfillment in the person and mission of Jesus Christ, on whom the Holy Spirit descended at his baptism.

In proclaiming Peter's explanation of how God's revelation in Jesus took place,

you have the opportunity to assist the assembly in making the connection between the events of Christmas and Easter. Accomplish this by speaking with great sincerity at the beginning of the reading about God's acceptance of all persons. Then, deliver the kerygma (the proclamation of Christ's teachings) with equal emphasis on each of its historical components. When you end the reading, leave the assembly wanting to hear the rest of the story—even though they know it.

Before we get to Easter in this liturgical year, we have to participate in spreading the Good News as we journey toward Jerusalem with Jesus. Our Baptism calls us to do nothing less.

GOSPEL Today's passage from the Gospel according to Luke marks a change in focus from the ministry of John the Baptist to that of Jesus. John himself knows his place; he is unworthy to help Jesus take off his sandals, and neither is he as strong. John also knows the

Convey the people's sense of expectation with excitement in your voice.

A reading from the holy Gospel according to Luke

The people were **filled** with **expectation**,
    and **all** were **asking** in their **hearts**
    whether **John** might be the **Christ**.
John **answered** them all, saying,
    "I am **baptizing** you with **water**,
    but **one mightier** than **I** is coming.
I am **not worthy** to **loosen** the **thongs** of his **sandals**.
He will **baptize** you with the **Holy Spirit** and **fire**."

Speak John's response candidly, but still offering the hope he does.

Take your time presenting the fact of Jesus' baptism and that he was praying.

After **all** the **people** had been **baptized**
    and **Jesus also** had been **baptized** and was **praying**,
    heaven was **opened** and the **Holy Spirit**
        descended upon him
    in **bodily form** like a **dove**.
And a **voice** came from **heaven**,
    "**You** are my **beloved Son**;
    with **you** I am well **pleased**."

Proclaim the voice's affirmation with a sense of personal satisfaction and delight.

difference between the baptisms each can perform. John baptizes with water, a common practice at the time, but Jesus will baptize with the Holy Spirit and fire. (Fire was thought to be a cleansing medium.) Jesus' baptism would be greater than John's.

The second section opens matter-of-factly with a statement about all the people John baptized, including Jesus. On the basis of this statement, Jesus' baptism appears to be just like everyone else's. As the sentence continues, however, we see

Jesus praying (as he frequently does in Luke's account) and we hear of the Holy Spirit coming upon Jesus from heaven. Finally a voice from heaven identifies Jesus as "my beloved Son."

Jesus' baptism by John was the same as everyone else's, but it led to something entirely different. His baptism would mark the beginning of a new period in his life. Interestingly, Luke places the genealogy of Jesus immediately after his baptism. Following the genealogy is the story of Jesus' temptation in the desert. Luke begins the temptation narrative noting that Jesus

returns from the Jordan filled with the Holy Spirit. The Spirit never leaves him throughout his journey to Jerusalem, and empowers him to fulfill his mission.

The Spirit we receive at Baptism does the same for us. Through the Spirit and through frequent prayer modeled on Jesus' prayer, we draw closer to God as God's beloved sons and daughters.

2ND SUNDAY IN ORDINARY TIME

Lectionary #66

READING I Isaiah 62:1–5

Isaiah = ī-ZAY-uh

Zion = ZĪ-uhn; ZĪ-ahn

A reading from the Book of the Prophet Isaiah

For **Zion's sake** I will **not** be **silent**,
    for **Jerusalem's sake** I will **not be quiet**,
until her **vindication shines** forth like the **dawn**
    and her **victory** like a **burning torch**.

Nations shall **behold** your **vindication**,
    and all the **kings** your **glory**;
you shall be **called** by a **new name**
    pronounced by the **mouth** of the LORD.
You shall be a **glorious crown** in the **hand** of the LORD,
    a **royal diadem** held by your **God**.
No more shall people call you "**Forsaken**,"
    or your land "**Desolate**,"
but you shall be called "**My Delight**,"
    and your land "**Espoused**."
For the LORD **delights** in you
    and makes your land his **spouse**.
As a **young man marries a virgin**,
    your **Builder** shall **marry you**;
and as a **bridegroom rejoices** in his **bride**
    so shall your **God rejoice** in **you**.

diadem = DĪ-uh-dem

Make the contrast clear between the old names, "Forsaken" and "Desolate" and the new names, "My Delight" and "Espoused" by lightening the tone of your voice on the new names.

Make eye contact with the assembly as you proclaim the final line with joy.

READING I Do you remember when we recently heard this reading proclaimed? This passage from Isaiah is the First Reading every year at the Vigil Mass for the Nativity of the Lord on Christmas Eve. In that liturgy, it is paired with Matthew's genealogy of Jesus and the story of the angel coming to Joseph in a dream telling him to welcome Mary into his home for she will give birth to Jesus. As we begin the counted Sundays of Ordinary Time, the reading is now coupled with the miracle story of the wedding feast at Cana.

The passage comes from the latter portion of the book of the prophet Isaiah, often referred to as Trito-Isaiah or Third Isaiah because it is believed to have been written by a different author than chapters 1–39 and chapters 40–55. Third Isaiah draws on Isaian themes, but develops them in light of the people's new situation. No longer are the people exiles in a foreign land. They have returned home to Jerusalem.

As the reading opens, we hear of Jerusalem's vindication and victory. The Lord has restored Israel. The Lord's people are not to keep their restoration to themselves. It is to shine forth for all to see. The names Jerusalem will be called from now on are ones that reflect the Lord's forgiveness for the people's association with pagan fertility cults. The Lord's generous mercy absolved the sin of the people's infidelity. The Lord desires to be as close to his people as spouses are to each other. Jerusalem's innocence, lost through the sin of worshiping other gods and now restored, means that she can now be compared to a virgin whom the Lord will marry. The spousal and wedding imagery provide the clear connections with today's Gospel.

Corinthians = kohr-IN-thee-uhnz

Make eye contact with the assembly as you address them as "Brothers and sisters."
Emphasize the contrast between "same" and "different."

Look up at different individuals each time "to another" occurs. Pause noticeably at the comma. Be careful not to have a sing-song rhythm.

Emphasize equally the "one and the same" Spirit and "all" as you summarize Paul's main point.

READING II   1 Corinthians 12:4–11

A reading from the first Letter of Saint Paul to the Corinthians

Brothers and sisters:
There are **different** kinds of **spiritual gifts** but the **same Spirit**;
    there are **different** forms of **service** but the **same Lord**;
    there are **different workings** but the **same God**
    who **produces all** of them in **everyone**.
To **each** individual the **manifestation** of the **Spirit**
    is **given** for some **benefit**.
To **one** is given through the **Spirit** the expression of **wisdom**;
    to **another**, the expression of **knowledge** according
        to the **same Spirit**;
    to **another**, **faith** by the same **Spirit**;
    to **another**, **gifts** of **healing** by the **one Spirit**;
    to **another**, mighty **deeds**;
    to **another**, **prophecy**;
    to **another**, **discernment** of **spirits**;
    to **another**, **varieties** of **tongues**;
    to **another**, **interpretation** of tongues.
But **one** and **the same Spirit** produces **all** of these,
    distributing them **individually** to **each person** as **he wishes**.

Use a narrative tone of voice to convey the setting.
Cana = KAY-nuh
Galilee = Gal-ih-lee

GOSPEL   John 2:1–11

A reading from the holy Gospel according to John

There was a **wedding** at **Cana** in **Galilee**,
    and the **mother** of **Jesus** was there.
Jesus and his **disciples** were **also** invited to the wedding.

READING II   For the first four Sundays of Ordinary Time, the Second Reading comes from the latter half of Paul's first Letter to the Corinthians; for the first three Sundays the epistle is from chapter 12. On the fourth Sunday, it is from chapter 15, the final chapter of 1 Corinthians. Chapter 12 is one of the most well-known chapters of all of Paul's writings. It focuses on the diversity of gifts in the Church and how the body of Christ is built up through the use of the gifts, without ranking them in order of importance.

The Corinthian community was mired in ugly divisions, which created disunity in the body of Christ. These divisions had to do with everything from economics, to what type of meat to eat, to whether or not women should cover their heads when they pray. The most divisive issue, however, was over the use of spiritual gifts and which gifts were most important. For Paul, these divisions made it seem like the Corinthians were dividing Christ himself, something which clearly could not happen.

In today's reading, Paul explains the diversity of gifts (*charismata*). This diver-

sity is good and acceptable because its source is one and the same Spirit. After laying out this fundamental belief, Paul proceeds to list the various gifts that are present in the community. Notice he mentions varieties of tongues and their interpretation last. *Glossolalia*, the Greek word for "speaking in tongues," always concludes Paul's lists of gifts, perhaps because this gift was the source of the most division in the community. In placing it last, Paul was attempting to reorder the mindset of the Corinthians, teaching them to recognize the equality of all spiritual gifts.

Speak Jesus' words as the polite address they are. His question is one of curiosity, not frustration or confrontation.

Emphasize the huge amount the jars could contain.

Pause between the statement of the headwaiter's lack of knowledge and the parenthetical remark about the servers' knowledge so as to draw the contrast between the two.

Proclaim the closing words of the headwaiter's statement with conviction; they are actually a confession of faith in Jesus.

Emphasize the words "the beginning" in the summary statement. Faith is a journey into belief.

When the **wine** ran **short**,
    the **mother** of **Jesus** said to him,
    "They have no **wine**."
And **Jesus** said to her,
    "**Woman**, how does **your** concern affect **me**?
My **hour** has **not yet come**."
His mother said to the **servers**,
    "**Do whatever** he **tells** you."
Now there were **six** stone **water** jars there for Jewish
        ceremonial **washings**,
    each holding **twenty** to **thirty gallons**.
Jesus **told** them,
    "**Fill** the jars with **water**."
So they **filled** them to the **brim**.
Then he told them,
    "**Draw** some out **now** and **take** it to the **headwaiter**."
So they **took** it.
And when the **headwaiter tasted** the **water** that had become **wine**,
    without knowing where it **came** from
    —although the **servers** who had **drawn** the water **knew**—,
    the **headwaiter** called the **bridegroom** and said to him,
"**Everyone** serves **good wine first**,
    and **then** when **people** have **drunk freely**, an **inferior** one;
    but **you** have **kept** the **good wine** until **now**."
Jesus did this as the **beginning** of his **signs** at **Cana** in **Galilee**
    and so **revealed** his **glory**,
    and his **disciples began** to **believe** in him.

The passage concludes with a restatement of the opening point of faith: one and the same Spirit creates and gives all of the gifts, not just certain gifts. It is by God's design and God's will that individuals in the Christian community have different, and equally necessary, gifts.

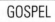 GOSPEL At the wedding feast at Cana, we see the first of seven signs in the Gospel according to John. There is no parallel in the synoptic accounts. The sign occurs at the beginning of Jesus' ministry and gives us insight into

who Jesus is. For John, a sign is more than a miracle. A sign reveals the abundant power and glory that Jesus brings to the world. This sign, turning water into "good wine," has obvious connections to the sacrificial meal of abundant feeding we know as the Eucharist.

The passage has three distinct sections. The first sets the scene. The second includes the preparation for the sign, the sign itself, and the headwaiter's public recognition of what Jesus has done. In this section, notice that Jesus does not do anything that causes the water to change into

wine; rather, his words coupled with the obedient actions of the servers yield the amazing transformation. The consequences of the sign follow in the last section: we learn more signs are to come, and that after this sign and the witness of the headwaiter, the disciples took the next step on their faith journey.

People love weddings! You will have their attention from the start. Practice different tones for each part, and emphasize allusions to Jesus' identity and ministry.

3RD SUNDAY IN ORDINARY TIME

Lectionary #69

READING I   Nehemiah 8:2–4a, 5–6, 8–10

A reading from the Book of Nehemiah

Ezra the **priest** brought the **law** before the **assembly**,
  which consisted of **men**, **women**,
  and those **children** old enough to **understand**.
Standing at one end of the open place that was before
      the Water **Gate**,
  he **read** out of the **book** from **daybreak** till **midday**,
  in the **presence** of the **men**, the **women**,
  and those **children** old enough to **understand**;
  and **all** the **people listened attentively** to the **book** of **the law**.
Ezra the scribe stood on a wooden **platform**
  that had been made for the occasion.
He **opened** the **scroll**
  so that **all** the **people** might **see** it
  —for he was standing **higher up** than any of the people—;
  and, as he **opened** it, **all** the people **rose**.
Ezra **blessed** the LORD, the **great God**,
  and **all** the **people**, their **hands** raised **high**, **answered**,
  "Amen, amen!"
Then they **bowed** down and **prostrated** themselves
      before the LORD,
  their faces to the **ground**.
Ezra read **plainly** from the **book** of the **law** of **God**,
  interpreting it so that **all** could **understand** what was **read**.

Nehemiah = nee-huh-MĪ-uh

Ezra = EZ-ruh

Make eye contact with different sections of the assembly on the opening verse, which describes those to whom Ezra brought the Law. You are doing the same in your proclamation.

Notice the repetition. Repeat your previous eye contact. Try a different technique for emphasizing "all the people" each time the phrase occurs.

Decrease the volume of your voice as you speak the parenthetical remark about Ezra standing higher.

Build in intensity to the people's proclamation "Amen, amen!" Decrease as you speak of them bowing down and prostrating themselves. Convey humility and reverence. Pause significantly to mark a transition to the next section.

READING I   This is the only Sunday of the three-year Lectionary cycle of readings on which we hear from the Book of Nehemiah. Ezra and Nehemiah were the two leaders most responsible for the religious formation of the Jewish community after the Babylonian exile. The two books of the Old Testament which now bear their names were originally one. In them, we read about Ezra as the one who led the people back to the Law and established it as the cornerstone of the Jewish community and Nehemiah as the one who spear-headed administrative reforms and engineered the task of rebuilding Jerusalem's walls.

Today's reading conjures up an image of the Liturgy of the Word. As you read of Ezra coming before an assembly so diverse in age, place yourself in Ezra's shoes. Like Ezra, each time you step up to proclaim the Word, you are standing at a prominent place within the worship space. We hear the composition of the assembly described twice, suggesting that Ezra never lost sight of the people to whom he brought the Word. Throughout your proclamation of the Word, one of your challenges is to be mindful of the people in the assembly and how they might respond to it.

There is a dynamic interplay between Ezra's proclamation of the Law and the people's attentive listening to it. The role of the assembly is not passive and solely receptive. Hearing and receiving the Word carries its own agency. The people in Ezra's assembly responded actively— standing, raising their hands, answering "Amen, amen!" and bowing down and prostrating themselves. It is all the people who respond. Seven times in the reading either the phrase "all the people" or the

Offer the words spoken in concert by
Nehemiah, Ezra, and the Levites with
encouragement.

Then **Nehemiah**, that is, His **Excellency**, and **Ezra**
      the priest-scribe
   and the **Levites** who were **instructing** the **people**
   said to **all** the **people**:
   "**Today** is **holy** to the LORD your **God**.
Do **not** be **sad**, and do **not** weep"—
   for **all** the **people** were **weeping** as they **heard** the **words**
      of the **law**.
He said further: "**Go**, **eat** rich **foods** and **drink** sweet **drinks**,
   and **allot portions** to those who had **nothing prepared**;
   for **today** is **holy** to our LORD.
Do **not** be **saddened** this **day**,
   for **rejoicing** in the LORD must be your **strength**!"

Use a tone of voice that communicates
optimism. The Lord is our strength.

READING II   1 Corinthians 12:12–30

Corinthians = kohr-IN-thee-uhnz

A reading from the first Letter of Saint Paul to the Corinthians

Brothers and **sisters**:
As a **body** is **one** though it has **many parts**,
   and **all** the **parts** of the **body**, though **many**, are **one** body,
      so also **Christ**.
For in **one Spirit** we were **all baptized** into **one body**,
   whether **Jews** or **Greeks**, **slaves** or **free** persons,
   and **we** were **all** given to **drink** of **one Spirit**.

Now the **body** is not a **single part**, but **many**.
If a **foot** should say,
   "**Because I** am **not** a **hand I** do **not belong** to the **body**,"
   it does **not** for this reason **belong any less** to the body.

Proclaim the opening verse slowly,
helping the assembly to hear it anew.
Slow the tempo even more on the final
words, "so also Christ."

The main point: a refrain that will repeat
in similar form two more times. Make eye
contact with the assembly as if you are
teaching this point to them.

word "all" occurs. Ezra was presenting the
Law not just to a select few, but to everyone in the assembly. Likewise, today the
Word is there for all who want to hear
and respond.

The Law Ezra proclaimed and his
interpretation of it were so powerful, perhaps even disconcerting, that we find the
cohort of Ezra, Nehemiah, and some of the
levitical clergy having to offer words of
encouragement to the people at the end
of the passage. Twice we hear them tell
the people not to be sad. Often you, too,
proclaim a message that the people have

difficulty hearing. This message is usually
one that challenges people to change or
live differently. Like the leaders, though,
you also communicate the hope that "today
is holy to our Lord" and invite the people to
feast on rich foods and drink sweet drinks
as the liturgy moves to the celebration of
the Eucharist.

READING II   Today is the second of three
consecutive Sundays on
which we hear from 1 Corinthians 12. The
reading picks up where last Sunday's left
off. Recall that in last Sunday's passage,

Paul laid the groundwork for his analogy of
the body which he develops in today's passage. The groundwork he laid consisted of
reminding the Corinthians that the source
of their different gifts is the same Spirit.

In today's passage, Paul begins by
drawing the connection between the one
Spirit and the Baptism which they all
share. In Baptism, they all drank of the
same Spirit and thus became members of
the one body. Similar to last Sunday's reading, after presenting his opening point,
Paul then goes on to develop it in relation
to something concrete the Corinthians can

A series of rhetorical questions. Remember to raise the tone of your voice slightly as you come to the end. Allow time for the assembly to bring the answer to mind.

A repetition of the main point. Pause after the transitional phrase, "But as it is," and then make eye contact with the assembly.

Emphasize "God" as you begin to describe how God designed the body.

In an hurried manner and with softer volume, contrast how the body of God's design is to respond to suffering and honor.

Or if an **ear** should say,
   "**Because I** am **not** an **eye I** do **not belong** to the **body**,"
   it does **not** for this reason **belong any less** to the body.
If the **whole body** were an **eye**, where would the **hearing** be?
If the **whole body** were **hearing**, where would the **sense**
     of **smell** be?
But as it **is**, **God** placed the **parts**,
   each one of them, in the **body** as he **intended**.
If they were **all one** part, **where** would the **body** be?
But as it **is**, there are **many parts**, yet **one** body.
The **eye** cannot say to the **hand**, "I do not **need** you,"
   nor again the **head** to the **feet**, "I do not **need** you."
Indeed, the **parts** of the body that seem to be **weaker**
   are all the more **necessary**,
   and those **parts** of the **body** that we consider less **honorable**
   we surround with **greater honor**,
   and our less **presentable** parts are treated with **greater propriety**,
   whereas our **more** presentable parts do not **need** this.
But **God** has so **constructed** the **body**
   as to give **greater honor** to a part that is **without** it,
   so that there may be **no division** in the body,
   but that the **parts** may have the **same concern** for **one another**.
If **one** part **suffers**, **all** the parts **suffer with** it;
   if **one** part is **honored**, **all** the parts **share its joy**.

understand. Last Sunday, he presented them with a list of spiritual gifts. This Sunday, he speaks practically about the interrelationship of the human body and its individual parts.

The words that the personified foot and ear say ("If a foot should say . . . ") reflect the twofold struggle in the Corinthian community about how to handle those who boast about their spiritual gifts and how to encourage those who do not have enough self-esteem to think their gifts are worthy of the body. Both segments of the community need to understand that they belong to the one body by virtue of their Baptism. Their contributions to the body are equally significant. This is a question of self-reflection and self-identity.

At the end of the first section on the human body, Paul asks a rhetorical question and then repeats his opening point. A good teacher, Paul uses this repetition to make sure those under his tutelage do not forget what he is trying to teach them. Paul's intent in the second section is to lead the Corinthians to understand how they are in relationship with others in the community. Perhaps to the Corinthians' surprise, Paul uses the analogy of the body to turn societal norms regarding who is dishonored and honored upside down.

In the concluding section, Paul's argument reaches its climax: the application to the Corinthian community. Using the word "now," he focuses the attention of the Corinthians on their present situation, just in case their attention wasn't already there. He then reminds them that they are indeed Christ's body. This is the first time in his letter that he uses the phrase "Christ's body." Previously he has spoken of the body being one and Christ being one,

The climactic repetition. Make eye contact with the assembly, identifying it as Christ's body and each person as an important part of his body.

Now **you** are **Christ's body**, and **individually parts** of it.
Some people **God** has designated in the **church**
    to be, **first**, **apostles**; **second**, **prophets**; **third**, **teachers**;
    then, **mighty deeds**;
    then **gifts** of **healing**, **assistance**, **administration**,
    and **varieties** of **tongues**.
Are **all apostles**? Are **all prophets**? Are **all teachers**?
Do **all** work **mighty deeds**? Do **all** have **gifts** of **healing**?
Do **all** speak in **tongues**? Do **all** interpret?

[Shorter: 1 Corinthians 12:12–14, 27]

Again, take your time with the rhetorical questions which conclude the reading.

GOSPEL   Luke 1:1–4, 4:14–21

A reading from the holy Gospel according to Luke

Use a stronger tone of voice on the main clauses of the one sentence prologue: "I too have decided," and "to write it down," as well as on Luke's reason for writing: "so that you may realize the certainty." Lower your tone and decrease slightly in volume on the parenthetical remarks.

Theophilus = thee-AWF-uh-luhs

Since **many** have **undertaken** to **compile** a **narrative** of the **events**
    that have been **fulfilled** among us,
    just as those who were **eyewitnesses** from **the beginning**
    and **ministers** of the **word** have **handed them down** to **us**,
I too have **decided**,
    after **investigating everything** accurately **anew**,
    to **write** it down in an **orderly sequence** for you,
    most **excellent Theophilus**,
    so that you may **realize** the **certainty** of the **teachings**
    you have received.

Jesus returned **to Galilee** in the **power** of the **Spirit**,
    and **news** of him **spread** throughout the **whole region**.
He **taught** in their **synagogues** and was **praised** by **all**.

Convey a sense of energy and excitement as you describe the power of the Spirit, the news of Jesus spreading, and the fact that the people of Galilee praised him.

---

but has not connected the two points as the body of Christ.

Notice in the list of gifts, as in last Sunday's list, the gift of tongues comes last. The order itself is not important. What is important is Paul's attempt to rein in the unconstrained pride that exists in the community among those who have this particular spiritual gift.

If you are proclaiming the longer reading, the passage ends with seven brief rhetorical questions to which we know the answers are seven "no's." These are powerful questions and, when proclaimed with

significant pauses after them, allow people time to recognize the "no" response deep inside of them.

GOSPEL   The two main sections of the Gospel are an interesting juxtaposition of verses. The first section is the prologue to Luke's work, with which some scholars believe Luke intends to introduce both his account of Jesus' life and his second volume, the Acts of the Apostles. The second section describes Jesus' proclamation in the Nazareth synagogue of his anointing by the Spirit and his

mission. It precedes the rejection he will face in his hometown, which we will hear next Sunday.

Both sections contain key Lucan themes: Jesus as the fulfillment of Scripture; the Spirit working in Jesus; and the announcement of the Good News, especially to the poor. The prologue is one lengthy and stylized sentence intended to serve many purposes. It lays out Luke's qualifications for writing his account of the Gospel. The Evangelist has accurately investigated the other accounts before

Proclaim the words Jesus speaks from the prophet Isaiah with potency and optimism. Jesus is the fulfillment of these words.

He came to **Nazareth**, where he had grown **up**,
 and went according to his **custom**
 into the **synagogue** on the **sabbath** day.
He **stood up** to **read** and was handed **a scroll** of the prophet **Isaiah**.
He **unrolled** the **scroll** and found the **passage** where it was **written**:
 The **Spirit** of the **Lord** is upon me,
  because **he** has anointed **me**
  to bring **glad tidings** to the poor.
 He has sent me to proclaim **liberty** to captives
  and **recovery** of **sight** to the blind,
  to let the **oppressed** go free,
  and to proclaim a year **acceptable** to the Lord.
Rolling up the **scroll**, he handed it back to the attendant
 and sat **down**,
 and the **eyes** of **all** in the **synagogue** looked **intently** at **him**.
He said to them,
 "**Today this** Scripture passage is **fulfilled** in your **hearing**."

Return to a narrative voice. Slow down and heighten the intensity, but not the volume, in your voice as you narrate the response of all in the synagogue.

Pause after the phrase introducing Jesus' concluding words. Make eye contact with the assembly as you emphasize the word "Today."

writing his own, which he will now present in an "orderly sequence." Luke bases this order not always on the correct historical sequence of events, but rather on his theme of Jesus as the fulfillment of God's promise in Scripture.

The reference to Theophilus as the addressee of the Gospel is a general reference to a believer or God-fearer. It literally means a "friend of God." (See also Acts 1:1.) Historical details are sometimes murky for Luke, but as the conclusion of the prologue indicates, what is unambiguous for

him is "the certainty of the teachings you have received."

The story of Jesus in the synagogue presented in the second section of today's Gospel includes the well-known quotation from the Book of Isaiah. Luke conflates and modifies Isaiah 58:6 and 61:1–2 in the words he places on Jesus' lips in order to serve his purpose of revealing Jesus' identity and mission as the One anointed by the Spirit and sent to bring Good News to the poor.

The ritual of Jesus rolling up the scroll, the reaction of all the people in the synagogue, and Jesus' concluding words

all elevate this scene from an anecdote to Jesus' own public declaration of his identity and mission. They prepare us for the events of Jesus' life that we will hear in the coming weeks of Ordinary Time. Leave the assembly with a sense that Jesus fulfills the Scripture passage in their midst today—not just historically long ago—but in the present as Luke's use of the word "today" intends.

4TH SUNDAY IN ORDINARY TIME

Lectionary #72

READING I   Jeremiah 1:4–5, 17–19

Jeremiah = jayr-uh-MĪ-uh

Testify to the divine providence of Jeremiah's call with assurance in your voice. The Lord will not abandon Jeremiah when he accepts the call.

Images of strength and power follow. Reflect the same characteristics in your tone of voice.

Draw attention to the phrase "says the Lord," by marking the preceding comma with an obvious pause.

A reading from the Book of the Prophet Jeremiah

The **word** of the LORD came to me, saying:
   Before I formed you in the **womb** I **knew you**,
      before you were **born** I **dedicated you**,
      a **prophet** to the **nations** I **appointed** you.

But **do** you **gird** your **loins**;
      stand up and **tell** them
      all that I **command** you.
Be **not crushed** on their account,
      as **though** I would **leave** you **crushed** before **them**;
for it is **I** this **day**
      who have made **you** a **fortified city**,
a **pillar** of **iron**, a **wall** of **brass**,
      against the **whole land**:
against Judah's **kings** and **princes**,
      against its **priests** and **people**.
They will **fight** against **you** but **not prevail** over you,
      for **I** am **with you** to **deliver** you, says the LORD.

READING I   In today's First Reading we hear the call of the prophet Jeremiah from the opening chapter of the prophet's book. In the first four lines we learn that the Lord knew Jeremiah intimately, even before he was in the womb. Before Jeremiah's birth, the Lord had called him to be a prophet, and a prophet not just among his own people, but "to the nations."

The reading skips, then, to later verses in God's dialogue with Jeremiah. Knowing what is missing will help you with your proclamation. We miss Jeremiah's objection that he is too young and doesn't know how to speak (Jeremiah 1:6). The Lord dismisses this objection and tells Jeremiah he will go to the people to whom God sends him, and he should not be afraid. The Lord then commissions the prophet, touching his mouth as a sign of putting his words in Jeremiah's mouth. The prophet then has two visions. First, he sees the branch of an almond tree, otherwise known as a watching tree. The vision signifies that the Lord will be watching out for Jeremiah— guarding him—but also making sure he boldly speaks the Lord's word. Next a boiling caldron appears from the north, the direction from which an invasion of Judah will take place. The invaders will destroy the country because of her idolatry.

The First Reading picks up after Jeremiah's two visions with the Lord telling the prophet that he must be resolute and unwavering in his commitment to bring the Lord's word to the people. The Lord called Jeremiah during the reign of King Josiah, a great reformer. However, with the defeat of Judah by Babylon and

Corinthians = kohr-IN-thee-uhnz

Instruct the assembly directly with the opening line.

Practice so as to avoid a sing-song delivery of the conditional verses which have a similar structure ("If . . . but . . . I . . . ")

Proclaim each of the characteristics of love in a tone of voice that matches their meaning. Also emphasize "not" before the negative characteristics.

Take your time with the words "Love never fails." This is the reason why the Corinthians should strive for the greatest spiritual gifts.

READING II 1 Corinthians 12:31 — 13:13

A reading from the first Letter of Saint Paul to the Corinthians

Brothers and **sisters:**
Strive **eagerly** for the **greatest** spiritual gifts.
But I shall **show** you a **still more excellent** way.

If I speak in **human** and **angelic** tongues,
    but do **not** have **love,**
    I am a resounding **gong** or a clashing **cymbal.**
And if I have the **gift** of **prophecy,**
    and **comprehend all mysteries** and **all knowledge;**
    if I have **all faith** so as to move **mountains,**
    but do **not have love,** I am **nothing.**
If I give away **everything** I **own,**
    and if **I hand** my **body over** so that I may **boast,**
    but do **not have love,** I **gain nothing.**

Love is **patient,** love is **kind.**
It is not **jealous,** it is not **pompous,**
    it is not **inflated,** it is not **rude,**
    it does **not** seek its own **interests,**
    it is not **quick-tempered,** it does not **brood** over **injury,**
    it does not **rejoice** over **wrongdoing**
    but **rejoices** with the **truth.**
It **bears all** things, **believes all** things,
    hopes all things, **endures all** things.

Love never fails.
If there are **prophecies,** they will be brought to **nothing;**
    if **tongues,** they will **cease;**
    if **knowledge,** it will be **brought** to **nothing.**

King Josiah's death, the people once again gave in to idolatrous practices. It was this fight against idolatry that Jeremiah would have to face head on, and for which the Lord would continuously strengthen him. The reading concludes with God's strong assurance of deliverance to the prophet, a deliverance which is ours as well.

READING II This cherished hymn on love, appropriately and often proclaimed at weddings, follows upon Paul's exhortation to the Corinthian community to live as the body of Christ. By

placing it at this point in his letter, Paul shows the Corinthians that love is the central, constitutive act that will maintain the unity of the body. This love, which reflects Christ's love, is the greatest spiritual gift.

The passage has three distinct sections. The first serves as an introduction. It includes the conditional, if-then statements that Paul personalizes with the pronoun "I." He knows that if he doesn't have love, but has all these other gifts, he is still nothing as an apostle and will have nothing to show for his ministry.

The second section describes the characteristics of love in both positive and negative terms. It builds to the climax that repeats the word "all" four times and the profound statement "Love never fails." Throughout all eternity love will triumph. The statement on the enduring nature of love is a reference to the gift of eternal love through Christ's Resurrection. Paul's conclusion also teaches that when we understand human love in relationship with divine love, God's love will always help overcome the limitations of the human love, gracing it with forgiveness and hope.

prophesy = PROF-uh-sī

The parallel structure of this philosophical section makes it difficult to proclaim. Use a reflective tone of voice as you take the assembly through the different time periods in life.

For we **know partially** and we **prophesy partially**,
　　but when the **perfect** comes, the **partial** will pass **away**.
When **I** was a **child**, I used to **talk** as a **child**,
　　think as a **child**, **reason** as a **child**;
　　when I became a **man**, I put **aside childish** things.
At **present** we see **indistinctly**, as in a **mirror**,
　　but **then face to face**.
At **present** I know **partially**;
　　then I shall know **fully**, as I am **fully known**.
So **faith**, **hope**, **love** remain, these **three**;
　　but the **greatest** of these is **love**.

[Shorter: 1 Corinthians 13:4–13]

GOSPEL Luke 4:21–30

Make eye contact with the assembly as you announce "Today."

Lighten the tone in your voice as your narrate the people's amazement. Emphasize the word "gracious," allowing your enunciation to communicate the grace that comes through the word.

Capernaum = kuh-PER-nee-*m; kuh-PER-nay-*m; kuh-PER-n*m

A reading from the holy Gospel according to Luke

Jesus began speaking in the **synagogue**, saying:
　　"**Today** this **Scripture** passage is **fulfilled** in your **hearing**."
And **all** spoke **highly** of him
　　and were **amazed** at the **gracious** words that came
　　　　from his **mouth**.
They **also asked**, "Isn't this the **son** of **Joseph**?"
He said to them, "**Surely** you will quote me this **proverb**,
　　'**Physician, cure** yourself,' and say,
　　'Do **here** in your **native place**
　　the things that we **heard** were **done** in **Capernaum**.'"

In the third section, Paul gives a personal reflection on his journey through life in relation to love. While he will only completely know in eternity the God who now knows him fully, what he does have to hang on to and live his life by in the present are the three divine virtues of faith, hope, and love. These three form a well-known and powerful triad. (See also 1 Thessalonians 1:3.) Paul stresses to the Corinthians that love is the greatest of the virtues. And, the Corinthians, who have many gifts to share with each other, desperately need love.

Love will hold them and us together as the body of Christ.

GOSPEL Like the prophet Jeremiah, in today's First Reading, Jesus, too, would face resistance, and he finds it quickly in his own hometown of Nazareth. The Gospel begins by repeating the concluding verse from last Sunday's reading. The word "today" emphasizes that Jesus fulfills Isaiah's words here and now. After hearing Jesus speak, the people initially extol him. Yet as the Gospel

proceeds, the tone changes dramatically.
　　While the people are amazed at the "gracious words" (words of grace) Jesus spoke, their curiosity about his identity gets the best of them. They ask among themselves about his family. Probably sensing their rising resistance, Jesus engages them. From this point forward we hear only Jesus' words, and he speaks like a prophet. His solemn statement, begun with the word "Amen," addresses one human aspect of their opposition head on. In Jesus' observation, Elijah and Elisha

Let your tone of voice correspond to Jesus' ominous and solemn declaration.

Use a serious, narrative tone of voice to tell the two short accounts of God's loving kindness extending to all people.

Elijah = ee-LĪ-juh

Zarephath = ZAYR-uh-fath

Sidon = SĪ-duhn

Elisha = ee-LI-shuh

Naaman = NAY-uh-muhn

Syrian = SEER-ee-uhn

Fill your voice with intensity as you speak the people's response to Jesus' words.

Allow serenity to contrast with the people's fury as you narrate Jesus' passing through the midst of the people.

And he said, **"Amen**, I say to you,
no **prophet** is **accepted** in his own **native place**.
Indeed, I tell you,
there were many **widows** in **Israel** in the days of **Elijah**
when the **sky** was **closed** for **three** and a **half years**
and a severe **famine** spread over the entire **land**.
It was to **none** of these that **Elijah** was **sent**,
but only to a widow in **Zarephath** in the land of **Sidon**.
Again, there were **many lepers** in Israel
during the time of **Elisha** the prophet;
yet not **one** of them was **cleansed**, but only **Naaman**
the **Syrian**."
When the people in the **synagogue heard** this,
they were all **filled** with **fury**.
They **rose** up, **drove** him out of the **town**,
and **led** him to the **brow** of the **hill**
on which their town had been **built**,
to **hurl** him down **headlong**.
But Jesus **passed through** the **midst** of them and **went away**.

both offered God's mercy, not to the insiders, but to people outside the Jewish tradition. The people who heard Jesus made the connection he intended them to: through him, God's mercy would continue to be extended to all, even those not thought to be among the chosen. As a result, the crowd is "filled with fury" and intend to throw Jesus down the hill on which the town was built. In a prelude to Easter, Jesus eludes them. The Gospel ends on this message of hope. God's mercy, through Christ, will forever extend to believers and nonbelievers, whether people like it or not.

5TH SUNDAY IN ORDINARY TIME

Lectionary #75

READING I   Isaiah 6:1–2a, 3–8

Isaiah = ī-ZAY-uh

Uzziah = uh-ZĪ-uh

Paint the picture of this reading's setting with a deliberate proclamation of the opening verse.

seraphim = SAYR-uh-fim

Use a reverent tone of voice as you proclaim the familiar words, "Holy, holy, holy . . ."

Place apprehension in your voice as you speak Isaiah's words of doom, which recognize his own sinfulness.

Begin to release the apprehension from your voice as you narrate the seraphim coming to Isaiah. Communicate the purging of Isaiah's sin with compassion fitting to God's tender mercy.

Speak Isaiah's acceptance of his call with confidence: his unclean lips are now lips that will proclaim the Lord's glory.

A reading from the Book of the Prophet Isaiah

In the year **King Uzziah** died,
  I **saw** the **Lord seated** on a **high** and **lofty throne**,
  with the **train** of his **garment filling** the **temple**.
Seraphim were stationed **above**.

They **cried** one to the other,
  "**Holy**, **holy**, **holy** is the LORD of hosts!
All the **earth** is **filled** with his **glory**!"
At the **sound** of that cry, the frame of the door **shook**
  and the house was **filled** with **smoke**.

Then I said, "**Woe** is me, I am **doomed**!
For I am a man of **unclean** lips,
  living among a **people** of **unclean lips**;
  yet my **eyes** have **seen** the **King**, the LORD of **hosts**!"
Then one of the **seraphim flew** to me,
  holding an **ember** that he had taken with tongs
    from the **altar**.

He **touched** my **mouth** with it, and said,
  "**See**, now that this has **touched** your **lips**,
  your **wickedness** is **removed**, your **sin purged**."

Then I **heard** the voice of the **Lord** saying,
  "**Whom** shall **I send**? **Who** will **go** for **us**?"
  "**Here I** am," I said; "send **me**!"

READING I   For the second Sunday in a row, we hear the call story of a prophet. Last Sunday we heard Jeremiah's call and this Sunday we hear Isaiah's. The Gospel paired with Jeremiah's call was that of Jesus' rejection in his hometown. Today the Gospel is Simon Peter's call to fish for people. Each pairing tells quite a different story of being called.

Isaiah's call begins with a vision of the Lord's transcendence. In the vision, angels cry out in words familiar to us from the Sanctus (the Holy, Holy, Holy), attesting to the Lord's holiness. The door frame shudders to symbolize the Lord's power, and smoke, often present in theophanies (experiences in which God reveals himself as God), fills the house. These symbols of the presence of God shake Isaiah to the core. He feels called because he has indeed experienced the Lord's presence, but is utterly afraid and genuinely convinced that he is unworthy to follow the call.

The seraphim (a term which literally means "fiery") approaches Isaiah holding an ember. Its approach shows God's willingness to be in relationship with him despite his unclean lips. Additionally, the angel holds an ember and, through an intimate gesture, touches Isaiah's lips, revealing that the Lord who calls Isaiah is a Lord of forgiveness and mercy.

Isaiah's vision concludes with the Lord vocalizing the call. Notice that the words of the call come in the form of an open-ended question. While we know Isaiah will respond affirmatively to the call, ask the Lord's question so that the assembly is left wondering what will come next. Will Isaiah, in fact, respond "send me?" Will each person in the assembly, in fact, respond "send me?"

Corinthians = kohr-IN-thee-uhnz

Use a conversational tone of voice to communicate Paul's reminder to the Corinthians of the Gospel he's preached.

Proceed deliberately through the summary of faith, allowing the assembly to hear each tenet.

Cephas = SEE-fuhs

Pick up the pace slightly as you narrate the multiple appearance stories Paul included.

Slow a little in order to emphasize Christ's appearance to Paul. "Born abnormally" was how Paul's opponents described him in order to negate his apostleship.

Conclude in the confidence of Paul's faith and ours that grace saves and works in us as we proclaim the Gospel.

READING II 1 Corinthians 15:1–11

A reading from the first Letter of Saint Paul to the Corinthians

I am **reminding** you, **brothers** and **sisters**,
    of the **gospel** I preached to you,
    which you indeed **received** and in which you also **stand**.
Through it you are also being **saved**,
    if you hold **fast** to the word I **preached** to you,
    unless you **believed** in **vain**.
For I **handed** on to you as of **first importance** what I also **received**:
    that **Christ died** for our **sins** in accordance with the **Scriptures**;
    that he was **buried**;
    that he was **raised** on the **third day**
        in accordance with the **Scriptures**;
    that he **appeared** to **Cephas**, then to the **Twelve**.
After that, Christ appeared to **more**
        than **five hundred** brothers **at once**,
    most of whom are still **living**,
    though some have **fallen asleep**.
After that he appeared to **James**,
    then to **all the apostles**.
Last of all, as to one born **abnormally**,
    he appeared to **me**.
For **I** am the **least** of the apostles,
    not fit to be **called** an apostle,
    because I **persecuted** the church of **God**.
But by the **grace** of God **I am** what **I am**,
    and his **grace** to me has **not** been **ineffective**.

Since we are given no details in the reading about whether Isaiah spent time reflecting on his response after the Lord asked the question, we are left to presume that having experienced the Lord's forgiveness, he needed no time to deliberate. His response is confident and faith-filled.

READING II On the last three Sundays, the Second Reading was from the twelfth chapter of 1 Corinthians. This Sunday the reading comes from the final chapter. The passage is the introduction to Paul's discussion of the Resurrection and its implications for the Corinthians. It explains how they are to live as the resurrected and transformed body.

Today's passage has three sections. In the first, Paul once again reminds the Corinthians of the Gospel that he preached to them, the Gospel they are to follow because it saves. This is the same Gospel they as a community are struggling to live by, that will guide them as they amend their relationships with one another.

Just in case his students, the Corinthians, have forgotten, in the second section Paul provides a summary of the Gospel he taught them. At the end of this summary, Paul mentions Christ's post-Resurrection appearances to Cephas and the Twelve. Scholars think Paul inserted the appearances that follow in order to situate himself in line with the other Apostles who witnessed the resurrected Christ and thus give his apostleship credibility.

The third section begins with Paul's own appearance story. The phrase "to one born abnormally" refers to the time when Paul persecuted Christians. By using this phrase he shows the power of God's grace:

Indeed, I have **toiled harder** than **all** of them;
    not I, however, but the **grace** of **God** that is **with** me.
Therefore, whether it be **I** or **they**,
    so we **preach** and so you **believed**.

[Shorter: 1 Corinthians 15:3–8, 11]

GOSPEL Luke 5:1–11

A reading from the holy Gospel according to Luke

While the **crowd** was **pressing** in on **Jesus** and **listening**
        to the **word** of **God**,
    he was standing by the **Lake** of **Gennesaret**.
He saw two **boats** there alongside the **lake**;
    the **fishermen** had **disembarked** and were **washing** their **nets**.
Getting into one of the boats, the one belonging to **Simon**,
    he asked him to **put out** a **short distance** from the **shore**.
Then he sat **down** and **taught** the crowds from the **boat**.
After he had finished **speaking**, he said to **Simon**,
    "**Put out** into **deep water** and **lower** your nets for a **catch**."
Simon said in reply,
    "**Master**, we have worked **hard all night** and have
        caught **nothing**,
    but at **your** command I **will** lower the nets."
When they had done this, they caught a **great number** of fish
    and their **nets** were **tearing**.

Gennesaret = geh-NES-uh-ret

Jesus commands Simon.

Convey Simon's objection matter-of-factly. He's explaining the facts to Jesus. Convey in the last half of Simon's reply that Simon accepts Jesus' authority.

Pick up the pace as you communicate the enormity of the catch of fish.

God could even save one who persecuted Christians. Paul's response to this grace was to work hard, according to Paul, harder than all of the other Apostles! This line seems to carry a little Pauline hubris. Paul's legitimate conclusion, though, is that the Corinthians believed because of his gospel labor. He now only wants them to respond rightly to the Gospel he and all the Apostles before him have preached, the Gospel of the Resurrection of the one body of Christ.

GOSPEL The positive response to Jesus' ministry detailed in this passage follows upon Jesus' rejection by the people of his hometown. Recall that the people were furious when Jesus suggested that the mercy of God, with which the Spirit anointed Jesus, would be offered to all people, Jew and Gentile alike.

Like God's call of Isaiah, who was in need of mercy in the First Reading, today's Gospel tells of Jesus' call of Simon Peter, also a sinful man. While Simon Peter is the focus of the passage, there is a community of fishers surrounding him. Those who are commercial fishers today will confirm that fishing is not a completely solo occupation. Partners are necessary to be successful. The way the evangelist Luke crafts this narrative shows that this is also the case with following Jesus.

Seeing the miracle of the nets being filled with fish after nothing had been caught all night, drew not only Simon Peter

Simon Peter's words are filled with faith, humility, and repentance, perhaps even embarrassment. Fill your voice with the same.

Zebedee = ZEB-uh-dee

Express Jesus' words "Do not be afraid" in a calm tone of voice. State the mission of his followers with directness, making eye contact with the assembly.

Be deliberate in your narration of the new followers' acceptance of Jesus' call.

They signaled to their **partners** in the **other** boat
  to come to **help** them.
They came and **filled both** boats
  so that the boats were in danger of **sinking**.
When **Simon Peter** saw this, he **fell** at the **knees** of Jesus and said,
  "**Depart** from me, **Lord**, for I am a **sinful man**."
For **astonishment** at the catch of fish they had made **seized** him
  and **all** those with him,
  and **likewise James** and **John**, the sons of **Zebedee**,
  who were **partners** of **Simon**.
Jesus said to **Simon**, "Do **not** be **afraid**;
  from now **on** you will be **catching men**."
When they brought their **boats** to the **shore**,
  they **left everything** and **followed him**.

to confess Jesus' identity as "Lord" (a post-Resurrection title), but also caused those with him, including his partners James and John, Zebedee's sons, to react with astonishment. Jesus had fished for them and they had been caught!

Luke describes them as being "seized" by Jesus and uses the plural pronoun "they" at the end of the section. This implies that probably most, if not all, of the people who were a part of the community of fishers, chose to follow Jesus. Now they would labor together to catch people to follow Jesus and become part of the community of disciples. These disciples, partners in faith, detached themselves completely from everything they knew and possessed. No longer in need of material possessions they, like the One they followed, would be filled and anointed with the Spirit.

ASH WEDNESDAY

Lectionary #219

READING I   Joel 2:12–18

Joel = JOH-*l

God speaks with urgency and longing.

A reading from the Book of the Prophet Joel

Even now, says the LORD,
    return to **me** with your **whole heart**,
    with **fasting**, and **weeping**, and **mourning**;
Rend your **hearts**, **not** your **garments**,
    and **return** to the LORD, your **God**.
For **gracious** and **merciful** is he,
    slow to **anger**, **rich** in **kindness**,
    and **relenting** in **punishment**.
Perhaps he will again **relent**
    and leave behind him a **blessing**,
Offerings and **libations**
    for the LORD, your **God**.

This is a rallying cry.
Zion = ZĪ-uhn; ZĪ-ahn

Blow the trumpet in **Zion**!
    proclaim a **fast**,
    call an **assembly**;
Gather the **people**,
    notify the **congregation**;
Assemble the **elders**,
    gather the **children**
    and the **infants** at the breast;
Let the **bridegroom quit** his room,
    and the **bride** her **chamber**.

READING I As you read today's passage from Joel you can hear the urgency in the prophet's message. Our reading begins "Even now," another way of saying, "It's late, but it's not too late." Obviously, something has gone terribly wrong. Joel even suggests that other nations, looking at what is happening in Israel, might ask, "Where is their God?" The people are suffering in such a way that it seems God might be absent.

A prophet has two roles: When the people are sinning, the prophet is to call them to repentance. When the people are suffering, the prophet is to offer them hope: God will be faithful to his promises. While today's reading begins with a call to repentance, it ends with hope. God does have concern for the Israelites and their land, and takes "pity on his people."

The reason why other nations might look at the Israelites and ask, "Where is their God?" is that the people have just experienced what we would call a natural disaster. By the time Joel prophesied, the Babylonian exile was over and the Temple had been rebuilt. Now, just when things might have become less difficult, the land was completely ravaged by a plague of locusts. All the crops were destroyed. The Israelites were in danger of starvation.

Joel interprets this catastrophic event as a sign that the day of the Lord, a day of judgment, is near. He begs the people to repent. He reminds them that God is "gracious and merciful . . . slow to anger, rich in kindness." Joel assures the people that it is not too late to repent so that God will "leave behind a blessing" not a punishment.

The priests' tone is beseeching.

Between the **porch** and the **altar**
 let the **priests**, the **ministers** of the LORD, **weep,**
And say, **"Spare,** O **LORD,** your **people,**
 and make not **your heritage** a **reproach,**
 with the **nations ruling** over them!
Why should they say among the **peoples,**
 'Where is their God?'"

The reading ends with reassurance.

Then the LORD was **stirred** to **concern** for his **land**
 and took **pity** on his **people.**

READING II   2 Corinthians 5:20—6:2

Corinthians = kohr-IN-thee-uhnz

A reading from the second Letter of Saint Paul to the Corinthians

Here, Paul is appealing on God's behalf.

Brothers and **sisters:**
We are **ambassadors** for **Christ,**
 as if **God** were **appealing** through **us.**
We **implore** you on behalf of **Christ,**
 be **reconciled** to **God.**
For **our sake** he made **him** to be **sin**
 who did **not know sin,**
 so that **we** might become the **righteousness**
 of **God** in **him.**

Read slowly, pausing after each unit of thought.

However, the whole nation must repent. An assembly must be called, attended by the old and the young, even nursing children. No exception is to be made; even those who are newly married and would usually be exempt from public duties must come. Priests and ministers must also repent and pray that God will spare the people

With the last sentence, the tone of the reading and of the Book of Joel changes. The Lord is "stirred to concern." Now, all will change. As you proclaim this reading,

the tone will change from entreaty to a clarion call to gather, to hope. On this Ash Wednesday emphasize especially the urgent need for repentance.

READING II Paul, like Joel, is imploring the people to "be reconciled to God." As with Joel, there is urgency in Paul's message: Paul tells the Corinthians that "now is the day of salvation."

In addition to being reconciled to God themselves, Paul teaches the Corinthians that both he and they are ambassadors for Christ in Christ's ministry of reconciliation.

Although Jesus never sinned, Jesus took on sin for the purpose of making human beings righteous. The Corinthians should "not . . . receive the grace of God in vain." Rather they should recognize that "now is the day of salvation" and not only accept the gift that is offered, but announce this Good News to all.

One way of being an ambassador for Christ, who calls all to be reconciled with God and each other, is to live in peace and reconciliation with one's neighbor. Earlier

Paul is still appealing. However, you could speak more softly here.

Working together, then,
we **appeal** to you **not** to receive the **grace**
of **God** in **vain**.
For he says:

*In an acceptable time I **heard** you,
and on the day of salvation I **helped** you.*

Now, increase your volume.

Behold, *now* is a **very acceptable time**;
behold, *now* is the **day of** *salvation*.

GOSPEL Matthew 6:1–6, 16–18

A reading from the holy Gospel according to Matthew

Jesus is instructing, not correcting his disciples.

Jesus said to his **disciples**:
"Take care **not** to **perform righteous deeds**
in order that people may **see** them;
otherwise, you will have **no recompense**
from your **heavenly Father**.

Jesus is drawing a contrast between his disciples and hypocrites.

When you give alms,
do **not blow** a **trumpet** before you,
as the **hypocrites** do in the **synagogues**
and in the **streets**
to **win** the **praise** of **others**.

Speak with authority. This phrase signals that Jesus is speaking with authority.

Amen, I say to you,
they have **received** their reward.
But when **you** give alms,
do **not** let your **left hand know** what your **right** is **doing**,
so that your **almsgiving** may be **secret**.
And your **Father** who sees in **secret** will **repay** you.

---

in 2 Corinthians Paul makes it clear that he himself needed to be reconciled with the Corinthians and that the Corinthians needed to be reconciled with each other. Ambassadors for Christ, who give witness to Jesus' gift of reconciliation, give witness by the way they themselves live.

You who have the privilege of proclaiming this reading are yourselves ambassadors for Christ in announcing reconciliation to all. Christ will be appealing through you, calling everyone to be "reconciled to God." Since it is Ash

Wednesday, give most emphasis to this call for reconciliation.

GOSPEL | Both of our previous readings stressed the absolute necessity and urgency of being in right relationship with God. Joel urged us to repent. Paul urged us to be reconciled. Our Gospel from Matthew discusses three practices that the Church calls us to take up during Lent, practices that help us grow into right relationship with God and with each other: almsgiving, prayer, and fasting.

Today's reading is part of a long sermon by Jesus, popularly called the Sermon on the Mount. Jesus tells the disciples that he has not come to destroy the Law, but to fulfill it (Matthew 5:17). Jesus teaches a new Law which is more demanding than the old Law, more demanding in the direction of love. Love, of course, is not a matter of appearance, but is a matter of the heart.

Jesus then applies this basic insight to almsgiving, prayer, and fasting. These practices, however, will be of no spiritual benefit unless they are done for the right

Again, speak with authority.

From here to the end, speak with an intimate and affectionate tone.

"**When you** pray,
    do **not** be like the **hypocrites**,
    who **love** to **stand** and **pray** in the **synagogues**
        and on **street corners**
    so that **others** may **see** them.
Amen, **I say to you**,
    they have **received** their **reward**.
But when **you** pray, **go** to your **inner room**,
    close the door, and **pray** to your **Father** in **secret**.
And your **Father** who **sees** in **secret** will **repay** you.

"**When you** fast,
    do **not** look **gloomy** like the **hypocrites**.
They neglect their **appearance**,
    so that they may **appear to others** to be fasting.
Amen, **I say to you**, they have **received their** reward.
But when **you** fast,
    anoint your **head** and **wash** your **face**,
    so that you may **not appear** to **be fasting**,
    except to your **Father** who is **hidden**.
And your **Father** who **sees** what is **hidden**
        will **repay** you."

reason: to serve God and to cooperate in the coming of God's Kingdom. "Righteous deeds" must not be practiced to elicit the admiration of others.

When giving alms, one must not "blow a trumpet" in order to draw attention to oneself; rather, almsgiving should be done in secret so that only God knows of this generous act. Prayer, too, should not be done in an ostentatious manner; rather,

when one prays, one should do so privately. God, who sees in secret, will hear and answer such a prayer. Finally, when one fasts, one should not turn it into a major production for the purpose of being admired; rather, a person who is fasting should appear as though he or she is not fasting. That is the fasting that the Father desires.

The tone of today's reading is intimate and instructional. Jesus is not accusing his disciples of the behaviors he describes; rather, he is teaching them to be different

from the "hypocrites" who perform religious acts not as an expression of love but as an expression of a need to be admired by others. Prayer, almsgiving, and fasting, when done out of love of God and neighbor, help us grow in holiness.

1st SUNDAY OF LENT

Lectionary #24

READING I   Deuteronomy 26:4–10

A reading from the Book of Deuteronomy

Moses spoke to the **people**, saying:
   "The **priest** shall **receive** the **basket** from **you**
      and shall set it in front of the **altar** of the LORD, your **God.**
   Then you shall **declare** before the LORD, your **God,**
      'My **father** was a **wandering Aramean**
      who went down to **Egypt** with a **small household**
      and **lived** there as an **alien.**
   But **there** he became **a nation**
      great, strong, and **numerous.**
   When the **Egyptians maltreated** and **oppressed** us,
      imposing **hard labor upon** us,
      we **cried** to the LORD, the **God** of our **fathers,**
      and he **heard** our **cry**
      and **saw** our **affliction,** our **toil,** and our **oppression.**
   He brought us **out** of **Egypt**
      with his **strong hand** and **outstretched arm,**
      with **terrifying power,** with **signs** and **wonders;**
      and **bringing** us into **this country,**
      he gave us **this land flowing** with **milk** and **honey.**
   Therefore, I have now brought you **the firstfruits**
      of the **products** of the **soil**
      which **you,** O LORD, have **given** me.'
   And having **set** them before the LORD, your **God,**
      you shall **bow down** in his **presence.**"

Deuteronomy = d<u>oo</u>-ter-AH-nuh-mee;
dyoo-ter-AH-nuh-mee
The narrator's voice sets the stage.
Moses is giving directions. Speak softly.
Moses = MOH-ziz; MOH-zis

This is a declaration. Raise your volume.
Speak slowly. Now, lower your volume.
Aramean = ayr-uh-MEE-uhn
Say this line slowly with awe and
gratitude.

Now speak more quickly.

Again, say this line slowly, with awe and
gratitude.

This is the conclusion of the peoples'
declaration.

This concludes Moses's instructions.
Drop your voice, since this is not part of
the declaration.

READING I   Today's First Reading takes place on the plains of Moab, after the Israelites' forty years of wandering in the desert, before they cross the Jordan and enter the promised land (around 1250 BC). However, it was not written until after the Babylonian exile (587–537 BC). Both the Israelites in the story, Moses' contemporaries, and the Israelites to whom the book is directed, the returning exiles, receive instructions on how to live in fidelity to God as they enter the promised land.

The exiles who returned to the holy land no longer had king or kingdom. They lived under Persian rule. But they still had their covenant relationship with God; they still had their Law. The returning exiles, like the ancestors who first entered the holy land, must remember their history and thank God for help through the centuries.

In today's reading, Moses is instructing the people about how to observe a yearly ritual in which they thank God for two things: for freeing them from slavery in Egypt and for giving them their land. In thanksgiving, the people are to offer God

the firstfruits of their crops. To begin the ceremony, the people bring the priest a basket of firstfruits that is placed before God's altar. Then the people will recall their history, from nomadic wandering to slavery in Egypt, God's rescue and guidance in the desert, God's gift of the promised land.

In gratitude, the people offer their firstfruits and "bow down in his presence." As you proclaim this story, remember that you are following Moses' instructions. You, like the Israelites, are reminding God's people of all that he has done for us.

Paul poses a question as part of his teaching.

In these two lines Paul is quoting Scripture. Read this thoughtfully.

Emphasize "that." Paul is referring back to the quotation.

This is Paul's conclusion. Read this slowly and with conviction.

Now Paul is explaining the conclusion he just drew. Increase your tempo.

Now, Paul is quoting Scripture again. Paul is drawing his conclusion again. Emphasize "no distinction" and "all."

Speak slowly and with conviction.

READING II — Romans 10:8–13

A reading from the Letter of Saint Paul to the Romans

Brothers and sisters:
What does Scripture say?
The word is near you,
  in your mouth and in your heart
  —that is, the word of faith that we preach—,
  for, if you confess with your mouth that Jesus is Lord
  and believe in your heart that God raised him from the dead,
  you will be saved.
For one believes with the heart and so is justified,
  and one confesses with the mouth and so is saved.
For the Scripture says,
  No one who believes in him will be put to shame.
For there is no distinction between Jew and Greek;
  the same Lord is Lord of all,
  enriching all who call upon him.
For "everyone who calls on the name of the Lord will be saved."

This is the narrator setting the stage. Use a matter-of-fact tone.
Jordan = JOHR-d*n

GOSPEL — Luke 4:1–13

A reading from the holy Gospel according to Luke

Filled with the Holy Spirit, Jesus returned from the Jordan
  and was led by the Spirit into the desert for forty days,
  to be tempted by the devil.
He ate nothing during those days,
  and when they were over he was hungry.

READING II — In the First Reading, the Israelites were celebrating their rescue from slavery. In the Second Reading, Paul is teaching the Romans, and us, that we have been saved from slavery to sin. The Israelites were putting their faith in God's covenant promises—that he would give them new life in the holy land. Paul is teaching the Romans, and us, to put our faith in Jesus Christ, who offers us eternal life.

When Paul asks, "What does Scripture say?" he answers his own question by quoting Deuteronomy 30:14 in which Moses

is teaching the people that the Law is already written in their hearts. Paul applies the words not to the Law, but to the word: "the word of faith that we preach." Not obedience to Law, but faith in Jesus Christ leads to salvation.

As he continues to teach that salvation depends on faith in Jesus Christ, Paul alludes to Isaiah 28:16c: "whoever puts his faith in it [God's covenant relationship with Zion] will not waver." Paul is teaching that no one who puts his faith in Jesus Christ will be shaken.

Christ offers salvation, not only to the Israelites, but to all. The "same Lord is Lord of all." It is this message of universal salvation that you should emphasize as you proclaim Paul's Good News to the Romans.

GOSPEL — As Luke's story of Jesus' temptation in the desert begins, Luke refers back to Jesus' baptism: Jesus is "filled with the Holy Spirit" as he returns from the Jordan, where he was baptized. The Spirit leads Jesus into the desert, not into temptation. While there, the devil tempts Jesus to abuse his power,

The devil sounds wily, not aggressive.

Jesus responds calmly and with confidence.
When the narrator speaks, drop your voice. This is background information.

Now the devil sounds magnanimous and grandiose.

Again, Jesus responds calmly and confidently.

Now the narrator gives us more background information.
The devil is getting frustrated. Raise your voice and sound more challenging.
Jerusalem = juh-ROO-suh-lem; juh-ROO-zuh-lem
parapet = PAYR-uh-puht; PAYR-uh-pet

In contrast to the devil, Jesus remains calm and assured. Here Jesus speaks with calm authority.

The narrator is concluding the story. Allow the words "for a time" to hang in the air. The story is far from over.

The **devil said** to him,
"**If** you are the **Son** of **God**,
    command this **stone** to become **bread**."
Jesus answered him,
"It is **written**, *One does **not live** on **bread alone**.*"
Then he took him up and **showed** him
    all the **kingdoms** of the **world** in a **single instant**.
The **devil said** to him,
"I shall **give** to you **all** this **power** and **glory**;
    for it has been **handed over to** me,
    and **I** may give it to **whomever I** wish.
All this will be **yours**, if you **worship** me."
Jesus said to him in **reply**,
"It is **written**:
    *You shall **worship** the **Lord**, your **God**,
        and **him alone** shall you **serve**.*"
Then he led him to **Jerusalem**,
    made him **stand** on the **parapet** of the **temple**, and said to him,
"**If you** are the **Son** of **God**,
    throw yourself down from here, for it is **written**:
    *He will command his **angels** concerning you, to **guard** you,*
    and:
        *With their **hands** they will **support** you,
        lest you dash your **foot** against a **stone**.*"
Jesus said to him in **reply**,
    "It **also** says,
    *You **shall not put** the **Lord**, your **God**, to the **test**.*"
When the **devil** had finished **every temptation**,
    he **departed** from him **for a time**.

to use it in self-serving ways rather than in service to others.

The three temptations that the devil offers Jesus are to abuse his power by using it to feed himself (turn stones into bread), to gain political power, and to put on a show—to prove that he can. As Jesus overcomes each temptation, he refers to the Book of Deuteronomy. First he quotes Moses, who reminded the people that human beings do "not live on bread alone." Rather, they live by "all that comes forth from the mouth of the LORD" (Deuteronomy 8:3). When overcoming the temptation to

worship the devil in order to gain political power, Jesus reminds the devil that only God should be worshipped (see Deuteronomy 6:13). Finally, when asked to prove his identity by throwing himself from the parapet of the temple, Jesus once more quotes Moses: "You shall not put the LORD, your God, to the test" (Deuteronomy 6:16).

When Moses says these words to the Israelites, and when Jesus says them to Satan, the Lord who is not to be tested is God. However, in the context of Luke's

account of the Gospel, the words take on a double meaning. Since Luke has already established Jesus' identity through his infancy narratives and his story of Jesus' baptism, the reader knows that the Lord who is not to be tempted is also Jesus Christ.

At the same time, Luke makes it clear that the human Jesus was tempted and will be tempted again. The devil departs from him "for a time." As you proclaim this reading, say Jesus' words with gentle firmness, but not with outrage. Jesus uses his time of temptation to teach the Word of God, even to the devil.

2ND SUNDAY OF LENT

Lectionary #27

READING I   Genesis 15:5–12, 17–18

A reading from the Book of Genesis

The **Lord God** took **Abram outside** and said,
  "Look up at the **sky** and count the **stars**, if you can.
Just so," he added, "shall **your descendants** be."
Abram put his **faith** in the **LORD**,
  who **credited** it to him as an act of **righteousness**.

He then **said** to him,
  "I am the **LORD** who brought you from **Ur** of the **Chaldeans**
  to give you **this land** as a **possession**."
"O **Lord GOD**," he asked,
  "how am I to **know** that I shall **possess** it?"
He **answered** him,
  "Bring me a three-year-old **heifer**, a three-year-old **she-goat**,
  a three-year-old **ram**, a **turtledove**, and a young **pigeon**."
Abram brought him **all** these, **split** them in **two**,
  and placed **each half opposite** the **other**;
  but the **birds** he did **not** cut up.
Birds of prey **swooped** down on the carcasses,
  but Abram **stayed** with them.
As the **sun** was about to **set**, a **trance** fell upon Abram,
  and a **deep**, **terrifying darkness enveloped** him.

When the sun had **set** and it was **dark**,
  there **appeared** a **smoking fire pot** and a **flaming torch**,
  which **passed between** those pieces.

Genesis = JEN-uh-sis
The narrator sets the stage.
Abram = AY-br*m
God is saying something wonderful, something full of hope.
Now the narrator speaks again. Have less affect in your voice when you read the narrator's lines.

Now God is speaking again. The tone is intimate and reassuring.
Abraham is truly puzzled and somewhat anxious.

God is giving directions.
heifer = HEF-er

Now the narrator continues the story.

Pause slightly after this line.
Say these five lines slowly and with awe.

 As this reading begins, God promises Abram that he will have many descendants, as many as the stars in the sky. This is not the first time God has made such a promise. Earlier, in Genesis 12, we read that God called Abram and told him to go to a new land that God would show him. After Abram's arrival, God promised that Abrams' descendants would inherit the land. But Abram's wife, Sara, was barren.

Knowing that this promise had been made before, and that, so far, Abram had no descendants, adds to the drama of today's reading. Even though he does not know how God will fulfill this promise, Abram believes that God will do so.

God then instructs Abram on how to celebrate the covenant with a ritual in which animals are cut in half, and Abram and God walk between the halves, God appearing as fire. This ritual created an unbreakable agreement in Abram's society. It was a way of saying that each party would rather be cut in half themselves than break the agreement.

Abram realizes that he is involved in a profound, life-changing experience. Later, God will once more make his presence known through a cloud and a fiery torch as he leads the people out of slavery.

As the reading ends, the narrator tells us the significance of what we have read. "It was on that occasion that the LORD made a covenant with Abram." As you proclaim the reading, try to convey both the drama and the significance of what is being described. World history has been profoundly affected by Israel's understanding of God's covenant relationship with Abraham and his descendants.

The narrator is concluding the story.

God speaks with sincerity and authority.

It was on **that** occasion that the LORD m...
    with **Abram**,
      saying: "To **your descendants** I **give this** ...
      from the **Wadi** of **Egypt** to the **Great River**,

READING II   Philippians 3:17—4:1

Philippians = fih-LIP-ee-uhnz

Paul is pleading with the Philippians. Begin with a loud and commanding voice.

Now lower your volume.

Say this line slowly.
Now increase your pace for the next four lines.

Now speak more slowly. Paul is drawing a contrast between the Philippians and these others.
Now Paul is teaching. Speak with authority.

Paul ends with an affectionate and positive tone.

A reading from the Letter of Saint Paul to the Philippians

Join with **others** in being **imitators** of **me**, brothers and sisters,
    and **observe those** who thus **conduct** themselves
    according to the model you have in **us**.
For **many**, as I have **often told** you
    and **now** tell you even in **tears**,
    conduct themselves as **enemies** of the **cross** of **Christ**.
Their **end** is **destruction**.
Their **God** is their **stomach**;
    their **glory** is in their "**shame**."
Their **minds** are occupied with **earthly** things.
But **our** citizenship is in **heaven**,
    and from **it** we **also** await a **savior**, the **Lord Jesus Christ**.
He will change our **lowly** body
    to **conform** with his **glorified** body
    by the **power** that enables him **also**
    to bring **all things** into **subjection** to **himself**.

Therefore, my **brothers** and **sisters**,
    whom I **love** and **long for**, my **joy** and **crown**,
    in **this way stand firm** in the **Lord**.

[Shorter: Philippians 3:20—4:1]

READING II   In today's reading Paul is very upset and is expressing himself with deep passion. This reading does not tell us what has caused Paul such distress. Many scholars think this particular section of Philippians is thought to be part of a separate letter (Philippians 3:2—4:3) inserted into a longer and much more joyful letter written to the same church. As the insertion begins, Paul is warning the Philippians to beware of those who are insisting on circumcision (see Philippians 3:2–11). Paul had taught the Philippians that salvation comes not by obedience to the Law, which required circumcision, but by faith in Jesus Christ. It angers Paul that anyone is teaching the opposite.

Rather than modeling themselves after these troublemakers, Paul wants the Philippians to model themselves on Paul and those who place their faith in Jesus Christ. He considers those who insist on obedience to the Law as "enemies of the cross of Christ." Why? Because they are as much as saying that Jesus' saving acts were unnecessary and therefore without effect.

Paul draws a sharp contrast between these false teachers, whose "minds are occupied with earthly things" and the Philippians who have heard and believed Paul's preaching: their "citizenship is in heaven." They, like Paul, await Jesus Christ, who rose from the dead and who will change their "lowly body to conform with his glorified body."

As Paul concludes, he expresses his deep love and longing for the Philippians. He urges them to "stand firm in the Lord." The tone in this reading changes from pleading to anger to love. As you proclaim

GOSPEL Luke 9:28b–36

A reading from the holy Gospel according to Luke

Emphasize Peter, John, and James. These three are often pictured as particularly close to Jesus.

As you describe the marvelous events, speak slowly and with awe.
Moses = MOh-ziz; MOH-zis
Elijah = ee-LĪ-juh
exodus = EK-suh-duhs

Now speak with conviction. There were witnesses to this marvelous event.
Jerusalem = juh-ROO-suh-lem; juh-ROO-zuh-lem
Peter is excited and enthusiastic.

This is the narrator's voice. Speak matter-of-factly. Then pause.

This is another marvelous and mysterious event. Speak with awe.

As you conclude the story speak softly and thoughtfully. There is mystery here.

Jesus took **Peter**, **John**, and **James**
   and went up the **mountain** to **pray**.
While he was **praying**, his **face changed** in **appearance**
   and his **clothing** became **dazzling white**.
And **behold**, **two men** were **conversing** with him, **Moses**
      and **Elijah**,
   who **appeared** in **glory** and spoke of his **exodus**
   that he was going to **accomplish** in **Jerusalem**.
Peter and his **companions** had been **overcome** by **sleep**,
   but becoming **fully awake**,
   they saw his **glory** and the **two men standing** with him.
As they were about to **part** from him, **Peter** said to **Jesus**,
   "**Master**, it is **good** that we are **here**;
   let us make **three tents**,
   one for **you**, one for **Moses**, and one for **Elijah**."
But he did **not know** what he was **saying**.
While he was **still speaking**,
   a **cloud came** and **cast** a **shadow** over them,
   and they became **frightened** when they **entered** the **cloud**.
Then from the cloud came a **voice** that said,
   "**This** is my **chosen Son**; listen to **him**."
After the **voice** had **spoken**, **Jesus** was found **alone**.
They fell **silent** and did not at that time
   tell **anyone** what they had **seen**.

---

the reading, do not hide Paul's passion, but try to leave your listeners with a sense of Paul's love for the Philippians and his insistence that faith in Jesus Christ is of preeminent importance.

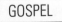 **GOSPEL** Today's Gospel is Luke's account of Jesus' Transfiguration. Remember that the gospel accounts are later writings than Paul's letters. They, like Paul's letters, are, to some extent, responding to questions on the minds of the people for whom they were written. Luke, like Paul, is responding to

questions that relate to the relative authority of the previous demands of the Law and the present teaching that Gentiles, too, are invited into covenant love, and are not required to obey all of the prescriptions of the Jewish law.

As today's Gospel begins, Jesus takes Peter, John, and James with him as he withdraws for prayer. They are privileged to catch a glimpse of Jesus' divinity: "his face changed in appearance and his clothing became dazzling white." Then they see that Jesus is talking with Moses, the Law-giver, and Elijah, the prophet. Peter wants

all three to stay. However, the narrator tells us that Peter did not understand. A voice from heaven tells them that Jesus is the one to whom they should listen. After that, Jesus is there alone.

Luke, like Paul, is teaching that if there is a conflict between following Jesus and obeying the Law, people should listen to Jesus. You can make this teaching clear to those who hear you proclaim the reading by emphasizing "him" when you read "This is my chosen Son; listen to him."

3RD SUNDAY OF LENT

Lectionary #30

READING I   Exodus 3:1–8a, 13–15

A reading from the Book of Exodus

Moses was tending the flock of his **father**-in-law **Jethro**,
  the **priest** of **Midian**.
Leading the flock across the **desert**, he came to **Horeb**,
  the **mountain** of God.
There an **angel** of the LORD **appeared** to Moses in **fire**
  flaming out of a **bush**.
As he **looked on**, he was **surprised** to see that the **bush**,
  though on **fire**, was **not consumed**.
So **Moses** decided,
  "I must go **over** to **look** at this **remarkable sight**,
  and see why the **bush** is **not burned**."

When the LORD saw him **coming over** to **look** at it more **closely**,
  God **called** out to him from the **bush**, "**Moses! Moses!**"
He answered, "**Here** I am."
God said, "**Come no nearer!**
Remove the **sandals** from your **feet**,
  for the **place** where you **stand** is **holy ground**.
I am the **God** of your **fathers**," he continued,
  "the God of **Abraham**, the God of **Isaac**, the God of **Jacob**."
Moses hid his **face**, for he was **afraid** to **look** at God.
But the LORD said,
  "I have **witnessed** the **affliction** of **my people** in **Egypt**

Margin notes

Exodus = EK-suh-duhs

Begin in a matter-of-fact tone of voice. You are merely setting the scene.
Moses = MOH-ZIZ; MOH-zis
Jethro = JETH-roh
Midian = MID-ee-uhn
Horeb = HOHR-eb
Now something marvelous is being recounted. Speak slowly and with awe.

Moses is puzzled but determined.

God speaks with authority but gently. God is introducing himself to Moses.

Abraham = AY-bruh-ham
Isaac = Ī-zik

Drop your voice for the narrator's lines.

God has come with wonderful news. Speak expansively and with joy.

READING I In a sense, today's reading is a continuation of the story that we read last week on the Second Sunday of Lent, the story from Genesis of God entering into a covenant relationship with Abraham. The reading itself draws our attention to that connection: When God introduces himself to Moses he says, "I am the God . . . of Abraham, the God of Isaac, the God of Jacob." Abraham is the father of Isaac; Isaac is the father of Jacob. In appearing to Moses, God is being faithful to the covenant God made with Abraham and his descendants.

However, today's reading is from the Book of Exodus, not the Book of Genesis. A great deal has happened between the two accounts. Abraham lived about 1850 BC, Moses about 1250 BC. Despite God's promise to Abraham that God would give him land, at the time of Moses the Israelites were not living in that land; they were slaves in Egypt. Today's reading describes this setting as it pictures God saying: "I have witnessed the affliction of my people in Egypt and have heard their cry of complaint against their slave drivers."

The Israelites had lived in the land that God promised Abraham for four generations. Three of them are named in today's reading: Abraham, Isaac, and Jacob. One of Jacob's sons was Joseph. Joseph, because of his brothers' treachery, ended up in Egypt. Later, Joseph's fellow Israelites also came to Egypt, due to a famine in the holy land. By the time of Moses, the Israelites had been in Egypt about five hundred years.

However, God had not forgotten the promises to Abraham. Just as God's presence was made known to Abraham by a

and have **heard** their **cry** of **complaint**
　　against their **slave drivers**,
　so I **know well** what they are **suffering**.
Therefore I have come down to **rescue** them
　　from the **hands** of the **Egyptians**
　　and **lead** them **out** of **that** land into a **good** and **spacious** land,
　　a land **flowing** with **milk** and **honey**."

Moses is not confident. He is uncertain and needs encouragement.

Moses said to **God**, "But when I **go** to the **Israelites**
　　and say to them, 'The **God** of your **fathers** has **sent** me to you,'
　if they **ask** me, '**What** is his **name**?' **what** am I to **tell** them?"
God replied, **"I am who am."**
Then he added, **"This** is what you shall tell the **Israelites**:
　I AM sent me to **you**."

Speak slowly and emphasize every word of "I am who am."
Israelites = IZ-ree-uh-lītz; IZ-ray-uh-lītz
Emphasize "I am."
Again, God speaks with authority. Speak with conviction.

God spoke **further** to **Moses**, "**Thus** shall you **say**
　　to the **Israelites**:
　The **LORD**, the **God** of your **fathers**,
　the God of **Abraham**, the God **of Isaac**, the God of **Jacob**,
　has **sent me** to **you**.

　"**This** is my **name forever**;
　　thus am I to be **remembered** through **all generations**."

READING II 1 Corinthians 10:1–6, 10–12

Corinthians = kohr-IN-thee-uhnz
Paul is teaching the Corinthians. Read each line slowly and pause after each line.

A reading from the first Letter of Saint Paul to the Corinthians

I do **not** want you to be **unaware**, **brothers** and **sisters**,
　　that our **ancestors** were **all under** the **cloud**
　　and all **passed through** the sea,

firebrand passing between cut animals, so is God's presence made known to Moses through fire flaming from a bush. God has come to rescue his people from slavery and to return them to the land originally promised to Abraham, "a good and spacious land, a land flowing with milk and honey."

After receiving his instructions, Moses asks God to reveal his name. God had not revealed his name to Abraham, so to do so was to enter in to an even greater degree of intimacy. God tells Moses that his name

is "I am who am." The name that God reveals to Moses is a form of the Hebrew verb "to be" and consists of four letters: YHWH. Without vowels the word is unpronounceable. In fact, the Israelites considered the name to be so holy that they refrained from pronouncing it, instead referring to God as Adonai, which means "Lord." The name suggests a variety of meanings: "I am always with you," "I cause to be all that happens," and, "I cause to be all that is." It is by this name that God has been remembered through all generations.

As you proclaim this reading, say, "I am who am" with great clarity and solemnity. In doing so you are becoming one of the countless generations that has remembered the name with which God revealed himself to Moses.

READING II In the Second Reading, Paul is using the story of the exodus to teach the Corinthians, and us, about our own spiritual journey. In doing so, he is using Old Testament people

Moses = MOH-ziz; MOH-zis

and **all** of them were **baptized** into **Moses**
    in the **cloud** and in the **sea**.
All **ate** the **same spiritual food**,
    and all **drank** the **same spiritual drink**,
    for they **drank** from a **spiritual rock** that **followed** them,
    and the **rock** was the **Christ**.

Say this line with great conviction.
Say this line more quickly.

Yet God was **not pleased** with **most** of them,
    for they were **struck down** in the **desert**.

Paul is not threatening but teaching.

These things **happened** as **examples** for **us**,
    so that **we** might not **desire evil** things, as **they** did.
Do not **grumble** as some of **them** did,
    and **suffered death** by the **destroyer**.
These things **happened** to **them** as an **example**,
    and they have been **written down** as a **warning** to **us**,
    upon whom the **end** of the **ages** has **come**.

Emphasize "end of the ages."
This is a warning—wise advice—rather than an angry threat.

Therefore, whoever **thinks** he is standing **secure**
    should **take care** not to **fall**.

GOSPEL   Luke 13:1–9

A reading from the holy Gospel according to Luke

The narrator is setting the stage. Speak matter-of-factly.
Galileans = gal-ih-LEE-uhnz
Pilate = PĪ-luht

Some people told **Jesus** about the **Galileans**
    whose **blood Pilate** had mingled with the **blood**
        of their **sacrifices**.
Jesus said to them in reply,

Jesus is teaching, trying to get the people to think by posing a question.

    "Do you **think** that because these **Galileans suffered**
        in **this way**
    they were **greater sinners** than **all other** Galileans?

---

and events as examples, or "types," to teach about New Testament people and events. At the time of the exodus, the people were "under the cloud," that is, they were lead by God. So are the Corinthians. The Israelites "passed through the sea." The Corinthians have also passed through the sea in that they have passed through the waters of Baptism. The Israelites had spiritual food (manna) and spiritual drink (water from the rock). Christians, too, have spiritual food and drink: the Eucharist.

Despite all that God had done for them, some of the Israelites sinned. As a result, they were struck down and did not reach the holy land. Paul tells the Corinthians that the fate of those rebellious Israelites serves as an example for them. They must not "desire evil things" or "grumble," as did some of the Israelites. They must examine themselves and "take care not to fall." As you proclaim the reading, emphasize this last line. During Lent, we, too, are called to examine ourselves and to take care that we do not fall.

GOSPEL Today's Gospel, like the reading from 1 Corinthians, is calling us to repent. As the reading begins, some people have told Jesus about the terrible fate that had befallen some of their fellow Galileans: they had been killed, and Pilate had mixed their blood with the blood of pagan sacrifices. Jesus asks the people if they think that this terrible fate is evidence that those killed had been greater sinners than other Galileans. Jesus assures them that this is not the

Say these two lines slowly and with great authority.

Now Jesus poses another question. Jesus is teaching, not speaking in anger. Siloam = sih-LOH-uhm

Jerusalem = juh-ROO-suh-lem; juh-ROO-zuh-lem

Again speak slowly and with authority.

Drop your voice for this line.

The owner is angry and impatient.

This line is the narrator's.

The gardener is kind and patient. Speak gently and persuasively.

This would be a last resort. The tone is not threatening, but regretful.

By no means!
But I **tell** you, if **you** do **not repent**,
    you will **all perish** as **they** did!
Or those **eighteen people** who were **killed**
    when the tower at **Siloam fell** on them—
    do you **think** they were **more guilty**
    than **everyone else** who lived in **Jerusalem?**
By no means!
But I **tell** you, if you do **not repent**,
    you will **all perish** as **they** did!' "

And he told them this **parable:**
    "There once was a person who had a **fig tree** planted
        in his **orchard,**
    and when he **came** in search of **fruit** on it but found **none,**
    he said to the **gardener,**
    'For **three years** now **I have come** in search of **fruit**
        on this **fig tree**
    but have found **none.**
So **cut** it **down.**
Why should it **exhaust** the **soil?'**
He said to him in **reply,**
    '**Sir, leave** it for **this** year **also,**
    and I shall **cultivate** the ground around it and **fertilize** it;
    it **may** bear **fruit** in the **future.**
If not you can **cut** it **down.' "**

case. They should not view such suffering as punishment for sin.

Jesus then offers another example. A tower had fallen and killed eighteen people. Were these people being punished because they were greater sinners than others? No, they were not. However, Jesus goes on to say that sin does cause terrible suffering. If the people don't repent, they, too, will perish. The lesson seems to be that while all suffering is not punishment for sin, the consequence of sin is inevitable suffering. To avoid suffering the people must repent.

Jesus then goes on to tell the people a parable. A person who owns an orchard is impatient because his fig tree is not producing fruit. He wants to cut it down. However, his gardener cautions patience. He suggests that the tree be given more time to become fruitful. However, in the final analysis, if the fig tree persists in not producing fruit it will, regrettably, have to be cut down. Jesus is teaching his listeners the urgency of repentance. They have not yet repented and produced good fruit. So far, they have not perished. However, at some point their opportunity to be fruitful will be over. Since they do not know when that time will be, they should repent now.

Today's Gospel could be misunderstood to be teaching that God is mean and punishing. Jesus came to reveal that God is love. Still, sin does have consequences. As you proclaim this reading, portray Jesus as teaching, not threatening. Make clear the regret in the gardener's voice that, in the end, unfruitful trees must be cut down.

3RD SUNDAY OF LENT, YEAR A

Lectionary #28

READING I   Exodus 17:3–7

Exodus = EK-suh-duhs

A reading from the Book of Exodus

In those days, in their **thirst** for **water**,
    the people **grumbled** against **Moses**,
    saying, **"Why did you ever make us leave Egypt**?

The people are very angry.

Was it just to have us **die** here of **thirst**
    with our **children** and our **livestock**?"
So **Moses** cried out to the LORD,
    "What shall **I do** with this **people**?

Moses is exasperated; he needs help and needs it now.

A little **more** and they will **stone me**!"
The LORD answered Moses,
    "Go over there in **front** of the **people**,

God is reassuring.

    along with **some** of the **elders** of **Israel**,
    holding in your **hand**, as you go,
    the **staff** with which you **struck** the **river**.

Horeb = HOHR-eb

I **will be standing** there in front of you on the **rock** in **Horeb**.

Here, God speaks with authority.

Strike the **rock**, and the **water** will **flow** from it
    for the **people** to **drink**."
This Moses did, in the presence of the **elders** of **Israel**.
The place was called **Massah** and **Meribah**,

Massah = MAS-uh
Meribah = MAYR-ih-bah

    because the **Israelites quarreled** there
    and **tested** the LORD, saying,

Emphasize this question.

    "Is the LORD **in** our **midst** or **not**?"

READING I   This reading takes place shortly after the exodus, the Israelites' dramatic escape from the Egyptians along a path God opened for them through the waters of the Red Sea. Now the people are beginning their forty years of wandering in the desert. We are soon reminded of the exodus, as God tells Moses to use the staff "with which you struck the river" (in Exodus 14:16) to strike a rock, out of which water will flow for the people. Despite the marvelous display of God's power and presence at the Red Sea, the Israelites are grumbling, asking, "Is the LORD in our midst or not?"

Why are the people complaining so bitterly? It is not just that they are thirsty. In addition, they are losing their conviction that God is with them and will protect them. They challenge Moses and he turns to God, who directs Moses so that water will be found and the people will know God is present. Moses already knows that God is with the Israelites. Through their own experience, through receiving the manna earlier (Exodus 16:1–15), and now being provided with water, the people are learning to share Moses' faith that God is in their midst.

As you proclaim the reading, try to convey the people's despair, Moses' frustration and helplessness, and God's constant presence and protection. Allow the question with which the reading concludes to hang in the air.

READING II   Romans 5:1–2, 5–8

A reading from the Letter of Saint Paul to the Romans

Brothers and **sisters:**
Since we have been **justified** by **faith,**

Pause after this line.
we have **peace with God through** our **Lord Jesus Christ,**
through whom we have gained **access** by **faith**

Pause after this line.
to this **grace** in which we **stand,**

Say this line with conviction.
and we **boast** in **hope** of the **glory** of **God.**

And **hope** does not **disappoint,**

Read slowly.
because the **love of God** has been **poured out** into our **hearts**
through the **Holy Spirit** who has been **given** to us.
For **Christ,** while we were **still helpless,**
died at the appointed **time** for the **ungodly.**
Indeed, only with **difficulty** does one **die** for a **just** person,

This line is something of an afterthought.
though **perhaps** for a **good** person one **might even**
find **courage** to **die.**
But **God proves** his **love for us**

Emphasize this line.
in that **while we were still sinners Christ died** for **us.**

GOSPEL   John 4:5–42

A reading from the holy Gospel according to John

The narrator's voice sets the stage.
Samaria = suh-MAYR-ee-uh
Sychar = SĪ-kahr

Jesus came to a town of **Samaria** called **Sychar,**
near the plot of land that **Jacob** had given to his son **Joseph.**
Jacob's well was there.
Jesus, tired from his journey, **sat down** there at the **well.**
It was about **noon.**

READING II This passage from the Letter to the Romans is a conclusion drawn from a core spiritual insight that Paul has just finished explaining: people do not earn salvation by obeying the Law that required circumcision and imposed certain eating restrictions regarding clean and unclean food; rather, we are saved through faith in Jesus Christ.

Paul now draws conclusions from it: "Since we have been justified by faith, we have peace with God . . . ." However, a gift can be refused. To receive the gift that has been freely offered, we must put our faith in Jesus Christ. Through Christ "we have gained access by faith to this grace in which we stand."

Christ's actions on our behalf are based entirely on God's love for his people. Without our deserving or earning anything, "the love of God has been poured out into our hearts through the Holy Spirit." Paul then meditates on just how much God loves us. It would be one thing if we were perfect people and somehow deserved this love, but we are not; rather, Christ died for us even though we were "ungodly."

Both Paul's explanations and his sentence structure are sometimes difficult. To proclaim this reading well, you will have to read it several times to make sure that you understand it. Then, as you proclaim the reading, emphasize God's love which has been poured out and which has been proven beyond all doubt by Christ's redeeming actions. This is Paul's main point.

A woman of **Samaria** came to **draw water**.
Jesus said to her,
  "**Give me a drink**."
His **disciples** had gone into the **town** to buy **food**.
The **Samaritan woman** said to him,
  "**How** can **you**, a **Jew**, ask **me**, a **Samaritan woman**,
    for a **drink**?"
—For **Jews** use **nothing** in common with **Samaritans**.—
Jesus **answered** and said to her,
  "**If you knew** the **gift** of God
  and **who** is saying to you, 'Give me a **drink**,'
  you would have **asked him**
  and he would have **given you living water**."
The woman **said** to him,
  "**Sir**, you do not even have a **bucket** and the **cistern** is **deep**;
  where then can you **get** this **living water**?
Are you **greater** than our **father Jacob**,
  who gave us this **cistern** and drank from it **himself**
  with his **children** and his **flocks**?"
Jesus **answered** and said to her,
  "Everyone who drinks **this water** will be **thirsty again**;
  but whoever drinks the water **I shall give** will **never thirst**;
  the water **I shall give** will become in him
  a **spring** of water **welling up** to **eternal life**."
The **woman** said to him,
  "Sir, **give me** this water, so that I may **not be thirsty**
  or have to keep **coming here** to **draw** water."

Jesus said to her,
  "**Go call** your **husband** and come **back**."
The woman **answered** and said to him,
  "I do **not have** a **husband**."
Jesus answered her,
  "You are **right** in saying, 'I do **not** have a **husband**.'

Side notes:
- Jesus' tone is conversational.
- Samaritan = suh-MAYR-uh-tuhn / The woman is astounded.
- Jesus is still low key and inviting.
- The woman is getting friendlier.
- Jesus' tone is becoming more serious.
- The woman does not understand. She is not entirely serious.
- There is a challenge here.
- Softer here.
- These words are factual and end affirming the woman, not accusing her.

GOSPEL To understand more fully what John is teaching his audience through the story of Jesus' encounter with the Samaritan woman at the well, it is helpful to know that John's gospel account was written toward the end of the first century AD for an audience that was asking, "Where is the risen Christ? We expected his return long before now." In response, the author writes his account of the Gospel that, on the surface level, is about Jesus during his public ministry, but, on a deeper level, is about the presence of the risen Christ in the lives of his audience.

Jesus is present through the Church and through what we have come to call the sacraments. Today's story is about the Sacrament of Baptism, "living water . . . welling up to eternal life."

To help his audience understand the deeper level of meaning in his stories, John pictures the characters in the story failing to think metaphorically and thus misunderstanding what Jesus says to them. This gives Jesus the opportunity to explain to the woman (and John to explain to his audience), the deeper level of meaning that his words contain. There are two

examples of this in today's reading: the Samaritan woman misunderstands what Jesus means by "water" and the disciples misunderstand what Jesus means by "food." (More about this later.)

With this background, let us examine the story from the beginning. Jesus, tired and hungry, initiates a conversation with a Samaritan woman by asking her for a drink. The unusual nature of this request is emphasized by having both the woman and the disciples react with surprise: The woman says, "How can you, a Jew, ask me, a Samaritan woman, for a drink?"

Now the woman is serious and a little puzzled.

Here Jesus speaks with authority.

For you have had **five** husbands,
  and the **one** you have now is **not** your **husband**.
What you have said is **true**."
The woman said to him,
  "**Sir**, I can **see** that you are a **prophet**.
Our **ancestors** worshiped on **this mountain**;
  but **you people** say that the place to worship is in **Jerusalem**."
Jesus said to her,
  "**Believe me**, woman, the hour is **coming**
  when you will **worship** the **Father**
  neither on **this mountain nor** in Jerusalem.
You people **worship** what you **do not understand**;
  we worship what we **understand**,
  because **salvation** is from the **Jews**.
But the **hour is coming**, and is now **here**,
  when **true worshipers** will **worship** the Father
    in **Spirit** and **truth**;
  and **indeed** the Father **seeks** such people to **worship** him.
God is **Spirit**, and those who **worship** him
  must worship in **Spirit** and **truth**."
The woman **said** to him,

The woman is becoming more certain.

  "**I know** that the **Messiah** is **coming**, the one called the **Christ**;
  when he **comes**, he will **tell** us **everything**."
Jesus said to her,

This is a solemn statement.

  "**I am he**, the one who is **speaking** with you."

At that moment his **disciples** returned,
  and were **amazed** that he was talking with a **woman**,
  but still no one said, "What are you **looking** for?"
  or "**Why** are you **talking** with **her**?"
The woman **left** her water jar
  and went into the **town** and said to the **people**,

Said with excitement.

  "**Come** see a man who told me **everything** I have **done**.

When the disciples return they are "amazed that he was talking with a woman." Jews considered Samaritans unclean and so would not ordinarily choose to have contact with them. In addition, it was socially unheard of for a man to initiate such a conversation with a woman he did not know.

As the story continues, our attention is drawn to the identity of Jesus Christ and his gift of living water. Jesus says to the woman, "If you knew the gift of God and who is saying to you, 'Give me a drink,' you would have asked him and he would have given you living water."

It is at this point that the woman misunderstands "living water." She tells Jesus that since he doesn't have a bucket he has no way of getting this living water out of the well. Her misunderstanding gives Jesus the opportunity to elaborate. The reader, if not the woman, now understands that Jesus is offering the Samaritan woman knowledge of him and eternal life through the waters of Baptism. As the story continues, the woman does come to realize with whom she is speaking.

The woman first realizes that Jesus is a prophet. She draws this conclusion because Jesus is aware that she has had five husbands and that the man she is now with is not her husband. But, as soon as she has this realization, she changes the subject. She asks about the difference in belief between the Jews and the Gentiles regarding where one should worship. Jesus tells her that the time will come when neither the mountain in Samaria nor the Temple in Jerusalem will be the designated places of worship. Worshippers "will worship the Father in Spirit and truth." By the time John is writing his gospel account, the temple has been destroyed (AD 70).

Could he **possibly** be the **Christ**?"
They went out of the town and **came** to him.
Meanwhile, the disciples **urged** him, "**Rabbi**, **eat**."
But he said to them,

Jesus is thoughtful.

"I have **food** to **eat** of which you **do not know**."
So the disciples **said** to one another,

The disciples are puzzled.

"Could someone have **brought** him something to **eat**?"
Jesus said to them,

This is said with great earnestness and some urgency.

"**My food** is to **do** the **will** of the **one who sent me**
and to **finish his work**.
Do you not say, 'In four months the **harvest** will be here'?
I **tell** you, **look up** and see the fields **ripe** for the **harvest**.
The reaper is **already** receiving **payment**
and **gathering crops** for eternal life,
so that the **sower** and **reaper** can **rejoice together**.
For here the saying is verified that '**One** sows and **another** reaps.'
I sent you to **reap** what you have **not worked** for;
others have done the work,
and **you** are **sharing** the **fruits** of **their** work."

Many of the **Samaritans** of that town began to **believe** in him
because of the **word** of the **woman** who **testified**,

This is said with awe.

"He told me **everything** I have **done**."
When the Samaritans **came** to him,
they **invited** him to **stay** with **them**;
and he **stayed** there **two days**.
Many more began to **believe in him** because of his **word**,
and they **said** to the woman,

This is said with excitement and certitude.

"We no longer **believe** because of **your word**;
for we have **heard** for **ourselves**,
and **we know** that this is **truly** the **savior of the world**."

[Shorter: John 4:5–15, 19b–26, 39a, 40–42]

John's audience worships in "Spirit and in truth."

The woman then brings up the subject of the expected messiah. Jesus says, "I am he, the one who is speaking with you." The woman is so excited by what Jesus has said that she leaves her bucket behind and runs to tell the townspeople what she has discovered. She wants them to help her discover whether this person could possibly be the Christ.

Now it is the disciples who misunderstand Jesus' words. They urge Jesus to eat. Jesus replies that he has food to eat that

they don't know about. They understand "food" literally and conclude that someone else has brought Jesus something to eat. Jesus than makes his meaning clear: "My food is to do the will of the one who sent me and to finish his work." The disciples are to be about God's work, too. They are to be "gathering crops for eternal life."

Because of the Samaritan woman's witness, many in the town come to believe in Jesus. Based not just on her testimony, but on their own experience, they recognize that Jesus "is truly the savior of the world."

As you proclaim this reading, you will take on the voices of many characters: Jesus, the Samaritan woman, the disciples, the crowd, and the narrator. Try to make their many tones clear to the congregation: playfulness, invitation, seriousness, puzzlement, excitement, and wonder. The author of this account of the Gospel and the Church that proclaims it want your audience to be like the woman and the crowd: able to profess faith in Jesus Christ and to accept Jesus' gift of eternal life.

4TH SUNDAY OF LENT

Lectionary #33

READING I   Joshua 5:9a, 10–12

Joshua = JOSH-oo-uh; JOSH-yoo-uh

Say this line with authority. God is speaking.

Now the narrator is speaking. Drop your voice.
Gilgal = GIL-gahl
Jericho = JAYR-ih-koh
Passover = PAS-oh-ver

This is very good news. Sound joyful.

Read "the manna ceased" slowly and then pause. An era is over.
manna = MAN-uh
Emphasize "Canaan." Speak with joy. A promise has been fulfilled.
Canaan = KAY-n*n

A reading from the Book of Joshua

The LORD said to **Joshua,**
   "**Today** I have **removed** the **reproach** of **Egypt** from you."

While the **Israelites** were encamped at **Gilgal** on the plains
      of **Jericho,**
   they celebrated the **Passover**
   on the evening of the **fourteenth** of the **month**.
On the day **after** the **Passover**,
   they **ate** of the **produce** of the **land**
   in the form of **unleavened cakes** and **parched grain**.
On that **same day after** the **Passover**,
   on which they ate of the **produce** of the **land**, the **manna ceased**.
No **longer** was there **manna** for the **Israelites**,
   who **that** year ate of the yield of the land of **Canaan**.

READING II   2 Corinthians 5:17–21

Corinthians = kohr-IN-thee-uhnz

Say this with wonder and joy.

A reading from the second Letter of Saint Paul to the Corinthians

Brothers and **sisters:**
Whoever is in **Christ** is a **new creation:**
   the **old** things have **passed away;**
   behold, **new** things have **come**.

READING I In today's reading from the Book of Joshua, the Israelites are camped "at Gilgal on the plains of Jericho." This means that they are finally back in the holy land, the land of Canaan, which had been promised to their ancestors some six hundred years earlier (around 1850 BC).

During most of those six hundred years the Israelites had lived in Egypt where they had been forced to go due to a famine in the holy land. While in Egypt, they had become slaves. However, God called Moses to lead the Israelites out of slavery, after which they spent forty years in the desert. Now (around 1200 BC), Moses has died and Joshua, after whom the book of Joshua is named, has become Moses' successor. Preceding today's reading, Joshua has led the people across the Jordan and into the promised land.

As the reading begins, the Lord assures Joshua that the long ordeal of slavery in Egypt is now completely over. God says, "I have removed the reproach of Egypt from you." The people celebrate this rescue from slavery by observing Passover.

The feast of Passover recalls the last plague visited on Egypt, the plague that resulted in the Israelites' escape. A terrible illness killed the first born of the Egyptians, but the angel of death "passed over" the homes of the Israelites.

While the Israelites wandered in the desert, God fed them with manna. Now that they are settled in the holy land, they no longer need the manna. They can eat the "produce of the land," the "yield of the land of Canaan." This marvelous news is emphasized because the story is not just about the end of an era in the history of the

Read slowly. Pause after "from God."

Pause after "reconciliation."

Now pick up your pace for the next three lines.

This is Paul's conclusion.

Now Paul is no longer explaining but imploring.
Say this slowly and with great conviction.

Again, read slowly as you conclude.

And **all this** is from **God**,
> who has **reconciled** us to **himself through Christ**
> and given us the **ministry** of **reconciliation**,
> **namely**, God was **reconciling** the **world** to **himself** in **Christ**,
> **not counting** their **trespasses against** them
> and **entrusting** to **us** the **message** of **reconciliation**.
So we are **ambassadors** for **Christ**,
> **as** if **God** were appealing **through** us.
We **implore** you on **behalf** of **Christ**,
> **be reconciled** to **God**.
For **our sake** he made **him** to be **sin** who did **not know** sin,
> so that **we** might become the **righteousness** of **God** in **him**.

GOSPEL   Luke 15:1–3, 11–32

A reading from the holy Gospel according to Luke

Pharisees = FAYR-uh-seez
Say the Pharisees' line with disgust.
parable = PAYR-uh-b*l
Jesus does not respond in kind. He is telling a story.
This is not a request but a demand.

Now Jesus is talking again.

Tax collectors and **sinners** were **all drawing near** to **listen** to **Jesus**,
> but the **Pharisees** and **scribes** began to **complain**, saying,
> "**This** man **welcomes sinners** and **eats** with them."
So to **them** Jesus addressed **this parable**:
"A man had **two sons**, and the **younger** son said to his father,
> '**Father** give me the **share** of your **estate** that should **come**
> > to me.'
So the father **divided** the property **between** them.
After a few **days**, the **younger** son collected **all** his **belongings**
> and **set off** to a **distant country**
> where he **squandered** his inheritance on a life of **dissipation**.

Pause after "dissipation."

Israelites. The story is primarily about God's faithfulness to his promises. God had promised the land to Abraham and his descendants, and now Abraham's descendants are living in the land, eating their own crops. As you proclaim this reading, try to make it clear to your listeners that you are proclaiming not just history, but wonderful news.

READING II The Second Reading, from 2 Corinthians, is also proclaiming a new era, a "new creation," this one initiated by Jesus Christ. Through

Christ, God has reconciled the world to himself. Therefore, disciples of Christ are called, not to be at odds with each other, but to be ministers of reconciliation.

As he writes to the Corinthians, Paul's message of reconciliation is heartfelt because the Corinthians are not only at odds with some of their own, but with Paul too. Paul had written them a tearful letter earlier, seeking reconciliation (see 2 Corinthians 2:4). In doing so, Paul was practicing what he is preaching now. Paul reminds the Corinthians that God does not

count peoples' trespasses against them, but instead reaches out to reconcile the world to himself. The Corinthians and Paul are supposed to be "ambassadors for Christ," bringing the good news of reconciliation to the whole world. They are not supposed to be people who are failing to be reconciled to each other.

Given this understanding of God's reconciling actions through Jesus Christ, and of his own and the Corinthians' role as ambassadors of this reconciliation, Paul implores the Corinthians to live lives reconciled to God. It was for their sake that

famine = FAM-in

Say "swine" with distaste. This is really sinking low.

The son is wily, still acting for his own good.

The son is practicing sounding penitent.

Pause after "father."

Speak quickly and with joy.

The father is full of joy and very excited.

Pause after "began."

When he had **freely spent everything**,
    a **severe famine struck** that country,
    and he found himself in **dire need**.
So he **hired** himself **out** to one of the local **citizens**
    who **sent** him to his **farm** to **tend** the **swine**.
And he **longed** to eat his **fill** of the **pods** on which the **swine fed**,
    but **nobody gave** him any.
Coming to his **senses** he thought,
    'How many of my father's hired **workers**
    have **more** than enough food to eat,
    but here am **I**, **dying** from **hunger**.
I shall **get up** and go to my **father** and I shall **say** to him,
    "**Father**, I have **sinned** against **heaven** and against **you**.
I no longer **deserve** to be called your **son**;
    treat me as **you** would **treat** one of your **hired workers**." '
So he **got up** and **went back** to his **father**.
While he was still a **long way off**,
    his **father** caught **sight** of him, and was **filled** with **compassion**.
He **ran** to his son, **embraced** him and **kissed** him.
His **son said** to **him**,
    '**Father**, I have **sinned** against **heaven** and against **you**;
    I no longer **deserve** to be called your **son**.'
But his **father** ordered his **servants**,
    '**Quickly** bring the **finest robe** and put it **on** him;
    put a **ring** on his **finger** and **sandals** on his **feet**.
Take the **fattened calf** and **slaughter** it.
Then let us **celebrate** with a **feast**,
    because this **son** of mine was **dead**, and has come to **life** again;
    he was **lost**, and has been **found**.'
Then the **celebration began**.

Christ, a person who did not know sin, suffered as he did. The effect of Christ's suffering was to make Christ's disciples (Paul, the Corinthians, and us) righteous. They (and we) must live as faithful recipients of such a great gift.

    As is often true, both Paul's sentence structure and his ideas are complicated. If you have the privilege of proclaiming this message of reconciliation, read it over several times so that you know when to pause and what to emphasize in order to make this Good News understandable to the assembly.

GOSPEL | Today's first two readings emphasize God's initiative in reaching out, in keeping promises, and in reconciling. The Gospel continues these themes, telling us how Jesus reached out to the Pharisees and scribes, who did not realize that they, too, were sinners, calling them to self-examination and conversion.

    As today's Gospel begins, the Pharisees and scribes are complaining because Jesus spends time with sinners. Of course, Jesus spends time with them, too, but they do not realize that when Jesus is with

them he is also spending time with sinners. Jesus tells them the parable of the prodigal son in order to teach them something about themselves, to call them to self-knowledge and conversion.

    In the parable a very loving father has two sons. The younger son asks for his inheritance, wastes it on a dissolute life, decides that his father's servants are better off than he is, and returns home out of self-interest. As soon as the father sees him, the father rushes out, welcomes him, and throws a big party to celebrate his return. This angers the older son who has

There is a radical change of tone here. Speak slowly and suspiciously.

Now the **older** son had been out in the **field**
and, on his way **back**, as he neared the **house**,
he heard the sound of **music** and **dancing**.
He **called** one of the **servants** and **asked** what this might **mean**.
The servant said to him,

The servant is excited and happy.

'Your **brother** has **returned**
and your **father** has **slaughtered** the **fattened calf**
because he has him **back safe** and **sound**.'
He became **angry**,
and when he **refused** to enter the **house**,
his **father** came **out** and **pleaded** with him.
He said to his father in reply,

The brother is angry and hurt.

'**Look**, **all these years** I **served** you
and **not once** did I **disobey** your **orders**;
yet you **never** gave me even a young **goat**
to **feast** on with my **friends**.
But when **your son** returns
who **swallowed** up your **property** with **prostitutes**,
for **him** you **slaughter** the **fattened calf**.'
He **said** to him,

The father is loving and compassionate.

'**My son**, **you** are here with me **always**;
everything I have is **yours**.
But **now** we must **celebrate** and **rejoice**,

Read the last two lines slowly.

because your brother was **dead** and has come to **life** again;
he was **lost** and has been **found**.' "

always obeyed the rules. When he realizes what is happening, he refuses to join the celebration. The father comes out to this son, too, and explains why the return of a sinner is worth celebrating. The story ends before we know whether the older brother realizes that he, too, is a sinner because he is self-righteous and refuses to love his own brother.

Jesus tells this story to the Pharisees and scribes because they are just like the older brother: they are self-righteous and judgmental. They can see that other people

sin, but they cannot see that they themselves also sin by their failure to forgive and to love. Even though the Pharisees and scribes are sinners and are criticizing Jesus, Jesus reaches out to them. They, like the older brother in the parable, are invited to the celebration. Will they accept the invitation that Jesus offers them, an invitation to the Kingdom of God, or will they fail to repent and thereby refuse the invitation?

To proclaim today's Gospel well, you will have to take on many voices: the narrator, the disdaining Pharisees, the demanding and wily younger brother, the loving, forgiving, and exuberant father, the angry and resentful older brother, and the earnest and still loving father. In proclaiming this reading you, too, will be a minister of reconciliation as you remind the congregation that God loves and forgives us and that we must love and forgive each other.

Lectionary #31

READING I   1 Samuel 16:1b, 6–7, 10–13a

A reading from the first Book of Samuel

Samuel = SAM-yoo-uhl

The LORD said to **Samuel**:
  "Fill your horn with **oil**, and be **on your way**.
I am **sending** you to Jesse of Bethlehem,
  for **I have chosen my king** from among his sons."

This direction is spoken with authority.
Jesse = JES-ee
Bethlehem = BETH-luh-hem

As **Jesse** and his **sons** came to the **sacrifice**,
  Samuel looked at **Eliab** and thought,
  "**Surely** the LORD's **anointed** is here before him."

Eliab = ee-LĪ-uhb
This is a thought; speak softly.

But the LORD said to **Samuel**:
  "**Do not judge** from his **appearance** or from his **lofty stature**,
  because I have **rejected** him.

Still soft, but with authority.

Not as **man** sees does **God** see,
  because **man** sees the **appearance**
  but the LORD looks into the **heart**."

Emphasize this very important insight.

In the **same** way **Jesse** presented **seven sons** before **Samuel**,
  but **Samuel** said to **Jesse**,
  "The LORD **has not chosen any one** of these."
Then **Samuel asked Jesse**,
  "Are these **all** the **sons** you have?"

Said gently; Samuel is disappointing Jesse.

Jesse replied,
  "There is still the **youngest**, who is tending the **sheep**."

Jesse is discounting the possibility that this son is important.

Now, Samuel speaks with authority.

Samuel said to **Jesse**,
  "**Send** for **him**;
  we will **not begin** the **sacrificial** banquet until **he** arrives here."

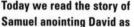

READING I Today we read the story of Samuel anointing David as God's chosen king while David is still a youth, tending his father's sheep. Samuel was a very important figure who lived at the time when the Israelites were transitioning from being a loose federation of twelve tribes to a united nation under one king (1020–1000 BC). Samuel functioned as judge, prophet, and priest, roles that would become distinct over the following centuries. In today's reading, Samuel is functioning primarily as a prophet, as one who speaks for God.

God tells Samuel to take his horn of oil and go to the house of Jesse because God has chosen his king from among Jesse's sons. In the context of 1 Samuel this is a controversial thing to do because Samuel has previously anointed Saul as king. However, Saul has disobeyed God (1 Samuel 13:8–14, 15) and must be replaced, as it turns out, by David. To anoint someone is of utmost importance. The word "messiah" means "the anointed one." In Israelite culture, priests, prophets, and kings were anointed. Whenever the Israelites were in difficulty, they expected God to send a

messiah, an anointed one, to rescue them. It was partially through priests, prophets, and kings that God kept his promises to be with and to protect the people.

Acting on God's instructions, Samuel goes to Jesse's home and meets all but one of his many sons. Initially, on seeing Eliab, Samuel thinks he has spotted God's choice, but God tells Samuel that Eliab, despite his impressive appearance, is not God's choice. Samuel is judging as human beings do, being swayed by appearance, and not as God judges, by looking into a person's

Use an admiring tone here.

Said in a decisive tone.

Speak with solemnity. An important ritual is being described.

Jesse **sent** and **had** the **young man** brought to them.
He was **ruddy**, a youth **handsome** to **behold**
    and making a **splendid appearance**.
The LORD said,
    "**There—anoint him**, for **this is the one!**"
Then **Samuel**, with the horn of **oil** in hand,
    anointed David in the presence of his brothers;
    and from **that day on**, the **spirit** of the LORD
        rushed upon **David**.

READING II   Ephesians 5:8–14

Ephesians = ee-FEE-zhuhnz

Paul's tone is encouraging. Things have changed for the better for the Ephesians.

Read this line slowly.

righteousness = RĪ-chuhs-ness
Paul is advising, not accusing.

Emphasize "expose them."

Read more slowly and increase the volume here.

Read this quotation as a proclamation.

A reading from the Letter of Saint Paul to the Ephesians

Brothers and **sisters**:
You were once **darkness**,
    but **now** you are **light** in the Lord.
Live as children of **light**,
    for **light** produces **every kind** of **goodness**
    and **righteousness** and **truth**.
Try to **learn** what is **pleasing** to the **Lord**.
Take **no part** in the **fruitless** works of **darkness**;
    rather **expose them**, for it is **shameful** even to **mention**
        the things done by them in **secret**;
    but everything **exposed** by the **light** becomes **visible**,
    for **everything** that becomes **visible** is **light**.
Therefore, it says:
    "**Awake**, O **sleeper**,
    and **arise** from the **dead**,
    and **Christ** will give you **light**."

heart. After seeing all the sons whom Jesse presents, Samuel says, "The Lord has not chosen any one of these."

Because he trusts God's instructions Samuel then asks Jesse if he has any other sons. Jesse says that he does, one so young that Jesse has dismissed the possibility that he might be God's choice. Samuel insists on seeing him. When David arrives, the Lord tells Samuel that David is God's choice. God says, "There – anoint him, for this is the one!" Samuel then anoints David, and the "spirit of the Lord rushed upon" him.

Two portions of this reading are particularly important for the elect who will be hearing this reading on the Fourth Sunday of Lent. One is that God sees into the heart. During the scrutinies, the elect are trying to see into their own hearts, to see as God sees. The second is that when David is anointed, the Spirit rushes upon him. Those preparing to be anointed in Baptism and Confirmation at the Easter Vigil will also receive the Spirit. As you proclaim the reading, give special emphasis to these two sections.

READING II Although the Letter to the Ephesians claims to have been written by Paul, scripture scholars think it is a pseudonymous letter, that is, a letter attributed to Paul by an admirer and follower, but not written by Paul. The letter seems to have been written a generation later.

By the time the letter was written, the recipients had evidently developed a well known baptismal hymn. As today's reading ends, the author quotes the hymn, saying: "Therefore, it [the hymn] says: 'Awake, O sleeper,/ and arise from the dead,/ and

GOSPEL   John 9:1–41

A reading from the holy Gospel according to John

The narrator sets the stage.

Rabbi = RAB-ī
The disciples are puzzled.

Jesus speaks with authority. Emphasize every word of this line.

A softer voice here.

The narrator is simply giving information.

Jesus' order is given gently.
The narrator explains the meaning of Siloam. Drop your voice.
Siloam = sih-LOH-uhm

Say this with firmness.

The man speaks with confidence.

(1) As **Jesus** passed by he saw a **man blind** from **birth**.
His **disciples asked** him,
   "**Rabbi**, **who sinned**, **this man** or his **parents**,
   that he was **born blind**?"
Jesus answered,
   "**Neither he nor** his **parents sinned**;
   it is so that the **works** of **God** might be made **visible**
      through **him**.
We have to do the **works** of the **one who sent me** while it is **day**.
Night is coming when **no one** can **work**.
While I am **in the world**, I am the **light of the world**."
(2) When he had said this, he **spat** on the **ground**
   and made **clay** with the **saliva**,
   and **smeared** the **clay** on his **eyes**, and said to him,
   "**Go wash** in the **Pool** of **Siloam**"—which means **Sent**—.
So he **went** and **washed**, and came **back** able to **see**.

(3) His **neighbors** and those who had seen him **earlier**
      as a **beggar said**,
   "Isn't **this** the **one** who **used** to **sit** and **beg**?"
Some said, "**It is**,"
   but others said, "**No**, he just **looks** like him."
He said, "**I am**."
So they said to him, "**How** were your **eyes opened**?"
He replied,
   "The **man** called **Jesus** made **clay** and **anointed** my **eyes**
   and told me, '**Go** to **Siloam** and **wash**.'
So I **went** there and **washed** and was able to **see**."

Christ will give you light.'" The death from which the person is arising is slavery to sin. The life to which the person is awakening is life lived in Christ.

Before being baptized, the people lived in darkness. Now they not only live in the light of Christ, they "are light in the Lord." To be that light for others, the Ephesians must "Try to learn what is pleasing to the Lord." This means that they will not do shameful things in secret, but will live in "goodness and righteousness and truth."

You will be proclaiming this reading, not only to the baptized, but also to those who are preparing for Baptism. They will soon be dying with Christ in order to rise with Christ. They, like the Ephesians, will be called to live in the light and to be light for others. As you proclaim this reading, use an inviting tone. Try to proclaim the last three lines so that those preparing for Baptism and those already baptized will be all the more receptive to the light that is Christ.

GOSPEL As is always true when reading the Gospel according to John, the story that we read today in which Jesus gives sight to a blind man, has more than one level of meaning. To understand the various levels of meaning it will be helpful to remember John's audience and theme. John is writing toward the end of the first century to fellow Christians who want to "see" the Son of Man return in glory on the clouds of heaven. Jesus'

And they said to him, "**Where is he**?"
He said, "I **don't know**."

(4) They brought the one who was **once blind** to the **Pharisees**.
Now **Jesus** had made **clay** and **opened** his **eyes** on a **sabbath**.
So then the **Pharisees** also asked him how he was able to **see**.
He said to them,
    "He put **clay** on my **eyes**, and I **washed**, and **now** I can **see**."
So some of the **Pharisees** said,
    "**This** man is **not** from **God**,
    because he does not **keep** the **sabbath**."
But **others** said,
    "**How** can a **sinful man** do such **signs**?"
And there was a **division** among them.
So they said to the **blind** man **again**,
    "What do **you** have to **say** about him,
    since he **opened your eyes**?"
He said, "**He** is a **prophet**."

(5) Now the **Jews** did **not believe**
    that he had been **blind** and **gained** his **sight**
    until they summoned the **parents** of the one
        who had **gained** his sight.
They asked them,
    "**Is this your son**, who you say was **born blind**?
How does he **now see**?"
His **parents** answered and said,
    "We **know** that this **is our son** and that he **was born blind**.
We do **not know** how he **sees now**,
    nor do we **know who opened** his **eyes**.
Ask him, **he** is of **age**;
    he can **speak** for **himself**."

Again, the man speaks with confidence.

Pharisees = FAYR-uh-seez

These lines are dismissive, disparaging.

Here the tone is true puzzlement.

There is a challenge in this question.

This is a solemn proclamation.

There is both a challenge and a threat in this question.

The parents want to avoid trouble. They are somewhat wily.

return was expected long before the end of the century. The author of the Gospel is trying to help his contemporaries open their eyes and see that the risen Christ is in their midst. To further this end, the author tells the story of a blind man who receives two kinds of sight, physical sight and spiritual insight: he recognizes Jesus as the Son of Man and worships him.

John makes it clear that we are to understand his story in two time periods—the time of Jesus and the blind man, as well as the time of John and his end-of-the-century audience—by conflating the two settings. Notice that when the blind man's parents are asked how their son can now see, they tell their interrogators to ask their son. Then the narrator's voice tells us that the blind man's parents said this because they were afraid. Why? Because those who were acknowledging Jesus as the Christ were being expelled from the synagogue.

This statement reflects the time of John and his audience, not the time of Jesus and his public ministry. In John's community, people who insisted on the divinity of Jesus Christ were being expelled from the synagogue. This was a very serious matter because Jews were excused from emperor worship. However, when a person was expelled from the synagogue, that person would no longer be exempt and so was subject to persecution, even martyrdom. By introducing into the story of Jesus and the blind man a detail that is contemporary with the author and audience, the author is making it clear to the readers that his story is just as much about them as it is about those who knew Jesus during Jesus' public ministry.

Drop your voice as you say the narrator's lines. This is background information.

His **parents** said this because they were **afraid**
    of the **Jews**, for the **Jews** had already **agreed**
        that if anyone acknowledged him as the **Christ**,
        he would be **expelled** from the **synagogue**.
For **this reason** his **parents** said,
    "**He** is of **age; question him**."

(6) So a **second** time they called the man who had been **blind**
    and said to him, "**Give God the praise**!
We **know** that this man is a **sinner**."
He replied,
    "If he is a **sinner**, I do **not know**.
One thing I **do** know is that I **was blind** and **now** I **see**."
So they said to him,
    "What did he **do** to you?
    How did he **open** your **eyes**?"
He answered them,
    "I **told** you **already** and you did **not listen**.
Why do you want to **hear it again**?
Do **you want** to become his disciples, **too**?"
They **ridiculed** him and said,
    "**You** are **that man's** disciple;
    we are disciples of **Moses**!
We **know** that **God** spoke to **Moses**,
    but **we** do **not know where this one** is **from**."
The man answered and said to them,
    "This is what is **so amazing**,
    that you do **not know** where he is **from**,
        yet he **opened** my **eyes**.
We **know** that **God** does **not listen** to **sinners**,
    but if one is **devout** and does **his will**, he **listens** to **him**."

Say, "Give God the praise" with false exuberance.

The once blind man speaks with quiet confidence.

A tone of impatience comes in here.

This is said with arrogant superiority.
Moses = MOH-ziz; MOH-zis

The man is being more bold now, not less.

The blind man, like John's audience, "sees" gradually. As the story begins, the man is both physically and spiritually blind. After receiving his physical sight, the man gains spiritual sight one step at a time. First the man concludes that Jesus is a prophet. Next he concludes that Jesus is not a sinner, as his interrogators insist, and that he must be from God. Otherwise Jesus would not have had the power to heal the man's blindness. John's audience, of course, sees an additional level of meaning in Jesus' being "from God." John began his gospel account by teaching that Jesus is the pre-existent Word who came from God. This pre-existent Word was not only with God, but is God (John 1:1).

After the man is thrown out, Jesus finds him and asks, "Do you believe in the Son of Man?" The man does not realize that he is in the presence of the Son of Man. John's audience is in the same situation. They are looking for the Son of Man, not realizing that the risen Christ is already in their midst. Jesus says, "You have seen him, the one speaking with you is he." On seeing Jesus, the once spiritually blind man worships him. This means that he recognizes Jesus' divinity, because only God should be worshiped.

In contrast to the blind man, who gains spiritual insight, the Pharisees become progressively more blind. First, because of their legalistic attitude toward the Sabbath regulations, they decide that Jesus cannot be from God even though he did heal a person's blindness. In their view, even healing should not be done on the Sabbath. Then, instead of coming

Here the man speaks adamantly.	It is **unheard of** that **anyone ever** opened the eyes
	    of a person born **blind**.
	If this man were **not** from **God**,
	    he would **not** be **able** to do **anything**."
	They answered and said to him,

The Jews are now outraged.	"You were **born totally** in **sin**, and are **you** trying to teach **us**?"
Say this line with harshness.	Then they **threw** him **out**.
	(7) When **Jesus** heard that they had **thrown** him **out**, he **found** him and **said**, "Do you **believe** in the **Son of Man**?"
Jesus speaks gently.	He **answered** and said,
The man is in awe.	**"Who is he**, sir, that I **may believe** in **him**?" **Jesus** said to him,
Speak slowly, in a quiet voice.	"You have **seen him**, the one **speaking** with you is **he**." He said,
Said with deep conviction.	**"I do believe**, Lord," and he **worshiped** him. Then **Jesus** said,

Jesus speaks with firmness.	"I came into this **world** for **judgment**,
	    so that those who **do not see** might **see**,
	    and those who **do see** might become **blind**."

	Some of the **Pharisees** who were with him **heard** this
The Pharisees are defensive.	and said to him, **"Surely we** are **not** also **blind**, are we?" Jesus said to them,
Jesus speaks with quiet firmness.	**"If** you **were blind**, you would have **no sin**; but now you are **saying**, 'We see,' so your **sin remains**."

[Shorter: John 9:1, 6–9, 13–17, 34–38]

to terms with the reality with which they are faced, they judge the once-blind man to be a sinner and throw him out. In their view, the blind man was "born totally in sin" because they believe that the man's original blindness was punishment for sin. Jesus tells the Pharisees that their pride and their judgmental attitude toward others are causing them to be spiritually blind. Jesus says, "But now you are saying, 'We see,' so your sin remains."

This reading, too, is chosen to help the elect and the whole congregation examine whether we are like the blind man or like the Pharisees. Are we growing in spiritual insight, or are we becoming progressively more blind? As you proclaim the reading, try to make the various characters come to life: the pompous, judgmental, and unreasonable Pharisees, the grateful and reasonable once-blind man, the frightened parents who want to avoid trouble, and Jesus, the great healer and

teacher. Then the baptized and the soon-to-be-baptized will be able to identify with the characters. Remember that the pool in which Jesus tells the man to wash is called Siloam, which means "sent." The pool is a symbol of Baptism. May we all strive to be like the blind man who obeyed Jesus, washed in the pool of Siloam, and became a faithful witness to his experience of Jesus Christ.

5TH SUNDAY OF LENT

Lectionary #36

READING I   Isaiah 43:16–21

Isaiah = i-ZAY-uh

These first seven lines are the narrator's voice, reminding the people of God's mighty acts on their behalf at the time of the Exodus.
Let your voice gradually rise in volume.

Lower your volume for this line, then pause.
Now God speaks. God is comforting and motivating the people, not correcting them.
Say this with excitement.

God is reminding the people that he takes care of his creatures.

jackals = JAK-ulz
ostriches = AHS-trij-*z

Emphasize "chosen people."
End with a voice brimming over with love.

A reading from the Book of the Prophet Isaiah

> **Thus** says the LORD,
>   who opens a **way** in the **sea**
>   and a **path** in the **mighty waters**,
> who **leads** out **chariots** and **horsemen**,
>   a **powerful army**,
> till they lie **prostrate** together, **never** to **rise**,
>   **snuffed out** and **quenched** like a **wick**.
> Remember **not** the events of the **past**,
>   the things of **long ago** consider **not**;
> **see**, I am doing something **new**!
>   **Now** it **springs forth**, do you not **perceive** it?
> In the **desert** I make a **way**,
>   in the **wasteland**, **rivers**.
> **Wild beasts honor** me,
>   **jackals** and **ostriches**,
> for I put **water** in the **desert**
>   and **rivers** in the **wasteland**
>   for my **chosen people** to **drink**,
> the people whom I **formed** for **myself**,
>   that they might **announce** my **praise**.

READING I Today's reading comes from the part of Isaiah that is called Second Isaiah (chapters 40–55). This portion of the Book of Isaiah was written during the time when the Israelites were in exile in Babylon (587–537 BC), a terribly traumatic time for the Israelites, filled with suffering. God had promised Abraham that his descendants would have the holy land. God had promised David that his descendants would be secure forever. What could it possibly mean that the Babylonians had conquered the holy land

and had taken all of the upper-class citizens into exile? The people could not help but ask: "Are we God's people, or not? Does God still love us, or not?"

In today's reading the narrator's voice reminds the exiles that God saved his people when they were in slavery in Egypt. God opened "a way in the sea," for them to escape Egypt, and God defeated the powerful army of their enemy. That enemy never conquered them again. They were "quenched like a wick."

Next, God speaks, telling the people that they can look to the present, not the

past, to see God's mighty actions on their behalf. God is doing something wonderful and new right now: "See, I am doing something new! Now it springs forth." God takes care of his creation. Even the animals honor him. Once the people understand the wonderful things that God is accomplishing for and through them, they will rest secure that they are God's Chosen People and they will praise God.

As you proclaim the reading, try to make clear the intimacy that exists between God and his people. God has chosen and cared for a people he created to be

READING II   Philippians 3:8–14

Philippians = fih-LIP-ee-uhnz

Paul's tone is passionate.

Say "rubbish" with disdain.
Say this line with great love.
Now, drop your voice and speak more quickly.

Emphasize "the righteousness from God"
This is a central point.

Now slow down again. Paul is finding meaning in his suffering.

Pause after this line.
Now increase your pace again.

Pause again after this line.

Paul ends with great hope and great passion.

A reading from the Letter of Saint Paul to the Philippians

Brothers and **sisters:**
I consider **everything** as a **loss**
  because of the **supreme good** of knowing **Christ Jesus** my **Lord.**
For **his** sake I have **accepted** the loss of **all things**
  and I **consider** them so much **rubbish,**
  that I may **gain Christ** and be **found** in **him,**
  not having any **righteousness** of my **own** based on the **law**
  but that which comes through **faith** in **Christ,**
  the **righteousness** from **God,**
  depending on **faith** to **know** him and the **power**
    of his **resurrection**
  and the **sharing of** his **sufferings** by being **conformed**
    to his **death,**
  if **somehow** I may **attain** the **resurrection** from the **dead.**

It is **not** that I have **already** taken hold of it
  or have already **attained perfect maturity,**
  but I **continue** my pursuit in **hope** that I **may possess** it,
  since I have **indeed been taken** possession **of** by **Christ Jesus.**
Brothers and **sisters, I** for **my** part
  do **not** consider **myself** to have **taken** possession.
Just one thing: **forgetting** what lies **behind**
  but **straining forward** to what lies **ahead,**
  I **continue** my **pursuit** toward the **goal,**
  the **prize** of God's upward **calling,** in **Christ Jesus.**

his own. The people should hold firm to this conviction, even in difficult times.

READING II In today's passage from Philippians, Paul is once more teaching that salvation comes through faith in Jesus Christ, not through observance of the Law. However, this time Paul teaches this central truth by applying it to himself. Paul is writing the Philippians from prison, and like the exiles in the First Reading, he is suffering. Like the exiles, he longs to find meaning in his suffering. Paul

finds that meaning by joining his suffering to that of his savior, Jesus Christ.

Paul tells the Philippians that when he looks back on his life and his past activities, which included persecuting Christians, he considers it all so much "rubbish." Paul now realizes that his righteousness is not something he earned by being faithful to the Law; rather, it is a gift from God that comes through faith in Jesus Christ.

While he is suffering, Paul has centered his faith on knowing Christ and the "power of his resurrection." He believes

that just as he is sharing in Christ's sufferings, is being conformed to Christ's Death, so he will he share in Christ's Resurrection.

This does not mean that Paul thinks he has attained perfection. He knows he has not. Nevertheless, Paul has been "taken possession of by Christ." Knowing that he belongs to Christ gives Paul the courage he needs to persevere, full of hope, even in a time of suffering.

As always, Paul's sentence structure is dense. Read this passage several times so that you know that you understand it. Then you will be able to make Paul's good

GOSPEL John 8:1–11

A reading from the holy Gospel according to John

The narrator is setting the stage.

Jesus went to the **Mount** of Olives.
But **early** in the **morning** he arrived again in the **temple** area,
    and **all** the **people** started **coming** to him,
    and he **sat** down and **taught** them.

Pause after this line.
Raise your volume slightly. The tension is rising.

Then the **scribes** and the **Pharisees** brought a **woman**
    who had been **caught** in **adultery**
    and made her **stand** in the **middle**.
They said to him,

Pharisees = FAYR-uh-seez

    "**Teacher**, **this woman** was **caught**
    in the **very act** of committing **adultery**.

The scribes and Pharisees are outraged and demanding.

Now in the **law**, **Moses** commanded us to **stone** such women.
So what do **you** say?"
They said this to **test** him,

Moses = MOH-ziz; MOH-zis

    so that they could have some **charge** to bring against him.

Drop your voice. The narrator is giving us background information.

Jesus bent down and began to **write** on the **ground** with his **finger**.
But when they continued **asking** him,
    he **straightened up** and said to them,
    "Let the **one among you** who is **without sin**
    be the **first** to throw a **stone** at her."

Jesus speaks gently but firmly.

Again he **bent** down and **wrote** on the **ground**.
And in **response**, they went **away one** by **one**,
    beginning with the **elders**.
So he was left **alone** with the **woman before** him.

Now the narrator is speaking again.

Then **Jesus straightened up** and **said** to her,
    "**Woman**, **where are** they?
Has **no one condemned** you?"
She replied, "**No one**, sir."
Then Jesus said, "**Neither** do **I condemn** you.
Go, and from now **on** do **not sin** any **more**."

Jesus speaks with love and gentleness.

The woman speaks with relief and gratitude.
Jesus still speaks lovingly, but his direction is given with firmness.

---

news much more understandable for those gathered for worship.

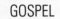 **GOSPEL** When the scribes and Pharisees ask Jesus about stoning a woman caught in adultery, they are trying to trap Jesus "so that they could have some charge to bring against him." If Jesus supports the Law when it prescribes the death penalty for those caught in adultery he will be acting against Roman law. Israel, an occupied country, did not have the authority to give anyone the death penalty. However, if Jesus does not support the Law of Moses, he will antagonize his fellow Jews.

Even though the scribes and Pharisees are trying to trap Jesus, he continues to try to teach them to stop being so judgmental of other people and to start examining their own inability to love their neighbor. Jesus does this simply by writing in the sand. We do not know what Jesus wrote. Some suggest that he wrote the sins he knew that various members of the accusing party had committed. After writing, Jesus says, "Let the one among you who is without sin be the first to throw a stone at her." Every single accuser leaves.

When Jesus is alone with the woman he does two loving things: he refuses to condemn her, and he instructs her to sin no more. In other words, in an attempt to affirm her, Jesus does not minimize the damage that sin causes. Still, the woman is offered forgiveness, not punishment. As you proclaim the reading, try to make it clear to your listeners just how much Jesus loves the woman, even though she is a sinner.

5TH SUNDAY OF LENT, YEAR A

Lectionary #34

READING I   Ezekiel 37:12–14

Ezekiel = ee-ZEE-kee-uhl

A reading from the Book of the Prophet Ezekiel

God's words are full of love and assurance. Emphasize every word of "O my people."

Thus says the **Lord GOD**:
O my people, I will **open** your **graves**
    and have you **rise** from them,
    and **bring** you **back** to the **land** of Israel.

Say this with great confidence. God is responding to the people's doubt.

Then you shall **know** that **I am the LORD**,
    when I open your **graves** and have you **rise** from them,
    O my people!

This is joyful news, indeed.

I will **put** my **spirit** in you that you may **live**,
    and I will **settle** you upon **your land**;
    thus you shall **know** that **I am the LORD**.

Say the promise with certitude and solemnity.

I have **promised**, and **I will do it**, says the LORD.

READING I   Ezekiel was a prophet from 593 to 571 BC. This means that Ezekiel prophesied both before and after the beginning of the Babylonian exile (587–537 BC) and the destruction of the first Temple in Jerusalem. In fact, Ezekiel himself was an exile in Babylon. He knew personally the devastation caused by being forcibly taken away from the holy land, the land that God had promised Abraham and his descendants.

As a prophet, Ezekiel spoke for God. In today's reading, Ezekiel is assuring the people that God still loves them, that they are still God's people, and that they will be returned to their land. Notice that as God first addresses the people, he says, "O my people." Then, after promising that he will bring them "back to the land of Israel," God once again says, "O my people." Ezekiel is teaching the exiles that they should not doubt God's love for them or God's fidelity to his covenant promises, even though they are in exile in Babylon.

For the Israelites, being in exile in Babylon was like being in the grave. Life as it should be lived was life in the holy land. Because we Christians believe in life after death, when we read Ezekiel's words (attributed to God because Ezekiel is speaking as a prophet), "I will open your graves," we may take the words literally rather than metaphorically. Ezekiel is not teaching that corpses would rise from the grave; he is teaching that those exiled in Babylon would return to the holy land. Ezekiel makes this clear as he pictures God saying, "I will put my spirit in you that you may live, and I will settle you upon your land." It is worth noting that Ezekiel lived several hundred years before the Israelites came to a belief in life after

READING II Romans 8:8–11

A reading from the Letter of Saint Paul to the Romans

Say the promise with certitude and solemnity.

Paul is complimenting the Romans as he teaches them.

Again, this is an adamant statement.

This is said with great reassurance.

This is Paul's great good news; speak with joy and confidence.

Brothers and **sisters:**
Those who are in the **flesh cannot please God.**
But **you** are **not** in the **flesh;**
    on the **contrary, you** are in the **spirit,**
    if only the **Spirit** of **God dwells in you.**
Whoever does not **have** the **Spirit** of **Christ**
        does **not belong** to him.
But if **Christ** is **in** you,   ·
    although the **body** is **dead** because of **sin,**
    the **spirit** is **alive** because of **righteousness.**
If the **Spirit** of the **One** who **raised Jesus** from the **dead**
        dwells in **you,**
    the One who **raised Christ** from the **dead**
    will give **life** to **your mortal bodies also,**
    through his **Spirit dwelling** in **you.**

GOSPEL John 11:1–45

A reading from the holy Gospel according to John

The narrator sets the stage.
Lazarus = LAZ-uh-ruhs
Bethany = BETH-uh-nee

(1) Now a man was **ill, Lazarus** from **Bethany,**
    the village of **Mary** and her sister **Martha.**
Mary was the one who had **anointed** the **Lord** with perfumed **oil**
    and **dried** his **feet** with her **hair;**
    it was **her brother Lazarus** who was **ill.**

death. This possibility did not enter the Israelites' thinking until about two hundred years before Christ.

However, in the light of Jesus' Passion, Death, and Resurrection, we now understand that life does not end with life on earth. As you proclaim the reading, fill your voice with confidence and hope. The exiles were receiving very good news. From a Christian perspective, it was not as good as the Good News revealed through Jesus Christ, but it was very good news indeed.

READING II The reading from Romans begins: "Those who are in the flesh cannot please God." At first glance this seems to say that human beings cannot please God. However, this is not Paul's intent. By living "in the flesh" Paul means allowing selfish desires rather than God's will to rule our lives. We can tell this because Paul goes on to tell the Romans: "But you are not in the flesh." The reason the Romans are no longer living in the flesh is that they are baptized. They now live in the Spirit; for the "Spirit of God dwells in" them.

Christians who live in the Spirit are not perfect. They are still tempted to sin, and sometimes do sin. The desires of the flesh sometimes prevail. It is this truth that Paul is acknowledging when he says, "although the body is dead because of sin." Nevertheless, Christians are not defeated by their lack of perfection. Why? Because, at the same time, "the spirit is alive because of righteousness." This is the righteousness that the baptized have received, not through obedience to the Law, but through faith in Jesus Christ.

There is a plea in these words.

Jesus is speaking thoughtfully and quietly. His words are mysterious.

glorified = GLOHR-ih-fīed

Read this line slowly but in a matter-of-fact way.

The tone here is resolved; the time has come.

Judea = joo-DE-uh; joo-DAY-uh
This is said with disbelief.
Rabbi = RAB-ī

Again, a quiet, thoughtful tone.

This is said with great confidence.

The disciples' tone is reassuring.
The narrator again explains things to us.

Say this slowly and solemnly.

Speak more quickly here.

So the **sisters** sent word to **Jesus** saying,
  "**Master**, the **one you love** is **ill**."
When **Jesus heard** this he said,
  "This **illness** is **not** to end in **death**,
  but is for the **glory** of **God**,
  that the **Son of God** may be **glorified** through it."
(2) Now **Jesus loved Martha** and her **sister** and **Lazarus**.
So when he heard that he was **ill**,
  he **remained** for **two days** in the **place** where he **was**.
Then **after** this he said to his disciples,
  "Let us go **back** to **Judea**."
The **disciples** said to him,
  "**Rabbi**, the **Jews** were just trying to **stone** you,
  and you want to go **back there**?"
Jesus answered,
  "Are there not **twelve hours** in a **day**?
If one walks during the **day**, he does not **stumble**,
  because he **sees the light** of this **world**.
But if one walks at **night**, he **stumbles**,
  because the **light** is **not in him**."
He said this, and then told them,
  "Our friend **Lazarus** is **asleep**,
  but I am **going** to **awaken** him."
So the disciples said to him,
  "**Master**, if he is **asleep**, he will be **saved**."
But **Jesus** was talking about his **death**,
  while **they** thought that he meant **ordinary sleep**.
So then **Jesus** said to them **clearly**,
  "**Lazarus** has **died**.
And I am **glad** for **you** that I was **not** there,
  that **you may believe**.
Let us **go** to him."

Not only does the Spirit give life on earth, the Spirit gives life *after* life on earth. Paul assures the Romans that just as Jesus rose from the dead, so will they: "the One who raised Christ from the dead will give life to your mortal bodies also."

The Jews began to entertain the possibility of life after death some two hundred years before Christ. During Paul's life, this is a question about which the Pharisees and Sadducees disagreed (see Acts 23:8). However, after Jesus rose from the dead

and appeared to many, the belief in life after death became central to Jesus' followers. It is this great good news that Paul is teaching the Romans.

As Christians, we believe that we will follow Christ's passage through death to eternal life; we believe in the resurrection of the body. As you proclaim Paul's great good news, make these central Christian beliefs stand out for those who hear you.

GOSPEL When we read the Gospel according to John, we know that we are to look for two levels of meaning. One level of meaning takes place in the plot, the interaction among Jesus, the disciples, Martha, and Mary. A second level of meaning takes place between the author of the Gospel and those in his late first-century audience who are asking, "Where is the risen Christ when we need him? We expected his return long before now."

Didymus = DID-uh-muhs

This is said with bravado.

The narrator continues the story.

So **Thomas**, called **Didymus**, said to his fellow **disciples**,
    "Let us **also** go to **die with him**."

(3) When **Jesus arrived**, he found that **Lazarus**
    had already been in the **tomb** for **four days**.
Now **Bethany** was near **Jerusalem**, only about **two miles away**.
And many of the Jews had come to **Martha** and **Mary**
    to **comfort** them about their brother.
When **Martha heard** that **Jesus** was coming,
    she went to **meet** him;
    but **Mary** sat at **home**.
Martha said to Jesus,

Jerusalem = juh-ROO-suh-lem;
juh-ROO-zuh-lem

Martha is full of grief. Speak slowly,
with anguish.

    "**Lord**, if **you** had **been here**,
    my **brother** would **not** have **died**.
But **even now** I **know** that **whatever you ask** of **God**,
    God will **give** you."
Jesus said to her,

Now, Martha speaks with hopeful faith.

    "Your **brother** will **rise**."
Martha said to him,

Jesus speaks gently, with love.
resurrection = rez-uh-REK-shuhn

    "I **know** he will rise,
    in the **resurrection** on the **last day**."
Jesus told her,
    "**I am** the **resurrection** and the **life**;
    whoever **believes** in **me**, even if he **dies**, will **live**,

Martha speaks with confidence.

    and **everyone** who **lives** and **believes** in **me** will **never die**.

Emphasize every word of this line.

Do you **believe** this?"
She said to him, "**Yes, Lord**.

This question is not so much a challenge
as it is encouragement.

I have come to **believe** that **you** are the **Christ**, the **Son of God**,
    the **one** who is **coming** into the **world**."

As is true throughout John's account, the author keeps instructing us to look for these two levels of meaning. For example, there are two "clues" that he gives us in today's reading: One is a statement that that doesn't make sense at the literal level of the plot, so we begin to look for a deeper meaning. The other is that when Jesus speaks metaphorically, he is understood literally, and this misunderstanding is explained. The core message of today's Gospel will be clearer once we understand these "clues" that the author has provided

to warn us that we should be looking for a deeper meaning.

First, a statement is made that doesn't make sense at the literal level. John tells us that Martha and Mary told Jesus that their brother, Lazarus, was ill, that Jesus loved Martha, Mary, and Lazarus, and that when Jesus heard that Lazarus was ill "he remained for two days in the place where he was." This is exactly the opposite of what we would expect. Why didn't Jesus go to his friends immediately?

Jesus' absence becomes central to the story when Martha says to Jesus, "Lord, if you had been here, my brother would not have died." This centers our attention solidly on the question of Jesus' absence versus Jesus' presence. This is the core question on the mind of John's audience.

To remind us that we need to think metaphorically to understand Jesus' full meaning, John uses a second device—Jesus speaks metaphorically but is understood literally. Jesus tells the disciples that "Lazarus is asleep." The disciples

Said with quiet conviction. Speak slowly.

Said very quietly.

Speak more quickly now.

Read more slowly.

Again, emphasize every word of this statement.

Jesus says this with anguish.

Pause here.

Said with puzzlement and incredulity.

This is said in a commanding voice.

(4) When she had said this,
    she **went** and **called** her **sister Mary secretly**, saying,
    "The **teacher** is **here** and is **asking** for **you**."
As soon as she heard this,
    she **rose quickly** and **went to him**.
For **Jesus** had not yet **come** into the **village**,
    but was still where **Martha** had **met** him.
So when the Jews who were **with** her in the house **comforting** her
    saw **Mary** get up **quickly** and go **out**,
    they **followed** her,
    presuming that she was going to the **tomb** to **weep** there.
When **Mary** came to where **Jesus** was and **saw** him,
    she **fell** at his **feet** and **said** to him,
    "**Lord, if you had been here**,
    my **brother** would not have **died**."
When **Jesus** saw her **weeping** and the Jews who had come
        with her **weeping**,
    he became **perturbed** and **deeply troubled**, and said,
    "**Where** have you **laid** him?"
They said to him, "**Sir, come** and **see**."
(5) And **Jesus wept**.
So the Jews said, "**See** how he **loved** him."
But **some** of them said,
    "Could not the **one** who **opened** the **eyes** of the **blind man**
    have done **something** so that **this man** would **not** have **died**?"

So **Jesus**, perturbed **again**, came to the **tomb**.
It was a **cave**, and a **stone** lay across it.
Jesus said, "**Take away the stone**."
Martha, the **dead** man's **sister**, said to him,
    "**Lord**, by **now** there will be a **stench**;
    he has been **dead** for **four days**."

understand Jesus literally. Their misunderstanding gives the narrator and Jesus the opportunity to explain the metaphorical level of meaning in Jesus' words. The narrator tells us that Jesus was talking about Lazarus' death, not ordinary sleep. Then Jesus speaks more clearly, saying, "Lazarus has died." By telling the story this way, the author is teaching his reading audience, including us, to think metaphorically as we read the Gospel.

At the level of the plot, the story of the raising of Lazarus is about Lazarus being given extended life on earth. However, at a deeper, metaphorical level, the story is about those who have faith in Jesus Christ being given eternal life. This deeper level of meaning is emphasized in the conversation between Jesus and Martha. Martha tells Jesus that had he been there her brother would not have died. Nevertheless, she does not think all is lost. She says, "But even now I know that whatever you ask of God, God will give you."

Jesus tells Martha: "I am the resurrection and the life; whoever believes in me, even if he dies, will live, and everyone who lives and believes in me will never die." With this dialogue, the author makes it clear that the story is not just about extended life on earth. The story is about eternal life.

Jesus then asks Martha if she believes what he has told her. Martha says, "I have come to believe that you are the Christ, the Son of God, the one who is coming into the world." Martha states exactly what John wants his late first-century audience to believe. As he concludes his account, the author tells us that he has written it so that people may know that "Jesus is the

Martha speaks with urgency.

Say this slowly and gently.

This is not an intimate prayer but said to be heard by the crowd, to build the listeners' faith.
Raise your volume here.

Drop your voice for the narrator's lines.
Read slowly and with awe.
Said quietly and with great relief.
The narrator makes a concluding remark to end the story.

Jesus said to her,
   "Did I not **tell** you that if you **believe**
   you will **see** the **glory** of **God**?"
(6) So they **took away** the **stone**.
And **Jesus raised** his **eyes** and said,
   "**Father**, I **thank** you for **hearing** me.
I know that you **always** hear me;
   but because of the **crowd** here I have said this,
   that **they may believe** that **you sent me**."
And when he had **said** this,
   he **cried out** in a **loud voice**,
   "**Lazarus, come out!**"
The **dead man came out**,
   tied hand and **foot** with **burial bands**,
   and his **face** was **wrapped** in a **cloth**.
So **Jesus** said to them,
   "**Untie him** and **let him go**."

(7) Now **many** of the **Jews** who had come to **Mary**
   and **seen** what he had done began to **believe** in **him**.

[Shorter: John 11:3–7, 17, 20–27, 33b–45]

Messiah, the Son of God, and that through this belief you may have life in his name" (John 20:31). ("Christ" and "Messiah" are synonyms. Each means "the anointed one.")

Notice that Martha doesn't say, "The one who came into the world," or, "The one who will come into the world." She says, "The one who is coming into the world." John doesn't want his audience to think of Jesus as one who came but is now gone, or to think of Jesus as someone who

is absent now but will come sometime in the future. He wants his audience to be able to see that the risen Christ is present with them through life, through death, and into eternal life. Christ is always "coming into the world."

Does Jesus' "absence" result in Lazarus' death? As the story began, Jesus had said, "This illness is not to end in death, but is for the glory of God, that the Son of God may be glorified through it." As the story proceeds, there is no question

that Lazarus is dead. He has been buried four days. Nevertheless, Jesus brings Lazarus back to life. With Christ, death is not death.

As you proclaim this reading, try to bring all the characters to life, but give special emphasis to Jesus' dialogue with Martha. John wants all of us to have Martha's faith so that we, too, will know Christ's presence and have eternal life.

PALM SUNDAY OF THE PASSION OF THE LORD

Lectionary #37

GOSPEL AT THE PROCESSION Luke 19:28–40

A reading from the holy Gospel according to Luke

Jesus proceeded on his **journey** up to **Jerusalem**.
As he drew near to **Bethphage** and **Bethany**
    at the place called the **Mount** of **Olives**,
    he sent **two** of his **disciples**.
He said, **"Go** into the **village opposite** you,
    and as you **enter** it you will **find** a **colt tethered**
    on which **no one** has **ever sat**.
Untie it and **bring** it here.
And if anyone should **ask** you,
    'Why are you **untying** it?'
    you will answer,
    'The **Master** has **need** of it.'"
So those who had been **sent** went **off**
    and found **everything just** as he had **told** them.
And as they were **untying** the **colt**, its **owners** said to them,
    "Why are you **untying** this **colt**?"
They answered,
    "The **Master** has **need** of it."
So they **brought** it to **Jesus**,
    threw their **cloaks** over the colt,
    and helped **Jesus** to **mount**.

The narrator sets the stage. Use a matter-of-fact tone.
Jerusalem = juh-ROO-suh-lem;
juh-ROO-zuh-lem
Bethphage = BETH-fuh-jee
Bethany = BETH-uh-nee
Now Jesus speaks. Jesus is giving precise instructions. There is both mystery and urgency in his words.

Say this line slowly and distinctly.
Now the narrator is speaking again.

There is some aggression in this question.
This is said with authority.
The narrator continues.

PROCESSION GOSPEL   In today's reading, Jesus is approaching Jerusalem, the culmination of a long journey that began in Luke 9:51. In Luke, this fact alone prepares us for something momentous to occur. A journey is the central organizing theme of Luke's two-volume work: Luke and Acts. Jerusalem is the holy city, the center of the action. The Gospel begins in Jerusalem with the angel's announcement to Zechariah that his wife, Elizabeth, will bear a son. Jesus will die in Jerusalem, and the Church will be born in Jerusalem. From Jerusalem the Good News will go out to the rest of the world.

As he approaches the city, Jesus instructs his disciples to go into a nearby village where they will find a colt that has never been ridden before. They are to bring the colt to Jesus. That Jesus is pictured as knowing exactly what will happen is the author's way of affirming that Jesus is in control of events as they unfold, that Jesus is doing his Father's will, and that God's purposes will be fulfilled through Jesus Christ.

Jesus' entry into Jerusalem on a colt is an allusion to a messianic prophesy from the book of Zechariah that says: "Exult greatly, O daughter Zion!/ Shout for joy, O daughter Jerusalem!/ Behold: your king is coming to you,/ a just savior is he,/ Humble, and riding on a donkey, / on a colt, the foal of a donkey" (Zechariah 9:9). In this passage the prophet, who lived in the fourth century BC, is offering his people hope of a renewed world order with Jerusalem at its center. At the time, the Israelites had not had their own king for over two hundred years.

As he **rode along**,
> the people were spreading their **cloaks** on the **road**;
> and **now** as he was approaching the **slope** of the **Mount**
>> of **Olives**,
> the **whole multitude** of his **disciples**
> began to **praise God aloud** with **joy**
> for **all** the **mighty deeds** they had seen.

They proclaimed:
> "**Blessed** is the **king** who **comes**
>> in the **name** of the **Lord**.
> **Peace** in **heaven**
>> and **glory** in the **highest**."

Some of the **Pharisees** in the crowd said to him,
> "**Teacher**, **rebuke** your **disciples**."

He said in reply,
> "I **tell** you, if **they keep silent**,
> the **stones** will **cry out**!"

Lectionary #38

**Slowly increase your speed and
your volume.**

**Say the proclamation with a loud and
joyful voice.**

Drop your voice for the narrator's line.
This is said with urgency and distaste.
Pharisees = FAYR-uh-seez
Speak Jesus' words slowly and solemnly.

READING I Isaiah 50:4–7

A reading from the Book of the Prophet Isaiah

> The **Lord GOD** has **given** me
>> a **well-trained tongue**,
> that I might know how to **speak** to the **weary**
>> a **word** that will **rouse** them.
> **Morning** after **morning**
>> he **opens** my **ear** that I may **hear**;
> and I have **not rebelled**,
>> have **not turned back**.

Isaiah = ī-ZAY-uh

Speak slowly and with confidence.

Increase both volume and speed here.

Slow down with "have not rebelled."

After returning with the colt, the disciples throw their cloaks over it and help Jesus mount. This, too, is an Old Testament allusion. When Jehu had been anointed king of Israel, those present took their garments, "spread [them] under Jehu . . . and cried out, 'Jehu is king!'" (2 Kings 9:13).

As Jesus rides along, the people, too, give up their cloaks to spread in Jesus' path. They begin to praise God for all the "mighty deeds" that they have seen Jesus perform. These deeds were not those of a political leader. They did not exhibit authority over the Roman occupiers, but over such things as illness and demonic possession.

The people then proclaim: "Blessed is the king who comes/ in the name of the Lord/. Peace in heaven/ and glory in the highest." In this proclamation, Luke is emphasizing Jesus' kingship even more than did Mark's gospel account, Luke's source.

In Mark the acclamation is: "Blessed is he who comes in the name of the Lord! [a quotation from Psalm 118:26]/ Blessed is the kingdom of our father David that is to come!" (Mark 11:9–10). Luke changes the emphasis in Mark from "kingdom" to "king." In doing so, Luke centers our attention on the identity of Jesus Christ. Jesus is king, but Jesus' "kingship" is far broader than one geographical area, than one "kingdom" on earth.

By adding, "Peace in heaven/ and glory in the highest," Luke reminds us of the multitude of heavenly hosts that praised God at the announcement of Jesus' birth to the shepherds. They sang: "Glory to God in the highest and on earth peace to those on whom his favor rests" (Luke 2:14). Both heaven and earth proclaim Jesus' kingship as he enters Jerusalem.

I **gave** my **back** to those who **beat** me,
  my **cheeks** to those who **plucked** my **beard**;
my **face** I did **not shield**
  from **buffets** and **spitting**.

The **Lord G**OD is **my** help,
  therefore I am **not disgraced**;
I have **set** my **face** like **flint**,
  knowing that I shall **not** be put to **shame**.

READING II   Philippians 2:6–11

A reading from the Letter of Saint Paul to the Philippians

Christ Jesus, though he was in the **form** of **God**,
  did not regard **equality** with **God**
  something to be **grasped**.
Rather, he **emptied** himself,
  taking the **form** of a **slave**,
  coming in **human likeness**;
  and found **human** in **appearance**,
  he **humbled** himself,
  becoming **obedient** to the point of **death**,
  even **death** on a **cross**.
Because of this, God **greatly exalted** him
  and **bestowed** on him the name
  which is **above every name**,
  that at the **name** of Jesus
  every knee should **bend**,
  of those in **heaven** and on **earth** and **under** the earth,
  and **every tongue confess** that
  Jesus Christ is **Lord**,
  to the **glory** of **God** the **Father**.

buffets = BUF-its

Speak these last two lines with confidence and determination.

Philippians = fih-LIP-ee-uhnz

Read slowly, pausing at commas. Paul is giving an amazing explanation for what was considered a scandal.

Emphasize this line. For the audience this is practically unbelievable.
Slowly increase both your tempo and your volume.

Now, slow down again.

This is a proclamation. Emphasize every word.

Some Pharisees think that this acclamation is inappropriate, to say the least. Obviously they understood its import. They tell Jesus to "rebuke your disciples." Jesus knows that the acclamation is true; he is a king. In refusing to silence the people, Jesus alludes to the prophet Habakkuk who, when condemning those who pursue "evil gain" for their household says that the "stone in the wall" and "the beam in the frame" of their homes will "cry out" against them (Habakkuk 2:11). Truth will not be suppressed. Jesus will fulfill his

Father's will, and heaven and earth will know that Jesus is king.

As you proclaim the reading, give the greatest emphasis to the people's proclamation. Their words clearly name the good news that we are celebrating today.

READING I In the context of a Lenten liturgy, when the Church proclaims today's suffering servant song from Isaiah, we understand the suffering servant to be Jesus. However, this reference to Christ was not always seen in Isaiah's words. The suffering servant

had previously been understood to be the prophet himself, and, later, the nation, Israel, suffering exile in Babylon.

When this song was originally written, it undoubtedly referred to a prophet known as Second Isaiah who prophesied to the exiles in Babylon in the sixth century BC. His prophesies appear in chapters 40–55 of the Book of Isaiah. Second Isaiah was a prophet of hope. He describes his role in the opening verses of today's reading: "The Lord God has given me/ a well-trained tongue,/ that I might know how to speak to the weary/ a word that will rouse

PASSION   Luke 22:14—23:56

The Passion of our Lord Jesus Christ according to Luke

When the narrator is speaking use a matter-of-fact tone.

(1) When the **hour came**,
   Jesus took his **place** at **table** with the **apostles**.
He **said** to them,
   "I have **eagerly desired** to eat this **Passover** with **you**
      before I **suffer**,
   for, I **tell you**, I **shall not eat** it **again**
   until there is **fulfillment** in the **kingdom** of **God**."

There is both urgency and dread in Jesus' tone.

Then he took a **cup**, gave **thanks**, and said,
   "**Take this** and **share** it among yourselves;
   for I **tell** you that from **this time on**
   I shall **not drink** of the **fruit** of the **vine**
   until the **kingdom** of **God comes**."

Say these words slowly and distinctly.

Now speak more quickly.

Then he took the **bread**, said the **blessing**,
   broke it, and **gave** it to them, saying,
   "**This** is my **body**, which will be **given** for **you**;
   do this in **memory** of me."

Again, say these words slowly and distinctly.

And likewise the **cup** after they had **eaten**, saying,
   "**This cup** is the **new covenant** in my **blood**,
   which will be **shed** for **you**.

Look up at the congregation as you say these lines.

(2) "And yet **behold**, the **hand** of the one who is to **betray** me
   is **with** me on the **table**;
   for the **Son of Man indeed goes** as it has been **determined**;
   but **woe to that man** by **whom** he is **betrayed**."
And they began to **debate** among themselves
   who among them would **do** such a **deed**.

The tone changes here to one of warning.

(3) Then an **argument** broke out among them
   about **which** of them should be **regarded** as the **greatest**.

This is the narrator again. Return to your matter-of-fact tone.

---

them." The hope that Second Isaiah offered the exiles was that God was accomplishing something wonderful through them. Their suffering was not in vain, and they were still God's beloved people.

As is often true of prophets, Second Isaiah's vocation brought him suffering. He has accepted this, not abandoning his vocation in order to avoid pain: "I gave my back to those who beat me,/ my cheeks to those who plucked my beard;/ my face I did not shield/ from buffets and spitting." The prophet is able to endure this suffering

because God is helping him. He knows that he "shall not be put to shame."

However, in the context in which Second Isaiah's suffering servant songs appear in the Book of Isaiah, the suffering servant is the personified nation, Israel, suffering exile in Babylon. By applying his own experience to that of the nation, Second Isaiah is encouraging the exiles to accept their suffering bravely, to believe that it has a purpose in God's plan for the world, to believe that God is still faithful to them, and to live in hope.

This suffering servant song was not originally considered to be a song about the messiah. After all, the messiah was expected to prevail over the enemy, as did Moses, as did David, as did God's other chosen leaders. However, after Christ suffered, died, and rose from the dead, the people struggled to find words to express the meaning that had been revealed through these mysterious and unexpected events.

In Second Isaiah, the Church found just the words it needed. In the light of the events surrounding Christ, Second Isaiah's words were understood to have a whole

Rather than being annoyed, Jesus is patient and teaches the Apostles.
Gentiles = JEN-tilez

He said to them,
    "The **kings** of the **Gentiles lord** it **over** them
    and those in **authority over** them are addressed as '**Benefactors**';
    but among **you** it shall **not be so**.
Rather, let the **greatest** among you be as the **youngest**,
    and the **leader** as the **servant**.
For **who** is **greater**:
    the one **seated** at table or the one who **serves**?
Is it not the **one seated** at **table**?
I am among you as the one who **serves**.
It is **you** who have **stood by** me in my **trials**;
    and I **confer** a **kingdom** on you,
    just as my **Father** has conferred **one** on **me**,
    that you may **eat** and **drink** at my **table** in my **kingdom**;
    and you will **sit** on **thrones**
    judging the **twelve** tribes of **Israel**.

Fill your voice with love. Even though the disciples are failing Jesus in some ways, he compliments them.

This is said with love and sadness.

(4) "**Simon**, **Simon**, **behold Satan** has demanded
    to **sift** all of you like **wheat**,
    but I have **prayed** that your **own faith** may **not fail**;
    and once you have **turned back**,
    you must **strengthen** your **brothers**."
He said to him,
    "**Lord**, **I** am prepared to go to **prison** and to **die** with you."
But he replied,
    "I **tell** you, **Peter**, before the **cock crows this day**,
    you will deny **three times** that you **know** me."

Peter is offended. He is defending himself.

Speak slowly and with sadness.

(5) He said to them,
    "When I **sent you forth** without a **money bag** or a **sack**
        or **sandals**,
    were you in **need** of anything?"

Now Jesus is teaching once more.

new level of meaning. Today, when you proclaim this reading, those gathered for worship will understand that Christ is the suffering servant. It is Christ who did not shield himself from "buffets and spitting." Through Christ's suffering God has accomplished something wonderful and new for the whole world.

As you proclaim today's reading with a "well trained tongue," you will realize that the words also apply to you and to those gathered for worship. We, Christ's disciples, are to accept unavoidable suffering, knowing that our suffering, united

with Christ's, can also accomplish great things. Read with confidence, knowing, without any doubt, that "the Lord God is [your] help."

READING II **Paul's Letter to the Philippians**, like the suffering servant song from Second Isaiah that we have just read, was written in the context of suffering. Although Paul writes this letter from prison, he is not discouraged. He has taken Christ as his model. Today's reading is part of what Paul has to say as he encourages the Philippians to

embrace Christ as their model, too. They, like Christ, should humbly and generously serve one another.

To teach this lesson of humble service even in the face of suffering, Paul turns to a hymn about Christ with which the Philippians were most probably familiar. The hymn is of great interest because of its "high Christology," that is, its emphasis on Jesus' divinity.

As the hymn begins, it claims that Jesus Christ existed before he became a human being. Although Jesus was "in the

Use a musing and ironic tone.

Now Jesus is serious again.

The disciples are anxious to please.

The meaning is not "two are sufficient," but, "That's it!" Jesus finally shows some exasperation.

The narrator continues the story.

This is said with urgency.

Jesus is in agony.

Read this description slowly in a solemn voice.

Jesus is correcting the disciples.

"**No**, **nothing**," they replied.
He said to them,
    "But **now** one who has a **money bag** should **take** it,
    and likewise a **sack**,
    and one who does **not** have a **sword**
    should **sell** his **cloak** and **buy** one.
For I **tell** you that **this Scripture** must be **fulfilled** in me,
    namely, *He was counted among the **wicked**;*
    and **indeed** what is written about **me** is coming to **fulfillment**."
Then they said,
    "**Lord**, **look**, there are **two** swords here."
But he replied, "**It is enough!**"

(6) Then going **out**, he **went**, as was his **custom**, to the Mount
    of **Olives**,
    and the **disciples followed** him.
When he **arrived** at the place he **said** to them,
    "**Pray** that you may **not undergo** the **test**."
After withdrawing about a **stone's throw** from them and **kneeling**,
    he **prayed**, saying, "**Father**, if you are **willing**,
    take this cup away from me;
    still, not **my** will but **yours** be done."
And to **strengthen** him an **angel from heaven appeared** to him.
He was in **such agony** and he **prayed** so **fervently**
    that his **sweat** became like **drops** of **blood**
    falling on the **ground**.
When he **rose** from **prayer** and **returned** to his **disciples**,
    he found them **sleeping** from **grief**.
He **said** to them, "**Why** are you **sleeping**?
Get up and **pray** that you may **not undergo** the **test**."

---

form of God," Jesus "did not regard equality with God something to be grasped;" rather, Jesus "emptied" and "humbled" himself by freely choosing to become a human being. In fact, Jesus even endured the most ignominious death possible, "death on a cross." Scripture scholars think that Paul added "death on a cross" to the pre-existing hymn to emphasize just how much Jesus had "emptied" himself to redeem the human race.

However, Jesus' abasement led, not to defeat, but to glorification. God has exalted Jesus, so much so that "at the name of Jesus every knee should bend of those in heaven and on earth and under the earth." This statement, through allusion, is another way of claiming that Jesus is God. In Isaiah, God says, "To me every knee shall bend . . . saying, 'Only in the Lord are just deeds and power'" (Isaiah 45:23b–24a). The hymn is teaching that Jesus should be treated as only God should be treated. Therefore, Jesus is God.

As you proclaim this hymn, allow your voice to crescendo with joy and certainty at the great Good New that it is teaching:

"Jesus Christ is Lord to the glory of God the Father."

PASSION   The story of Jesus' last meal with his disciples, his agony in the garden, arrest, trials before Jewish and Roman authorities, Crucifixion, and Death are very familiar to all of us. In fact, the story is so familiar that we may not realize that the four gospel accounts do not all tell the story in exactly the same way. Each gospel writer molds the story to fit the needs of his audience. Luke is writing to Gentiles. He wants his

There is both grief and accusation in this question.

Judas = JOO-duhs

Again the disciples are eager to please.

(7) While he was **still speaking**, a **crowd** approached
   and in **front** was **one** of the **Twelve**, a man named **Judas**.
He went up to **Jesus** to **kiss** him.
Jesus said to him,
   "**Judas**, are you **betraying** the **Son** of **Man** with a **kiss**?"
His disciples **realized** what was about to happen, and they asked,
   "**Lord**, shall we **strike** with a **sword**?"
And **one** of them struck the high priest's **servant**
   and **cut** off his right **ear**.

This is a command. Raise your voice.

But **Jesus** said in reply,
   "**Stop**, **no more** of this!"
Then he **touched** the servant's ear and **healed** him.
And Jesus said to the **chief priests** and **temple guards**
   and **elders** who had **come** for him,

This is said with great self-possession. Jesus is challenging those who have come to arrest him.

   "Have you come out as against a **robber**, with **swords**
      and **clubs**?
Day after **day** I was **with** you in the **temple** area,
   and you did **not seize** me;
   but **this** is **your hour**, the time for the **power** of **darkness**."

Drop your voice as the narrator continues the story.

(8) After **arresting** him they **led** him **away**
   and took him into the **house** of the **high priest**;
   Peter was following at a **distance**.
They lit a **fire** in the **middle** of the **courtyard** and **sat around** it,
   and **Peter** sat down **with** them.
When a **maid** saw him **seated** in the **light**,
   she looked **intently** at him and said,

Raise your voice for this accusation.

   "**This man too** was with him."
But he **denied** it saying,

Peter is adamant.

   "**Woman, I do not know** him."

Gentile audience to understand just how all-inclusive and how forgiving Jesus is. Luke thus chooses to include details that emphasize Jesus as one who teaches, heals, and forgives even as he is being tortured and crucified.

(1) The story begins with the institution of the Eucharist. While celebrating the Passover with the Apostles, Jesus takes the bread and wine used to celebrate God's rescue of the people from slavery in Egypt and gives them a whole new meaning. Taking the bread, Jesus says, "This is my body, which will be given for you; do this in memory of me." Taking the cup Jesus says, "This cup is the new covenant in my blood, which will be shed for you"

Jesus wants the Apostles to know that he will still be with them, even after he is crucified. He also wants them to understand his Death and all that his Death will accomplish within the context of their covenant relationship with God. A new understanding of that covenant will come with Jesus' Resurrection. The invitation to covenant love will be extended to the whole human race, not just to the Israelites.

(2) Jesus then tells the Apostles that he knows that one of them is going to betray him. (3) This comment causes them to debate who that person might be, and to argue over which one of them is the greatest. Jesus has every reason to be totally exasperated with his Apostles, but instead of berating them, Jesus teaches them and compliments them. First, he reminds the Apostles that they are not to be the kind of leaders who lord it over others; rather, they are to be servant leaders, as Jesus himself has been. Jesus has lived among them as "one who serves."

Again, a loud accusation.

Peter is placating.

Said with certitude.

Galilean = gal-ih-LEE-uhn

Peter is still placating.

Read slowly and pause.

Continue more quickly and with sadness.

A short while **later** someone **else** saw him and said,
   "**You too** are **one** of them";
   but **Peter** answered, "My **friend**, I am **not**."
About an hour **later**, still **another** insisted,
   "**Assuredly**, this man **too** was **with** him,
   for he **also** is a **Galilean**."
But **Peter** said,
   "My **friend**, I do **not know** what you are **talking** about."
Just as he was **saying** this, the **cock crowed**,
   and the **Lord turned** and **looked** at Peter;
   and **Peter remembered** the **word** of the **Lord**,
   how he had **said** to him,
   "Before the **cock crows** today, you will **deny** me **three times**."
He **went out** and **began** to **weep bitterly**.

The men who held Jesus in **custody** were **ridiculing** and
      beating him.
They **blindfolded** him and **questioned** him, saying,
   "**Prophesy! Who is it** that **struck** you?"
And they **reviled** him in saying **many other things against** him.

Use a cruel and taunting tone.

prophesy = PROF-uh-sī

(9) When **day** came the council of **elders** of the people **met**,
   both **chief priests** and **scribes**,
   and they brought him **before** their **Sanhedrin**.

Sanhedrin = san-HEE-druhn

The Sanhedrin is trying to sound reasonable.

Jesus is not cowed. He speaks with quiet authority.

They said, "If **you are** the **Christ, tell us**,"
   but he **replied** to them, "If I **tell you**, **you** will **not believe**,
   and if I **question**, you will **not respond**.
But from **this time on** the Son of **Man** will be **seated**
   at the **right hand** of the **power** of **God**."
They all asked, "**Are** you then the **Son** of **God**?"
He replied to them, "**You** say that I am."
Then they said, "What further **need** have **we** for **testimony**?
We have **heard** it from his **own mouth**."

The Sanhedrin is inviting Jesus to incriminate himself.

Jesus avoids the trap.

The Sanhedrin's tone is self righteous and judgmental.

Then, even though he knows that his Apostles are going to desert him and Peter is going to deny him, Jesus sees past their failures to the final strength and fidelity after Pentecost. He compliments them on standing by him thus far and promises them that they will be reunited with him in his kingdom. In other words, the terrible failures that we will read about soon are temporary failures.

(4) Peter's denial will also be a temporary failure. True, Peter will deny Jesus three times, but after that he will return and have a leadership role in the church. Jesus tells Peter, " . . . once you have turned back, you must strengthen your brothers."

(5) Jesus then continues to teach the Apostles, and they continue to misunderstand. He asks them if they lacked anything when they obeyed his instructions about setting forth "without a money bag or a sack or sandals." They acknowledge that they lacked nothing. Jesus then asks if now, because he will soon be violently separated from them, they will disobey all those instructions. Will they start to try to provide for themselves rather than trust God's providence to provide for them? Will they even run out and buy swords?

The Apostles misunderstand Jesus' ironic tone and take his words to be new instructions, instructions to disobey what Jesus had previously told them to do even though being obedient to those instructions had resulted in their needing nothing. They did not realize that Jesus was simply questioning whether or not they would remain faithful to what they had already been taught.

Pilate = PĪ-luht

This is said with anger and distaste.
Caesar = SEE-zer

Pilate wants to know the answer.
Jesus avoids the trap again.

This is announced with authority.

Said with insistence and anger.
Judea = joo-DEE-uh; joo DAY-uh
Galilee = GAL-ih-lee

Herod = HAYR-uhd
Jerusalem = juh-ROO-suh-lem;
juh-ROO-zuh-lem

The narrator continues the story.
Have a bemused tone. How ironic!

(10) Then the **whole assembly** of them **arose** and **brought** him
  before **Pilate**.
They brought **charges** against him, saying,
  "We found this man **misleading** our people;
  he **opposes** the payment of **taxes** to **Caesar**
  and **maintains** that **he** is the **Christ**, a **king**."
Pilate asked him, "**Are you** the **king** of the **Jews**?"
He said to him in reply, "**You** say so."
Pilate then addressed the **chief priests** and the **crowds**,
  "I find this man **not guilty**."
But they were **adamant** and said,
  "He is **inciting** the **people** with his **teaching**
    throughout **all Judea**,
  from **Galilee** where he **began even** to **here**."

(11) On hearing **this** Pilate asked if the **man** was a **Galilean**;
  and upon learning that he was under **Herod's** jurisdiction,
  he sent him to **Herod**, who was in **Jerusalem** at that time.
Herod was **very glad** to see **Jesus**;
  he had been **wanting** to see him for a **long time**,
  for he had **heard** about him
  and had been **hoping** to **see** him perform some **sign**.
He **questioned** him at **length**,
  but he gave him **no answer**.
The **chief priests** and **scribes**, meanwhile,
  stood by **accusing** him **harshly**.
Herod and his **soldiers** treated him **contemptuously**
    and **mocked** him,
  and after **clothing** him in **resplendent garb**,
  he **sent** him back to **Pilate**.
Herod and **Pilate** became **friends that very day**,
  even though they had been **enemies** formerly.

Based on their misunderstanding, the Apostles show Jesus that they already have two swords.

(6) Now, Jesus does express his exasperation saying, "It is enough." The meaning of Jesus' words is not "Two swords are sufficient," but, "That's it, I've had enough!" Jesus will teach the Apostles that he does not want them to take up swords at the time of the arrest.

(7) When they do just that, one of them cutting off the high priest's servant's ear, Jesus says, "Stop, no more of this!" Then

Jesus, even though he is being arrested by this servant of the high priest, heals his ear.

Luke, like his source, Mark, pictures Jesus in true agony in the garden. Jesus' sweat is like "drops of blood falling on the ground." Jesus does not want to die, especially now, when the disciples understand so little. Jesus prays: "Father, if you are willing, take this cup away from me; still, not my will but yours be done"

However, Luke, unlike Mark, does not highlight the disciples' failure to stay awake and pray as Jesus has instructed. In Mark, Jesus returns to them three times,

only to find them sleeping. In Luke, this happens only once, and Luke says that the disciples are sleeping because of "grief." Jesus does not admonish them for their failure; rather, he simply says, "Get up and pray that you may not undergo the test."

(8) Luke also tells the painful story of Peter's threefold denial of Jesus. Again, Peter, when accused of having been with Jesus, says the very ironic words: "Woman, I do not know him." As Peter says this, his intention is to lie. He not only knows Jesus, he just, a few hours previously, had

Pilate has authority, but he wants to please the crowd.

(12) **Pilate** then summoned the **chief priests**, the **rulers**
and the **people**
and said to them, "**You** brought **this man** to **me**
and **accused** him of **inciting** the **people** to **revolt**.
I have conducted my investigation in **your presence**
and have **not found** this man **guilty**
of the **charges** you have brought **against** him,
nor did **Herod**, for **he** sent him **back** to us.
So **no capital crime** has been **committed** by him.
Therefore I shall have him **flogged** and then **release** him."

Barabbas = buh-RAB-uhs

But **all together** they **shouted out**,
"**Away** with this man!
Release Barabbas to us."
—Now **Barabbas** had been **imprisoned** for a **rebellion**
that had taken place in the **city** and for **murder**.—
Again Pilate **addressed** them, **still wishing** to **release** Jesus,
but they **continued** their **shouting**,

This is even louder and more angry.
crucify = KROO-sih-fi
Pilate speaks with less authority. He seems to be pleading with the crowd to be reasonable.

"**Crucify** him! **Crucify** him!"
Pilate addressed them a **third** time,
"**What evil** has this man **done**?
I found him **guilty** of **no capital crime**.
Therefore I shall have him **flogged** and then **release** him."
With **loud shouts**, however,
they **persisted** in calling for his **crucifixion**,
and **their** voices **prevailed**.

This is a tragic statement.

The **verdict** of **Pilate** was that their **demand** should be **granted**.
So he **released** the man who had been **imprisoned**
for **rebellion** and **murder**, for whom they **asked**,

Pause after this line.

and he **handed Jesus over** to them to **deal** with as they **wished**.

declared that he was ready to go to prison or to die with Jesus. However, as readers, we know that Peter is telling the truth. Peter does not yet know what the reader knows about Jesus: Jesus is divine. Peter will understand this only after the Resurrection.

However, Luke adds a detail to the story that appears nowhere else. After Peter has denied knowing Jesus, Luke tells us that "the Lord turned and looked at Peter." Peter's reaction to whatever he sees in Jesus' look is to weep. Given the fact that in the Gospel according to Luke Jesus is constantly forgiving those who

are harming him, we can only conclude that Peter is weeping because he saw love, not accusation, in Jesus' eyes.

(9) Like Mark, Luke tells us that Jesus is brought before the Sanhedrin, the Jewish court, and found guilty because he does not deny being the Son of God.

(10) However, when Jesus is brought before Pilate, the charge is not blasphemy but that Jesus is somehow a threat to Roman rule: they accuse Jesus of opposing the payment of taxes to Caesar and claiming to be a king. Even though Pilate finds no guilt in Jesus he does not release him.

(11) Instead he sends Jesus to Herod. Herod, too, finds no guilt in Jesus, but sends him back to Pilate. Luke tells us that Herod and Pilate had been enemies before, but now they become friends. Jesus' power to heal extends even to his enemies.

(12) Although Pilate is the one in authority and Jesus is the prisoner, in the eyes of the reader Pilate loses his stature while Jesus does not. Pilate, despite his proclamation that he finds no guilt in Jesus, succumbs to the demands of the

Cyrenian = sī-REE-nee-uhn

(13) As they **led him away**
    they took hold of a certain **Simon**, a **Cyrenian**,
    who was coming in from the **country**;
    and after **laying** the **cross** on him,
    they **made** him **carry** it **behind Jesus**.
A **large crowd** of people **followed Jesus**,
    including **many women** who **mourned** and **lamented** him.
Jesus **turned** to them and **said**,

Jesus speaks quietly and with sadness.

    "**Daughters** of **Jerusalem**, do **not** weep for **me**;
    weep instead for **yourselves** and for your **children**
    for **indeed**, the **days are coming** when **people** will **say**,
    '**Blessed** are the **barren**,
    the **wombs** that never **bore**
    and the **breasts** that never **nursed**.'
At **that time** people will say to the **mountains**,
    '**Fall upon us!**'
    and to the **hills**, '**Cover us!**'
    for if these things are done when the **wood** is **green**
    what will **happen** when it is **dry**?"
Now **two others**, **both criminals**,
    were **led** away **with** him to be **executed**.

(14) When they came to the **place** called the **Skull**,
    they **crucified** him and the **criminals** there,
    one on his **right**, **the other** on his **left**.
Then **Jesus** said,

This is a heartfelt prayer.

    "**Father**, **forgive** them, they **know not** what **they do**."
They **divided** his **garments** by **casting lots**.

crowd and turns Jesus over to the people "to deal with as they wished."

(13) In Luke's account, not everyone in the crowd is against Jesus. Some women of Jerusalem are there who mourn and lament him. Jesus, once more, sees the occasion as a time to teach. He admonishes the women of Jerusalem not to weep for him but for themselves and their children. Jesus warns them that times of suffering are in Jerusalem's future.

(14) Jesus' desire to forgive extends even to those who crucify him. At the very time that Jesus is being crucified, he forgives those responsible, praying, "Father, forgive them, they know not what they do"

(15) In addition, Jesus forgives one of the criminals who is crucified with him. This criminal admits that he deserves the harsh punishment that he is receiving. At the same time, this guilty man defends Jesus' innocence and asks Jesus to remember him when Jesus comes into his kingdom. Jesus tells the condemned man, "today you will be with me in Paradise."

Scripture scholars suggest that Luke portrays Jesus using the word "Paradise" rather than "kingdom" here because Luke is teaching the saving effect of Jesus' Passion and Death. "Paradise" is an allusion to the story of the man and woman in the garden who are pictured as committing the first sin. The harm that Adam's sin caused the whole human race is now being reversed. The human race is being redeemed from slavery to sin by Jesus' Passion and Death.

The **people stood** by and **watched**;
    the **rulers**, meanwhile, **sneered** at him and said,
        "He **saved others**, let him **save himself**
        if he is the **chosen** one, the **Christ** of **God**."
Even the **soldiers** jeered at him.
As they **approached** to **offer** him **wine** they called **out**,
        "If **you** are King of the **Jews**, **save yourself**."
Above him there was an **inscription** that read,
        "**This** is the **King** of the **Jews**."

(15) Now **one** of the **criminals** hanging there **reviled** Jesus, saying,
        "Are you **not** the **Christ**?
        Save yourself and **us**."
The **other**, however, **rebuking** him, said in reply,
        "Have **you no fear** of **God**,
        for **you** are subject to the **same condemnation**?
And **indeed**, **we** have been **condemned justly**,
        for the sentence **we received corresponds** to our **crimes**,
        but **this** man has done **nothing criminal**."
Then he said,
        "**Jesus**, **remember** me when you **come** into your **kingdom**."
He replied to him,
        "**Amen**, **I** say to **you**,
        today you will be **with** me in **Paradise**."

(16) It was **now** about **noon** and **darkness** came
        over the **whole land**
    until **three** in the **afternoon**
    because of an **eclipse** of the **sun**.
Then the **veil** of the **temple** was **torn** down the **middle**.
Jesus cried out in a **loud voice**,
        "**Father**, into **your hands** I **commend** my **spirit**";
    and when he had **said** this he **breathed** his **last**.

Use a sneering tone.

This is a taunt.

This is another taunt.

The tone is "rebuking."

This is said with gentleness.

Jesus speaks with authority and love.

This is a loud cry.

(16) Luke teaches the cosmic significance of Jesus' Death by telling us that there was an eclipse of the sun as Jesus was dying, and that the veil of the Temple was torn down the middle. As Jesus dies, he willingly turns over his Spirit to his Father saying, "Father, into your hands I commend my spirit." These last words are very different than the lament that we heard in Mark's account, "My God, my God, why have you forsaken me?" Luke pictures Jesus full of trust. Jesus has followed his Father's will. He has revealed God's love in everything that he has done.

(17) The very first words spoken after Jesus' Death do not come from one of Jesus' disciples, but from a Roman centurion, a Roman soldier. He states, "This man was innocent beyond doubt." His words echo those of Pilate who saw no guilt in Jesus. The crowd who had gathered to watch the Crucifixion, and who earlier had said nothing as they witnessed the soldiers jeering at Jesus, has experienced a change of heart: "They returned home beating their breasts." Jesus' healing grace is operative even after his Death.

(18) Jesus' teaching and healing power is also still at work in Joseph of Arimathea, a member of the Sanhedrin who did not consent to the plan to trap and condemn Jesus. Joseph was "awaiting the kingdom of God." Remember, announcing the imminent in-breaking of the Kingdom of God was central to Jesus' preaching. Joseph takes Jesus' body and buries it

[Here all kneel and pause for a short time.]

centurion = sen-TOOR-ee-uhn;
sen-TYOOR-ee-uhn

Said with awe and conviction.

(17) The **centurion** who **witnessed** what had **happened glorified God** and said,
    "**This man** was **innocent beyond doubt.**"
When **all** the **people** who had **gathered** for this spectacle **saw**
    what had **happened**,
    they returned **home beating** their **breasts**;
    but **all** his **acquaintances stood** at a **distance**,
    including the **women** who had **followed** him from **Galilee**
    and **saw** these events.

Pause at the end of the line.

(18) Now there was a **virtuous** and **righteous** man
    named **Joseph**, who,
    though he was a **member** of the **council**,
    had **not consented** to their **plan** of action.
He came from the **Jewish** town of **Arimathea**
    and was **awaiting** the **kingdom** of **God**.
He went to **Pilate** and **asked** for the **body** of **Jesus**.
After he had taken the **body down**,
    he **wrapped** it in a **linen cloth**
    and **laid** him in a **rock-hewn tomb**
    in which **no one** had **yet** been **buried**.

Arimathea = ayr-ih-muh-THEE-uh

It was the **day** of **preparation**,
    and the **sabbath** was about to **begin**.
The **women** who had come from **Galilee** with him
    followed behind,
    and when they had **seen** the **tomb**
    and the **way** in which his **body** was **laid** in it,
    they **returned** and **prepared spices** and **perfumed oils**.
Then they **rested** on the **sabbath** according to the **commandment**.

Now speak more quickly. The narrator is
concluding the story.

[Shorter: Luke 23:1–49]

with great dignity—wrapping it in a linen cloth and laying it in a new tomb. Jesus' burial is fitting for the King that he is.

Luke says nothing about any of the Twelve being present at Jesus' Death or burial. He does say that Jesus' "acquaintances" were standing at a distance, among them some women who had followed Jesus from Galilee. These women stay until the very end, watching where Jesus is buried and preparing spices. They will be the first to discover the empty tomb

when they bring the spices for Jesus' burial on the day after the Sabbath, only to discover that Jesus has been raised from the dead (Luke 24:1–8).

As you proclaim Luke's account of Jesus' Last Supper, Jesus' Passion, and his Death, try to enter the drama so that all of the many characters come alive: Jesus, who remains loving and forgiving in every circumstance; Peter, who boasts of his strength and fidelity and then denies knowing Jesus; the cruel men who ridicule and beat Jesus; Pilate, who possesses authority but succumbs to the

wishes of the crowd; the raucous crowd that demands his Crucifixion; the jeering soldiers; and the solemn centurion who, against all odds, sees Jesus' goodness and innocence. The goal is to have the gathered community enter into the story, not simply with palms, as they are invited to do during the procession before Mass, but with their whole being.

HOLY THURSDAY: MASS OF THE LORD'S SUPPER

Lectionary #39

Exodus = EX-uh-duhs
Moses = MOH-ziz; MOH-zis
Aaron = AYR-uhn
Egypt = EE-jipt

God is giving instructions to Moses and Aaron, not giving a proclamation to the whole community. Read slowly and with moderate volume.

Israel = IZ-ree-uhl; IZ-ray-uhl

Emphasize "whole assembly of Israel." This is to be a community ritual.

READING I   Exodus 12:1–8, 11–14

A reading from the Book of Exodus

The LORD said to **Moses** and **Aaron** in the land of **Egypt**,
  "This month shall stand at the **head** of your **calendar;**
  you shall reckon it the **first month** of the **year.**
Tell the **whole community** of **Israel:**
  On the **tenth** of **this month every one** of your **families**
  must procure for itself a **lamb, one apiece** for **each household.**
If a family is **too small** for a **whole** lamb,
  it shall **join** the **nearest household** in **procuring** one
  and shall **share** in the **lamb**
  in proportion to the number of **persons** who **partake** of it.
The **lamb** must be a **year-old male** and **without blemish.**
You may take it from either the **sheep** or the **goats.**
You shall **keep** it **until** the **fourteenth day** of **this month,**
  and **then**, with the **whole assembly** of Israel present,
  it shall be **slaughtered** during the **evening twilight.**
They shall take **some** of its **blood**
  and apply it to the **two doorposts** and the **lintel**
  of **every house** in which they **partake** of the **lamb.**
That same night they shall eat its **roasted flesh**

  with **unleavened bread** and **bitter herbs.**

READING I The setting for today's reading is just before the last plague, which resulted in the Israelites being able to leave Egypt, thus ending hundreds of years of enslavement. However, the time of the setting is obviously not the same as the time of the person telling the story. How can we tell? Because today's reading pictures God giving Moses and Aaron instructions on how to celebrate Passover, how to celebrate God's mighty intervention in history on the Israelites' behalf. The celebration, of course, developed after the event.

Scripture scholars surmise that this instruction concerning the Passover celebration was inserted into an earlier story about the plagues. Therefore, as the story now stands, the instruction on how to celebrate this saving event, how to celebrate the Passover, is interwoven with the instruction on what the Israelites must do to be spared from the final plague.

The tenth and last plague involved the death of "every firstborn of the land [of Egypt], both man and beast." However, the firstborn of the Israelites' would be spared. According to God's instruction, the Israelites

were to put blood on the doorposts and lintels of their homes. God would "pass over" those homes. Thus, "no destructive blow will come upon" the Israelites.

As the reading begins, God tells Moses and Aaron to consider this month as "the first month of the year." Before the exodus experience the Israelites already had a Passover celebration in the first month of the year, the month of the spring equinox, that marked the shepherds' moving from the winter fields to the summer fields. This celebration also involved marking with blood—the shepherds put blood on their

Increase your pace here.

"**This** is how you are to **eat** it:
with your **loins girt**, **sandals** on your **feet** and your **staff**
in **hand**,
you shall eat like those who are in **flight**.
It is the **Passover** of the LORD.

Emphasize this line.
God is reassuring Moses and Aaron, not threatening the Egyptians.

For on this **same night** I will go through **Egypt**,
striking down every firstborn of the **land**, both **man** and **beast**,
and **executing judgment** on **all** the **gods** of Egypt—**I**, the **LORD**!
But the **blood** will mark the **houses** where **you are**.

Emphasize "you."
Again emphasize "you."

Seeing the **blood**, I will **pass over you**;
thus, when I **strike** the land of **Egypt**,
no destructive blow will come upon **you**.

Again emphasize "you."

"**This day** shall be a **memorial feast** for you,
which **all your generations** shall celebrate
with **pilgrimage** to the LORD, as a **perpetual institution**."

Raise your volume for this conclusion.

READING II   1 Corinthians 11:23–26

Corinthians = kohr-IN-thee-uhnz

A reading from the first Letter of Saint Paul to the Corinthians

Read this with solemnity and reverence.
Paul is recalling something holy.

Brothers and **sisters**:
I **received** from the **Lord** what I also **handed on** to **you**,
that the **Lord Jesus**, on the night he was **handed over**,
took bread, and, **after** he had **given thanks**,
broke it and said, "**This is my body** that is for **you**.

Emphasize Jesus' words of consecration.

Do this in **remembrance** of me."
In the **same way also** the **cup**, after **supper**, saying,
"**This cup** is the **new covenant** in **my blood**.

tents as a way of promoting the fertility of the sheep and of protecting the newborn sheep from any evil spirits.

In the celebration of Passover that is described in today's reading, some of the features of this nomadic feast are appropriated and their meaning reinterpreted. The Passover being celebrated is no longer the shepherds' passing from one field to another, but God's passing over the houses of the Israelites during the last plague and the Israelites' passing over from slavery to freedom.

Other features are added to the Passover celebration: The Israelites are to have sandals on their feet and a staff in their hands. They are to eat the Passover meal "like those who are in flight." The Israelites are to celebrate this event as a "perpetual institution."

We read this passage from Exodus on Holy Thursday because, in Mark, Matthew, and Luke's gospel accounts, Jesus is pictured as celebrating Passover on the night before he dies. On that night Jesus reinterprets once more the meaning of the feast. At this Passover celebration, Jesus becomes

the lamb whose blood gives life, and the Passover becomes Jesus' Passover through death to eternal life. As you proclaim the reading, emphasize those lines that make this connection clear. The "Passover of the LORD" is to be celebrated forever.

READING II On Holy Thursday we read about Jesus' institution of the Eucharist, not from the four Evangelists, but from the earliest account that we have, from Paul's First Letter to the Corinthians. This letter dates to about AD 56, almost a

Now it is Paul, not Jesus, who is speaking. This is Paul's concluding instruction.

Do this, as **often** as you **drink it**, in **remembrance** of **me**."
For as **often** as you **eat** this **bread** and **drink** the **cup**,
    you **proclaim** the **death** of the **Lord** until he **comes**.

GOSPEL   John 13:1–15

A reading from the holy Gospel according to John

The narrator is giving us background information.

Before the **feast** of **Passover**,
    Jesus knew that his **hour** had **come**
    to pass from **this world** to the **Father**.
He **loved** his **own** in the **world**, and he **loved them** to the **end**.
The **devil** had already induced **Judas**, son of **Simon** the **Iscariot**,
        to **hand him over**.

Judas = JOO-duhs
Iscariot = ih-SKAYR-ee-uht
Pause after, "So," then raise your volume. We are starting the immediate drama here.

So, **during supper**,
    fully aware that the Father had put **everything** into his power
    and that he had **come from God** and was **returning to God**,
    he **rose** from **supper** and **took off** his **outer garments**.
He took a **towel** and **tied** it around his **waist**.
Then he **poured water** into **a basin**
    and began to **wash** the **disciples' feet**
    and **dry** them with the **towel** around his **waist**.
He came to **Simon Peter**, who said to him,

Peter is not just asking a question, but is objecting.

Jesus is reassuring Peter.

    "**Master**, are you going to wash **my** feet?"
Jesus answered and **said** to him,
    "**What I am doing**, you do **not understand now**,
    but you **will** understand **later**."

Peter is adamant.

Peter said to him, "You will **never wash my feet**."

decade before our earliest account of the Gospel, attributed to Mark and dated around AD 65.

Paul's story of the institution of the Eucharist is his theological basis for teaching the Corinthians how they should behave at their Eucharistic gatherings and how they should treat each other (see 1 Corinthians 11:17–34). When the Corinthians gathered for Eucharist, they had a meal together. At that meal, some people were getting drunk while others were going hungry. Paul couldn't believe

that people would behave in such a manner at a Eucharistic gathering. In today's reading he is reminding the Corinthians that Jesus served others. A person living as a disciple of Jesus Christ would never simply ignore the needs of others.

To demonstrate Jesus' total gift of self to others, Paul tells the Corinthians that, on the night before Jesus died, he took bread, gave thanks, and said, "This is my body that is for you. Do this is remembrance of me." Then, taking the cup, Jesus said, "This cup is the new covenant in my blood. Do this, as often as you drink it, in remembrance

of me." Since Jesus gave his body and blood for their salvation, how could the Corinthians possibly celebrate Eucharist in remembrance of Christ and, at the same time, ignore the poor in their midst?

This reading is selected for Holy Thursday because of its description of Eucharist. As you proclaim the reading, give the most emphasis to Jesus' words of institution. This is the only text that is proclaimed on Holy Thursday that includes an account of Jesus instructing us to celebrate Eucharist in remembrance of him.

Jesus is persuading.

This is said whole-heartedly.

There is a warning in Jesus' words.

This is an aside, said by the narrator.

The story resumes here.

Jesus speaks with gentle authority.

Read this final lesson slowly.

Jesus answered him,
"**Unless** I **wash** you, you will have **no inheritance** with me."
Simon Peter said to him,
"**Master**, then not **only** my **feet**, but my **hands**
and **head** as **well**."
Jesus said to him,
"Whoever has **bathed** has **no need**
except to have his **feet** washed,
for he is **clean all over**;
so you are **clean**, but **not all**."
For he **knew** who would **betray** him;
for **this reason**, he said, "**Not all** of you are **clean**."

So when he had **washed** their **feet**
and put his **garments** back **on** and **reclined** at **table** again,
he said to them, "Do you **realize** what I have **done** for you?
You call me '**teacher**' and '**master**,' and **rightly so**, for **indeed** I am.
If **I**, therefore, the **master** and **teacher**, have **washed your feet**,
you ought to **wash one another's feet**.
I have given you a **model** to **follow**,
so that as **I have done** for **you**, **you** should also **do**."

GOSPEL | The Gospel according to John was written for an end-of-the-century audience who was wondering why the Son of Man had not yet returned on the clouds of heaven as expected. John is teaching his audience that the risen Christ is already in their midst. While at one level John's stories are about Jesus during his public ministry, at another level John's stories are about the presence of the risen Christ in the lives of John's audience and in our lives. Today's account is a perfect example.

Jesus uses the occasion of his last meal with the disciples to set an example of service by washing their feet. Peter objects to the Lord performing such a menial task. Jesus tells Peter, "Unless I wash you, you will have no inheritance with me." Jesus then tells Peter that whoever has bathed "is clean all over."

With this explanation, we realize that Jesus is not talking simply about washing a disciple's feet. Jesus is talking about Baptism. It is Baptism that causes a person to have an inheritance with Christ. It is Baptism that makes one entirely clean.

Through Baptism, the risen Christ remains with his people.

Jesus then goes on to explain how his disciples should live. Jesus says, "you ought to wash one another's feet." Emphasize this line as you proclaim the reading. Those who share Eucharist on Holy Thursday are to live as Eucharistic people. We must serve others.

GOOD FRIDAY: PASSION OF THE LORD

Lectionary #40

READING I   Isaiah 52:13 — 53:12

A reading from the Book of the Prophet Isaiah

Isaiah = ĭ-ZAY-uh

Use an exultant tone. God is announcing good news.

Now the narrator is speaking and is drawing a contrast. Lower your voice.

With this line, increase your volume and sound jubilant.

Now the kings of other nations are speaking. Their good news is almost unbelievable!
Again this is a contrast. Lower your volume.

Speak with more volume and with authority. Now the truth is understood.

See, my **servant** shall **prosper**,
    he shall be **raised high** and **greatly exalted**.
Even as many were **amazed** at him—
    so **marred** was his **look beyond human semblance**
    and his **appearance beyond** that of the **sons** of **man**—
so shall he **startle many nations**,
    because of **him kings** shall stand **speechless**;
for those who have **not** been **told** shall **see**,
    those who have **not heard** shall **ponder** it.

Who would **believe** what **we** have **heard**?
    To **whom** has the **arm** of the LORD been **revealed**?
He grew up like a **sapling** before him,
    like a **shoot** from the **parched earth**;
there was in him **no stately bearing** to make us **look** at him,
    nor appearance that would **attract** us to him.
He was **spurned** and **avoided** by people,
    a man of **suffering**, **accustomed** to **infirmity**,
one of those from whom people **hide** their **faces**,
    spurned, and **we** held him in **no esteem**.

Yet it was **our infirmities** that **he bore**,
    our sufferings that **he endured**,
while we thought of him as **stricken**,
    as one **smitten** by **God** and **afflicted**.

READING I   On Good Friday, when you proclaim this reading from Isaiah about a servant of the Lord who suffered for the sins of all nations but was raised up and greatly exalted, you and those who hear you will be thinking of Jesus Christ. Jesus is the one who bore our infirmities. Jesus is the one who was "pierced for our offenses." Jesus is the lamb who went before the shearer. Through Jesus' suffering many have been justified.

However, when this reading was first proclaimed, those who heard it were not thinking about Jesus Christ, but about the nation, Israel, in exile in Babylon. Only in hindsight, in the light of subsequent events, did the words take on the meaning we now hear in them. To understand how Isaiah's words have been fulfilled in Jesus Christ, we will first explain what Isaiah's prophesy meant in its original setting. We will then see how Isaiah's prophecy took on a fuller meaning after Jesus' Passion, Death, and Resurrection.

Chapters 40–55 of the Book of Isaiah are from a prophet known as Second Isaiah. This prophet lived during the Babylonian exile (587–537 BC), one of the most painful and mysterious times in Israel's history, second only to the time of slavery in Egypt before the exodus. Second Isaiah offered hope to the exiles at a time when they truly needed reassurance.

After all, the Israelites had understood themselves to be God's Chosen People. They had understood that God would keep their nation and their Temple secure. Now, both the nation and the Temple were destroyed, and all of the upper-class citizens were living in exile in Babylon. This terrible turn of events caused the people to

Speak slowly and with sorrow.

Say this with awe.
Increase your speed here.

Again, read slowly to emphasize the contrast.

Read this with sadness. This is a tragic turn of events.

Emphasize the servant's total innocence.

This is the mystery. Why is the innocent servant, Israel, suffering?

Pause, then speak with authority. The people are being assured that their suffering does have purpose.

But he was **pierced** for **our offenses**,
  crushed for **our sins**;
upon **him** was the chastisement that makes **us whole**,
  by **his stripes we were healed**.
We had **all** gone **astray** like **sheep**,
  each following his **own way**;
but the LORD laid upon **him**
  the **guilt** of us **all**.

Though he was **harshly treated**, he **submitted**
  and **opened not** his **mouth**;
like a **lamb** led to the **slaughter**
  or a **sheep** before the **shearers**,
  he was **silent** and **opened not** his **mouth**.
Oppressed and **condemned**, he was **taken away**,
  and **who** would have **thought any more** of his **destiny**?
When he was **cut off** from the **land** of the **living**,
  and **smitten** for the **sin** of his **people**,
a **grave** was assigned him among the **wicked**
  and a **burial place** with **evildoers**,
though he had done **no wrong**
  nor spoken **any falsehood**.
But the LORD was pleased
  to **crush** him in **infirmity**.

If he gives **his life** as an **offering** for **sin**,
  he shall **see** his **descendants** in a **long life**,
  and the **will** of the LORD shall be **accomplished** through **him**.

Because of his **affliction**
  he shall **see** the **light** in **fullness** of **days**;

ask: "Are we truly God's people? Is God truly our God? If so, what is the meaning of our present suffering?"

Through the beautiful prophecy that we read today, Second Isaiah offers the people hope. He does this by presenting a variety of voices who remark on the situation of the audience, that is, the exiles in Babylon. The exiles, as a group, are referred to as God's "servant."

The first voice to speak is God's: "See, my servant shall prosper, he shall be raised high and greatly exalted." This, all

by itself, is wonderful news. God calls the nation "my servant." The Israelites still are God's people. God is still their God. In addition, in the future, Israel will once more prosper. The exile in Babylon is temporary.

The next voice to speak is that of the narrator. This voice acknowledges how much the people have suffered: "so marred was his [the servant's] look beyond human semblance." Nevertheless, something marvelous was going to be accomplished through this servant, something that would cause kings of other nations to stand speechless.

Next we hear from the kings themselves. Their lines begin with: "Who would believe what we have heard?" The kings had thought nothing of this suffering people. They certainly had not held them in any esteem. Yet the kings of all nations have benefited from the suffering of God's servant, Israel. Oppressed and condemned, the people had been taken away from "the land of the living," their nation, Israel. But through the servant's suffering, the will of the Lord will be accomplished.

through his **suffering**, my **servant** shall **justify many**,
and their **guilt** he shall **bear**.
Therefore I will **give** him his **portion** among the **great**,
and he shall **divide** the spoils with the **mighty**,
because he **surrendered** himself to **death**
and was **counted** among the **wicked**;
and he shall take away the **sins** of **many**,
and win **pardon** for their **offenses**.

READING II   Hebrews 4:14–16; 5:7–9

A reading from the Letter to the Hebrews

Brothers and **sisters:**
Since we have a **great high priest** who has **passed**
through the **heavens**,
Jesus, the **Son** of **God**,
let us **hold fast** to our **confession**.
For we do **not** have a **high priest**
who is **unable** to **sympathize** with our **weaknesses**,
but **one** who has **similarly** been **tested** in **every way**,
yet without sin.
So let us **confidently approach** the **throne** of **grace**
to receive **mercy** and to find **grace** for **timely help**.

In the days when **Christ** was in the **flesh**,
he offered **prayers** and **supplications** with **loud cries** and **tears**
to the one who was **able** to **save him** from **death**,
and he was **heard** because of his **reverence**.

Finally, God speaks again. God says, "through his suffering, my servant shall justify many." In God's voice, Second Isaiah assures the exiles that through Israel's suffering in Babylon other nations will come to know God and will receive "pardon for their offenses."

Some five hundred years later, when the earliest Christians were struggling with the scandal of Jesus' Crucifixion and Death, as well as with the hope engendered by Jesus' Resurrection and post-Resurrection appearances, they turned to Second Isaiah's suffering servant song to

help them interpret the meaning of these mysterious events. In the light of Jesus, Second Isaiah's words took on a whole new level of meaning. Jesus was the suffering servant who took on the sins of all nations, who revealed God's love to his people, and who justified the human race. Jesus' suffering also has meaning.

As you proclaim Second Isaiah's song, emphasize those lines that we hear as referring to Jesus. Because we understand Jesus to be the suffering servant, the

Lamb of God who takes away the sins of the world, we proclaim this reading on Good Friday.

READING II The Second Reading on Good Friday also centers our attention on the meaning of Jesus' suffering; however, it does not start with this topic. It starts with an exhortation urging the people to "hold fast" to their "confession." What is their confession?

The Letter to the Hebrews presents Jesus as the perfect High Priest who has offered the perfect sacrifice: himself.

Son though he **was**, he learned **obedience** from what he **suffered**;
and when he was made **perfect**,
he became the **source** of **eternal salvation** for **all** who
obey him.

PASSION   John 18:1—19:42

The Passion of our Lord Jesus Christ according to John

Jesus went out with his **disciples** across the **Kidron valley**
to where there was a **garden**,
into which **he** and his **disciples entered**.
Judas his **betrayer also** knew the place,
because **Jesus** had **often met there** with his **disciples**.
So **Judas** got a band of **soldiers** and **guards**
from the **chief priests** and the **Pharisees**
and went there with **lanterns**, **torches**, and **weapons**.
Jesus, **knowing everything** that was **going** to **happen** to **him**,
went out and said to them, "**Whom** are you **looking** for?"
They answered him, "**Jesus** the **Nazorean**."
He said to them, "**I AM**."
Judas his **betrayer** was **also** with them.
When he said to them, "**I AM**,"
they **turned away** and **fell** to the **ground**.
So he **again** asked them,
"**Whom** are you **looking** for?"
They said, "**Jesus** the **Nazorean**."
Jesus answered,
"**I told** you that **I AM**.
So if you are **looking** for **me**, let **these men go**."

Increase your volume. This is a proclamation of good news, explaining the source of our confidence and hope.

The narrator's voice begins the story. This is background information.
Kidron = KID-ruhn

Judas = JOO-duhs

Pharisees = FAYR-uh-seez

Emphasize this line. It is claiming Jesus' divinity.
Jesus speaks with calm authority.

Emphasize "I AM." This is another claim of divinity.

Drop your voice.
Nazarene = NAZ-uh-reen

Pause after this line.

Again emphasize "I AM."

Because Jesus has done this, the Hebrews (and we) can "confidently approach the throne of grace to receive mercy."

As the reading begins, the author tells us that Jesus is "a great high priest who has passed through the heavens." The words "passed through the heavens" refer to Jesus' Resurrection from the dead. This means that Jesus is still alive. Jesus' priesthood is not limited to that time when he offered himself in sacrifice; rather, Jesus continues to be a priest because he is still alive. Jesus has an eternal priesthood.

Because Jesus was "tested in every way, yet without sin" Jesus' sacrifice of himself was the perfect sacrifice. Therefore, unlike the sacrifices that the Jewish priests offered every year in the Temple for the forgiveness of sin, Jesus' sacrifice need never be repeated. Because Jesus is the perfect High Priest who offered the perfect sacrifice, the Hebrews can be confident that they will receive mercy from the "throne of grace."

After the exhortation to remain faithful to this confession, the author of Hebrews centers our attention on Jesus' suffering. He says that Jesus "offered prayers and supplications with loud cries and tears to the one who was able to save him from death, and he was heard because of his reverence." How can the author claim that Jesus was heard when he prayed not to die? After all, Jesus suffered a very painful death. The author makes this claim because Jesus is still alive. Jesus' Death did not end in death, but in eternal life.

This is the narrator giving us background information. Lower your voice.

Malchus = MAL-kuhs

Jesus is correcting Peter, but privately.

Again, the narrator takes up the story.

Annas = AN-uhs
Caiaphas = KAY-uh-fuhs; KĪ-uh-fuhs

Pause here.

Emphasize "another disciple." This is the beloved disciple.

This is said with incredulity.
This is said with firmness.
The narrator continues the story.

This was to **fulfill** what he had **said**,
  "I have not lost **any** of those you **gave** me."
Then **Simon Peter**, who had a **sword**, **drew** it,
  struck the **high priest's slave**, and **cut off** his **right ear**.
The slave's name was **Malchus**.
Jesus said to **Peter**,
  "**Put** your **sword** into its **scabbard**.
Shall I not **drink** the **cup** that the **Father gave me**?"

So the **band** of **soldiers**, the **tribune**, and the **Jewish guards**
    seized Jesus,
  bound him, and **brought** him to **Annas** first.
He was the **father-in-law** of **Caiaphas**,
  who was **high priest** that year.
It was **Caiaphas** who had counseled the **Jews**
  that it was **better** that **one man** should **die**
    rather than the **people**.

Simon Peter and **another disciple followed Jesus**.
Now the **other disciple** was **known** to the **high priest**,
  and **he entered** the courtyard of the high priest **with Jesus**.
But **Peter** stood at the gate **outside**.
So the **other disciple**, the **acquaintance** of the **high priest**,
  went out and **spoke** to the **gatekeeper** and brought **Peter in**.
Then the **maid** who was the **gatekeeper** said to **Peter**,
  "**You** are **not one** of **this** man's **disciples**, are you?"
He said, "**I am not**."
Now the **slaves** and the **guards** were **standing**
    around a **charcoal fire**
  that they had made, because it was **cold**,
  and were **warming** themselves.
Peter was **also** standing there keeping **warm**.

What, then, was the purpose for Jesus' painful Death? The author of Hebrews claims that Jesus "learned obedience from what he suffered, and when he was made perfect, he became the source of eternal salvation for all who obey him." Jesus' suffering, like the suffering of the Israelites, was not in vain.

Again, as you proclaim the reading, stress those passages that address the reason for Jesus' suffering. On Good Friday we once again remember that through Jesus' suffering, he became the source of eternal salvation for all nations.

GOSPEL Every year we hear two accounts of Jesus' Passion and Death: one on Palm Sunday and one on Good Friday. On Palm Sunday the selection is from whichever synoptic gospel account is being proclaimed that year: Matthew if it is Cycle A, Mark if it is Cycle B, and Luke if it is Cycle C. Since this liturgical year is Cycle C, we read Luke. On Good Friday, however, we always hear John. John's account of Jesus' Passion and Death is unique in many respects.

To understand all that John wishes to teach us, it's important to understand a few things about John's audience, theme, and method. As we will see, John's purpose in composing his gospel account is apparent throughout his writing, but is especially evident as he tells the story of Jesus' Passion and Death.

The Gospel according to John was written later than the other gospel accounts. Most of it was written about AD 90. Some additions were made some ten years later. By AD 90, the time of Jesus'

The **high priest questioned Jesus**
    about his **disciples** and about his **doctrine**.
Jesus answered him,
    "**I have spoken publicly** to the **world**.
I have **always taught** in a **synagogue**
    or in the **temple area** where **all** the **Jews gather**,
    and in **secret** I have said **nothing**. **Why ask me?**
Ask those who **heard** me what I **said** to them.
They know what I said."
When he had **said** this,
    one of the **temple guards** standing there **struck** Jesus and said,
    "Is **this** the way you **answer** the **high priest**?"
Jesus answered him,
    "If I have spoken **wrongly**, **testify** to the wrong;
    but if I have spoken **rightly**, **why** do you **strike** me?"
Then **Annas** sent him bound to **Caiaphas** the **high priest**.

Now **Simon Peter** was **standing** there keeping **warm**.
And they said to him,
    "**You** are **not** one of **his disciples**, are you?"
He denied it and said,
    "**I am not**."
One of the **slaves** of the high priest,
    a **relative** of the one whose ear **Peter** had cut off, said,
    "Didn't I **see you** in the garden with **him**?"
Again Peter **denied** it.
And **immediately** the **cock crowed**.

Then they brought **Jesus** from **Caiaphas** to the **praetorium**.
It was **morning**.
And they **themselves** did **not enter** the praetorium,
    in order **not** to be **defiled** so that they could **eat** the **Passover**.

Margin notes:

Jesus speaks with calm authority.

The narrator is speaking. Lower your voice.

This is said with outrage.

Again Jesus is calm and in control.

The narrator is speaking again.

This is said with incredulity.

Emphasize every word.

He is quite sure of what he saw.

This is tragic. Pause after this line.

The narrator continues the story.
praetorium = prih-TOHR-ee-uhm

---

expected return on the clouds of heaven was long overdue. John's audience was asking, "Where is the risen Christ? He was supposed to have returned long before now." In answer to this question, John is teaching his audience that the risen Christ is not absent, but present. So, as John tells the story of Jesus during his public ministry, he is, at the same time, telling the story of the risen Christ's presence in John's community through the Church and through what we have come to call the sacraments. Because John is trying to help those in his audience see that the risen Christ is in

their midst, he constantly emphasizes Jesus' divinity. As we will soon see, even as John tells the story of Jesus' Passion and Death, he has Jesus' divinity show through in extraordinary ways.

From the very beginning of John's account, Jesus is presented as the Lamb of God who takes away the sins of the world. John the Baptist refers to Jesus with these words before Jesus' public ministry even begins (see John 1:29, 36). As John tells the story of Jesus' Passion and Death, he will once more emphasize that Jesus is the

new Passover Lamb who takes away the sins of the world.

With this background in mind, let us now look carefully at the details in John's Passion narrative, many of which appear only in John. By noticing what is unique to John, we will be able to discern John's message.

As today's reading begins, Jesus is leaving his last meal with his disciples before his Death. In the synoptic gospel accounts, that last meal was the Passover meal. In John, it is not. In John, the Passover falls twenty-four hours later; the

Pilate = PĪ-luht

Pilate initially speaks with great authority.

This is said with great anger.

Pilate wants no part of their plans.

This is the narrator giving background information. Drop your voice.

Again Pilate is in charge and speaks with authority.

Jesus is not threatened. He, not Pilate, is actually in charge.

Pilate is interested.

Said quietly and earnestly.

Said with great interest.

So **Pilate** came out to **them** and said,
  "**What charge** do you **bring** against **this man?**"
They **answered** and said to him,
  "If he were **not** a **criminal,**
  we would not have **handed** him over to **you.**"
At **this,** Pilate **said** to them,
  "Take him **yourselves,** and judge him according to **your law.**"
The **Jews answered** him,
  "We do not have the **right** to **execute anyone,** "
  in order that the **word** of **Jesus** might be **fulfilled**
  that he **said** indicating the **kind** of **death** he would **die.**
So **Pilate** went back into the **praetorium**
  and **summoned Jesus** and said to him,
  "Are **you** the **King** of the **Jews?**"
Jesus answered,
  "Do **you** say this on your **own**
  or have others **told** you about me?"
Pilate answered,
  "**I am not** a **Jew,** am I?
Your **own nation** and the **chief priests** handed **you** over to **me.**
What have you **done?**"
Jesus answered,
  "**My** kingdom does not **belong** to **this** world.
If my kingdom **did** belong to **this** world,
  my attendants would be **fighting**
  to keep me from being **handed over** to the Jews.
But as it **is, my** kingdom is **not here.**"
So **Pilate** said to him,
  "**Then** you **are** a **king?**"
Jesus answered,
  "**You** say I am a **king.**

Passover and the Sabbath fall on the same day. That means that in John's account, Jesus is killed not on the afternoon after the Passover meal, but on the afternoon before the Passover meal, just when the Passover lambs are being slain. John makes this timing of the Passover clear when he explains why those who brought Jesus to the praetorium do not themselves enter it. They want to avoid defilement so that they can eat the Passover meal later that evening. This change in the timing of the Passover is one of the many ways in which

John teaches that Jesus is the Lamb of God. Jesus, the new Passover lamb, is slain on the afternoon before the Passover meal.

Notice that in John there is no agony in the garden. Jesus does not pray to be relieved of his suffering and Death. In fact, when Peter tries to defend Jesus with a sword, Jesus says, "Put your sword into its scabbard. Shall I not drink the cup that the Father gave me?" Far from dreading his Death, Jesus is intent on doing what he has come to do.

As he tells the story of Jesus' arrest, John emphasizes Jesus' divinity in three

ways. First, John tells us that Jesus knows everything that is going to happen to him. Throughout the gospel account, John pictures Jesus as omniscient, as all knowing. Since only God is omniscient, to picture Jesus in this way is to claim that Jesus is God.

In addition, John pictures Jesus identifying himself to the arresting soldiers with the words, "I AM." We might miss the significance of Jesus' words if it were not for the arresting soldiers' remarkable response: when Jesus identifies himself

Say this slowly and with solemnity.

Pause after this profound question.

Emphasize every word. This is a refrain.

The crowd is angry.

This is the narrator's comment.

Barabbas = buh-RAB-uhs

The soldiers are having a good time
making fun of Jesus. They don't know
that their words are true.

Emphasize every word of this refrain.

This is said in a mocking way, not in a
respectful way.

This is said with anger.

For **this** I was **born** and for **this** I came **into** the **world**,
   to **testify** to the **truth**.
Everyone who **belongs** to the **truth listens** to **my** voice."
Pilate said to him, "**What is truth?**"

When he had **said** this,
   he **again** went out to the **Jews** and **said** to them,
   "**I find no guilt** in **him.**
But you have a **custom** that I **release one prisoner**
      to you at **Passover.**
Do you want me to release to you the **King** of the **Jews**?"
They cried out again,
   "Not **this** one but **Barabbas!**"
Now **Barabbas** was a **revolutionary.**

Then **Pilate** took **Jesus** and had him **scourged.**
And the **soldiers** wove a **crown** out of **thorns**
      and **placed** it on his **head,**
   and **clothed** him in a **purple cloak,**
   and they **came** to **him** and said,
   "**Hail, King** of the **Jews!**"
And they **struck** him **repeatedly.**
Once **more Pilate** went out and **said** to them,
   "**Look,** I am bringing him **out** to **you,**
   so that **you** may know that **I find no guilt in him.**"
So **Jesus** came out,
   wearing the **crown** of **thorns** and the **purple cloak.**
And he said to them, "**Behold,** the **man!**"
When the **chief priests** and the **guards** saw him they cried out,
   "**Crucify** him, **crucify** him!"
Pilate said to them,
   "Take him **yourselves** and crucify him.

with these words the arresting soldiers turn away and fall to the ground. What is happening here? Why do they fall to the ground?

These two details, Jesus' self-identification and the soldiers' response, are two more ways in which John is teaching Jesus' divinity. Jesus' statement, "I AM," is an allusion to the name God revealed to Moses at the burning bush. When Moses asks God how he is to answer those who ask what God's name is, God replies: "This is what you shall tell the Israelites: I AM has sent me to you . . .

This is my name forever;/ this is my title for all generations" (Exodus 3:14b, 15b). Throughout John's gospel account, Jesus makes a number of "I am" statements, all of which are allusions to this scene in Exodus and reminders to John's audience that Jesus is God.

As John tells the story, even the arresting soldiers, for just an instant, catch a glimpse of Jesus' divinity and respond appropriately: they fall to the ground. John is not expecting us to understand this detail as historical reporting. The moment passes as though it had never been described. The

soldiers continue to arrest Jesus. This is one of many literary devices that John uses to teach his audience to see two levels of meaning in his story. The story of Jesus' Passion is not the story of a defeated human being; rather, it is the story of a divine person being faithful as he completes the job he has become incarnate to accomplish. In John, Jesus' divinity always shines through.

Unlike the synoptic gospel accounts, John's account includes no Sanhedrin trial. Instead, Jesus appears before two

Again emphasize every word of this refrain.	I find no guilt in him."
	The Jews **answered**,
This is said with anger and outrage.	"We have a **law**, and **according** to that **law** he **ought** to **die**,
	because he made **himself** the **Son** of **God**."
	Now when **Pilate** heard **this** statement,
	he became **even more afraid**,
	and went **back** into the **praetorium** and **said** to Jesus,
Pause here. John's audience knows that Jesus is from God.	"**Where** are you **from**?"
	Jesus did **not answer** him.
	So **Pilate** said to him,
Pilate is both fearful and in disbelief.	"Do you **not speak** to **me**?
	Do you **not know** that I have power to **release** you
	and I have **power** to **crucify** you?"
	Jesus answered him,
Jesus is still calm and unperturbed.	"You would have **no power** over **me**
	if it had **not** been **given** to you from **above**.
	For **this reason** the one who **handed** me **over** to you
	has the **greater sin**."
The narrator continues the story.	**Consequently**, **Pilate** tried to **release** him;
	but the Jews cried out,
The crowd is angry and demanding.	"If you release **him**, you are **not** a Friend of **Caesar**.
	Everyone who makes himself a **king opposes Caesar**."
	When **Pilate** heard **these** words he **brought Jesus** out
	and seated him on the **judge's bench**
	in the place called **Stone Pavement**, in **Hebrew**, **Gabbatha**.
Gabbatha = GAB-uh-thuh	It was **preparation** day for **Passover**, and it was about **noon**.
	And he said to the Jews,
Pilate is mocking, not honoring Jesus.	"**Behold**, your **king**!"
	They cried out,
Again, the crowd is angry and insistent.	"Take him **away**, take him **away**! **Crucify** him!"

high priests: Annas, and his father-in-law, Caiaphas. At this point today's reading mentions a character who appears only in John's account. This person, usually referred to as the "beloved disciple," appears twice in today's reading: helping Peter get in to the high priest's courtyard, and standing at the foot of the cross. This person is never named. Again, to leave a very important person unnamed, as John does with both the beloved disciple and with Jesus' mother, is to employ a literary device that is used to teach the audience

the significance of what is being described. Both the beloved disciple and Jesus' mother become more than individual people in John's account; they become symbols. The beloved disciple becomes a symbol for the priority of love in one's relationship with Jesus; Jesus' mother becomes a symbol for the Church.

   The beloved disciple first appears in John's gospel account at the Last Supper. He appears with Peter in four different stories: at the Last Supper, here in the high priest's courtyard, at the empty tomb, and at Jesus' post-Resurrection appearance.

In every instance, the beloved disciple appears to be closer to Jesus than is Peter. Scripture scholars conclude that through this character, John is teaching the priority of love. Authority, represented by Peter, is necessary and good. However, it is a loving relationship with Jesus Christ that is most important. As John's gospel account ends, Peter will be affirmed in his authority because he loves (John 21:15–17).

   After appearing before the high priests, Jesus is taken to Pilate. It is clear from the beginning that the charges

Pilate said to them,
  "Shall I **crucify** your **king?**"
The chief **priests** answered,
  "We have **no king** but Caesar."
Then he handed him over to **them** to be **crucified**.

So they **took Jesus**, and, **carrying** the **cross himself**,
  he went out to what is called the **Place** of the **Skull**,
    in **Hebrew**, **Golgotha**.
There they **crucified** him, and with him **two others**,
  one on **either side**, with **Jesus** in the **middle**.
Pilate also had an **inscription written** and **put** on the **cross**.
It read,
  "**Jesus** the **Nazorean**, the **King** of the **Jews**."
Now many of the Jews **read** this inscription,
  because the place where **Jesus** was crucified was near the **city**;
  and it was written in **Hebrew**, **Latin**, and **Greek**.
So the **chief priests** of the **Jews** said to **Pilate**,
  "Do not write 'The **King** of the **Jews**,'
  but that he **said**, 'I am the **King** of the **Jews**'."
Pilate answered,
  "What I have **written**, I have **written**."

When the soldiers had **crucified** Jesus,
  they **took** his **clothes** and **divided** them into **four shares**,
  a share for **each soldier**.
They **also** took his **tunic**, but the **tunic** was **seamless**,
  woven in **one piece** from the **top down**.
So they said to one another,
  "Let's **not tear** it, but cast **lots** for it to **see** whose it will **be**,"

Said with irony.

Said with great adamancy.

Drop your voice here.

Read slowly and with sadness.

Golgotha = GAWL-guh-thuh

Read this as a proclamation.

The chief priests are ingratiating.

Pilate is fed up with the chief priests.

The soldiers have no sense of tragedy.
They are going about their business.

---

against Jesus are not clear and that Pilate has no interest in convicting a person in whom he finds no guilt. The charge against Jesus is not specific, just that he is a criminal. The people have brought Jesus to Pilate because they do not have the authority to execute anyone. In a political sense, Pilate has power and Jesus does not. However, as the story unfolds, Jesus becomes, in the minds of the readers, more powerful, and Pilate less powerful.

In answer to Pilate's questions, Jesus does not deny that he is a king. Jesus says, "For this I was born and for this I came into the world, to testify to the truth." In the name of truth Jesus tells Pilate that his kingdom is not of this world. Although Pilate finds no guilt in Jesus, in order to please the crowd, he turns Jesus over to be crucified.

Pilate is not the only one who fails the test of being faithful to the truth. The chief priests who want Jesus crucified are Jews living in an occupied country. They do not truly recognize Caesar as their king. First, God is their king. In addition, based on their understanding of God's covenant promises to David, they are full of messianic hopes. They expect God to intervene on their behalf and re-establish their nation. So, when the chief priests cry out, "We have no king but Caesar," they are not speaking the truth. They are being unfaithful to their deepest messianic hopes.

In John, Jesus carries his cross by himself. Why would a divine person need any help? Pilate has a sign posted that declares Jesus to be King of the Jews in three languages. Jesus is not deserted at the foot of the cross. Mary Magdalene,

<table>
<tr><td>**Drop your voice here.**</td><td>in order that the passage of **Scripture** might be **fulfilled**
   that says:
     *They divided my **garments** among them,
     and for my **vesture** they cast **lots**.*</td></tr>
</table>

Say this with sadness. Then pause.

This is what the **soldiers did.**
Standing by the **cross** of **Jesus** were his **mother**
   and his mother's sister, **Mary** the wife of **Clopas**,
   and **Mary** of **Magdala**.

Clopas = KLOH-puhs
Magdala = MAG-duh-luh

When Jesus saw his **mother** and the **disciple** there whom he **loved**
   he said to his **mother**, "**Woman**, **behold**, your **son**."

Read Jesus' words slowly and clearly.

Then he said to the **disciple**,
   "**Behold**, your **mother**."
And from **that hour** the **disciple** took **her** into **his** home.

Pause here.

After **this**, aware that **everything** was now **finished**,
   in order that the **Scripture** might be **fulfilled**,
   Jesus said, "**I thirst**."
There was a **vessel filled** with **common wine**.

Jesus still speaks with authority.

So they put a **sponge soaked** in **wine** on a **sprig** of **hyssop**
   and **put** it up to his **mouth**.

Emphasize "hyssop."
hyssop = HIS-uhp

When **Jesus** had taken the **wine**, he said,
   "**It is finished**."

Emphasize every word.
Speak slowly and with great solemnity.

And **bowing** his **head**, he **handed over** the **spirit**.

[Here all kneel and pause for a short time.]

Speak more quickly here.

Now since it was **preparation day**,
   in order that the **bodies** might not remain on the **cross**
     on the **sabbath**,
   for the **sabbath day** of that week was a **solemn** one,
   the **Jews** asked **Pilate** that their **legs** be broken
   and that they be **taken down**.

Mary, the wife of Clopas, the beloved disciple, and Jesus' mother are all there.

When Jesus sees his mother and the beloved disciple, he says to his mother: "Woman, behold your son." To the beloved disciple he says, "Behold your mother" Jesus calls his mother "Woman," both here and at Cana, because she is the new Eve, the new mother of all the living in the new spiritual order that Jesus has established. Jesus' mother, the "Woman," stands for the Church, the mother of the disciples of Jesus Christ.

As Jesus approaches death, and right after his Death, John twice more reminds us that Jesus is the new Passover lamb. First, when the soldiers offer Jesus wine to drink, they lift the sponge up on a sprig of hyssop, the same plant that was used to put the blood of the Passover lamb on the lintels of the houses of the Israelites so that the Lord would pass over them. Then, after Jesus dies, the soldiers decide not to break his bones, just as the bones of the Passover lamb were to remain unbroken (Numbers 9:12).

Jesus' last words on the cross also show that Jesus has remained in control and in charge, even as he accepts death on a cross. John tells us that Jesus' last words are, "It is finished." Jesus came to do a job, he has done it, and now it is finished. Jesus freely "hand[s] over the spirit."

Rather than break Jesus' bones, the soldiers pierce his side. "Immediately blood and water flowed out." Once more John is teaching that the risen Christ is present in what we have come to call the

So the **soldiers came** and **broke** the legs of the **first**
and then of the **other** one who was **crucified** with Jesus.
But when they came to **Jesus** and saw that he was **already dead**,

Emphasize this line.

they did **not break his** legs,
but **one** soldier thrust his **lance** into his **side**,

Emphasize this line.
Say this with great conviction.

and **immediately blood** and **water flowed out**.
An **eyewitness** has **testified**, and his **testimony** is **true**;
he **knows** that he is speaking the **truth**,
so that **you also** may **come** to **believe**.
For this happened so that the **Scripture** passage might be **fulfilled**:
*Not a **bone** of it will be **broken**.*
And again **another** passage says:
*They will look upon **him** whom they have **pierced**.*

The narrator's voice concludes the story.
Arimathea = ayr-ih-muh-THEE-uh

After **this**, **Joseph** of **Arimathea**,
secretly a **disciple** of Jesus for **fear** of the **Jews**,
asked **Pilate** if he could **remove** the **body** of Jesus.
And **Pilate permitted** it.
So he **came** and **took** his body.

Nicodemus = nik-uh-DEE-muhs
myrrh = mer
aloes = AL-ohz
This is amazing, a great extravagance.

Nicodemus, the one who had **first** come to him at **night**,
also came bringing a mixture of **myrrh** and **aloes**
weighing about **one hundred pounds**.
They took the **body** of Jesus
and bound it with **burial cloths** along with the **spices**,
according to the **Jewish burial custom**.

Emphasize "garden."

Now in the place where he had been **crucified** there was a **garden**,
and in the **garden** a **new tomb**, in which **no one**
had **yet** been **buried**.
So they **laid Jesus there** because of the **Jewish preparation** day;
for the **tomb** was **close by**.

sacraments: Baptism and Eucharist. The same symbols, water for Baptism and wine for Christ's blood, were used in John's story of the wedding feast at Cana, where Jesus established a new spiritual order and the disciples saw his glory.

John's story of the Passion begins and ends in a garden. Jesus is arrested in a garden, and Jesus is buried with honors given only to kings in a garden. The garden is one of John's many allusions to the Book of Genesis. Remember, the two books

begin with exactly the same words: "In the beginning." Scripture scholars surmise that John emphasizes the garden because in this story the effect of the sin that was committed in the garden in Genesis is reversed. Through his Passion and Death, Jesus has freed the human race from its slavery to sin.

As you proclaim the story of Jesus' Passion, try to enter into the emotions of each character: Jesus is always confident and self assured. In contrast, nearly everyone else is petty or weak in some

way: Peter denies Jesus, Pilate becomes weaker and weaker as he tries to please the crowd, and the chief priests are belligerent and demanding. Through it all, the narrator's voice simply moves the story along, sometimes without emotion, sometimes with deep sadness.

HOLY SATURDAY: EASTER VIGIL

Lectionary #41

READING I   Genesis 1:1—2:2

A reading from the Book of Genesis

Genesis = JEN-uh-sis

In the **beginning**, when **God** created the **heavens** and the **earth**,
    the **earth** was a **formless wasteland**, and **darkness**
        covered the abyss,
    while a **mighty wind swept** over the **waters**.

abyss = uh-BIS

Then God **said**,
    "**Let there be light**," and there **was light**.
God saw how **good** the light **was**.
God then separated the **light** from the **darkness**.
God called the **light** "**day**" and the **darkness** he called "**night**."
Thus **evening** came, and **morning** followed—the **first day**.

Emphasize every one of God's words.
Drop your voice when the narrator speaks.

Pause here.

Then God said,
    "**Let** there be a **dome** in the **middle** of the **waters**,
    to separate **one** body of water from the **other**."
And so it **happened**:
    God made the **dome**,
    and it **separated** the water **above** the dome
        from the water **below** it.
God called the **dome** "**the sky**."
Evening came, and **morning** followed—the **second day**.

Read God's words as a proclamation.

Now the narrator is speaking again.

Pause.

Then God said,
    "**Let** the **water under** the sky be **gathered** into a **single basin**,
    so that the **dry land** may **appear**."

Again God proclaims.

READING I At the Easter Vigil, when we celebrate Christ's Resurrection and our new life in Christ, we recall not only all of salvation history, starting with Abraham, our father in faith (who lived around 1850 BC), but all of creation, all that exists. The Easter Vigil liturgy begins the story of Jesus Christ before creation: "In the beginning . . . ." This is to say that the ramifications of Jesus' Incarnation, Death, and Resurrection affect not just followers of Jesus Christ who lived during or after Jesus' public

ministry. The story of Jesus Christ encompasses all that has been, all that is, and all that will ever be.

To understand more fully what the inspired author of the creation story is teaching us, we must correctly understand the kind of writing we are reading. The story does not purport to teach history or science. To interpret the story as though it were addressing these topics is simply to change the subject and miss the message. We know the author is not teaching history because, by definition, history rests on accounts of events that were witnessed

and about which we have oral or written tradition. That is certainly not true of this story. We know the author is not teaching science because, by definition, science studies material forms and recurring phenomena. A story in which the main character is God is not presenting itself as teaching science. God is not the object of the scientific study.

What kind of writing, then, are we reading? The creation story is an imaginative and symbolic story that probes mysteries that are still, to some extent, beyond

This is now a refrain. Emphasize "happened."

And so it **happened**:
    the water **under** the sky was **gathered** into **its** basin,
    and the **dry land appeared**.
God called the **dry land** "the **earth**,"
    and the **basin** of the **water** he called "**the sea**."

This, too, is now a refrain. Emphasize "good."

God **saw** how **good** it was.

Once more God proclaims.

Then God said,
    "Let the **earth** bring forth **vegetation**:
    every kind of **plant** that bears **seed**
    and **every kind** of **fruit tree** on **earth**
    that bears **fruit** with its **seed** in it."

Emphasize "happened."

And so it **happened**:
    the earth brought forth **every kind** of **plant** that bears **seed**
    and **every kind** of **fruit tree** on **earth**
    that bears **fruit** with its **seed** in it.

Emphasize "good."

God **saw** how **good** it was.

Pause.

Evening came, and **morning** followed—the **third day**.

Say this with majesty.

Then God said:
    "Let there be **lights** in the **dome** of the **sky**,
    to separate **day** from **night**.
Let them **mark** the **fixed times**, the **days** and the **years**,
    and serve as **luminaries** in the **dome** of the **sky**,
    to shed **light** upon the **earth**."

Emphasize "happened." God speaks and things happen.

And so it **happened**:
    God made the **two great lights**,
    the **greater** one to govern the **day**,
    and the **lesser** one to govern the **night**;
    and he made the **stars**.
God set them in the **dome** of the **sky**,
    to shed **light** upon the **earth**,
    to govern the **day** and the **night**,
    and to separate the **light** from the **darkness**.

---

our comprehension. The story responds to such questions as: How did all that exists come into existence? Who is God? Who are we in relationship to God? Who are we in relationship to each other and to our world? If we bring questions like these to the creation story, we will open ourselves to understand what the inspired author intends to teach.

In addition to understanding the kind of writing we are reading, we need to know something about the time of the original author and his audience. When did the author live? What were the needs of

his audience? What were their shared presumptions?

We can tell from reading the story that the author lived in a society that was organized around a work week: six days of labor and a Sabbath day. How? Because the author uses the work week to structure his story. By using this literary device, the author is teaching that creation is God's work. We can also tell from the story that the author lived at a time when the world was thought to be flat. This is apparent from his description of the second day

when the water above the dome is separated from the water beneath the dome. At the time, everyone presumed that the earth was flat and that it had a dish, or a dome, over it.

Although the story is not scientific, it is systematically ordered. On the first three days the author pictures God separating one thing from another: light from darkness, the water above the dome from the water beneath the dome, and the dry land beneath the dome from the sea. The next three days are spent populating that which has been separated: the sun and moon are

Emphasize "good."

Pause after each day.

Emphasize "abundance."

Emphasize "happened."

Continue to emphasize the words that stress abundance.

winged = wingd; WING-uhd

Continue to emphasize "good." This refrain is central to the author's message.

Again, the author is describing abundance.

Emphasize "all kinds" all three times.

This line is all important. Read slowly and solemnly.

Again this is all important. Read these three lines slowly.

God **saw** how **good** it was.

Evening came, and **morning** followed—the **fourth day**.

Then God said,
"Let the **water teem** with an **abundance** of **living creatures**,
and on the **earth** let **birds fly beneath** the **dome** of the **sky**."
And so it **happened**:
God created the **great sea monsters**
and **all kinds** of **swimming creatures** with which
the **water teems**,
and **all kinds** of **winged birds**.
God **saw** how **good** it was, and God **blessed** them, saying,
"Be **fertile**, **multiply**, and **fill** the **water** of the **seas**;
and let the **birds multiply** on the **earth**."
Evening came, and **morning** followed—the **fifth day**.

Then God said,
"Let the **earth bring forth all kinds** of **living creatures**:
cattle, **creeping** things, and **wild animals** of **all kinds**."
And so it **happened**:
God made **all kinds** of **wild animals**, **all kinds** of **cattle**,
and **all kinds** of **creeping** things of the **earth**.
God **saw** how **good** it was.

Then God said:
"Let us make **man** in our **image**, after our **likeness**.
Let them have **dominion** over the **fish** of the **sea**,
the **birds** of the **air**, and the **cattle**,
and over **all** the **wild animals**
and **all** the **creatures** that **crawl** on the **ground**."
God created **man** in **his image**;
in the **image** of **God** he **created** him;
male and **female** he **created** them.

put in the sky, fish and birds are put in their respective places, animals and human beings are put on the dry land. After six days, God's work is completed.

Scripture scholars surmise that this creation story was written about 450 BC, after the Babylonian exile, to teach some truths central to the Israelites, but not believed by the Babylonians. What are these core truths, and how are they being taught? One core truth is that there is one God who created all that exists. The Babylonians believed in many gods. Among these gods were the sun and the

moon. The inspired author of the creation story teaches that the sun and the moon are material things created by God. They measure the days, the nights, and the seasons, but they are not gods. They are the creation of the one God.

Another core truth is that matter is good. The Babylonians believed that spirit was good, but not matter. Notice how this story stresses the goodness of matter through a refrain. On all but the second day, after God creates, God sees how good creation is. On the sixth day, when God

looks at everything he has made, he finds it "very good."

Among what is "very good" are human beings. In the Babylonian creation story, human beings are created out of the corpse of a rebellious and defeated god. In this creation story, male and female human beings are created in the image of a loving God who wants his creatures to flourish.

Human beings, male and female, are to have dominion over creation. For males and females, made in God's image, to have "dominion" over the rest of creation does not mean that they have permission to

<table><tr><td>

Now increase your tempo.

</td><td>

God **blessed** them, saying:
  "Be **fertile** and **multiply**;
  fill the earth and **subdue** it.
Have **dominion** over the **fish** of the **sea**, the **birds** of the **air**,
  and **all** the **living things** that **move** on the **earth**."
God **also** said:

</td></tr>
<tr><td>

Emphasize "every" and "all." "All" is repeated five times.

</td><td>

  "**See**, I give you **every seed-bearing plant all over** the **earth**
  and **every tree** that has seed-bearing **fruit** on it to be **your food**;
  and to **all** the animals of the land, **all** the birds of the air,
  and **all** the living creatures that **crawl** on the ground,
  I give **all** the green plants for food."
And so it **happened**.
God **looked** at **everything** he had made, and he **found** it
    very good.

</td></tr>
<tr><td>

Emphasize "very good." The refrain has been altered to emphasize just how good all of creation is.

</td><td>

Evening came, and **morning** followed—the **sixth day**.

Thus the **heavens** and the **earth** and **all** their **array**
    were **completed**.
Since on the **seventh** day God was **finished**

</td></tr>
<tr><td>

Emphasize "work." Creation is God's work.

</td><td>

  with the **work** he had been **doing**,
  he **rested** on the **seventh** day from **all** the **work**
    he had **undertaken**.

[Shorter: Genesis 1:1, 26–31a]

</td></tr>
</table>

READING II   Genesis 22:1–18

<table><tr><td>

Genesis = JEN-uh-sis
Emphasize this first line. This is the narrator's interpretation of the story that follows.
Abraham is eager to respond to the LORD.
Abraham = AY-bruh-ham

</td><td>

A reading from the Book of Genesis

God put **Abraham** to the **test**.
He called to him, "**Abraham**!"
"**Here I am**," he replied.

</td></tr>
</table>

exploit or to use the rest of creation for selfish purposes. The men and women who are made in God's image will have dominion as God does, using their authority to love and care for each other and for all of creation.

While in exile in Babylon, the Israelites may well have gotten out of the practice of observing the Sabbath. After all, the Babylonians did not structure time into a six-day workweek and a Sabbath. However, on their return to the holy land, they were encouraged once more to observe the

Sabbath. The story reinforces this teaching by picturing even God resting on the seventh day.

As you proclaim the story of creation, emphasize the goodness of creation, constantly taught by the author through the refrain. Emphasize, too, that human beings, male and female, are created in God's image. This truth is at the core of our many social justice teachings. To the extent that we live as creatures made in God's own image, we are indeed very good.

READING II When we move from a story about creation to a story about the patriarch, Abraham, we move from an imaginative and symbolic story that has its roots in a universal experience—we all exist—to an imaginative and symbolic story that has its roots in historical events. Abraham lived within the bounds of history, around 1850 BC, in the Middle East. Even though the stories about Abraham are tied to history, the stories have little in common with what we call historical writing. These stories are legends, passed down from generation to generation by

Say God's words softly. God knows that this is terrible news for Abraham.

Isaac = Ī-zik

Moriah = moh-RĪ-uh

Now the narrator is speaking. This is sad and mysterious.

Then God said:
"Take your **son Isaac**, your **only one**, whom you **love**,
and go to the **land** of **Moriah**.
There you shall **offer** him **up** as a **holocaust**
on a **height** that I will **point out** to you."
Early the next morning **Abraham saddled** his **donkey**,
took with him his **son Isaac** and **two** of his **servants** as **well**,
and **with** the **wood** that he had **cut** for the **holocaust**,
set out for the **place** of which **God** had **told** him.

On the **third day Abraham** got **sight** of the place from **afar**.
Then he said to his **servants**:

Abraham is not lying. He is walking in faith and speaking with calm assurance.

"**Both** of you **stay here** with the **donkey**,
while the **boy** and **I** go on over **yonder**.
We will **worship** and then **come back** to you."

The narrator continues the story.

Emphasize "son Isaac's shoulders." This foreshadows Jesus.

Thereupon Abraham took the **wood** for the **holocaust**
and **laid** it on his **son Isaac's shoulders**,
while **he himself** carried the **fire** and the **knife**.
As the two walked on **together**, **Isaac** spoke
to his **father Abraham**:
"**Father!**" Isaac said.
"**Yes, son,**" he replied.

Isaac is excited and innocent. He has no sense of tragedy.

Isaac continued, "**Here** are the **fire** and the **wood**,
but **where** is the **sheep** for the **holocaust**?"
"**Son**," Abraham answered,

Abraham says this with great faith.

"**God himself** will **provide** the **sheep** for the **holocaust**."
Then the **two continued** going **forward**.

When they came to the **place** of which **God** had **told** him,
Abraham built an **altar** there and arranged the **wood** on it.

The narrator continues to build dread and suspense in the listeners.

Next he **tied up** his **son Isaac**,
and **put** him on **top** of the **wood** on the **altar**.

---

oral tradition, with many details added to make the story interesting and applicable to new generations.

At its core, the story was originally about Abraham coming to the realization that his God was a loving God who did not desire child sacrifice. Child sacrifice was widely practiced in Abraham's Canaanite culture. Just as the first-born males of animals were offered to God, so were the first-born males of human beings. This practice was finally outlawed by the Israelites around 1250 BC (see Exodus 13:13–14).

First-born sons were to be redeemed, not sacrificed.

Why was Abraham able to grow beyond the expectations of his culture, to perceive that God would not want child sacrifice? Abraham had previously had a profound personal experience of God's presence and God's love (see Genesis 12:1–8; 15:1–21). God had entered into a covenant relationship with Abraham, promising Abraham protection, land, and descendants. Abraham was to have faith in God. It was through Isaac that God's promises to Abraham were being fulfilled.

Therefore, Abraham had faith that God would not want Isaac sacrificed as a first-born male.

In today's Second Reading, we can see how the storyteller emphasizes Abraham's faith in God's fidelity to his promises as well as Abraham's readiness to respond to God. When God calls Abraham, Abraham always responds, "Here I am." Abraham is ready and willing. The poignancy of Abraham's dilemma is emphasized with the words, "Take your son, Isaac, your only one, whom you love."

This is said with urgency.

Abraham is calm. These are the same words he used in response to God's call. The messenger speaks with authority.

Then he **reached** out and **took** the **knife** to **slaughter** his **son**.
But the LORD's **messenger called** to him from **heaven**,
    "**Abraham, Abraham!**"
"**Here I am**," he answered.
"**Do not** lay your **hand** on the **boy**," said the messenger.
"**Do not** do the **least thing** to him.
I **know now** how **devoted you** are to **God**,
    since you **did not withhold** from **me** your **own beloved son**."

Now the narrator is speaking. Lower your volume.

As **Abraham** looked **about**,
    he spied a **ram caught** by its **horns** in the **thicket**.
So he **went** and **took** the **ram**
    and **offered it** up as a **holocaust** in **place** of his **son**.

Yahweh-yireh = YAH-way-YEER-ay

Abraham **named** the site **Yahweh-yireh**;
    hence people **now** say, "On the **mountain** the LORD will **see**."

Again the LORD's **messenger** called to **Abraham** from **heaven**
    and said:

Again, the messenger speaks with great authority.
abundantly = uh-BUHN-d*nt-ly

Fill your voice with joy. This is great good news.

"**I swear** by **myself**, **declares** the LORD,
that because you **acted** as you **did**
in **not withholding** from **me** your **beloved son**,
I will **bless** you **abundantly**
and make **your descendants** as **countless**
as the **stars** of the **sky** and the **sands** of the **seashore**;
your descendants shall take **possession**
of the **gates** of their **enemies**,
and in **your descendants all** the **nations** of the **earth**
    shall find **blessing**—

Say this with solemnity and awe. This is key to God's covenant with his people.

all this because **you obeyed my command**."

[Shorter: Genesis 22:1–2, 9a, 10–13, 15–18]

After completing the trip, Abraham tells the servants to stay while he and Isaac go elsewhere. Abraham says, "We will worship and then come back to you." At first the reader assumes that Abraham is lying, that he is hiding his mission from the servants, and that only Abraham will return to them. The same seems to be the case when Isaac asks, "where is the sheep for the holocaust?" Abraham does not tell Isaac that he is the sacrifice; rather, he says, "God himself will provide the sheep for the holocaust." What

appears to the reader to be deceitful turns out to be the absolute truth. Abraham is walking in faith.

Abraham's faith is well placed. God does provide an animal to be sacrificed, a ram. Isaac is spared. Then God renews his covenant promises: Abraham's descendants will be "as countless as the stars." In Abraham's "descendants all the nations of the earth shall find blessing." Why? Because Abraham obeyed God. Abraham's obedience was rooted in faith.

While the story about the sacrifice of Isaac was originally about Abraham's

growing beyond his culture's expectation of child sacrifice, this does not seem to be the primary lesson in the story's present form. As the story begins, the author says, "God put Abraham to the test." After child sacrifice was no longer an issue, the story continued to be told with a new emphasis. It interprets Abraham's suffering as he sought to understand and do God's will as a test—a test that Abraham passed. Abraham put his faith in God's love and acted in accordance with God's will as he understood it. So must we.

Exodus - EK-suh-duhs

God is empowering Moses, encouraging him to be a leader and act with authority.
Israelites = IZ-ree-uh-līts; IZ-ray-uh-līts

God is assuring Moses that he need not fear the Egyptians.
Egyptians = ee-JIP-shunhz

Say, "I am the Lord," slowly and with authority.

Now the narrator is speaking. At first we are given background information.

Israel = IZ-ree-uhl; IZ-ray-uhl
Say this in a lowered tone.

At this point the story becomes marvelous. Raise your volume and speak with awe.
Moses = MOH-ziz; MOH-zis

READING III   Exodus 14:15—15:1

A reading from the Book of Exodus

The LORD said to **Moses**, "**Why** are you **crying out** to **me**?
Tell the **Israelites** to **go forward**.
And **you**, lift up your **staff** and, with **hand outstretched**
    over the **sea**,
  split the **sea** in **two**,
  that the **Israelites** may **pass through it** on **dry land**.
But I will make the **Egyptians** so **obstinate**
  that they will go in **after** them.
Then I will receive **glory** through **Pharaoh** and **all** his **army**,
  his **chariots** and **charioteers**.
The **Egyptians** shall **know** that **I am** the LORD,
  when I receive **glory** through **Pharaoh**
  and his **chariots** and **charioteers**."

The **angel** of **God**, who had been **leading Israel's camp**,
  now moved and went **around behind** them.
The **column** of **cloud also**, **leaving** the **front**,
  took up its place **behind** them,
  so that it **came between** the **camp** of the **Egyptians**
  and that of **Israel**.
But the **cloud** now became **dark**, and thus the **night passed**
  without the **rival camps** coming **any closer together**
    all night long.
Then **Moses stretched out** his **hand** over the **sea**,
  and the LORD **swept** the **sea**
  with a **strong east wind throughout** the **night**
  and so **turned** it into **dry land**.

As you proclaim the reading, try to help your listeners understand the poignancy of this story and how Abraham was always present and faithful to God even under the most difficult of circumstances. It is Abraham's faith and his trust in God's love that we are to emulate.

READING III   The next reading in the Easter Vigil sweep of salvation history is the story of the exodus, of the Israelites being freed from slavery in Egypt so that they can return to the land

that God had promised Abraham. The Book of Exodus comes right after the Book of Genesis in the Bible, but about six hundred years separate the settings of the two books: Abraham lived about 1850 BC. The exodus occurred about 1250 BC. Abraham's descendants had gone to Egypt because of a famine in the holy land. Once there, they became slaves and were not able to escape until God intervened on their behalf.

As always, to understand the revelation in this story we must consider the literary form and the social setting of the

storyteller and his audience. The literary form is a legend, that is, an imaginative and symbolic story with an historical core. At the core of the story is an event through which the Israelites experienced God's power and presence. The Israelites escaped Egypt. They did not save themselves; God saved them: "Thus the Lord saved Israel on that day."

As was true with the Abraham story, our present account of this marvelous event is layered: several accounts by different storytellers have been combined into our finished product. For instance, one

Read slowly and victoriously.

When the **water** was thus **divided**,
    the **Israelites marched** into the **midst** of the **sea** on **dry land**,
    with the **water** like a **wall** to their **right** and to their **left**.

Now increase your speed.
Pharaoh's = FAYR-ohs

The **Egyptians followed** in **pursuit**;
    all Pharaoh's **horses** and **chariots** and **charioteers**
        went **after** them
    right into the **midst** of the **sea**.

Now drop both your volume and your speed.

In the **night watch** just before **dawn**
    the LORD **cast** through the **column** of the **fiery** cloud
    upon the **Egyptian** force a **glance** that **threw** it into a **panic**;
    and he so **clogged** their **chariot wheels**
    that they could **hardly drive**.

Emphasize "Israel" and "them."

With **that** the Egyptians **sounded** the **retreat** before **Israel**,
    because the LORD was **fighting** for **them against** the **Egyptians**.

God is not only instructing but encouraging Moses.

Then the LORD told **Moses**, "**Stretch out** your **hand over** the **sea**,
    that the **water** may **flow back** upon the **Egyptians**,
    upon their **chariots** and their **charioteers**."

The narrator is speaking. Again, this is marvelous.

So **Moses stretched out** his **hand** over the **sea**,
    and at **dawn** the **sea flowed back** to its **normal depth**.

Increase your speed here.

The **Egyptians** were **fleeing head on** toward the **sea**,
    when the LORD **hurled** them **into** its **midst**.

This is good news from Israel's point of view.

As the **water flowed back**,
    it **covered** the **chariots** and the **charioteers**
        of **Pharaoh's whole army**
    which had followed the **Israelites** into the **sea**.
Not a **single one** of them **escaped**.
But the **Israelites** had marched on **dry land**
    through the **midst** of the **sea**,
    with the **water** like a **wall** to their **right** and to their **left**.

Again a triumphant tone is appropriate.

Thus the LORD **saved** Israel on **that day**
    from the **power** of the **Egyptians**.

---

account says that God caused the waters to part with "a strong east wind" while the other account describes the waters parting because Moses stretched out his hand over the sea. The two accounts weave together nicely because both attribute the Israelites' escape to God's intervention.

Since the authors are attributing events to their ultimate cause, God, they also picture God as being the cause for the Egyptians' actions. God is pictured as making the Egyptians obstinate, and of clogging the Egyptians' chariot wheels. As we read the story, we find this strange because we know that people have free will and that God also loves the Egyptians. At the time this story was written, the Israelites had a keen awareness that God loved them, but they did not yet realize that God also loved their enemies. They do not come to this realization until after the Babylonian exile (587–537 BC).

The story of the exodus became central to the Israelites' self-identity. The marvelous event of their escape was interpreted as an example of God's faithfulness to his promises. As you proclaim the reading, try to give your listeners a sense of awe that such a marvelous event would occur. The authors want their audience to know that God intervened in human history to save his people. The Church wants us to know that God can and does do the same thing today.

READING IV We move now from the experience of the exodus, an exultant time, to the experience of the exile, a shattering time. Again, hundreds of years have passed between the setting of this reading and the setting of the previous

Lower your volume and decrease your speed. This is the narrator drawing a lesson from the marvelous events.

This is said with great gratitude and joy.

When **Israel** saw the **Egyptians** lying **dead** on the **seashore**
and **beheld** the **great power** that the LORD
had **shown against** the Egyptians,
they **feared** the LORD and **believed** in **him**
and in his **servant Moses.**

Then **Moses** and the **Israelites** sang **this song** to the LORD:
I will **sing** to the LORD, for he is **gloriously triumphant;**
horse and **chariot** he has **cast** into the **sea.**

READING IV   Isaiah 54:5–14

Isaiah = ī-ZA-uh

Isaiah's tone is one of comfort and hope.
Emphasize "Lord of hosts."
Israel = IZ-ree-uhl; IZ-ray-uhl

Emphasize "God of all the earth."
This is wonderful news.

Now, God is speaking. Read the "brief moment" line quickly, the "great tenderness" line slowly.
Read quickly.

Read slowly.

A reading from the Book of the Prophet Isaiah

The **One** who has **become** your **husband** is your **Maker;**
his **name** is the LORD of **hosts;**
your **redeemer** is the **Holy One** of **Israel,**
called **God** of **all** the **earth.**
The LORD calls you **back,**
like a **wife forsaken** and **grieved** in **spirit,**
a wife **married** in **youth** and **then cast off,**
says **your God.**
For a **brief moment** I **abandoned** you,
but with **great tenderness** I will **take** you **back.**
In an **outburst** of **wrath,** for a **moment**
I **hid** my **face** from you;
but with **enduring love** I take **pity** on you,
says the LORD, your **redeemer.**

---

reading, from 1250 BC to 587–537 BC. A great deal has happened in the meantime.

After the exodus and the wandering in the desert, the Israelites returned to the holy land. By 1000 BC the land was securely theirs, the twelve tribes were united, and they had a period of peace under the famous King David. During David's reign, the people began to understand the presence of their king, their kingdom, and later their temple, as signs of their covenant relationship with God. Because of Nathan's prophecy to David (see 2 Samuel

7:1–17), the people believed that their king and their nation would be secure forever.

Events did not confirm this expectation. In 922 BC, the kingdom divided. In 721 BC, the northern kingdom was conquered by the Assyrians. In 587 BC, the southern kingdom was conquered by the Babylonians. All of the upper class citizens were forced to go into exile in Babylon. It is to these exiles, suffering and disillusioned, that the prophet known as Second Isaiah prophesied. (The Book of Isaiah contains the work

of three different prophets, referred to as First, Second, and Third Isaiah.)

As the reading begins, it is the prophet's voice that we hear, speaking to personified Jerusalem. Second Isaiah reminds Jerusalem that her redeemer is not only "the Holy One of Israel," but also, "God of all the earth." Then Second Isaiah has God speak, acknowledging the terrible pain and disillusionment that events have caused ("For a brief moment I abandoned you,") but insisting that God's covenant love for his people still exists: "but with enduring love I take pity on you."

God is explaining his reasons for no longer being angry.
Noah = NOH-uh
deluge = DEL-ooj; DEL-oozh

This is a solemn promise.

This is what the exiles need to hear.

This is extravagant love, indeed.
carnelians = kahr-NEEL-yuhnz

sapphires = SAF-īrz

carbuncles = KAHR-bung-k*lz

This is wonderful news.

Speak with great confidence. This is a promise.

This is for **me** like the **days** of **Noah**,
   when I swore that the **waters** of **Noah**
   should **never again deluge** the **earth**;
so I have **sworn not** to be **angry** with you,
   or to **rebuke** you.
Though the **mountains** leave their **place**
   and the **hills** be **shaken**,
my love shall **never leave you**
   nor **my covenant** of peace be **shaken**,
   says the LORD, who has **mercy** on **you**.
O **afflicted one**, **storm-battered** and **unconsoled**,
   I lay your **pavements** in **carnelians**,
   and your **foundations** in **sapphires**;
I will make your **battlements** of **rubies**,
   your **gates** of **carbuncles**,
   and **all** your **walls** of **precious stones**.
All your **children** shall be **taught** by the LORD,
   and **great** shall be the **peace** of your **children**.
In **justice** shall you be **established**,
   far from the **fear** of **oppression**,
   where **destruction cannot** come **near you**.

READING V Isaiah 55:1–11

Isaiah = i-ZAY-uh

God is calling God's people to return.
Say "come" with longing. It is a refrain.

God is promising them a plentiful life after their return.

A reading from the Book of the Prophet Isaiah

Thus says the LORD:
All you who are **thirsty**,
   come to the **water**!
You who have **no money**,
   come, receive **grain** and **eat**;

God then recalls the time of Noah when God made a promise never again to flood the whole earth. Now God is making another promise. God says, "my love shall never leave you nor my covenant of peace be shaken."

God then describes Jerusalem renewed. Her streets and walls will all be made from precious stones. Jerusalem's children will return, where they will be taught by God. Then Jerusalem will no longer have anything to fear: "destruction cannot come near [her]."

As you proclaim Second Isaiah's words of hope, give greatest emphasis to God's promises of steadfast love. These are the words that the exiles most needed to hear. We, too, need to hear them. God's love will never depart from us, either.

READING V In the Fifth Reading, we are again proclaiming words of hope from Second Isaiah that were originally addressed to the exiles in Babylon. The exiles are hungering and thirsting for their old covenant relationship

with God. After all, God had promised Abraham that his descendants would inherit the land in which the exiles used to live. God had promised David that David's line and David's kingdom would be secure forever. To the exiles it appeared that God had broken those promises. They no longer lived on the land, and they no longer had a kingdom—or perhaps the exiles had simply misunderstood covenant love. Perhaps God was not their God, and they were not God's people after all.

This is an ironic question. Why behave so foolishly?

God is pleading, not just inviting.

This line is all important. This is what the exiles need to hear.

God is teaching the exiles that their present suffering has not been without purpose. They, like David, are God's chosen witnesses.

Israel = IZ-ree-uhl; IZ-ray-uhl

Now the prophet is exhorting the people. The tone is one of invitation and encouragement, not blame.

Now the Lord is once more speaking.

The rest of the reading is all one sentence. God is comparing the fruitfulness of rain to the fruitfulness of God's word.

come, without **paying** and without **cost**,
> **drink wine** and **milk!**

Why spend your **money** for what is not **bread**,
> your **wages** for what **fails** to **satisfy?**

Heed me, and you shall **eat well**,
> you shall **delight** in **rich fare.**

Come to me **heedfully**,
> **listen**, that you may have **life.**

I will **renew** with **you** the **everlasting covenant**,
> the benefits assured to **David.**

As I made him a **witness** to the **peoples**,
> a **leader** and **commander** of **nations**,

so shall **you summon** a **nation** you **knew not**,
> and **nations** that **knew you not** shall **run** to you,

because of the LORD, your **God**,
> the **Holy One** of Israel, who has **glorified you.**

Seek the LORD while he may be **found**,
> **call him** while he is **near.**

Let the **scoundrel forsake** his **way**,
> and the **wicked man** his **thoughts**;

let him **turn** to the LORD for **mercy**;
> to our **God**, who is **generous** in **forgiving.**

For **my thoughts** are not **your** thoughts,
> nor are **your** ways **my** ways, says the LORD.

As **high** as the **heavens** are **above** the **earth**,
> so **high** are **my ways** above **your ways**
> and **my thoughts** above **your thoughts.**

For **just** as from the **heavens**
> the **rain** and **snow** come **down**

As the reading begins, God is calling his people back. All who are thirsty are to come to the water. Even those without money are to come and receive food. The people need only "heed" God, and all their needs will be met. That the people must listen to God is repeated: "Come to me heedfully, listen, that you may have life." Listening to God will lead to an abundant banquet: "you shall delight in rich fare." A sumptuous banquet is often a biblical symbol for being in right relationship with God.

What constitutes this abundant life to which God invites his people? An abundant life is one lived in the secure knowledge of God's covenant love. God says, "I will renew with you the everlasting covenant." Just as God made promises to David, and David was a witness of God to other nations, so shall the Israelites become a witness of God to other nations: "nations that knew you not shall run to you." In other words, there is a purpose in the exiles' present suffering. Their suffering is not in vain, and God has not stopped loving and caring for them. Instead, God is using

them to bring other nations to a knowledge of God.

To experience this right relationship with God, the Israelites must repent: "Let the scoundrel forsake his way, and the wicked man his thoughts." They must turn to God, who is "generous and forgiving."

The passage ends with a beautiful poem in which God compares the fruitfulness of his word to the fruitfulness of rain and snow. The rain and snow give "seed to the one who sows and bread to the one who eats." In the same way, God's

and do **not return** there
　　till they have **watered** the **earth**,
　　making it **fertile** and **fruitful**,
giving **seed** to the **one** who **sows**
　　and **bread** to the **one** who **eats**,
so shall **my word be**
　　that **goes forth** from **my mouth**;
my word shall **not return** to me **void**,
　　but shall **do my will**,
　　achieving the **end** for which I **sent** it.

This is the second part of the comparison.

Increase your volume and speak slowly as you proclaim this conclusion.

READING VI　Baruch 3:9–15, 32—4:4

A reading from the Book of the Prophet Baruch

Hear, O **Israel**, the **commandments** of **life**:
　　listen, and **know prudence**!
How **is** it, **Israel**,
　　that **you** are in the **land** of your **foes**,
　　grown **old** in a **foreign land**,
defiled with the **dead**,
　　accounted with those **destined** for the **netherworld**?
You have **forsaken** the **fountain** of **wisdom**!
　　Had you **walked** in the **way** of **God**,
　　you would have **dwelt** in **enduring peace**.
Learn where **prudence** is,
　　where **strength**, where **understanding**;
that you may **know also**
　　where are **length** of **days**, and **life**,
　　where **light** of the **eyes**, and **peace**.

Baruch = buh-ROOK

Baruch is commanding attention; proclaim these first two lines with authority.

Now drop your voice. Baruch is asking the exiles a question.
Israel = IZ-ree-uhl; IZ-ray-uhl

Pause after the question.
Raise your voice. This is an accusation.
This is one of the author's central points.

This is no longer an accusation but an appeal.

Pause after this line.

Word will achieve "the end for which [God] sent it."

As in the previous reading from Second Isaiah, the parts of the reading that deserve the most emphasis are the parts that give hope and that express God's love, God's commitment, and God's purpose. These beautiful words fill our hearts with joyful expectation, just as they did the hearts of the exiles to whom they were originally proclaimed.

READING VI This reading is attributed to Baruch, Jeremiah's scribe, who lived during the Babylonian exile. However, scripture scholars deduce that this attribution is an example of a commonly used literary device called "pseudonymity." The actual author lived some three hundred years after the exile, in the second or first century BC, during the time of the diaspora. ("Diaspora" refers to the dispersion of people from their homeland.) Since the Babylonian exile, the Jews had been spread throughout the Middle East. In the fourth century, the Greeks conquered that part of the world.

The unknown author of Baruch was writing to the Jews of the diaspora, comparing their situation to that of the exiles in Babylon. He is urging diaspora Jews not to succumb to the temptation of embracing the values of the Greek culture rather than living in fidelity to the Torah, the Jewish Law, which is a source of wisdom.

First, the author asks why the people have found themselves in exile: "How is it, Israel, that you are in the land of your

Baruch poses a second question.	Who has **found** the **place** of **wisdom**, who has **entered** into **her treasuries**?

Say this with gentle conviction.	The **One** who **knows all things** knows **her**;
	  he has **probed** her by his **knowledge**—
	the One who **established** the **earth** for **all time**,
	  and **filled** it with **four-footed beasts**;

Fill your voice with awe.	he who **dismisses** the **light**, and it **departs**,
	  calls it, and it **obeys** him **trembling**;
	before whom the **stars** at their **posts**
	  shine and **rejoice**;

The stars are always ready to serve.	when he **calls** them, they **answer**, "**Here we are!**" **shining** with **joy** for their **Maker**.

Emphasize every word of this line.	**Such is our God**;
	  no other is to be **compared** to him:
	He has **traced** out the **whole way** of **understanding**,
	  and has **given** her to **Jacob**, his **servant**,

The "her" is personified Wisdom.	to **Israel**, his **beloved son**.

The "she" is also personified Wisdom.	**Since then** she has **appeared** on **earth**,
	  and **moved** among **people**.
	She is the **book** of the **precepts** of **God**,
	  the **law** that **endures forever**;
	all who **cling** to **her** will **live**,
	  but those will **die** who **forsake** her.

Now, Baruch is pleading with the people. This, too, is central to the author's purpose.	**Turn**, O **Jacob**, and **receive** her:
	  walk by her **light** toward **splendor**.
	Give **not** your **glory** to **another**,
	  your **privileges** to an **alien race**.

Baruch is reminding the Israelites that they are blessed because God has chosen to reveal himself to them. This is said with gratitude.	**Blessed** are **we**, O **Israel**; for what **pleases God** is **known** to **us**!

foes?" He then answers his own question. It is because Israel has not been faithful: "You have forsaken the fountain of wisdom!" Had the Israelites remained faithful, instead of being exiled they would have lived in "enduring peace."

The author then recites a poem in praise of wisdom. God, who created the whole world, knows Wisdom and has given her to the Israelites, "has given her to Jacob, his servant, to Israel, his beloved son." Wisdom is "the book of the precepts

of God, the law that endures forever." Those who remain faithful to the Law will live. Those who do not will die.

The author then exhorts his contemporaries to remain faithful to the Law, to "walk by her light toward splendor." They are not to give their "privileges to an alien race," that is, they are not to embrace the values of Greek civilization rather than those of the Torah. The author ends with a reminder that Israel has been greatly blessed to have received God's Law, God's wisdom: "Blessed are we, O Israel; for what pleases God is known to us!"

The tone in this reading changes from line to line. In the first line the author is demanding to be heard. The tone then changes to one of thoughtfulness. Next, the tone is accusing. The song to Wisdom should be proclaimed with awe. The final call to repentance is a plea, and the last two lines a blessing. An effective proclamation of this reading will include these many tones.

READING VII Ezekiel 36:16–17a, 18–28

A reading from the Book of the Prophet Ezekiel

The **word** of the LORD **came** to me, **saying:**
   Son of **man**, when the **house** of Israel **lived** in **their** land,
      they **defiled** it by their **conduct** and **deeds.**
Therefore I **poured** out my **fury upon** them
      because of the **blood** that **they poured** out on the **ground,**
      and because they **defiled** it with **idols.**
I **scattered** them among the **nations,**
      dispersing them over **foreign lands;**
      according to their **conduct** and **deeds** I **judged** them.
But when they **came** among the **nations wherever** they **came,**
      they **served** to **profane my holy name,**
      because it was **said** of **them:** "**These** are the **people** of the LORD,
      yet they had to **leave** their **land.**"
So I have **relented** because of **my holy name**
      which the **house** of Israel **profaned**
      among the **nations** where they **came.**
Therefore say to the **house** of Israel: **Thus says** the Lord GOD:
      Not for **your sakes** do I **act, house** of Israel,
      but for the **sake** of **my holy name,**
      which you **profaned** among the **nations** to which you **came.**
I will **prove** the **holiness** of **my great name,**
         profaned among the **nations,**
      in whose **midst** you have **profaned** it.
Thus the **nations shall know** that **I am** the LORD,
         says the **Lord GOD,**
      when in **their sight** I **prove** my **holiness** through **you.**

READING VII Today's prophecy from Ezekiel was originally addressed to the exiles in Babylon. Once more, the question of why the people are in exile is raised. Since God promised the Israelites land and a kingdom, and they now have neither, does that mean that God has been unfaithful? No. God explains that the Israelites lost the land because they defiled it with idols. The Israelites were judged according to their deeds.

However, God is now going to save the Israelites, not because they deserve to be saved, but because the Israelites are profaning God's name in the countries in which they are living. He wants other nations to recognize his holiness. When God saves the Israelites, the other nations will take note. God says: "Thus the nations shall know that I am the Lord . . . when in their sight I prove my holiness."

For this purpose, God will gather the Israelites back to the holy land. God will "sprinkle clean water upon [them] to cleanse [them] from all [their] impurities." The Israelites will receive a new heart and a new spirit so that they live holy lives. The reading ends with a promise that the exiles long to hear. God says: "You shall live in the land I gave your fathers; you shall be my people, and I will be your God."

Since this reading is being proclaimed at the Easter Vigil, where the elect will receive Baptism, give special emphasis to God's promise to sprinkle water on the people and to cleanse them from their impurities. For the elect, this promise is being fulfilled during this Easter Vigil. They will receive God's Spirit within them. They will know that they are God's people, and God will be their God.

The tone changes here to graciousness and mercy.

Emphasize these lines since the Church will be celebrating Baptism and Confirmation at the Vigil.

This is the good news that the exiles long to hear.

For I will **take you away** from among the **nations**,
> **gather you from all** the **foreign lands**,
> and **bring** you **back** to **your own land**.
I will **sprinkle clean water upon** you
> to **cleanse** you from **all** your **impurities**,
> and from **all** your **idols** I will **cleanse** you.
I will give you a **new heart** and place a **new spirit within** you,
> taking from your **bodies** your **stony hearts**
> and **giving** you **natural hearts**.
I will **put my spirit within you** and make **you live** by **my statutes**,
> **careful** to **observe my decrees**.
You shall **live** in the **land** I **gave** your **fathers**;
> **you** shall be **my people**, and I will be **your God**.

EPISTLE   Romans 6:3–11

A reading from the Letter of Saint Paul to the Romans

The overall tone of this reading is explanatory.
Paul is reminding the Romans of what they have previously been taught.
This is Paul's first point.

This is Paul's second point.

Paul restates both points.

Brothers and **sisters**:
Are you **unaware** that **we** who were **baptized** into **Christ Jesus**
> were **baptized** into his **death**?
We were **indeed buried with him** through **baptism** into **death**,
> so **that**, **just** as **Christ** was **raised** from the **dead**
> by the **glory** of the **Father**,
> **we too** might **live** in **newness** of **life**.

For **if** we have **grown** into **union with him**
> through a **death** like **his**,
> we shall **also** be **united with him** in the **resurrection**.

EPISTLE   The reading from Romans is a catechetical lesson on the meaning and ramifications of Baptism. As the reading begins, Paul reminds the Romans that those who have been baptized have been baptized into Christ's Death. This death is symbolized by the elect's submersion in the waters of Baptism. Paul describes the significance of this symbolic action when he says, "We were indeed buried with him through baptism into death."

However, those who enter the baptismal waters rise from those baptismal waters. They rise to a new life, a life in which they are no longer slaves to sin. Paul tells the Romans, "you too must think of yourselves as being dead to sin and living for God in Christ Jesus."

In addition, those who have joined Christ in his Death and burial are also joined with Christ in his Resurrection. Paul says, "For if we have grown into union with him through a death like his, we shall also be united with him in the resurrection."

Through the baptismal waters, Christians die with Christ and rise to new life: new life on earth because we are no longer slaves to sin, and new life for eternity because, with Christ, we will pass through death to eternal life. This is the good news that you will be proclaiming at the Easter Vigil. Paul's writing is dense, and he repeats his points several times. Read them over until you are sure you understand Paul's meaning. Then proclaim them with great joy.

Paul explains that Christians are no longer slaves to sin.

We **know** that our **old self** was **crucified** with **him**,
  so that our **sinful body** might be **done away with**,
  that we might **no longer** be in **slavery** to **sin**.
For a **dead person** has been **absolved** from **sin**.

Paul restates each point a third time.

If, **then**, we have **died** with **Christ**,
  we **believe** that we shall **also live** with **him**.
We **know** that **Christ**, **raised** from the **dead**, **dies no more**;
  death no **longer** has **power** over him.
As to his **death**, he **died** to **sin once** and for **all**;
  as to his **life**, he **lives** for **God**.

Here Paul states the ramification of what he has taught. This is how the Romans should live.

Consequently = KON-suh-kwent-lee

Consequently, **you too** must think of **yourselves**
    as being **dead** to **sin**
    and **living** for **God** in **Christ Jesus**.

GOSPEL   Luke 24:1–12

A reading from the holy Gospel according to Luke

The women are sad. This is a heartbreaking situation.
Galilee = GAL-ih-lee

At **daybreak** on the **first day** of the **week**
  the **women** who had come from **Galilee with** Jesus
  took the **spices** they had **prepared**
  and **went** to the **tomb**.

This is very mysterious.

They found the **stone rolled away** from the **tomb**;
  but when they **entered**,
  they did **not** find the **body** of the **Lord Jesus**.
While they were **puzzling** over this, **behold**,
  two men in **dazzling garments appeared** to them.

Now something amazing happens.

They were **terrified** and **bowed** their **faces** to the **ground**.

GOSPEL | As you proclaim today's Gospel, it is important that you not project onto the people in the story the understanding that we, as post-Resurrection people, have. The women in the story, the Apostles, and Peter are slowly coming to a realization of the good news that Jesus has risen from the dead. Even though Jesus had told the Apostles and the women that he would rise, no one understood Jesus' words, nor expected Jesus to be alive after he had been crucified, died, and was buried.

The women who come with the spices had witnessed the burial (see Luke 23:55–56). Now, as they approach the tomb once more, they find that the stone has been rolled back and that Jesus' body is not there. Obviously, the women did not expect Jesus to rise from the dead. If they had, the empty tomb would have filled them with joy and confirmed their hopes. Instead, they are puzzled.

Two men in dazzling clothes then appear and explain the significance of the empty tomb to the women. They announce the core Easter proclamation: "he has

been raised." The men then remind the women of what Jesus had said earlier, that he would be crucified but would "rise on the third day."

The women thus become the first witnesses to the Easter good news, the first evangelizers. They go to the Apostles and all the others to tell them what they have witnessed. The Apostles, too, have not been expecting a resurrection. If they had, the women's witness would have filled them with joy and confirmed their hopes.

The two men ask this question gently. They don't want the women to be afraid.

This is astounding good news. Say this with joy.

Galilee = GAL-ih-lee

Say this line with calm certitude. Then pause.

Now speak more quickly and with excitement.

Now speak matter-of-factly.

Say this with sadness.

Again, speak more quickly as you conclude the story.

They **said** to them,
  "**Why** do you **seek** the **living** one among the **dead**?
He is **not here**, but he has been **raised**.
Remember what he **said** to you while he was **still** in **Galilee**,
    that the **Son** of **Man** must be **handed over** to **sinners**
    and be **crucified**, and **rise** on the **third day**."
And they **remembered** his words.
Then they **returned** from the **tomb**
    and **announced all these things** to the **eleven**
    and to **all** the **others**.
The women were **Mary Magdalene**, **Joanna**,
      and **Mary** the mother of **James**;
    the **others** who **accompanied** them also told this
      to the *apostles*,
    but their **story** seemed like **nonsense**
    and they did **not believe** them.
But **Peter** got up and **ran** to the tomb,
    bent down, and **saw** the **burial** cloths **alone**;
    then he went **home amazed** at what had **happened**.

Instead, the women's story "seemed like nonsense and they did not believe them."

Peter does not completely dismiss the women's words. He runs to the tomb and is amazed at what has happened. That is not to say that Peter has come to full belief. This will occur when Jesus appears to Peter (see Luke 24:34).

As you proclaim the reading, try to enter into the process of coming to understanding and belief that Luke is describing. The women are puzzled, then terrified.

The Apostles are dismissive. They did not believe. Peter is amazed, but he has more to learn. Entering into this process will help you and those who listen to you appreciate more fully the extraordinary nature of the Good News that we celebrate. Jesus died and was buried. However, Jesus now lives. Jesus has conquered death, both for himself and for us. Alleluia.

EASTER SUNDAY

Lectionary #42

READING I   Acts 10:34a, 37–43

A reading from the Acts of the Apostles

Peter proceeded to speak and **said**:
"**You know** what has happened **all over Judea**,
    beginning in **Galilee** after the **baptism**
    that **John** preached,
    how **God** anointed **Jesus** of **Nazareth**
    with the **Holy Spirit** and **power**.
He went about **doing good**
    and **healing all** those **oppressed** by the **devil**,
    for **God** was **with him**.
We are **witnesses** of **all** that he **did**
    both in the **country** of the Jews and in **Jerusalem**.
They **put** him to **death** by **hanging** him on a **tree**.
This **man God raised** on the **third day** and **granted**
        that **he be visible**,
    not to **all** the people, but to **us**,
    the **witnesses** chosen by **God** in **advance**,
    who **ate** and **drank** with him **after** he **rose** from the **dead**.
He **commissioned us** to **preach** to the **people**
    and **testify** that **he** is the **one appointed** by **God**
    as **judge** of the **living** and the **dead**.
To **him all** the **prophets** bear **witness**,
    that **everyone** who **believes** in **him**
    will **receive forgiveness** of sins through **his name**."

Peter is speaking with great confidence.
Judea = joo-DEE-uh; joo-DAY-uh
Galilee = GAL-ih-lee

Emphasize this line
Nazareth = NAZ-uh-reth

Emphasize this line.

Jerusalem = juh-ROO-suh-lem;
juh-ROO-zuh-lem

Say this with amazement.

Now speak again with great confidence.

Emphasize "him," "him," and "his."

READING I   On Easter Sunday the Church proclaims Peter's first sermon to the Gentiles. This is a very important speech because it contains the basic kerygma, the core truths of Christianity.

Up until this time, Peter had thought that his mission was to his own people, the Israelites. However, Peter had a dream in which a sheet descended from heaven filled with clean and unclean animals. A voice said, "Get up, Peter. Slaughter and eat." Peter refused, saying he would not

eat anything unclean. The voice said, "What God has made clean, you are not to call profane" (Acts 10:13–15). Following this dream, the servants of Cornelius came and asked Peter to come to Cornelius' house. Cornelius was a Gentile, and under normal circumstances Peter would not have entered the home of a Gentile because he would have considered it unclean. However, based on the dream, Peter went. Today's reading is part of what Peter said to Cornelius and his household.

After giving a short description of Jesus' powerful public ministry, Peter

teaches the Gentiles the core truths of Christianity: Jesus was crucified and died. Jesus rose from the dead. Jesus is judge of the living and the dead. Jesus fulfills the words of the prophets. Those who believe in Jesus receive forgiveness of sin.

Peter assures the Gentiles that he knows what he is talking about: Peter and the other disciples witnessed Jesus' public ministry, witnessed Jesus' post-Resurrection appearances, and were commissioned by Jesus to testify to the truth. This truth, faithfully passed on by the Apostles, is once more faithfully passed on

Colossians = kuh-LOSH-uhnz

Emphasize "seek what is above." Paul is exhorting.

Speak slowly and distinctly. Paul is probing a mystery.

Say "glory" with joy. This is good news indeed.

READING II   Colossians 3:1–4

A reading from the Letter of Saint Paul to the Colossians

Brothers and **sisters**:
If then you were **raised** with **Christ**, **seek** what is **above**,
    where **Christ** is seated at the **right hand** of **God**.
Think of **what** is **above**, not of what is on **earth**.
For you have **died**, and your **life** is **hidden with Christ** in **God**.
When **Christ your life appears**,
    then **you too** will **appear with him** in **glory**.

Or:

Corinthians = kohr-IN-thee-uhnz

This question is a reminder, not a challenge; the Corinthians know this.
Now the tone changes to a command.

Emphasize this line.
paschal = PAS-kuhl
Use a celebratory tone for the last three lines.

READING II   1 Corinthians 5:6b–8

A reading from the first Letter of Saint Paul to the Corinthians

Brothers and **sisters**:
Do you **not know** that a **little yeast leavens all** the **dough**?
Clear out the **old** yeast,
    so that you may become a **fresh** batch of **dough**,
    inasmuch as you are **unleavened**.
For our **paschal lamb**, **Christ**, has been **sacrificed**.
Therefore, let us **celebrate** the **feast**,
    not with the **old yeast**, the **yeast** of **malice** and **wickedness**,
    but with the **unleavened bread** of sincerity and **truth**.

by the Church's proclamation on Easter Sunday. As you proclaim the Good News, emphasize the core truths that Peter teaches the Gentiles, especially that Jesus rose from the dead.

READING II COLOSSIANS. As the reading from Colossians begins, the author is reminding the people that they "were raised with Christ." This is a reference to the Colossians' baptism. The author has earlier said, "You were buried with him in baptism, in which you were also raised with him through faith in the power

of God, who raised him from the dead" (Colossians 2:12). When the Colossians entered the waters of Baptism they died with Christ, and when they emerged from those waters they were raised with Christ.

That the Colossians have been raised with Christ affects the way they live their lives. Instead of being concerned with things of earth, including some false teachers, they should "seek what is above where Christ is seated at the right hand of God."

To say that Christ is seated at God's right hand is to allude to Psalm 110:1 and to

claim that Christ, the Messiah, is the Son of God. This reference is based on a conversation described in the Gospel according to Matthew (22:44) between Jesus and the Pharisees. Jesus points out that in Psalm 110:1, David, to whom the psalms are attributed, says, "The Lord said to my lord,/ 'Sit at my right hand/ until I place your enemies under your feet." (Matthew 22:44; Psalm 110:1). Jesus explains to the Pharisees that if David called the messiah "Lord," the messiah can't be David's son. Jesus, the Messiah, is God's own Son.

GOSPEL   John 20:1–9

A reading from the holy Gospel according to John

On the **first day** of the **week**,
  Mary of **Magdala** came to the **tomb early** in the **morning**,
  while it was **still dark**,
  and saw the **stone removed** from the **tomb**.
So she **ran** and **went** to Simon **Peter**
  and to the **other** disciple whom **Jesus loved**, and **told** them,
  "They have **taken** the **Lord** from the **tomb**,
  and we **don't know where** they **put** him."
So **Peter** and the **other disciple** went out and **came** to the **tomb**.
They **both ran**, but the **other** disciple ran **faster** than Peter
  and **arrived** at the tomb **first**;
  he **bent down** and saw the **burial** cloths there, but did
    not go **in**.
When **Simon Peter** arrived **after** him,
  he went into the **tomb** and **saw** the **burial cloths** there,
  and the cloth that had **covered** his **head**,
  not with the **burial cloths** but **rolled up** in a **separate place**.
Then the **other disciple also** went in,
  the one who had **arrived** at the **tomb first**,
  and **he saw** and **believed**.
For they did **not yet understand** the Scripture
  that he had to **rise** from the **dead**.

Speak slowly. What happens is very mysterious.
Magdala = MAG-duh-luh

Now increase your pace.

Mary is very upset.

The narrator continues the story. Speak slowly again.

Say this with puzzlement.

Emphasize this line, then pause.
The narrator is explaining Peter's puzzlement.

Since Christ is seated at God's right hand, Christ's victory is complete and his glory can be seen. The Colossians' victory in Christ is not yet visible. However, when Christ appears, the Colossians "will appear with him in glory."

The Easter Good News is not only that Christ has risen from the dead, but that those who are baptized into Christ will also rise from the dead. This is the Good News that you should emphasize as you proclaim the reading.

1 CORINTHIANS. In today's reading from 1 Corinthians, Paul is admonishing the people because they have allowed a person who is living with his father's wife to remain in the community. The man who is sinning is referred to as "old yeast." Paul is warning the Corinthians that this man's actions, "a little yeast," can have a very negative effect on "all the dough," that is, on the larger community. Paul is telling the Corinthians that the man should no longer be allowed to be part of the community: "Clear out the old yeast."

By giving this direction while using the imagery of yeast, unleavened bread, and the paschal lamb, Paul is relying on his readers' familiarity with the feast of Unleavened Bread and the feast of Passover. Originally these were two separate feasts, but later they were combined. Both celebrate the exodus. The feast of Unleavened Bread originally celebrated the barley harvest. All the old yeast from the previous harvest would be thrown out, and new, unleavened bread from the new harvest would be made. The unleavened bread symbolized purity, a new beginning. Once attached to the Passover celebration, it also celebrated the haste with

Lectionary #46

AFTERNOON GOSPEL   Luke 24:13–35

A reading from the holy Gospel according to Luke

As the story begins, the narrator is setting the stage by giving us background information.
Emmaus = eh-MAY-uhs

That **very day**, the **first day** of the **week**,
  two of **Jesus' disciples** were going
    to a village seven miles from **Jerusalem** called **Emmaus**,
    and they were **conversing** about **all** the **things**
      that had **occurred**.
And it **happened** that while they were **conversing** and **debating**,
  Jesus himself drew **near** and **walked** with them,
    but their **eyes** were **prevented** from **recognizing** him.

Say this with amazement and excitement.
Say this with regret.

He **asked** them,
  "**What** are you **discussing** as you **walk** along?"
They **stopped**, looking **downcast**.

Jesus is starting an apparently casual conversation.
Cleopas = KLEE-oh-puhs

One of them, named **Cleopas**, said to him in **reply**,
  "Are **you** the **only visitor** to **Jerusalem**
  who does **not know** of the **things**
    that have **taken place** there in these **days**?"

Cleopas speaks with disbelief.
Jerusalem = juh-ROO-suh-lem; juh-ROO-zuh-lem

Jesus' tone is still casual.

And he **replied** to them, "What **sort** of things?"
They **said** to him,

The disciples speak with great emotion. They are deeply distressed.
Nazarene = NAZ-uh-reen

  "The **things** that **happened** to **Jesus** the **Nazarene**,
  who was a **prophet mighty** in **deed** and **word**
  before **God** and **all** the **people**,
  how our **chief priests** and **rulers** both **handed** him **over**
  to a **sentence** of **death** and **crucified** him.
But **we** were **hoping** that he would be the **one** to **redeem Israel**;
  and besides all **this**,
  it is **now** the **third day** since this took **place**.

Here the disciple's tone changes from distress to puzzlement.

---

which the Israelites had to flee Israel. They did not have time for the dough to rise.

The paschal lamb refers to the lamb eaten during the Passover celebration, a remembrance of the blood of the lamb that was put on the lintels of the Israelites' homes during the last plague. Seeing the lamb's blood, the Lord passed over the homes of the Israelites, sparing their first born and making it possible for them to escape slavery.

Paul is reminding the Corinthians that they are "unleavened": they have new life and have been made pure by their Baptism.

Through Baptism they have been joined to the new Paschal Lamb, Jesus Christ, who was sacrificed and whose blood gives eternal life. The Israelites should, therefore, celebrate as renewed people, full of "sincerity and truth."

As you proclaim the reading, emphasize the words, "let us celebrate the feast." These words remind us that we, too, are unleavened bread, cleansed by the Passover lamb, and that we, too, are called to celebrate our feast, Easter, with sincerity and truth.

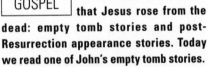 Two kinds of stories claim that Jesus rose from the dead: empty tomb stories and post-Resurrection appearance stories. Today we read one of John's empty tomb stories.

It is Easter Sunday morning when Mary Magdala discovers that the stone in front of Christ's tomb is rolled back. Her conclusion is that someone has removed Jesus' body. She runs to tell this alarming news to Simon Peter and to "the other disciple whom Jesus loved."

This other disciple whom Jesus loved, often referred to as the "beloved disciple,"

Some **women** from our **group**, however, have **astounded** us:
  they were at the **tomb early** in the **morning**
  and did **not** find his **body**;
  they came **back** and **reported**
  that they had **indeed** seen a **vision** of **angels**
  who **announced** that he was **alive**.
Then **some** of those **with** us **went** to the **tomb**
  and found things **just** as the **women** had **described**,
  but **him** they did **not see**."
And he **said** to them, "Oh, how **foolish** you are!
How slow of **heart** to **believe all** that the **prophets spoke**!
Was it not **necessary** that the **Christ** should **suffer** these things
  and **enter** into his **glory**?"
Then **beginning** with **Moses** and **all** the **prophets**,
  he **interpreted** to them what referred to **him**
  in **all** the **Scriptures**.
As they **approached** the village to which they were **going**,
  he gave the **impression** that he was going on **farther**.
But they **urged** him, "**Stay** with us,
  for it is **nearly evening** and the **day** is **almost over**."
So he went in to **stay** with them.
And it **happened** that, while he was **with** them at **table**,
  he took **bread**, said the **blessing**,
  broke it, and **gave** it to them.
With **that** their **eyes** were **opened** and they **recognized** him,
  but he **vanished** from their **sight**.

This is not said with joy because the disciples didn't believe the women.

The disciples are discouraged.
Jesus is challenging the disciples' lack of belief.

Now the narrator is speaking. Speak slowly.
Moses = MOH-ziz; MOH-zis

The disciples speak with urgency.

Now the narrator speaks again.

Emphasize these words that allude to Eucharist.

Speak with joy, then amazement.

appears only in John's gospel account. The beloved disciple is first mentioned at the Last Supper and remains a major figure through the post-Resurrection appearance stories. The fact that this person is never named is John's way of telling us that the beloved disciple functions in the story, not only as a person, but as a symbol. The beloved disciple symbolizes the absolute importance of having a loving personal relationship with Jesus Christ.

Notice that after Mary Magdala delivers her news, the beloved disciple and Peter both run to the tomb. The beloved disciple arrives first, but waits respectfully for Peter to catch up. Peter enters the tomb first, but he comes to no conclusion about what has happened. The beloved disciple enters the tomb, and "he saw and believed."

John is teaching that although authority, represented by Peter, is completely necessary and deserves respect, it is love that enables a disciple of Jesus Christ to arrive first and to believe in the Resurrection even without a post-Resurrection appearance. Remember that this lesson is central to the Gospel according to John. John is writing to end-of-the-century Christians who want to see Jesus return on the clouds of heaven. John is teaching them to recognize that Jesus is already in their midst. In this story, John is teaching about the indispensible role that love plays in one's ability to see and believe in the risen Christ. As you proclaim this reading, emphasize, "he saw and believed." We, too, are invited to see and believe.

AFTERNOON GOSPEL This account from Luke of Christ's post-Resurrection appearance is also set on Easter Sunday. Two disciples

The disciples speak with joy and wonder.

Speak more quickly. This is said with great excitement.

The narrator's voice concludes the story. Emphasize the last line.

Then they said to each other,
  "Were not our **hearts burning within us**
  while he **spoke** to us on the **way** and **opened** the Scriptures
    to us?"
So they **set out** at **once** and **returned** to **Jerusalem**
  where they found **gathered** together
  the **eleven** and those **with** them who were **saying**,
  "The **Lord** has **truly** been **raised** and has **appeared** to **Simon!**"
Then the **two recounted**
  what had taken **place** on the **way**
  and how he was made **known** to them in the **breaking** of **bread**.

are walking along, upset and discouraged because their hopes have been dashed. Jesus, the one they thought might be the messiah, has died and been buried. They have heard some astounding news from some women who claimed that Jesus' tomb was empty and that some angels claimed that Jesus was alive! Of course, the two disciples do not believe this story.

As the two walk along, the risen Christ joins them, "but their eyes were prevented from recognizing him." This stranger in their midst asks what they are discussing. After hearing the reason for their distress, Jesus "interpreted to them what referred to him in all the Scriptures." Here Luke is teaching what was also taught in the First Reading from Acts: Jesus fulfills the words of the prophets.

Not until they prevail on the stranger to stay with them for a meal do they recognize Jesus' identity. When Jesus takes bread, says a blessing, breaks the bread, and gives it to the disciples, their "eyes were opened and they recognized him."

The allusions to Eucharist are obvious. Luke is teaching that Jesus is truly present in the Eucharist. However, the risen Christ is also present when two are gathered in his name. He is present in the stranger whom we meet on life's journey. And he is present in the Scripture proclaimed. As you proclaim this reading, try to make it possible for those who hear you to recognize the risen Christ in their midst.

2ND SUNDAY OF EASTER (DIVINE MERCY SUNDAY)

Lectionary #45

READING I   Acts 5:12–16

A reading from the Acts of the Apostles

The narrator is reporting wonderful news. Speak with awe.

Speak quickly here. The narrator is simply setting the stage.

Solomon's = SOL-uh-muhnz
portico = POHR-tih-koh

Now speak more slowly. Emphasize "believers in the Lord."

Many **signs** and **wonders** were **done** among the **people**
    at the **hands** of the **apostles**.
They were **all together** in Solomon's **portico**.
None of the others **dared** to **join** them, but the **people**
        esteemed them.
Yet **more** than **ever**, **believers** in the **Lord**,
    great numbers of **men** and **women**, were added **to** them.
Thus they **even carried** the **sick** out into the **streets**
    and **laid** them on **cots** and **mats**
    so that when **Peter** came **by**,
    at least his **shadow** might **fall** on **one** or **another** of them.
A **large number** of **people** from the **towns**
    in the **vicinity** of **Jerusalem also** gathered,
    bringing the **sick** and those **disturbed** by **unclean spirits**,
    and they were **all cured**.

Jerusalem = juh-ROO-suh-lem;
juh-ROO-zuh-lem

Say this with amazement.

READING I   In the Acts of the Apostles, Luke interweaves stories about individual events with summary statements that function as transitions between those stories. Today we read one of the summary statements. Everything that follows in today's reading is an elaboration of the first sentence: "Many signs and wonders were done among the people at the hands of the apostles."

"Signs and wonders" served the same purpose in the early Church as they did in Jesus' ministry: they added authority to the content of the Apostles' preaching, and they gave evidence of the imminent in-breaking of the Kingdom of God. Notice that the signs and wonders resulted in greater numbers of "believers in the Lord."

This summary is describing the ministry in and around Jerusalem. Like Luke's gospel account, Acts has a geographic structure. While the Gospel will first take root in Jerusalem, it will then spread to Samaritan towns and finally to the ends of the then-known world. As the reading ends, it tells us that the Good News is already spreading: large numbers of people are coming from other towns. As you proclaim this reading, emphasize that the Church continued to grow as the Apostles carried on Jesus' ministry. We know that the Church is still growing today as we, the body of Christ, carry on that same ministry.

READING II   The Book of Revelation is written in a literary form that we do not have in our culture, so it is often misunderstood. This kind of writing is called "apocalyptic literature." Apocalyptic literature was a very popular kind of writing for a period of four hundred years. It

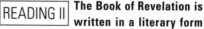

A reading from the Book of Revelation

Revelation = rev-uh-LAY-shuhn

The author is introducing himself to the readers. Speak slowly.

Patmos = PAT-muhs; PAT-mahs

This is a command. Raise your volume.
Here the tone begins with puzzlement and then turns to awe.
Emphasize "one like a son of man."

Now speak quickly.
Say the son of man's words slowly and with confidence.

Again, this is a command. Speak with authority.

I, **John**, your **brother**, who **share** with you
    the **distress**, the **kingdom**, and the **endurance** we have
        in **Jesus**,
    found myself on the **island** called **Patmos**
    because I proclaimed **God's word** and gave **testimony** to **Jesus**.
I was **caught up** in **spirit** on the **Lord's** day
    and **heard behind** me a **voice** as **loud** as a **trumpet**, which said,
    "**Write** on a **scroll** what you **see**."
Then I **turned** to **see whose voice** it **was** that **spoke** to me,
    and when I **turned**, I saw **seven gold lampstands**
    and in the **midst** of the **lampstands** one **like** a **son** of **man**,
    wearing an **ankle-length robe**, with a **gold sash**
        around his **chest**.

When I caught **sight** of him, I **fell down** at his **feet** as though **dead**.
He **touched** me with his **right hand** and said, "Do **not** be **afraid**.
I am **the first** and **the last**, the **one** who **lives**.
Once I was **dead**, but **now** I am **alive forever** and **ever**.
I hold the **keys** to **death** and the **netherworld**.
Write down, therefore, what you have **seen**,
    and what is **happening**, and what **will happen afterwards**."

was always written to people facing persecution, it was always written in code, and it always offered hope, assuring those who were being persecuted that the end time, the end of their present suffering, was near.

Notice, as the author begins he says that he shares his audience's "distress." He himself is in exile, living on the island of Patmos, because he "gave testimony to Jesus." The author then describes a vision in which he is instructed to write what he sees. The claim to have had a vision is a convention of apocalyptic writings. To understand what the author wants to teach us we must be able to "crack" the code he uses to describe his vision.

In the vision, John sees "one like a son of man" wearing a long robe and a gold sash. By the time John is writing, toward the end of the first century AD, the title "Son of Man" has become a well-known title for Jesus. You will remember that Jesus used this title in reference to himself when he warned his disciples about his future suffering in Luke 9:22. The title is an allusion to the Book of Daniel, the other apocalyptic work in the canon. In Daniel, God, who sits on a throne and is clothed in white, gives authority over other nations to the "son of man" (Daniel 7:13–14).

However, in John's vision, the figure of the Son of Man and God are merged. It is the Son of Man who is dressed in the long white robe. It is the Son of Man who has authority, not only over other nations, but over death and the netherworld. The author is teaching that Jesus Christ is God.

In the vision, the son of Man identifies himself to John as Jesus, who has risen from the dead. The Son of Man says: "I was

GOSPEL John 20:19–31

A reading from the holy Gospel according to John

On the **evening** of that **first day** of the **week**,
    when the **doors** were **locked**, where the **disciples** were,
    for **fear** of the **Jews**,
    Jesus came and **stood** in their **midst**
    and said to them, "**Peace** be with **you**."
When he had **said** this, he **showed** them his **hands** and his **side**.
The **disciples rejoiced** when they **saw** the **Lord**.
Jesus said to them **again**, "**Peace** be with **you**.
As the **Father** has **sent me**, so **I** send **you**."
And when he had **said** this, he **breathed** on them and **said**
        to them,
    "**Receive** the **Holy Spirit**.
Whose **sins** you **forgive** are **forgiven** them,
    and whose **sins** you **retain** are **retained**."

Thomas, called **Didymus**, one of the **Twelve**,
    was not **with** them when **Jesus came**.
So the **other** disciples said to him, "We have **seen** the **Lord**."
But **he** said to them,
    "**Unless** I **see** the **mark** of the **nails** in his **hands**
    and **put** my **finger** into the **nailmarks**
    and **put** my **hand** into his **side**, I will **not believe**."

Now a **week later** his **disciples** were **again** inside
    and **Thomas was with** them.
Jesus came, although the **doors** were **locked**,
    and **stood** in their **midst** and said, "**Peace** be with **you**."

The narrator begins by setting the scene. Speak in a matter-of-fact tone of voice.

Now speak with amazement and awe. Emphasize "Peace be with you." This will become a refrain.

Say Jesus' words slowly and with authority.

Drop your voice for the narrator's lines. breathed = bree**th**d

Again say Jesus' words slowly and with authority.

Didymus = DID-uh-muhs

The disciples speak with great excitement.

In contrast, Thomas speaks slowly and adamantly.

Increase your speed for the narrator's line.

Emphasize Jesus' greeting.

---

dead, but now I am alive forever and ever." As you proclaim the reading, these are the words to emphasize. Because the reading places our hope in Jesus, who has conquered death, we read this selection on the Second Sunday of Easter.

 GOSPEL Today's Gospel begins on Easter eve, with the disciples locked in a room because of their fear. Remember, Mary Magdalene has already told them about the empty tomb, and the beloved disciple has already believed. To

this frightened group, Jesus appears and says, "Peace be with you." The peace that Jesus offers to the fear-filled disciples will be received only when the disciples believe the Easter good news.

After offering them peace, Jesus shows the disciples his hands and his side. This is to say that the Jesus who is appearing to them is the same person who died and was buried. On realizing that it truly is Jesus, the disciples rejoice. This fulfills a promise that Jesus made at his last meal when he said that he would return, and

that when he returned the disciples would rejoice (John 16:22). Jesus then commissions the disciples to carry on his mission to the world: "As the Father has sent me, so I send you."

In John's gospel account, Jesus bestows the Holy Spirit on his disciples. Jesus breaths on the disciples on Easter evening. Jesus breathes on the disciples (one of many references to the creation story in the Book of Genesis), saying, "Whose sins you forgive are forgiven them, and whose sins you retain are retained." Remember, at the very beginning of John's

Jesus speaks to Thomas with gentleness and love.

Then he said to **Thomas**, "**Put** your **finger here** and **see** my **hands**,
and **bring** your **hand** and **put** it into my **side**,
and **do** not be **unbelieving**, but **believe**."
Thomas **answered** and said to him, "**My Lord and my God!**"
Jesus **said** to **him**, "Have you **come** to **believe**
because you have **seen** me?
Blessed are **those** who **have not seen** and **have believed**."

Thomas is in awe and worships.
Jesus' tone remains gentle and loving.

Now **Jesus** did **many other signs** in the **presence** of his **disciples**
that are **not written** in this book.
But **these are written** that you may **come to believe**
that **Jesus** is the **Christ**, the **Son** of **God**,
and that **through this belief** you may have **life** in **his name**.

Read the narrator's conclusion slowly. It explains his reason for writing his account of the Gospel.

gospel account, Jesus is identified as the Lamb who "takes away the sin of the world" (John 1:29). Now the disciples, too, will take away sins by baptizing.

Thomas is not present when Jesus appears. On hearing the good news, Thomas declares that he will not believe unless he himself can touch Jesus' wounds. Although no one is aware of Jesus' presence when Thomas says this, a week later, when Jesus appears again, Jesus is obviously fully aware of exactly what

Thomas has said. In other words, Jesus is with the disciples all the time, both when they see him and when they do not. When Jesus offers Thomas the opportunity to do exactly as he wished, Thomas no longer has the need to do so. Instead, he worships Jesus, saying, "My Lord and my God!"

What Jesus then says to Thomas is what the author of the Gospel according to John is saying to his end-of-the-century audience who awaits Jesus' return. Jesus says: "Blessed are those who have not seen and have believed." The author then

concludes by stating that this is his purpose. He wants his readers to believe that "Jesus is the Christ," and to have "life in his name." As you read this explanation, you will be proclaiming why the Church has selected this reading for today: we, too, are to believe that Jesus is the Christ and so have life in his name.

3RD SUNDAY OF EASTER

Lectionary #48

READING I   Acts 5:27b–32, 40b–41

A reading from the Acts of the Apostles

The narrator sets the stage. Use a matter-of-fact voice.
 	
Sanhedrin = san-HEE-druhn
 	
The high priest's tone is accusatory and arrogant.
 	
Jerusalem = juh-ROO-suh-lem;
juh-ROO-zuh-lem
 	
Drop your voice for the narrator's line.
Peter speaks with confidence and earnestness but not anger.
	When the **captain** and the **court officers** had **brought**
	    the **apostles** in
	and made them **stand** before the **Sanhedrin**,
	    the **high priest questioned** them,
	    "We gave you **strict orders**, did we **not**,
	    to **stop teaching** in **that name**?
	Yet you have **filled Jerusalem** with your **teaching**
	    and want to **bring this man's blood** upon **us**."
	But **Peter** and the **apostles** said in reply,
	    "We must **obey God** rather than **men**.
	The **God** of our ancestors **raised Jesus**,
	    though **you** had him **killed** by **hanging** him on a **tree**.
	God exalted him at his **right hand** as **leader** and **savior**
	    to grant **Israel repentance** and **forgiveness** of **sins**.
	We are **witnesses** of these things,
	    as is the **Holy Spirit** whom **God** has **given** to those who
	        obey him."

Say this with an ironic tone. This is an order the Apostles cannot obey.
 	
The narrator shares the Apostles' joy. Sound happy as you conclude.
	The **Sanhedrin ordered** the apostles
	    to **stop speaking** in the **name** of Jesus, and **dismissed** them.
	So they **left** the **presence** of the **Sanhedrin**,
	    rejoicing that they had been found **worthy**
	    to **suffer dishonor** for the **sake** of the **name**.

READING I Last Sunday the reading from Acts told us just how successful the Apostles' ministry was in Jerusalem. People were coming from surrounding towns, and all were being healed. Between that reading and today's reading, the high priest has had the Apostles arrested, only to have an angel release them. After having resumed their preaching, the Apostles are brought in to appear before the Sanhedrin.

As we join the story, the high priest is reminding the Apostles that they have already been given strict orders to stop teaching in Jesus' name. The members of the Sanhedrin are angry, not only because of the Apostles' successful ministry, but because the Apostles are telling people about the Sanhedrin's role in Jesus' Crucifixion. The Sanhedrin wanted Jesus silenced.

In reply to the Sanhedrin, Peter and the Apostles make a number of very important claims. First, they claim that they "must obey God rather than men." Next, they claim that this Jesus, who was crucified, has been raised from the dead and is now exalted at God's right hand as "savior." To say this is, of course, to claim

Jesus' divinity. This savior is to "grant Israel repentance and forgiveness of sins." The Apostles also claim to be witnesses of all these things.

The Sanhedrin lets the Apostles go, ordering them to stop preaching in Jesus' name. This is, of course, an order that the Sanhedrin knows the Apostles will not obey. The Apostles regard their mistreatment by the Sanhedrin as an honor. Like Jesus, they are suffering, and their suffering is in Jesus' name.

As you proclaim the reading, emphasize the main claims. During Easter

Revelation = rev-uh-LAY-shuhn

John is describing his vision.
Speak with awe.

creatures = CREE-cherz

As the reading directs, say these lines in a loud voice.

Now John is speaking again.
Speak with awe.

Speak loudly and passionately.

Only the "Amen" is loud. The rest is John's description, said with awe.

The narrator introduces the story.
Tiberias = ti-BEER-ee-uhs
Simon = SI-muhn

Emphasize each name. Speak slowly.
Nathanael = nuh-THAN-ay-uhl
Cana = KAY-nuh
Galilee = GAL-ih-lee
Zebedee's = ZEB-uh-deez
Didymus = DID-uh-muhs

READING II   Revelation 5:11–14

A reading from the Book of Revelation

I, **John**, **looked** and **heard** the voices of **many angels**
   who **surrounded** the **throne**
   and the **living creatures** and the **elders**.
They were **countless** in **number**, and they **cried out**
   in a **loud voice**:
   "**Worthy** is the **Lamb** that was **slain**
      to receive **power** and **riches**, **wisdom** and **strength**,
      honor and **glory** and **blessing**."
Then I heard **every creature** in **heaven** and on **earth**
   and **under** the **earth** and in the **sea**,
   everything in the **universe**, cry out:
   "To the **one** who **sits** on the **throne** and to the **Lamb**
      be **blessing** and **honor**, **glory** and **might**,
      forever and **ever**."
The **four living creatures** answered, "**Amen**,"
   and the **elders** fell **down** and **worshiped**.

GOSPEL   John 21:1–19

A reading from the holy Gospel according to John

At that time, **Jesus revealed** himself **again** to his **disciples**
      at the **Sea** of **Tiberias**.
He **revealed** himself in **this way**.
Together were **Simon Peter**, **Thomas** called **Didymus**,
   Nathanael from **Cana** in **Galilee**,
   Zebedee's sons, and **two others** of his **disciples**.

Time, we, too, are celebrating Jesus' Resurrection, exaltation, and saving power. We, too, realize that we must obey God, not human beings.

READING II In today's reading from Acts, the Apostles claimed that Jesus was exalted at God's right hand. The reading from Revelation is claiming the same thing. As is typical in apocalyptic literature (the literary form in which the Book of Revelation is written), the person to whom the book is attributed, John, is describing a vision. To understand what

the author is teaching we have to unlock the code in which the vision is described. Apocalyptic literature was written in code because it was addressed to a persecuted audience. The author wanted the persecuted people, but not the persecutors, to understand the message.

John is describing the heavenly court. All creation is recognizing that Jesus is divine. However, Jesus is not called by his name. Jesus is called "the Lamb." We are so familiar with the term "Lamb of God," and it has circulated so much in our culture after some two thousand years of

Christian influence, that we may not realize how enigmatic it would be to a person outside Christian circles in the Roman world of the first century AD. "Lamb" is code for "Jesus" for two reasons: Jesus is the paschal lamb of a new Passover: Jesus' blood gave eternal life, as the blood of a lamb gave extended life on earth to the first born of the Israelites during the last plague before the exodus (see Exodus, chapters 11 and 12). In addition, Jesus is the new Suffering Servant lamb described in Isaiah (see Isaiah 53:7). Through Jesus'

Peter speaks casually.	**Simon Peter** said to them, "**I am** going **fishing**."
The others speak casually, too.	They said to him, "**We also** will **come with** you."
	So they **went out** and got into the **boat**,
Emphasize that they caught nothing.	but **that night** they caught **nothing**.
	When it was already **dawn**, **Jesus** was **standing** on the **shore**;
	but the **disciples** did not **realize** that it was **Jesus**.
Jesus appears to be making pleasant conversation.	Jesus said to them, "**Children**, have you **caught anything** to **eat**?"
	They answered him, "**No**."
Now Jesus' tone gains authority.	So he said to them, "**Cast** the **net** over the **right side** of the **boat**
	and you will **find** something."
Emphasize the marvelous catch.	So they **cast** it, and were **not** able to **pull** it **in**
	because of the **number** of **fish**.
Say "It is the Lord" with joy and excitement.	So the **disciple** whom **Jesus loved** said to **Peter**, "It is the **Lord**."
	When **Simon Peter heard** that it was the **Lord**,
	he **tucked in** his **garment**, for he was **lightly clad**,
	and **jumped** into the sea.
	The **other** disciples **came** in the **boat**,
	for they were **not far** from **shore**, only about a **hundred yards**,
Continue to emphasize the marvelous catch.	**dragging** the **net** with the **fish**.
	When they **climbed out** on **shore**,
	they **saw** a charcoal **fire** with **fish** on it and **bread**.
Jesus continues to speak casually.	**Jesus said** to them, "**Bring** some of the **fish** you just **caught**."
	So **Simon Peter** went over and **dragged** the **net ashore**
	full of one **hundred fifty-three large fish**.
The marvelous catch is being emphasized once more.	Even though there were so **many**, the **net** was **not torn**.
	Jesus said to them, "**Come**, have **breakfast**."
	And **none** of the **disciples dared** to ask him, "**Who are** you?"
Say this with awe.	because they **realized** it was the **Lord**.
Emphasize the words that remind us of Eucharist.	**Jesus** came over and **took** the **bread** and **gave** it to them,
	and in like **manner** the **fish**.

suffering and Death, all nations will come to know their God.

In John's vision, the worship that is due only to God is given both to the one who sits on the throne and to the Lamb. "Every creature in heaven and on earth and under the earth and in the sea," cries out in worship. In this scene, John is teaching that the risen Christ is already victorious in the heavenly court. Jesus Christ has conquered death and is divine.

The message to the original audience was that those who were experiencing persecution should remain faithful to Christ and they, too, would rise from the dead. The message that you, as reader, will be proclaiming on the Third Sunday of Easter to those gathered in worship is much the same: Those who put their faith in Christ will not only die with Christ, but will rise with Christ. We will someday be in the heavenly throne room, joining all of creation to give praise to our redeemer, Jesus Christ.

GOSPEL In today's post-Resurrection appearance story, the disciples have fished all night to no avail.

A person on the shore whom they do not recognize tells them to cast their nets on the right side. They follow the stranger's direction and have a huge catch of fish. Based on this sign alone, one of the disciples realizes who gave them the direction. The beloved disciple tells Peter, "It is the Lord."

In all of the stories in which the beloved disciple and Peter appear together, the beloved disciple believes first. We will see as the story continues that the author is teaching that love is most important. Love, represented by the beloved disciple,

Pause slightly after this line.

This was now the **third time** Jesus was **revealed** to his **disciples**
after being **raised** from the **dead**.

Jesus speaks gently.

Peter speaks gently, too.

When they had **finished breakfast**, Jesus said to Simon **Peter**,
"**Simon**, son of **John**, do **you love** me more than **these**?"
Simon Peter answered him, "**Yes**, Lord, you **know** that
I love you."
Jesus said to him, "**Feed** my **lambs**."
He then said to **Simon Peter** a **second** time,
"**Simon**, son of **John**, do **you love** me?"
Simon Peter answered him, "**Yes**, Lord, you **know**
that **I** love you."

Jesus continues to speak gently.

Peter is slightly louder, slightly more insistent.

Jesus said to him, "**Tend my sheep**."
Jesus said to him the **third** time,
"**Simon**, son of **John**, do **you love** me?"
Peter was **distressed** that Jesus had said to him a **third** time,
"Do **you love** me?" and he **said** to him,

Jesus still speaks gently.

"**Lord**, **you know everything**; you **know** that I **love** you."
Jesus said to him, "**Feed** my **sheep**.
Amen, **amen**, I say to you, when you were **younger**,
you used to **dress yourself** and **go** where **you** wanted;
but when you **grow old**, you will **stretch** out your **hands**,
and **someone else** will **dress** you
and **lead** you where you do **not want** to go."

Peter is getting exasperated. He speaks with great insistence.

Now Jesus' tone changes. He speaks with authority and is giving a warning.

He said this **signifying** by what **kind** of **death** he would
glorify God.
And when he had **said** this, he said to him, "**Follow** me."

Now the narrator is explaining Jesus' words.

Look up at the congregation when you say, "Follow me."

[Shorter: John 21:1–14]

is the basis for belief and must also be the basis for authority, represented by Peter.

After the disciples arrive on the shore of the Sea of Tiberias, Jesus feeds them with bread and fish. In a previous story, set on the same shore, Jesus fed the crowd with bread and fish and then gave his "I am the bread of life" discourse (see John 6). We are, of course, invited to connect the two stories and understand that Jesus is present in the Eucharist. Jesus continues to be the bread of life for his disciples.

After the meal is finished, Jesus gives Peter the opportunity to profess his love three times, just as Peter had denied Jesus three times. Each time Peter professes his love, Jesus gives Peter pastoral responsibility for Jesus' flock. Here the author is stressing once again that authority must be rooted in love. Peter is to model himself on Jesus, the Good Shepherd, and be willing to lay down his life for the sheep (see John 10:1–18).

Finally, Jesus warns Peter that the day will come when others will lead him where Peter does not want to go. Scripture

scholars think this is a reference to Peter's martyrdom. The Gospel according to John was written some thirty years after Peter is thought to have been martyred in Rome (AD 64).

As you proclaim this Gospel during the Easter season, try to emphasize the ideas that John is teaching, not only to his original audience, but to us: The risen Christ is present. Christ continues to feed us. Our faith must be rooted in love. We, too, are called to follow Christ.

4TH SUNDAY OF EASTER

Lectionary #51

READING I Acts 13:14, 43–52

A reading from the Acts of the Apostles

The narrator's voice is giving us factual information. Emphasize "synagogue" and "Jews."

Barnabas = BAHR-nuh-buhs
Perga = PER-guh
Antioch = AN-tee-ahk
Pisidia = pih-SID-ee-uh

Emphasize "following Sabbath." Paul and Barnabas are still operating in a Jewish context.

Raise your voice as you describe the Jews' outrage.

Speak with authority rather than anger.

Gentiles = JEN-tils

This is a quotation. Read this slowly and thoughtfully.

Now return to your normal tone and pace.

Paul and **Barnabas** continued on from **Perga**
and reached **Antioch** in **Pisidia**.
On the **sabbath** they **entered** the **synagogue** and **took** their **seats**.
Many Jews and worshipers who were **converts** to **Judaism**
followed **Paul** and **Barnabas**, who **spoke** to them
and **urged** them to **remain faithful** to the **grace** of **God**.

On the **following sabbath** almost the **whole city** gathered
to **hear** the **word** of the **Lord**.
When the **Jews** saw the **crowds**, they were **filled** with **jealousy**
and with **violent abuse contradicted** what **Paul said**.
Both **Paul** and **Barnabas** spoke out **boldly** and **said**,
"It was **necessary** that the **word** of **God** be **spoken** to **you first**,
but since **you reject** it
and **condemn** yourselves as **unworthy** of **eternal life**,
we **now turn** to the **Gentiles**.
For **so** the **Lord** has **commanded** us,
*I have made you a **light** to the **Gentiles**,
that you may be an **instrument** of **salvation**
to the **ends** of the **earth**.*"

The **Gentiles** were **delighted** when they **heard** this
and **glorified** the **word** of the **Lord**.

READING I   As you read today's selection from Acts, it will be helpful to keep in mind that Luke wrote Acts for Gentiles. In this reading, Luke is careful to explain that Paul, the Jewish Apostle to the Gentiles, did not neglect his own people; rather, when Paul entered a town, he went first to the Jews. Only later did he extend his message to the Gentiles.

That is what we will see in this reading. Paul and Barnabas are in Antioch, and they enter the Jewish synagogue on the Sabbath. The reading leaves out what Paul preaches in the synagogue. For that, we

must read Acts 13:17–41, in which Paul speaks eloquently of how Jesus, who has risen from the dead, is the fulfillment of God's promises to the Jewish people's ancestors. As a result of Paul's preaching, many Jews follow Paul and Barnabas, as we learn at the beginning of the reading.

One week later, many who are not Jews come to hear Paul preach. At this point we hear the reaction of those who did not follow Paul and Barnabas. These Jews become angry and openly contradict what Paul says. Paul's response is not addressed to all the Jews, but to those

specific Jews who are now rejecting and abusing Paul and Barnabas.

Paul explains that God has commanded him to go to the Gentiles. To support this statement, Paul applies to himself the words from the prophet Isaiah (see Isaiah 49:6). These words were originally addressed to the Israelites who were in exile in Babylon. Isaiah was offering the exiles hope that God was accomplishing something wonderful through them. They would be God's instrument to bring other nations to a knowledge of God. Paul sees

Pause after this line.

All who were **destined** for **eternal life** came to **believe**,
and the **word** of the **Lord continued** to **spread**
through the **whole region**.
The **Jews**, however, incited the **women** of **prominence**
who were **worshipers**
and the **leading men** of the **city**,
stirred up a **persecution** against **Paul** and **Barnabas**,
and **expelled** them from their **territory**.

Pause after this line.
Increase your speed. The disciples are
moving on.

So they shook the **dust** from their **feet** in **protest against** them,
and went to **Iconium**.
The **disciples** were **filled** with **joy** and the **Holy Spirit**.

READING II   Revelation 7:9, 14b–7

Revelation = rev-uh-LAY-shuhn

A reading from the Book of Revelation

John is describing a vision of God's
throne room in heaven. Speak with awe.

Speak slowly and emphasize every word.
The crowd is vast beyond imagination.

I, **John**, had a **vision** of a **great multitude**,
which **no one** could **count**,
from **every nation**, **race**, **people** and **tongue**.
They stood before the **throne** and before the **Lamb**,
wearing **white robes** and holding **palm branches**
in their **hands**.

The elder is explaining the meaning of
the vision.

Then **one** of the **elders said** to me,
"**These** are the **ones** who have **survived** the time
of **great distress**;
they have **washed** their **robes**
and made them **white** in the **blood** of the **Lamb**.

"For **this reason** they **stand** before **God's throne**
and **worship** him **day** and **night** in his **temple**.

---

these words being fulfilled in his own mission to the Gentiles.

Faced with persecution, and having accomplished their goal of teaching the Good News of Jesus Christ to Jews and Gentiles, Paul and Barnabas move on to another town. As you proclaim the reading, emphasize that both Jews and Gentiles believed the Good News of Jesus Christ. It is important for people to understand that Paul, the Apostle to the Gentiles, also preached to, and converted, many of his fellow Jews.

READING II Once more we read a message of hope taught in code to persecuted Christians. In today's selection, John is again describing a vision of the heavenly throne room. A great multitude is present, worshipping both God and the Lamb. Here, John is teaching that Jesus Christ is God.

In addition, John is teaching that those who have been martyred because of their faith not only died with Christ but have risen with Christ. Again, this message of hope is taught in code so that only those who are being persecuted will understand it.

In John's vision, he sees that the people are dressed in white robes. The elder explains the meaning of the vision: "These are the ones who have survived the time of great distress; they have washed their robes and made them white in the blood of the Lamb." The "Lamb" is Christ. The "blood of the Lamb" refers to Jesus' saving Death. To have washed one's robes in the blood of the Lamb is to have lived and died in fidelity to Jesus. The martyrs are not dead. They are alive and will never suffer again. "God will wipe away every tear from their eyes."

Say these lines with love and gentleness.

Raise your volume in joy and gratitude as you read the last two lines.
tear = teer

Say the first three lines with gentle certitude.

Now, raise your volume. A threat is envisioned.

Drop your voice. Jesus is explaining why no one can take them.

Say the last line with gratitude and confidence.

The one who **sits** on the **throne** will **shelter** them.
They will **not hunger** or **thirst** anymore,
   nor will the **sun** or **any heat strike** them.
For the **Lamb** who is in the **center** of the **throne**
   will **shepherd** them
     and **lead** them to **springs** of **life-giving water**,
     and **God** will **wipe away every tear** from their **eyes**."

GOSPEL John 10:27–30

A reading from the holy Gospel according to John

Jesus said:
"My **sheep hear** my **voice**;
   I **know** them, and they **follow me**.
I give them **eternal life**, and they shall **never perish**.
No one can take them out of **my hand**.
My **Father**, who has given them **to me**, is **greater** than **all**,
   and **no** one can take them out of the **Father's hand**.
The **Father** and I are **one**."

The end of this reading contains some of the most beautiful words of comfort in the entire Bible. As you proclaim these words, speak lovingly and gently. The words are just as true when addressed to us.

GOSPEL To understand today's Gospel, we must recall the social setting in which John wrote his gospel account. John was writing to a community of Jews who had split because some in the community insisted on the divinity of Jesus Christ. Those Jews who insisted on Jesus' divinity had been

expelled from the synagogue. This left them vulnerable to Roman persecution because they were no longer exempt from emperor worship.

Today's reading is part of a conversation that Jesus is pictured having with some Jews who do not believe in him (like some in John's community). Immediately before today's passage, Jesus has said, " . . . but you do not believe, because you are not among my sheep" (John 10:26). Jesus then goes on to describe his sheep in contrast to the people to whom Jesus is speaking. Jesus' sheep know Jesus' voice,

believe in Jesus, and follow Jesus. Jesus will give them eternal life.

Jesus then goes on to explain his relationship with his Father. Jesus says that his sheep have been given to him by his Father, that no one can take them away from him because no one is greater than his Father, and therefore the sheep will always be safe. Then Jesus adds, "The Father and I are one." As you proclaim this short Gospel, say Jesus' words slowly and solemnly. Jesus is God. This is the faith of the Church, in John's time and in our own.

5TH SUNDAY OF EASTER

Lectionary #54

READING I   Acts 14:21–27

A reading from the Acts of the Apostles

After **Paul** and **Barnabas** had proclaimed the **good news**
    to that **city**
    and made a **considerable number** of **disciples**,
    they returned to **Lystra** and to **Iconium** and to **Antioch**.
They **strengthened** the **spirits** of the **disciples**
    and **exhorted** them to **persevere** in the **faith**, saying,
    "It is **necessary** for us to undergo **many hardships**
    to **enter** the **kingdom** of **God**."
They appointed **elders** for them in **each church** and,
    with **prayer** and **fasting**, **commended** them to the **Lord**
    in whom they had **put** their **faith**.
Then they traveled through **Pisidia** and reached **Pamphylia**.
After proclaiming the word at **Perga** they went down to **Attalia**.
From there they sailed to **Antioch**,
    where they had been **commended** to the **grace** of **God**
    for the **work** they had now **accomplished**.
And when they **arrived**, they called the **church together**
    and **reported** what **God** had **done** with them
    and how he had **opened** the **door** of **faith** to the **Gentiles**.

As you begin, read the first two lines quickly.

Barnabas = BAHR-nuh-buhs
Read the names of the cities slowly.
Lystra = LIS-truh
Iconium = ī-KOH-nee-uhm
Antioch = AN-tee-ahk
This is an exhortation. Say this persuasively.

Pause after this line.

Again, read the names of the cities slowly.
Pisidia = pih-SID-ee-uh
Pamphylia = pam-FIL-ee-uh
Perga = PER-guh
Attalia = at-uh-LI-uh
Antioch = AN-tee-ahk

Now increase your pace and fill your voice with joy and gratitude.

Gentiles = JEN-tīls

READING I In last week's reading from Acts, we learned that when Paul and Barnabas left Antioch of Pisidia they were being persecuted. Today we read that they "returned to Lystra and to Iconium and to Antioch." It was extremely brave of them to do this. On their first visit, the people in Iconium had threatened to stone them (Acts 14:5), and Paul had been stoned and left for dead in Lystra (Acts 14:19). This is the context in which Paul and Barnabas exhort the disciples to persevere, saying, "It is necessary for us to undergo many hardships to enter the kingdom of God."

As Paul and Barnabas visit each town, they establish formal church structures: "They appointed elders for them in each church and, with prayer and fasting, commended them to the Lord."

Luke reminds us that Paul and Barnabas had themselves been formally appointed by the church in Antioch, Syria, to the missionary journey that was now coming to a close: "They sailed to Antioch, where they had been commended to the grace of God for the work they had now accomplished." Having been formally appointed by that church, they return and report "what God had done with them and how he had opened the door of faith to the Gentiles."

As you proclaim this reading, emphasize both the statement that stresses the necessity of suffering and the statement that stresses the joyful reporting of all that God had accomplished, even in the face of suffering. These themes will be emphasized again in today's Gospel.

READING II   Revelation 21:1–5a

Revelation = rev-uh-LAY-shuhn

Say "new heaven" and "new earth" with great joy.

Now speak with awe.
Jerusalem = juh-ROO-suh-lem;
juh-ROO-zuh-lem

As the reading directs, use a loud voice, full of conviction.

Pause after this line.

Drop your voice for this line.
This is God's voice. Speak with authority.

A reading from the Book of Revelation

Then **I**, **John**, saw a **new heaven** and a **new earth**.
The **former** heaven and the **former** earth had **passed away**,
    and the **sea** was **no more**.
I also saw the **holy city**, a **new Jerusalem**,
    coming down out of **heaven** from **God**,
    prepared as a **bride adorned** for her **husband**.
I heard a **loud voice** from the **throne** saying,
    "**Behold**, **God's dwelling** is **with** the **human race**.
He will **dwell** with them and they will be **his people**
    and **God himself** will **always** be with them as **their God**.
He will **wipe every tear** from their **eyes**,
    and there shall be **no more death** or **mourning**, **wailing** or **pain**,
    for the **old order** has **passed away**."

The **One** who sat on the **throne** said,
    "**Behold**, I make **all things new**."

READING II Today we read John's vision of the final triumph of good over evil. We can more easily understand just how wonderful John's good news is if we remember the situation of John's audience. John's contemporaries were being severely persecuted; many of their loved ones had already been martyred. One can easily imagine the questions John's audience would ask while experiencing such persecution: Where is Jesus now, when we need him? Why does evil seem to be prevailing over good?

Is this all there is to life: suffering and then death?

As is true of all of John's visions, the action precipitates from heaven. This is to say that Jesus' victory is already complete in heaven. Although the ramifications of that victory are not yet fully experienced on earth, they will be in the future. That is why the new Jerusalem is descending from heaven.

In addition to the image of a city, the image of a bride is used to describe the final victory of good over evil. While the image of a city emphasizes the communal

nature of Jesus' final victory, the image of a bride emphasizes the intimacy that exists between Jesus and Jesus' people. This intimacy is described at length: God "will dwell with them and they will be his people and God himself will always be with them as their God."

In addition, suffering will be no more. God will "wipe every tear from their eyes." There will be no more death, mourning, or pain. The people should not give up hope or try to avoid martyrdom; rather, they should be faithful and believe that God will "make

Judas = JOO-duhs

Jesus is speaking with great solemnity. Read slowly.

Here the tone changes. Jesus is speaking intimately and with great affection.

Speak this line slowly.

Now increase your pace.

Again read slowly.

GOSPEL   John 13:31–33a, 34–35

A reading from the holy Gospel according to John

When **Judas** had **left** them, **Jesus** said,
    "**Now** is the **Son of Man glorified**, and **God** is **glorified in him**.
If **God** is glorified in him,
    God will **also glorify** him in **himself**,
    and **God** will **glorify** him **at once**.
My **children**, I will be with you only a **little while longer**.
I give you a **new commandment**: love one another.
As **I** have loved **you**, so **you also** should **love one another**.
This is how **all** will **know** that **you** are **my disciples**,
    if **you** have **love** for **one another**."

---

all things new." As you proclaim the reading, try to communicate the great hope that John is offering. The people should put their hope in Christ because Christ has conquered evil.

GOSPEL   The setting for today's Gospel is Jesus' last meal with his disciples before he dies. Jesus knows that he is going to die, and he knows that Judas is going to betray him. As soon as Judas leaves, Jesus begins to discuss the meaning of his coming Crucifixion.

Remember that the Crucifixion was a scandal, not only for Jesus' disciples, but for John's audience. If Jesus really was divine, if Jesus really was God's own Son, then why did Jesus die on a cross? In today's Gospel, Jesus explains to his disciples that his Crucifixion was not a shame, but a victory. In John, Jesus' Crucifixion and his glorification are treated as a single event. Jesus refers to the fact that he will soon be gone: "My children, I will be with you only a little while longer." Jesus is going to glorify God. At the same time, God

will glorify Jesus. God will glorify the Son of Man "at once."

Just as Jesus will be laying down his life for his people, so must the disciples lay down their lives for each other. Jesus gives them a new commandment, to love one another, not just as they love themselves, but as Jesus has loved them. The identifying mark of Christians will be their self-sacrificing love for each other. This is the Good News and challenge that you want to emphasize as you proclaim the reading.

6TH SUNDAY OF EASTER

Lectionary #57

READING I Acts 15:1–2, 22–29

A reading from the Acts of the Apostles

Some who had come down from **Judea** were **instructing**
　　the **brothers**,
　　"**Unless** you are **circumcised** according to the **Mosaic practice**,
　　you **cannot** be **saved**."
Because there arose **no little dissension** and **debate**
　　by **Paul** and **Barnabas** with them,
　　it was decided that **Paul**, **Barnabas**, and **some** of the **others**
　　should go up to **Jerusalem** to the **apostles** and **elders**
　　about this question.

Say this with great authority.
Mosaic = moh-SAY-ik

Now the narrator is speaking. Emphasize
"no little dissension and debate."

The **apostles** and **elders**, in agreement with the **whole church**,
　　decided to choose **representatives**
　　and to send them to **Antioch with Paul** and **Barnabas**.
The ones **chosen** were **Judas**, who was called **Barsabbas**,
　　and **Silas**, **leaders** among the brothers.
This is the **letter** delivered by them:

"The **apostles** and the **elders**, your **brothers**,
　　to the brothers in **Antioch**, **Syria**, and **Cilicia**
　　of **Gentile** origin: **greetings**.
Since we have **heard** that some of **our number**
　　who went out without **any mandate** from **us**
　　have **upset** you with their **teachings**
　　and **disturbed** your **peace** of **mind**,
　　we have with **one accord** decided to choose **representatives**

Emphasize "the whole church."

Barnabas = BAHR-nuh-buhs
Jerusalem = juh-ROO-suh-lem;
Juh-ROO-zuh-lem
Antioch = AN-tee-ahk
Judas = JOO-duhs
Silas = SĪ-luhs
Read this as though you were reading an
announcement. Raise your voice.
Syria = SEER-ee-uh
Cilicia = suh-LISH-ee-uh
Gentile = GEN-til

READING I The action in today's reading takes place immediately after Paul's first missionary journey, when he and Barnabas have returned to Antioch. Paul, of course, had been converting both Jews and Gentiles, and the Gentiles were not circumcised. Now, some were saying that unless the Gentiles were circumcised, they could not be in right relationship with God; they could not be saved. In other words, all Christians must also be Jewish and follow the Jewish Law. Paul and Barnabas argue against these false teachers. In addition, they decide to go to Jerusalem to talk with the leaders of the Jerusalem church about the issue.

Today's reading then skips verses 15:3–21. In these verses, we learn that when Paul and Barnabas arrive in Jerusalem and present the false teaching, some of the Pharisees who had become Christians also think that Gentiles should be circumcised and required to keep the Law of Moses. This disagreement sets the stage for the first church council, the Council of Jerusalem.

At the meeting, Peter reminds everyone about his experience. He had gone to Cornelius' house only to discover that God had already sent his Spirit upon the Gentiles (see Acts 10). Both Jew and Gentile are saved through grace, not through observance of the Law, he argues. James also speaks, pointing out that the conversion of the Gentiles fulfills the words of the prophets. James does not want to require circumcision.

Today's passage then picks up the story again. Paul, Barnabas, and some chosen representatives are to return to Antioch with the Council's decision.

and to **send** them to you along with our **beloved Barnabas**
and **Paul**,
who have dedicated their **lives** to the **name**
of our **Lord Jesus Christ**.
So we are sending **Judas** and **Silas**
who will **also convey** this **same message** by **word** of **mouth**:
'It is the **decision** of the **Holy Spirit** and of **us**
not to **place** on you **any burden** beyond **these necessities**,
namely, to **abstain** from **meat sacrificed** to **idols**,
from **blood**, from **meats** of **strangled animals**,
and from **unlawful marriage**.
If you keep **free** of **these**,
you will be doing what is **right. Farewell.**'"

READING II   Revelation 21:10–14, 22–23

A reading from the Book of Revelation

The **angel** took me in **spirit** to a **great, high mountain**
and **showed** me the **holy city Jerusalem**
coming **down** out of **heaven** from **God**.
It **gleamed** with the **splendor** of **God**.
Its **radiance** was like that of a **precious stone**,
like **jasper**, **clear** as **crystal**.
It had a **massive, high wall**,
with **twelve gates** where **twelve angels** were stationed
and on which **names** were **inscribed**,
the **names** of the **twelve tribes** of the **Israelites**.

Circumcision will not be required of Gentiles, nor will observance of the Mosaic Law. Only some eating restrictions and some laws involving sexual activity will be required. As you proclaim the reading, remember that the way the decision was reached is just as important as the decision itself. Make it clear to your listeners that consultation and communal discernment under the inspiration of the Holy Spirit were hallmarks of the early Church.

READING II Once again we read some of John's description of the "new Jerusalem," one of the symbols John uses to describe the final victory of good over evil. In the line immediately before today's reading, an angel says to John, "Come here. I will show you the bride, the wife of the Lamb" (Revelation 21:9). The new Jerusalem described in today's reading is that bride, the wife of the Lamb, the redeemed community of God's people.

This redeemed community has massive walls with twelve gates, three facing in every direction. The names of the twelve tribes are inscribed on the gates. The stones in the foundation of the walls are inscribed with the names of the Twelve Apostles. This is to say that both the story of the twelve tribes and the story of the Twelve Apostles define and are foundational to the identity of the redeemed community, which is now open to all.

The new Jerusalem does not need a Temple. Traditionally the Temple had been understood to be the place where God

There were **three** gates facing **east**,
  three **north**, three **south**, and three **west**.
The **wall** of the city had **twelve courses** of **stones**
    as its **foundation**,
  on which were inscribed the twelve **names**
  of the twelve **apostles** of the **Lamb**.

I saw **no temple** in the **city**
  for its **temple** is the **Lord God almighty** and the **Lamb**.
The **city** had **no need** of **sun** or **moon** to **shine** on it,
  for the **glory** of **God** gave it **light**,
  and its **lamp** was the **Lamb**.

This is an explanation, not a description. Speak more matter-of-factly.

Now let awe return to your tone as you conclude.

GOSPEL John 14:23–29

A reading from the holy Gospel according to John

Jesus said to his **disciples**:
  "Whoever **loves** me will **keep** my **word**,
  and my **Father** will **love him**,
  and we will **come** to him and **make** our **dwelling with** him.
Whoever does **not** love me does **not** keep my words;
  yet the **word** you **hear** is **not mine**
  but **that** of the **Father** who **sent** me.

"I have **told** you this while I am **with** you.
The **Advocate**, the **Holy Spirit**,
  whom the **Father** will **send** in **my name**,
  will **teach** you **everything**
  and **remind** you of **all** that I **told** you.

This is an intimate conversation. Speak with warmth and gentleness.

Now speak with more authority.

Now Jesus is reassuring the disciples. Advocate = AD-voh-k*t

Sound encouraging.

---

dwells. Now, God dwells in the whole city; God dwells in and among his people. Nor does the city need a sun or moon. In this community, God is the only source of light, and the Lamb is the lamp that reveals that light.

Because the Book of Revelation teaches hope through symbolic language, it is often difficult to understand. Proclaim the reading slowly so that your listeners have time to translate the symbols into ideas. To live in the new Jerusalem, we, too, need to let God become our light.

GOSPEL Today we continue to read Jesus' farewell discourse to his Apostles on the night before he died. Remember that John's audience is living at the end of the first century and is looking for the presence of the risen Christ. Jesus has not returned in glory on the clouds of heaven, as expected. As John pictures Jesus speaking to his disciples, John is directly addressing the question on the mind of his audience.

Today's reading is a continuation of a passage in which Jesus assures the disciples that he will be with them after his

Death. Jesus has just said: "I will not leave you orphans; I will come to you. In a little while the world will no longer see me, but you will see me, because I live and you will live" (John 14:18–19). John is teaching his end-of-the-century audience, and us, that Jesus is not absent, but present.

As today's reading begins, Jesus tells the disciples that the bond of unity between himself, his Father, and them, the bond that will enable them to experience Jesus' presence, is love. Those who love Jesus will not be separated from him; rather, both

Now Jesus is comforting the disciples.

A note of persuasiveness enters here.

Conclude with gentle authority.

Peace I **leave** with you; my **peace** I **give** to you.
Not as the **world** gives do **I give** it to **you**.
Do **not** let your **hearts** be **troubled** or **afraid**.
You heard me **tell** you,
　'I am **going away** and I will come **back** to you.'
If you **loved** me,
　　you would **rejoice** that I am **going** to the **Father**;
　　for the **Father** is **greater** than **I**.
And now I have **told** you this before it **happens**,
　　so that **when** it **happens** you may **believe**."

Jesus and his Father will dwell with those who love them: "Whoever loves me will keep my word, and my Father will love him, and we will come to him and make our dwelling with him."

In addition, Jesus tells his disciples that they will receive "the Advocate, the Holy Spirit" who "will teach [them] everything and remind" them of all that Jesus has told them. The disciples obviously do not understand everything they are being taught. However, after the Resurrection, and with the help of the Holy Spirit, they will begin to understand what at this point is incomprehensible to them.

Next, Jesus offers the disciples peace. He does not want them to be "troubled or afraid." In an additional effort to comfort them, Jesus again emphasizes that he will return: "You heard me tell you, 'I am going away and I will come back to you.'"

Finally Jesus (and John) returns the emphasis to love. Jesus says: "If you loved me, you would rejoice that I am going to the Father." Love always acts for the other's good. Jesus has come from the Father, has done the Father's will, and now returns to the Father. When the disciples truly love Jesus, they will recognize that even though Jesus has returned to the Father, the Father, Son, and Spirit still dwell within and among them.

As you proclaim this reading, emphasize the absolute priority of love. It is love that will enable not only the disciples, but John's audience, and us, to experience the presence of the risen Christ in our midst.

THE ASCENSION OF THE LORD

Lectionary #58

READING I   Acts 1:1–11

A reading from the beginning of the Acts of the Apostles

Luke is giving background information. Speak matter-of-factly.

Theophilus = thee-AWF-uh-luhs

In the **first** book, **Theophilus**,
    I dealt with **all** that **Jesus did** and **taught**
    until the **day** he was **taken up**,
    after giving **instructions** through the **Holy Spirit**
    to the **apostles** whom he had **chosen**.

Here let some awe and excitement enter your tone.

He presented himself **alive** to them
    by **many proofs** after he had **suffered**,
    appearing to them during **forty days**
    and **speaking** about the **kingdom** of **God**.
While **meeting** with them,

Repeat the instructions slowly and with firmness.

Jerusalem = juh-ROO-suh-lem; juh-ROO-zuh-lem

    he **enjoined** them **not** to **depart** from **Jerusalem**,
    but to **wait** for "the **promise** of the **Father**
    about which you have heard me **speak**;
    for **John baptized** with **water**,

Emphasize "Holy Spirit." Then pause.

    but in a few days **you** will be **baptized** with the **Holy Spirit**."

The Apostles are excited.

When they had **gathered together** they asked him,
    "**Lord**, are you at **this time** going to **restore**
    the **kingdom** to **Israel**?"

Jesus answers gently. He has to correct the Apostles, but he wants them to have hope.

He **answered** them, "It is **not** for you to **know** the **times**
        or **seasons**
    that the **Father** has **established** by his **own authority**.

This is a promise and very exciting news.

But you will receive **power** when the **Holy Spirit** comes **upon** you,
    and you will be **my witnesses** in **Jerusalem**,

READING I   Today's reading from Acts begins with Luke's introduction to this second volume of his two volume work: the Gospel according to Luke and the Acts of the Apostles. Luke ends his gospel account and begins Acts with an account of the Ascension.

In the Gospel we will read today, Luke places the Ascension on Easter Sunday night, on the evening of the same day that the empty tomb was discovered. However, in Acts, the Ascension is pictured as being forty days after Easter. Our liturgical calendar follows the account in Acts.

That the same author describes the Ascension as occurring at different times shows that Luke is not teaching history. He is teaching about spiritual realities. Luke's account of the Ascension is a kind of book end, dividing Christ's mission carried out by Jesus Christ on earth and Christ's mission carried out by Jesus' disciples under the inspiration of the Holy Spirit. The number "forty" that Luke uses is a symbolic number, signifying the time of fulfillment when God's will has been accomplished.

Jesus' instructions to the Apostles appear at the end of the Gospel and at the beginning of Acts. However, in Acts the disciples ask Jesus if he is going to "restore the kingdom to Israel." They are still thinking in political terms, not spiritual terms. They have not yet understood that Jesus' kingdom is a spiritual and eternal kingdom.

Jesus then instructs the Apostles that they will be Jesus' witnesses to the ends of the earth. After this commissioning, Jesus is lifted up and is no longer visible. As was true at the empty tomb, two men dressed in white interpret the meaning of

Judea = <u>joo</u>-DEE-uh; <u>joo</u> DAY-uh
Samaria = suh-MAYR-ee-uh

Now the narrator is speaking.

Speak with awe.

The "men" speak with authority.
Galilee = GAL-ih-lee

throughout **Judea** and **Samaria**,
and to the **ends** of the **earth**."
When he had **said** this, as they were **looking on**,
he was **lifted up**, and a **cloud took** him from their **sight**.
While they were looking **intently** at the **sky** as he was **going**,
suddenly two men dressed in **white garments**
stood beside them.
They said, "**Men** of **Galilee**,
why are you **standing** there looking at the **sky**?
This **Jesus** who has been **taken up** from you into **heaven**
will **return** in the **same way** as you have **seen** him
going into **heaven**."

READING II   Ephesians 1:17–23

Ephesians = ee-FEE-zhuhnz

Paul is offering a blessing.

The next thirteen lines are all one
sentence. Read slowly, pausing after
each comma.

A reading from the Letter of Saint Paul to the Ephesians

Brothers and **sisters**:
May the **God** of our **Lord Jesus Christ**, the **Father** of **glory**,
give you a **Spirit** of **wisdom** and **revelation**
resulting in **knowledge** of him.
May the **eyes** of your **hearts** be **enlightened**,
that you may know what is the **hope** that belongs to **his call**,
what are the **riches** of **glory**
in **his inheritance** among the **holy ones**,
and what is the **surpassing greatness** of **his power**
for us who **believe**,
in accord with the **exercise** of his **great might**:
which he **worked** in **Christ**,
raising him from the **dead**
and **seating** him at his **right hand** in the **heavens**,

---

the event for the Apostles and for the readers. Jesus has ascended to heaven, but Jesus will return.

In the meantime, the Apostles should not spend their time "looking at the sky." They have a mission to fulfill: to be witnesses of Jesus Christ in Jerusalem, throughout Judea and Samaria, indeed, to the ends of the earth. Since the Apostles' mission is now our mission, make eye contact with the assembly and read the commissioning slowly and clearly.

READING II   **EPHESIANS.** In the reading from Ephesians, the author is offering a prayer or a blessing. He prays that the Ephesians may have knowledge of God, of the hope to which they are called, of the riches of their spiritual inheritance, and of God's great power. This power has been illustrated in what God has done in and through Jesus Christ.

This mighty God has raised Jesus from the dead and seated him at God's own right hand in heaven. Jesus' authority far surpasses that of any other known authority, power, or dominion. This Jesus, who is

head of all things, has been given to the "church, which is his body." This Jesus has been given to us.

This beautiful blessing is expressed in very long sentences. Therefore, as you read the sentences, read slowly and pause after each comma. Also, make sure you understand the reading yourself before you try to proclaim it. Your intonations and your pacing will make the reading understandable to those who hear you. Try to proclaim the reading so that those gathered receive the same blessing that the author wished to give the Ephesians.

far above **every principality**, **authority**, **power**, and **dominion**,
and **every name** that is **named**
not only in **this age** but **also** in the one to **come**.
And he put **all things** beneath his **feet**
and gave him as **head** over **all things** to the **church**,
which is his **body**,
the **fullness** of the **one** who **fills all things** in **every way**.

Or:

READING II Hebrews 9:24–28; 10:19–23

A reading from the Letter to the Hebrews

Christ did not enter into a **sanctuary** made by **hands**,
a **copy** of the **true** one, but **heaven itself**,
that he might now **appear** before **God** on **our behalf**.
Not that he might offer himself **repeatedly**,
as the **high** priest enters **each year** into the **sanctuary**
with **blood** that is **not** his **own**;
if **that** were **so**, he would have had to **suffer repeatedly**
from the **foundation** of the **world**.
But **now once for all he** has **appeared** at the **end** of the **ages**
to take away **sin** by **his sacrifice**.
Just as it is **appointed** that **men** and **women die once**,
and after **this** the **judgment**, so also **Christ**,
offered once to take away the **sins** of **many**,
will appear a **second** time, **not** to take away **sin**
but to bring **salvation** to those who **eagerly await** him.

Therefore, **brothers** and **sisters**, since through the **blood** of **Jesus**
we have **confidence** of **entrance** into the **sanctuary**

Side notes (left column):

Say these lines with awe.
principality = prin-suh-PAL-uh-tee
Pause here.
Emphasize "all things," which is repeated several times.
authority = uh-THOHR-ih-tee
dominion = doh-MIN-yuhn

The author is teaching.

This is a contrast.

Obviously, this is not true.

Now the true argument is being presented. Emphasize this sentence.

Now the author offers an analogy.

The author is drawing a conclusion. Sound encouraging.

HEBREWS. Today's reading from Hebrews is part teaching and part exhortation. The author explains that Jesus offered the perfect sacrifice for sin: himself. Because this was a perfect sacrifice, it never need be repeated. Jesus is himself in the heavenly sanctuary and has paved the way for us to be there, too.

As the reading begins, the author compares Jesus' sacrifice for sin to the sacrifice offered by the Jewish high priest on the Day of Atonement. Those priests entered the sanctuary of the Temple, a sanctuary made by human hands. Jesus, by

contrast, entered the heavenly sanctuary. Therefore, Jesus now appears "before God on our behalf."

The animal sacrifice that the priests offer in the Temple must be repeated every year. Jesus' sacrifice need never be repeated. When Jesus appears again, it will not be to offer sacrifice, but "to bring salvation to those who eagerly await him."

After this explanation, the tone of the reading changes to exhortation. The Hebrews, and we, are exhorted to approach the heavenly sanctuary "with a sincere heart and in absolute trust." This trust is

well placed, as is our hope, because "he who made the promise is trustworthy."

The first part of the reading is difficult to understand. However, once you master the author's meaning, you will be able to proclaim this good news, both the explanation and the exhortation, so that your listeners realize anew that they, too, expect to join Jesus in heaven.

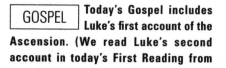

GOSPEL Today's Gospel includes Luke's first account of the Ascension. (We read Luke's second account in today's First Reading from

by the **new** and **living way** he opened for us through the **veil**,
that is, **his flesh**,
and since we have "a **great priest** over the **house** of **God**,"
let us **approach** with a **sincere heart** and in **absolute trust**,
with our hearts **sprinkled clean** from an **evil conscience**
and our **bodies washed** in **pure water**.
Let us hold **unwaveringly** to our **confession** that gives us **hope**,
for he who made the **promise** is **trustworthy**.

This is an exhortation.

Conclude the exhortation with a tone of certainty.

GOSPEL   Luke 24:46–53

A reading from the holy Gospel according to Luke

Jesus said to his **disciples**:
"**Thus** it is **written** that the **Christ** would **suffer**
and **rise** from the **dead** on the **third day**
and that **repentance**, for the **forgiveness** of **sins**,
would be **preached** in **his name**
to **all** the **nations**, **beginning** from **Jerusalem**.
You are **witnesses** of these things.
And **behold** I am sending the **promise** of my **Father** upon you;
but **stay** in the **city**
until you are **clothed** with **power** from on **high**."

Then he **led** them out as far as **Bethany**,
raised his **hands**, and **blessed** them.
As he **blessed** them he **parted** from them
and was **taken up** to **heaven**.
They did him **homage**
and then returned to **Jerusalem** with **great joy**,
and they were **continually** in the **temple praising God**.

Jesus is explaining the scandal of his Crucifixion.

Emphasize "all the nations."
Jerusalem = juh-ROO-suh-lem;
juh-ROO-zuh-lem

Read this line slowly, then pause

Now the narrator is speaking.

Bethany = BETH-uh-nee

Speak slowly.
Increase your tempo as you conclude.

Acts.) In the Gospel, the Ascension takes place on Easter night, after Jesus' post-Resurrection appearance to the disciples in Jerusalem. On that same day the women have discovered the empty tomb, and Jesus has appeared to two disciples on the road to Emmaus. Now Jesus is appearing to the disciples. He has shown them his hands and feet, invited them to touch him, and even eaten a piece of fish to demonstrate that he is not a ghost. (See Luke 24:36–46.)

As we join the story, Jesus is explaining that "it is written that the Christ would suffer and rise from the dead on the third day." The disciples sorely needed an explanation of the Crucifixion. That Jesus should have died such an ignominious death had shattered their faith.

Jesus goes on to tell the disciples that they are to preach "repentance for the forgiveness of sins" in Jesus' name to all nations. Before doing this, however, they are to stay in Jerusalem until they are "clothed with power from on high."

After saying this, Jesus blesses the disciples and is taken up to heaven. The disciples recognize Jesus' divinity because they "do him homage." They then return to Jerusalem, full of joy and praising God, while they await the coming of the Spirit.

Jesus commissions the disciples as witnesses and promises them the Holy Spirit. As you proclaim Jesus' words, look up at people in the assembly. Try to help them realize that they, too, are commissioned to be witnesses of Jesus Christ and are promised the Spirit.

7TH SUNDAY OF EASTER

Lectionary #61

READING I   Acts 7:55–60

A reading from the Acts of the Apostles

This is the narrator speaking. Read slowly and distinctly.

Stephen, **filled** with the **Holy Spirit**,
   looked up **intently** to **heaven** and **saw** the **glory** of **God**
   and **Jesus** standing at the **right hand** of **God**,

Now Stephen is speaking. He is having a vision and is full of awe.

   and **Stephen** said, "**Behold**, I see the **heavens opened**
   and the **Son** of **Man** standing at the **right hand** of **God**."

The narrator speaks again. Speak more quickly. Pause after "stone him."

But they **cried out** in a **loud voice**,
   covered their **ears**, and **rushed** upon him **together**.
They **threw** him **out** of the city, and began to **stone** him.
The **witnesses** laid down their **cloaks**

Now speak more slowly again. These two lines are foreshadowing things to come.
Saul = sawl

   at the **feet** of a young man named **Saul**.
As they were **stoning Stephen**, he **called out**,

Stephen calls out in a loud voice.

   "**Lord Jesus, receive my spirit**."
Then he **fell** to his **knees** and **cried out** in a **loud voice**,

Stephen calls out again.
Lower your volume for the narrator's conclusion.

   "**Lord**, do **not hold** this **sin against** them";
   and when he **said** this, he fell **asleep**.

READING I Today's reading is not the first time we meet Stephen in the Acts of the Apostles. Stephen was one of the men who was selected to administer the goods of the community when the Apostles found that this responsibility was taking them away from their major responsibility of preaching the Word (Acts 6:1–7). Stephen became a very effective teacher and so attracted the ire of some of the members of the synagogue. After being accused of blasphemy by false witnesses, Stephen preached to the Sanhedrin, putting Jesus Christ and his mission in the context of all

of Jewish salvation history. Stephen's preaching infuriated the Sanhedrin. At this point our Lectionary reading picks up the story.

As Luke describes Stephen's martyrdom, Luke makes it clear that Stephen's ministry is a mirror image of Jesus' ministry. First, Stephen has a vision of the risen Christ in glory in heaven. When he tells the members of the Sanhedrin about his vision, they are furious; they take him outside the city, and stone him to death. Stephen's words as he dies recall Jesus' words as he died: "Lord Jesus, receive my spirit" (Luke

23:46), and "Lord do not hold this sin against them" (Luke 23:34). Luke then says that Stephen "fell asleep." This is Luke's way of affirming that Stephen is not dead, but will be with the risen Christ in heaven.

As he tells the story of Stephen's martyrdom, Luke also introduces the person who will be the main focus of the second half of Acts: Saul, also called Paul. Before his conversion, Paul was among those who persecuted Christians.

As you proclaim the reading, emphasize those parts of Stephen's ministry that reflect Jesus' ministry. One of Luke's main

Revelation = rev-uh-LAY-shuhn

John sets the stage.

Now Jesus speaks. Raise your volume and speak slowly.

Alpha = AL-fuh
Omega = oh-MAY-guh

Say this with conviction. These are words of comfort for those whose loved ones have suffered martyrdom.

Again, raise your volume and speak slowly.

This is an invitation. Say "come" in a heartfelt tone.

This line offers great hope.
Say this as an ardent prayer.

READING II Revelation 22:12–14, 16–17, 20

A reading from the Book of Revelation

I, John, heard a **voice** saying to me:
    "**Behold**, I am **coming soon**.
I bring **with** me the **recompense** I will give to **each**
    according to his **deeds**.
I am the **Alpha** and the **Omega**, the **first** and the **last**,
    the **beginning** and the **end**."

Blessed are they who **wash** their **robes**
    so as to have the **right** to the **tree** of life
    and enter the **city** through its **gates**.

"**I, Jesus**, sent my **angel** to give you **this testimony**
        for the **churches**.
I am the **root** and **offspring** of **David**,
    the **bright morning star**."

The **Spirit** and the **bride** say, "**Come**."
Let the **hearer** say, "**Come**."
Let the **one** who **thirsts** come **forward**,
    and the **one** who **wants it** receive the **gift** of **life-giving water**.

The **one** who gives this **testimony** says, "**Yes**, I am **coming soon**."
Amen! **Come, Lord Jesus!**

points is that Jesus' disciples are carrying on Jesus' own ministry under the power of the Holy Spirit.

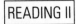 In today's passage from Revelation, John is once again having a vision in which Jesus, who is God, speaks. We know the speaker is the risen Christ because the voice says, "I am the Alpha and the Omega, the first and the last, the beginning and the end." God had previously identified himself as the Alpha and the Omega as the book began (see Revelation 1:8).

The victorious Christ says to John, "Behold, I am coming soon." This is wonderful news for those in John's persecuted audience. They are waiting for the risen Christ to come and make his victory over evil and death manifest in their lives. Not only is Christ coming soon, but Christ will "bring . . . the recompense" according to each person's deeds. In other words, when Christ comes, judgment will occur. Those who have been persecuting John's audience will be held accountable for their evil actions. Those innocent Christians who have endured persecution will be

rewarded. Those who have been martyred will join the victorious Christ in heaven. They have washed their robes in the blood of the Lamb, (see Revelation 7:13–17), and so will have eternal life.

The bride who says, "Come," stands for the redeemed community of God's people, the Church (Revelation 21:9–11), and the redeemed community longs for Jesus to come. In addition, that community invites others to join it, to receive "the gift of life-giving water," to receive Baptism. As the reading ends, the victorious Christ again

GOSPEL John 17:20–26

A reading from the holy Gospel according to John

Lifting up his **eyes** to **heaven**, Jesus **prayed** saying:
"**Holy Father**, I pray **not only** for **them**,
    but also for those who will **believe** in **me** through **their word**,
    so that they may **all** be **one**,
    as **you**, **Father**, are in **me** and I in **you**,
    that they **also** may be in **us**,
    that the **world** may **believe** that **you** sent me.
And **I** have given **them** the **glory you** gave **me**,
    so that **they** may be **one**, as **we** are **one**,
    I in **them** and **you** in **me**,
    that they may be brought to **perfection** as **one**,
    that the **world** may **know** that **you** sent **me**,
    and that **you loved them** even as **you loved me**.
Father, **they** are **your gift** to me.
I **wish** that where **I** am **they also** may be **with me**,
    that they may **see my glory** that **you** gave me,
    because **you loved me** before the **foundation** of the **world**.
Righteous Father, the **world also** does **not** know **you**,
    but **I know you**, and **they know** that **you** sent **me**.
I made **known** to them **your name** and **I will** make it **known**,
    that the **love** with which **you loved me**
    may be in **them** and **I** in **them**."

The first line is the narrator's voice introducing Jesus' prayer.

The next six lines are one sentence. Read slowly and pause at each comma.

Emphasize the "you" in "you sent me." This will be repeated.

Emphasize "one" all three times.

Again, emphasize the "you" in "you sent me."

This is a wish. Use a softer tone.

Now speak with firmness for the last four lines.

---

promises, "I am coming soon" and the community responds, "Come, Lord Jesus!"

Because the Book of Revelation is written in symbolic language, it is difficult to understand. Make sure you understand the symbols yourself before proclaiming the reading so that, by your intonations and pauses, you can make the symbols understandable to the congregation.

GOSPEL   Today we read the conclusion of Jesus' prayer at his last meal with the disciples. Jesus prays not only for the disciples, but for "those

who will believe in me through their word." In other words, Jesus prays for us.

There are two main thoughts in this prayer. The first is that it is vitally important for Jesus' disciples to remain united with each other. This is absolutely essential so that others may also come to believe. Only if Christians remain united will the world believe that Jesus was sent by the Father.

The second main idea is that this necessary union is established through love. As the Father and Jesus love each other, so does Jesus love his disciples, and so must

his disciples love each other. Only if they remain in God's love will the disciples be able to see Jesus' glory, the glory Jesus has with the Father.

Unity and love are the ideas to be emphasized as you proclaim the reading. Try to look up at the congregation as you read so that those gathered before you will understand that Jesus said this prayer for them.

PENTECOST SUNDAY: VIGIL

Lectionary #62

READING I   Genesis 11:1–9

Genesis = JEN-uh-sis

The narrator is beginning to tell us a story.

Shinar = SHEE-nahr; SHĪ-nahr

The people are anxious to get started.
mortar = MOHR-t*r

These are great plans! The people are full of themselves.
bitumen = bih-TOO-m*n; bih-TYOO-m*n; bĭh-TYOO-m*n

God is pictured like a human being. He is offended at the peoples' prideful actions.

Emphasize this "Let us" in contrast to the people's "let us."

This is the narrator speaking.

A reading from the Book of Genesis

The **whole world** spoke the **same language**, using the **same words**.
While the **people** were **migrating** in the **east**,
    they came upon a **valley** in the land of **Shinar** and **settled** there.
They **said** to one another,
    "**Come**, let us **mold bricks** and **harden** them with **fire**."
They used **bricks** for **stone**, and **bitumen** for **mortar**.
Then they said, "**Come**, let us **build ourselves** a **city**
    and a **tower** with its **top** in the **sky**,
    and so make a name for **ourselves**;
    otherwise we shall be **scattered all over** the **earth**."

The LORD **came down to see** the **city** and the **tower**
    that the **people** had **built**.
Then the LORD said: "**If now**, while they are **one people**,
    all speaking the **same language**,
    they have **started** to do **this**,
    nothing will later **stop** them from **doing**
        whatever they **presume** to **do**.
Let us then go **down there** and **confuse** their **language**,
    so that **one** will **not understand** what **another says**."
Thus the LORD **scattered** them from there **all over** the **earth**,
    and they **stopped building** the **city**.

READING I   **GENESIS.** The story of the tower of Babel is proclaimed on the Vigil of Pentecost because, by the end of the story, people speak different languages and can't understand each other. This sad situation will be reversed on Pentecost: people who speak different languages will understand each other.

However, the story, if misunderstood, could lead to some false conclusions about God and about whether or not God wants human beings to have ingenuity and to flourish. To understand what the story is teaching we must consider the kind of writing we are reading, the literary form, as well as the placement of this story in the early chapters of Genesis, right before the call of Abraham.

The story of the tower of Babel was originally an "etiology." An etiology is a story that explains why something is as we know it is from experience. The original author of the story knew from experience that people spoke different languages. He composed this story to explain why this is the case. The word "babel" is a play on the Hebrew word *balal*, which means "confusion." In the original social context, by naming the tower "babel," the author was probably poking fun at the Babylonians who built towers called "ziggurats."

The story of the tower of Babel illustrates the negative effects of human pride. The human beings in the story want to make a name for themselves. They want to build a tower that will go all the way to heaven. They say, "Come, let us build ourselves . . . a tower with its top in the sky, and so make a name for ourselves; otherwise we shall be scattered all over the earth."

Here the narrator is insulting Babylon.
Babel = BAB-*l; BAY-b*l

That is why it was called **Babel,**
because **there** the Lord **confused** the **speech** of **all** the **world.**
It was from **that place** that he **scattered** them **all over** the **earth.**

Or:

Exodus = EK-suh-duhs

READING I   Exodus 19:3–8a, 16–20b

A reading from the Book of Exodus

Here God initially speaks in terms of intimacy and gentleness.
Israelite = IZ-ree-uh-lit; IZ-ray-uh-lit
Egyptians = ee-JIP-shuhnz

Moses went up the **mountain** to **God.**
Then the Lord **called** to him and said,
    "**Thus** shall you **say** to the **house** of Jacob;
    tell the **Israelites:**
    You have **seen for yourselves** how I treated the **Egyptians**
    and how I **bore you up** on **eagle wings**
    and brought you **here** to **myself.**

Now raise your voice and speak slowly. This passage is core to the Israelites' self identity.

Therefore, if you **hearken** to my **voice** and **keep** my **covenant,**
    you shall be my **special possession,**
    dearer to me than **all other people,**
    though all the **earth** is **mine.**
You shall be to me a **kingdom** of **priests,** a **holy nation.**

Emphasize this line.
Now drop your voice again.
Now the narrator is giving us background information.

That is what you must **tell** the **Israelites."**
So **Moses went** and **summoned** the **elders** of the **people.**
When he set before them
    all that the Lord had **ordered him** to tell them,
    the **people all answered together,**
    "**Everything** the Lord has **said, we will do."**

Say this with total conviction and commitment; then pause.

This story appears in Genesis because it is one of four "sin stories" that sets the stage for an account of salvation history, an account that begins with God calling Abraham. By the end of the sin stories, human beings are not obeying God's original instructions to "fill the earth" (Genesis 1:28); rather, they are isolated from God and each other, and lack the power to undo the harm they have caused.

The story of the tower of Babel includes what is called an "anthropomorphic" picture of God; that is, God is pictured as a human being. God is angry

because human beings have become prideful, so he decides to thwart their efforts. Human beings cannot build a structure that joins heaven and earth.

As you proclaim the story, do not hesitate to enter into the mood of the characters. The human beings are full of pride. God is teaching them a lesson. However, the lesson that the Church is teaching us is that human beings cannot save themselves. Only God and God's initiative can bridge the chasm that sin has caused between heaven and earth.

EXODUS. As this reading begins, Moses is going up Mount Sinai to meet God, and God gives Moses instructions about what to tell the Israelites, who are encamped at the foot of the mountain. First, the Israelites are to reflect on their experience of the exodus. It was God who enabled the Egyptians to escape slavery in Egypt: "I bore you up on eagle wings and brought you here to myself." Now God is reminding the Israelites that if they listen to his voice and remain faithful to their covenant relationship, he will make them a "kingdom of priests, a holy nation." Moses

Read these lines with awe.

On the **morning** of the **third day**
> there were **peals** of **thunder** and **lightning**,
> and a **heavy cloud** over the **mountain**,
> and a **very loud trumpet blast**,
> so that **all** the **people** in the camp **trembled**.

Say this with confidence. After all, the people know they are dear to God.

But **Moses led** the **people out** of the **camp** to **meet God**,
> and they stationed themselves at the **foot** of the **mountain**.

Now return to a tone of awe
Sinai = SĪ-nī

Mount Sinai was **all wrapped** in **smoke**,
> for the LORD **came down upon** it in **fire**.
The smoke **rose** from it as though from a **furnace**,
> and the **whole mountain trembled violently**.

Let your voice get louder and louder, too.

The **trumpet** blast grew **louder** and **louder**,
> while **Moses** was **speaking**,
> and **God** answering him with **thunder**.

Drop your voice for the last two lines.

When the LORD **came down** to the **top** of **Mount Sinai**,
> he summoned **Moses** to the **top** of the **mountain**.

Or:

<hr>

READING I   Ezekiel 37:1–14

Ezekiel = ee-ZEE-kee-uhl

A reading from the Book of the Prophet Ezekiel

Ezekiel is speaking. He is setting the stage for the conversation that follows.

The **hand** of the LORD came **upon** me,
> and he **led me out** in the **spirit** of the LORD
> and **set** me in the **center** of the **plain**,
> which was now **filled** with **bones**.

Emphasize "bones."

He made me **walk** among the **bones** in **every direction**
> so that I **saw** how **many they were** on the **surface** of the **plain**.

Say this with amazement.

How dry they were!

returns to the people, summons the elders, and repeats God's message to them. All the people respond "Everything the LORD has said, we will do."

This Lectionary selection then skips several verses in which God instructs Moses to tell the people to sanctify themselves for two days, because on the third day, God will reveal himself on Mt. Sinai. The symbols used to describe God's theophany (appearance) on the mountain are thunder, lightning, trumpet blasts, smoke, fire, and the trembling of the whole earth.

This scene, proclaimed on the Vigil of Pentecost, is a foreshadowing of the coming of the Spirit upon the early Church when the Spirit descended as tongues of fire. Therefore, as you proclaim the reading, give special emphasis to the line: "for the LORD came down upon it in fire."

EZEKIEL. Today's prophecy from Ezekiel was originally directed toward the Israelites when they were in exile in Babylonia. The exile was a terribly traumatic time for the Israelites. They believed

that they were in a covenant relationship with God and that God had promised them their nation. Now the nation was conquered and they were living in foreign lands. Their feelings are expressed near the end of today's reading when the house of Israel says, "Our bones are dried up, our hope is lost, and we are cut off." Through Ezekiel's prophecy, God is offering the people hope that they will live again, that they will return to their homeland.

As the account begins, Ezekiel sees a plain full of dry bones and is asked, "Can these bones come to life?" One would

God asks this question. God is testing Ezekiel's faith.

Ezekiel passes the test. He knows God can do anything.

God is speaking with great authority.

prophesy = PROF-uh-sī

Emphasize "come to life."

sinews = SIN-yoos

Emphasize this whole line.

Now drop your voice. Ezekiel is speaking.

Say this with awe.

Say this with disappointment.

God again speaks with great authority.

Emphasize "spirit."

Emphasize "come to life."

Say this with excitement and amazement.

Israel = IZ-ree-uhl; IZ-ray-uhl

Now God is explaining the meaning of the vision.

The people have been saying this with despair.

He asked me:
> Son of man, can these bones come to life?

I answered, "Lord GOD, you alone know that."
Then he said to me:
> Prophesy over these bones, and say to them:
> Dry bones, hear the word of the LORD!

Thus says the Lord GOD to these bones:
> See! I will bring spirit into you, that you may come to life.
> I will put sinews upon you, make flesh grow over you,
>   cover you with skin, and put spirit in you
>   so that you may come to life and know that I am the LORD.

I, Ezekiel, prophesied as I had been told,
    and even as I was prophesying I heard a noise;
    it was a rattling as the bones came together, bone joining bone.
I saw the sinews and the flesh come upon them,
    and the skin cover them, but there was no spirit in them.
Then the LORD said to me:
> Prophesy to the spirit, prophesy, son of man,
>   and say to the spirit: Thus says the Lord GOD:
> From the four winds come, O spirit,
>   and breathe into these slain that they may come to life.

I prophesied as he told me, and the spirit came into them;
    they came alive and stood upright, a vast army.
Then he said to me:
> Son of man, these bones are the whole house of Israel.

They have been saying,
    "Our bones are dried up,
    our hope is lost, and we are cut off."

---

expect Ezekiel to say, "No," just as one might expect the exiles to be without hope. However, Ezekiel responds, "Lord GOD, you alone know that." Ezekiel believes that anything is possible with God.

First God gives the bones sinew, flesh, and skin. However, the bones are still not alive. Then God gives the bones spirit: ". . . the spirit came into them; they came alive and stood upright." This line, of course, deserves special emphasis on the Vigil of Pentecost.

God explains to Ezekiel that the bones are the house of Israel. God's message to the Israelites is: "I will open your graves and have you rise from them, and bring you back to the land of Israel. Then you shall know that I am the LORD." The reading is teaching not only the exiles, but us, that all things are possible with God, and that God will give us new life in the Spirit, too.

JOEL. Joel was a prophet after the exile was over and the Israelites had returned to the holy land. In today's reading, Joel is warning the people about a coming "day of the LORD," when God would

intervene in human history, and good would finally prevail over evil. Whether or not the day of the Lord was to be welcomed or dreaded depended entirely on how the people had been living their lives. If the people had been faithful, the day of the Lord would be glorious; if the people had been unfaithful, the day of the Lord would be the day of reckoning.

Earlier in the book, Joel's warning of the coming of the day of the Lord was a threat. The people had experienced a terrible infestation of locusts that had

Now God is speaking with compassion and assurance.

Therefore, **prophesy** and **say** to them: **Thus says** the **Lord** GOD:
> O my **people**, I will **open** your **graves**
> and have you **rise** from them,
> and **bring you back** to the **land** of Israel.

Then **you shall know** that **I am** the LORD,
> when I **open** your **graves** and have you **rise from** them,
> O my **people**!

I will put **my spirit** in **you** that **you may live**,
> and I will **settle you** upon **your land**;
> thus you shall **know** that **I am** the LORD.

I have **promised**, and **I will do it**, says the LORD.

Emphasize "O my people." It is being repeated.

Say these concluding lines with earnestness. God is promising and God will keep his promises.

Or:

Joel = JOH-*l

God is promising something wonderful!

Emphasize "pour out my spirit." This is being repeated.

These are signs of God's presence. They are meant to instill great awe, not fear.

READING I   Joel 3:1–5

A reading from the Book of the Prophet Joel

> **Thus** says the LORD:
> I will **pour out** my **spirit** upon **all flesh**.
> Your **sons** and **daughters** shall **prophesy**,
>> your **old men** shall **dream dreams**,
>> your **young men** shall **see visions**;
> even upon the **servants** and the **handmaids**,
>> in **those days**, I will **pour out** my **spirit**.
> And I will work **wonders** in the **heavens** and on the **earth**,
>> **blood**, **fire**, and **columns** of **smoke**;
> the **sun** will be **turned** to **darkness**,
>> and the **moon** to **blood**,

---

destroyed all their crops. Joel interpreted this event as punishment for sin. He called on the people to repent, and they did. Now, the day of the Lord will be a joyful day for the Israelites because they are in right relationship with God.

On the great day of the Lord, God will pour out his spirit "on all flesh," on males and females, on the old and the young, even on slaves. God will make his presence known in fire and smoke, as he did during the exodus and on Mount Sinai. The sun will become dark, and the moon turn to

blood. In other words, the day of the Lord will be truly earth shattering, a "great and terrible day": great for the Israelites because they have repented, terrible for other nations who have not repented.

Now that they have repented, have "call[ed] on the name of the LORD," the Israelites will be rescued. The Lord will call the survivors in Jerusalem. Therefore, as you proclaim the reading, do not use a threatening tone, but an encouraging and

hope-filled tone. Joel's words of encouragement prepare us for Pentecost, as we look forward to celebrating the pouring out of God's Spirit on the Church.

READING II In his Letter to the Romans, Paul explains the life in the Spirit that Christians are living. In today's selection, Paul reminds both the Romans, and us, of what has already been accomplished and of what remains to be accomplished in our life in the Spirit.

It is "great" for the audience, "terrible" for other nations.

Those in Judah are the faithful remnant. This is good news for them.

Zion = ZĪ-ahn

Jerusalem = juh-ROO-suh-lem; juh-ROO-zuh-lem

at the **coming** of the **day** of the LORD,
 the **great** and **terrible day**.
Then **everyone** shall be **rescued**
 who **calls** on the **name** of the LORD;
for on **Mount Zion** there shall be a **remnant**,
 as the LORD **has said**,
and in **Jerusalem survivors**
 whom the LORD shall **call**.

READING II   Romans 8:22–27

A reading from the Letter of Saint Paul to the Romans

Brothers and **sisters**:
We know that **all creation** is **groaning** in **labor pains**
 even until now;
 and not only **that**, but **we ourselves**,
 who have the **firstfruits** of the **Spirit**,
 we also groan within **ourselves**
 as we **wait** for **adoption**, the **redemption** of our **bodies**.
For in **hope** we were **saved**.
Now **hope** that **sees** is not **hope**.
For who **hopes** for what one **sees**?
But if we **hope** for what we **do not see**, we **wait** with **endurance**.

In the **same way**, the **Spirit too comes** to the **aid** of our **weakness**;
 for we do **not know how** to **pray** as we **ought**,
 but the **Spirit** himself **intercedes** with **inexpressible groanings**.

Speak slowly and emphasize "groaning in labor pains." This metaphor emphasizes the "already but not yet" nature of our life in the Spirit.

Say this with longing.

Now speak more quickly. With hope we can move forward.

The Spirit's coming is very good news; our hope rests in the Spirit.

Paul starts with what Christians know from experience: "We know that all creation is groaning in labor pains even now, and not only that, but we ourselves who have the firstfruits of the Spirit, we also groan within ourselves." Paul and his fellow Christians are the "firstfruits of the Spirit" because they have already received the Spirit. The Spirit is alive and working in and through them. At the same time, the Spirit has not yet accomplished God's will in and through creation. All of creation, including human beings, groans for the Spirit's work to flourish and be completed.

Paul affirms that Christians have already been saved: "in hope we were saved." However, since we have not yet seen the full ramifications of that fact, redemption is also a hope. Therefore, we wait with endurance for the full accomplishment of God's will.

During this "already but not yet" time in God's redemptive plan, "the Spirit . . . comes to the aid of our weakness." Because our knowledge is limited, yet we desire God's will, we do not always know how to pray. This lack on our part need not be a worry for us because the Spirit prays on our behalf, and the Spirit does know how to pray. God, who searches hearts, understands the Spirit's prayer. The Spirit intercedes with God on our behalf. Since you are proclaiming this reading on the Vigil of Pentecost, emphasize that we are the firstfruits of the Spirit and that the Spirit intercedes for us, God's holy ones.

The "one who searches hearts" is God. This is consoling news. It comforts us and adds to our hope.

And the one who **searches hearts**
> **knows** what is the **intention** of the **Spirit**,
> because he **intercedes** for the **holy ones**
> **according** to **God's will**.

GOSPEL   John 7:37–39

A reading from the holy Gospel according to John

The narrator's voice sets the stage.

On the **last** and **greatest day** of the **feast**,
> **Jesus stood up** and **exclaimed**,

Jesus is exclaiming. So should you.

> "Let **anyone** who **thirsts come** to **me** and **drink**.
As **Scripture** says:
> *Rivers of living water will flow from within him*
> > who **believes** in me."

Emphasize "living water" and "who believes in me."

Emphasize "the Spirit." This is why we are reading this passage on Pentecost.

He said this in reference to the **Spirit**
> that those who came to **believe** in **him** were to **receive**.

Drop your voice here. This is background information.

There **was**, of course, **no Spirit yet**,
> because **Jesus** had **not yet** been **glorified**.

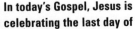

In today's Gospel, Jesus is celebrating the last day of the seven-day Feast of Tabernacles. He is speaking to a large crowd. Jesus invites all who thirst to come to him and drink. He then says, "Rivers of living water will flow from within him who believes in me."

The "living water" to which Jesus is referring is Baptism. Jesus has earlier told the woman at the well that the water he gives "becomes . . . in [her] a spring of water welling up to eternal life" (John 4:14). The author's voice tells us that Jesus said this statement "in reference to the Spirit." At Baptism Christians receive the Spirit.

The reading concludes, "There was, of course, no Spirit yet, because Jesus had not yet been glorified." John is clearly not talking about the existence of the Spirit but about the reception of the Spirit. When the Apostles and their companions receive the Spirit, they will be filled with understanding, courage, and power that they did not previously have.

This reading is selected for the Vigil of Pentecost because of Jesus' reference to the "Spirit that those who came to believe in him were to receive." Give this line special emphasis as you proclaim the reading.

PENTECOST SUNDAY: DAY

Lectionary #63

READING I Acts 2:1–11

A reading from the Acts of the Apostles

When the **time** for **Pentecost** was **fulfilled,**
    they were **all in one place together.**
And **suddenly** there came from the sky
    a **noise** like a **strong driving wind,**
    and it **filled** the **entire house** in which they **were.**
Then there appeared to them **tongues** as of **fire,**
    which **parted** and came to **rest** on **each one of them.**
And they were **all filled** with the **Holy Spirit**
    and began to **speak** in **different tongues,**
    as the **Spirit enabled** them to **proclaim.**

Now there were **devout Jews** from **every nation** under **heaven**
    staying in **Jerusalem.**
At this **sound,** they **gathered** in a **large crowd,**
    but they were **confused**
    because **each one** heard them speaking in his **own language.**
They were **astounded,** and in **amazement** they asked,
    "Are not **all these people** who are **speaking Galileans**?
Then how does **each** of **us hear** them in his **native language**?
We are **Parthians, Medes,** and **Elamites,**
    inhabitants of **Mesopotamia, Judea** and **Cappadocia,**

Side notes:

Pentecost = PEN-tih-kost; PEN-tih-kawst
Emphasize "all" and "together." This is important to Luke.
Raise your voice here and increase your tempo.

Now speak more slowly and lower your voice.

Say this with amazement.
tongues = tungs

Emphasize "every nation under heaven."
Jerusalem = juh-ROO-suh-lem; juh-ROO-zuh-lem

The people ask this with amazement and confusion.
Galileans = gal-ih-LEE-uhnz
Parthians = PAHR-thee-uhnz
Medes = meedz
Elamites = EE-luh-mīts
Mesopotamia = mes-uh-poh-TAY-mee-uh
Judea = joo-DEE-uh; joo-DAY-uh
Cappadocia = kap-uh-DOH-shuh; kap-uh-DOH-shee-uh

READING I As today's reading begins, Luke tells us that the time of Pentecost had come, and "they were all in one place together." The Jewish feast of Pentecost was the feast on which the Jews celebrated Moses having received the Law on Mount Sinai. Luke has earlier said that the gathered group included the Apostles, some women, Mary the Mother of Jesus, and his brothers. In all, there were about one hundred and twenty persons (Acts 1:13–15).

The coming of the Spirit on Pentecost is described as being like a strong wind and like tongues of fire. These are traditional symbols representing the coming of God (see Isaiah 66:15a, 18). Notice that in Luke's description, the tongues of fire separate and come to rest on each person. Pentecost is not just a celebration of the descent of the Holy Spirit on the Apostles, but the descent of the Holy Spirit on the whole gathered Church.

Next, Luke describes the effect of the coming of the Spirit: the preaching of the Good News of Jesus Christ to every nation.

Luke does this by appropriating a gift of the Spirit known from experience, *glossolalia,* also called the "gift of tongues." (It appears in Mark 16:17; Acts 10:44–48; 19:6; and 1 Corinthians 12:14.) He reinterprets it as the ability to speak in foreign languages. Luke is teaching that it is the Spirit who enables the Church to fulfill Jesus' commission to be his "witnesses in Jerusalem, throughout Judea and Samaria, and to the ends of the earth" (Acts 1:8). Today, the Good News of Jesus Christ is still proclaimed in every language to every

Pontus = PON-tuhs
Asia = AY-zhuh
Phrygia = FRIJ-ee-uh
Pamphylia = pam-FIL-ee-uh
Egypt = EE-jipt
Say the last two lines slowly and with awe.
Libya = LIB-ee-uh
Cyrene = si-REE-nee

Pontus and Asia, Phrygia and Pamphylia,
Egypt and the districts of Libya near Cyrene,
as well as travelers from Rome,
both Jews and converts to Judaism, Cretans and Arabs,
yet we hear them speaking in our own tongues
of the mighty acts of God."

READING II   1 Corinthians 12:3b–7, 12–13

Corinthians = kor-IN-thee-uhnz

A reading from the first Letter of Saint Paul to the Corinthians

Brothers and sisters:
No one can say, "Jesus is Lord," except by the Holy Spirit.

Emphasize "Holy Spirit." Because this reading speaks of the Spirit it has been chosen for Pentecost.
Emphasize "same." It is repeated three times.

There are different kinds of spiritual gifts but the same Spirit;
    there are different forms of service but the same Lord;
    there are different workings but the same God
    who produces all of them in everyone.
To each individual the manifestation of the Spirit
    is given for some benefit.

Now, the word "one" is being repeated.
Emphasize "one" all five times that it is repeated.

As a body is one though it has many parts,
    and all the parts of the body, though many, are one body,
    so also Christ.
For in one Spirit we were all baptized into one body,
    whether Jews or Greeks, slaves or free persons,
    and we were all given to drink of one Spirit.

Say "one Spirit" with conviction. We want these words to remain in everyone's mind.

Or:

---

nation. As you proclaim this reading, you will be one of those Spirit-filled people, carrying out Jesus' commission.

 CORINTHIANS. In today's passage from 1 Corinthians, Paul is addressing the problem of division, a problem that plagued the early Church and that continues to plague the Church today. What is one to do when church members passionately disagree with each other or when some feel superior to others?

Paul teaches the Corinthians, and us, that unity can and must be maintained even in the face of differences. All who claim Jesus as Lord are operating under the inspiration of the one Holy Spirit. That Spirit gives people different spiritual gifts and different works to perform. Such gifts are not given just for the sake of the individual who receives them, but for the good of the whole community. Therefore, they should not result in pride but in service.

To explain further, Paul draws on the analogy of a human body. The body has many parts, and those parts have different

functions. Nevertheless, the parts make up a single body. All the functions, though different, are for the good of that one body. The same is true of the Church, the body of Christ. There is only one Spirit, and all were baptized into the one body of Christ in that one Spirit. This fact supersedes any other fact that might cause division, such as whether a person is Jewish or Greek or whether a person is a slave or a master. Such differences become inconsequential for those who have been baptized into the body of Christ and who have drunk of the same Spirit.

READING II Romans 8:8–17

A reading from the Letter of Saint Paul to the Romans

Brothers and **sisters:**
Those who are in the **flesh cannot please God.**
But **you** are **not** in the **flesh;**
on the **contrary, you** are in the **spirit,**
if only the **Spirit** of **God dwells** in you.
Whoever does **not** have the **Spirit** of **Christ** does **not belong**
to him.
But if **Christ** is **in** you,
although the **body** is **dead** because of **sin,**
the **spirit** is **alive** because of **righteousness.**
If the **Spirit** of the **one** who **raised Jesus** from the **dead dwells**
in **you,**
the **one** who **raised Christ** from the **dead**
will give **life** to **your mortal bodies also,**
through his **Spirit** that **dwells** in **you.**
Consequently, brothers and **sisters,**
we are **not debtors** to the flesh,
to live **according** to the flesh.
For if you live according to the **flesh,** you will **die,**
but if by the **Spirit** you put to **death** the **deeds** of the **body,**
you will **live.**

For those who are **led** by the **Spirit** of **God** are **sons** of **God.**
For you did not receive a **spirit** of **slavery** to fall back into **fear,**
but you received a **spirit** of **adoption,**
through whom we cry, "**Abba, Father!**"

Margin notes:

Say this with conviction.
Emphasize the contrast.

Speak slowly and emphasize "Spirit of God."
Now increase your pace.

Now slow down again.

Pause after this line.
Read this entire sentence slowly, pausing with each comma.

Now Paul is beginning to draw his conclusion. Increase your pace slightly.

Say this sentence slowly. This is Paul's central point.

Now Paul is persuading.

Abba = AH-bah

Paul is both teaching and persuading as he insists on unity. You will be both teaching and persuading as you proclaim this reading to a Church that still suffers from divisions. Since today is Pentecost, and the Holy Spirit is the source of our unity, emphasize all that Paul has to say about the Spirit.

ROMANS. In today's Second Reading, Paul is teaching Roman Christians the ramifications of having the Spirit dwell within them. First, because the Spirit dwells in them, the Romans are no longer slaves to sin. They do not live according to the flesh.

A person who does live according to the flesh "cannot please God." Such is not the case for the Romans, who have the Spirit dwelling in them.

Not only can the Romans please God, they have become children of God. Because the Spirit dwells in them, the Romans are not slaves who must live in fear, but adopted sons and daughters who have a very close relationship with God. They address him in terms of intimacy and endearment: "Abba, Father!"

As children of God, the Romans are "joint heirs with Christ." The same Spirit who raised Jesus from the dead dwells in them and so will raise their mortal bodies, too. Of course, those who share Christ's Resurrection will also share Christ's suffering: "if only we suffer with him so that we may also be glorified with him."

What was true for the Romans is just as true for us. As you proclaim this reading on Pentecost, emphasize those lines that are teaching the ramifications of the Spirit's dwelling in us. We, too, are no longer slaves to sin but are adopted sons and daughters of God and coheirs with Jesus of eternal life.

Emphasize "children of God."

Say the last two lines slowly.

The **Spirit himself** bears **witness** with **our spirit**
    that we are **children** of **God**,
    and if **children**, then **heirs**,
    heirs of **God** and **joint heirs** with **Christ**,
    if only we **suffer** with him
    so that we may **also** be **glorified** with him.

GOSPEL John 20:19–23

A reading from the holy Gospel according to John

The narrator is setting the stage.

On the evening of that **first day** of the **week**,
    when the **doors** were **locked**, where the **disciples** were,
    for **fear** of the Jews,
    Jesus came and **stood** in their **midst**
    and said to them, "**Peace** be **with you**."
When he had said this, he **showed** them his **hands** and his **side**.
The disciples **rejoiced** when they **saw** the **Lord**.
Jesus said to them **again**, "**Peace** be **with you**.
As the **Father** has **sent me**, so **I send you**."
And when he had said this, he **breathed** on them
    and said to them,
  "**Receive** the **Holy Spirit**.
Whose **sins** you **forgive** are **forgiven** them,
    and whose **sins** you **retain** are **retained**."

Or:

Emphasize this line. It will be repeated. Jesus is not simply giving a greeting, but a gift.

Again, emphasize "Peace be with you." This is Jesus' commission to his disciples. Speak slowly and clearly. breathed = breethd

On the Solemnity of Pentecost, this is the most important line.

GOSPEL | **JOHN 20.** In John's post-Resurrection story, Jesus bestows the Spirit upon the disciples on Easter night. The disciples are behind locked doors, disillusioned and full of fear, when Christ suddenly appears in their midst. Jesus' first words are not a reprimand; rather, Jesus offers the disciples the gift of peace.

To assure the disciples that he really is Jesus, the person who suffered, died, and was buried, Jesus shows the disciples his hands and his side. John then tells us that "the disciples rejoiced when they saw the Lord." Earlier, at Jesus' last meal with the disciples, he had told them that he was going, but that they would see him again, and when they did, their hearts would be full of joy (see John 16:19–22). That promise has now been fulfilled.

After once more offering them the gift of peace, Jesus commissions the disciples. As the Father has sent Jesus, so Jesus sends the Apostles. They are to continue Jesus' mission in the world. To accomplish this mission, the disciples will need the Holy Spirit. Jesus breathes on the disciples and says, "Receive the Holy Spirit. Whose sins you forgive are forgiven them, and whose sins you retain are retained." Since Jesus is, from the very beginning of John's gospel account, identified as the "Lamb of God who takes away the sin of the world" (see John 1:29), some scripture scholars conclude that these words regarding forgiving or retaining sin, spoken in the context of a commissioning,

GOSPEL John 14:15 –16, 23b–26

A reading from the holy Gospel according to John

Jesus said to his disciples:
  "If you **love** me, you will **keep** my **commandments**.
and I will ask the **Father**,
  and he will give you another **Advocate** to be **with** you **always**.

"Whoever **loves me** will **keep** my **word**,
  and my **Father** will **love** him,
  and we will **come** to him and **make** our **dwelling with** him.
Those who do **not** love me do **not** keep my words;
  yet the word you **hear** is **not mine**
  but that of the **Father** who **sent** me.

"I have **told** you this while I am **with** you.
The **Advocate**, the **Holy Spirit** whom the **Father**
    will **send** in **my name**,
  will teach you **everything**
  and **remind** you of **all** that I **told** you."

This is an intimate conversation. Speak with warmth and gentleness.

Advocate = AD-voh-k*t

Say this with conviction.

Now speak with more authority.

Now Jesus is reassuring the disciples.

Sound encouraging.

are a reference to the effect of Baptism. To the extent that the disciples are able to spread the Good News so that people receive Baptism, to that extent people will be freed from sin. To the extent that the disciples fail to do this, people's sins will remain.

As you proclaim this reading on Pentecost Sunday, give the greatest emphasis to the line "Receive the Holy Spirit." We know that we, too, received the Holy Spirit at Baptism, our sins have been forgiven, and the Spirit continues to dwell within us.

JOHN 14. At Jesus' last meal with his disciples, he reminds them that love is the bond that unites him with his Father, and love is also the bond between Jesus and his disciples. Those who love Jesus keep his commandments, and both the Father and Jesus dwell in that person.

In addition, Jesus promises the disciples that after he is gone, the Father will send an Advocate, the Holy Spirit, who will teach the disciples everything and remind them of all that Jesus told them. This Holy Spirit will be with the disciples always.

On Pentecost, we celebrate the fulfillment of Jesus' promise that the Father would send the Holy Spirit. As you proclaim this reading, emphasize that promise, which appears both as the reading begins and as it concludes. We are celebrating not only the initial coming of the Spirit on the Church, but the ongoing coming of the Spirit. The Spirit is still teaching us and reminding us of the revelation that we received through Jesus Christ.

THE MOST HOLY TRINITY

Lectionary #166

READING I Proverbs 8:22–31

Proverbs = PRAH-verbz

Use a warm tone of voice to tell of the intimate relationship between the Lord and wisdom before creation.

prodigies = PROD-uh-jees

A reading from the Book of Proverbs

Thus says the **wisdom** of **God**:
"The LORD **possessed** me, the **beginning** of his **ways**,
    the **forerunner** of his **prodigies** of long **ago**;
from of **old** I was **poured forth**,
    at the **first**, **before** the **earth**.
When there were no **depths** I was brought **forth**,
    when there were no **fountains** or **springs** of **water**;
before the **mountains** were **settled** into place,
    before the **hills**, I was **brought forth**;
while as yet the **earth** and **fields** were not **made**,
    nor the first **clods** of the **world**.

"When the **Lord** established the **heavens** I was **there**,
    when he marked out the **vault** over the **face** of the **deep**;
when he made **firm** the skies **above**,
    when he fixed **fast** the **foundations** of the **earth**;
when he set for the **sea** its **limit**,
    so that the **waters** should not **transgress** his **command**;
then was **I beside** him as his **craftsman**,
    and **I** was his **delight** day by day,
playing before him all the while,
    playing on the surface of his **earth**;
    and **I** found **delight** in the human **race**."

Emphasize the different time references and the different elements of creation.

A "clod" is a lump of earth or clay.

Pause significantly after the stanza on the preexistence of Wisdom as the text transitions to the Lord's acts of creation.

Emphasize Wisdom's presence in all the acts of the Lord's creation.

Lighten your tone of voice as you speak of Wisdom playing before the Lord and delighting in the human race. All of creation is beautiful!

READING I Today is the only Sunday in Year C that we hear from the Book of Proverbs, from the genre of writing known as wisdom literature. Its purpose is to teach wisdom, the practical knowledge of how to love God and others as one lives in the world. Proverbs contains a section of lengthy instructional poems (chapters 1–9), from which today's passage comes, as well as sections composed of pithy, two-line maxims or proverbs (10–29), and a final section of shorter poems

(30–31), which concludes by describing wisdom as the fear of the Lord.

Today's passage is part of the second speech by Wisdom, personified as a character. In the first half of today's reading, Wisdom speaks of her deep union with the Lord from the beginning. She was the firstborn of all creation, born before any of nature's features that now define earth's landscape. Before all else, the Lord brought Wisdom forth, giving birth to her.

In the second half of the reading, Wisdom describes her role in creation. She was indeed present as part of the Lord's creative acts. Wisdom tells us that she participated in creation as the Lord's craftsman. Wisdom was co-creating with the Lord, delighting in the Lord's creation. In the conclusion of Wisdom's speech (not a part of the Lectionary reading), Wisdom addresses her children, calling them to follow her instructions. To do so will lead to life, life in the Lord. Wisdom's intention is

READING II Romans 5:1–5

A reading from the Letter of Saint Paul to the Romans

Brothers and sisters:
Therefore, **since** we have been **justified** by **faith**,
    we have **peace** with **God** through our **Lord Jesus Christ**,
    through whom we have gained **access** by **faith**
    to this **grace** in which we **stand**,
    and we **boast** in **hope** of the **glory** of **God**.
Not **only** that, but we even **boast** of our **afflictions**,
    knowing that **affliction** produces **endurance**,
    and **endurance**, proven **character**,
    and proven **character**, **hope**,
    and **hope** does **not disappoint**,
    because the **love** of **God** has been poured **out** into our **hearts**
through the **Holy Spirit** that has been **given** to **us**.

The main clauses in the first stanza after "we have been justified . . . " are "we have peace" and "we boast in hope." Emphasize them equally. Lower your tone of voice on the parenthetical statement between them.

Stronger on "we even boast"; lighter on "knowing that affliction." Proceed, following the punctuation at a methodical pace. Each noun is equally important.

Keep a strong voice for the entire climactic "why" statement that concludes the reading.

to playfully draw her children to the Lord, the Creator of all life. Thus, a hopeful, joyful proclamation is appropriate as you invite the assembly to come to the Lord and play.

READING II This reading is Paul's two-sentence gift to us. In the first sentence, Paul confirms that we are justified, or saved, by faith. The first effect of our justification is peace with God through Jesus Christ. We know Jesus Christ through faith and, therefore, are

firmly planted in the grace of reconciliation that comes through him.

Justification also leads us to hope, the second effect of our right relationship with God through Jesus Christ. To "boast" in something means to brag or show off. It might make sense to most people for Christians to boast in the hope we have in God's glory now and in the future, but Paul also encourages the justified to boast in their afflictions. The cognitive dissonance here makes your proclamation challenging. Who would brag about the adversity they face? Yet Paul teaches us that we can

logically boast in the face of our difficulties, because through our endurance, they lead to the development of Christian character and to hope.

Paul is not telling us that we must earn God's love through our afflictions and the amount of suffering we endure; rather, he teaches that through our afflictions we can still hope. Why? Because God's love grounds this hope, so it will never let us down. God freely gives this love to us. Boast of God's freely given love as you proclaim this reading!

Use a calm and straightforward tone to convey Jesus' realistic assessment of the disciples' readiness.

The introduction of the Spirit is encouraging.

Emphasize the verbs which tell what the Spirit will do: "guide," "speak," "declare," "glorify," "take," and "declare."

Use a warm tone to impart the intimate communion between the Father and Son.

Make eye contact on the final phrase.

GOSPEL John 16:12–15

A reading from the holy Gospel according to John

Jesus said to his **disciples:**
"I have **much more** to tell you, but you **cannot bear** it **now.**
But when he **comes,** the **Spirit** of **truth,**
  he will **guide** you to **all truth.**
He will **not** speak on his **own,**
  but he **will speak** what he **hears,**
  and will **declare** to you the things that are **coming.**
He will **glorify** me,
  because he will **take** from what is **mine** and **declare** it to you.
Everything that the **Father** has is **mine;**
  for this **reason** I told you that he will **take** from what is **mine**
  and **declare** it to **you.**"

GOSPEL The Gospel is from the part of the Last Supper discourse in which Jesus reveals to his disciples that he will send the Advocate, the Holy Spirit, to them when he returns to the One who sent him. This passage describes who the Spirit is and what the Spirit will do. As the Gospel begins, Jesus is being realistic about how much information his disciples can handle at this moment. They don't need to know everything that will transpire in terms of his suffering and Death. What they do need to know is that Jesus will not abandon them.

Jesus identifies the Spirit as the Spirit of truth. Truth in John's gospel account refers to Jesus, the Word incarnate. Thus, Jesus tells the disciples it is his own Spirit which will come. The Spirit will speak, declare, glorify, and take, all in reference to Jesus. Through the Spirit's actions, the disciples will participate in the relationship between the Spirit and Jesus. Jesus' words in the final verse affirm the intimate communion that exists between him and the Father and extend this communion to the disciples. The assembly, like the disciples, participates in this communion. This

declaration about the Spirit is not a prediction of the future; rather, it is the truth that the disciples can bear at this point in their faith journey: God through Jesus Christ in the Holy Spirit will always be with them. The disciples are one with the Triune (three-in-one) God.

Lectionary #169

READING I — Genesis 14:18–20

A reading from the Book of Genesis

In those days, **Melchizedek**, king of **Salem**,
  brought out **bread** and **wine**,
  and being a **priest** of **God Most High**,
  he **blessed Abram** with these **words**:
  "**Blessed** be **Abram** by **God Most High**,
    the **creator** of **heaven** and **earth**;
  and blessed be **God Most High**,
    who **delivered** your **foes** into your **hand**."
Then **Abram** gave him a **tenth** of **everything**.

Genesis = JEN-uh sis

In the opening lines, highlight Melchizedek's actions. Use a prayerful and solemn tone to speak his words of blessing.
Melchizedek = mel-KIZ-uh-dek or mel-KEEZ-uh-dek
Salem = SAY-luhm
Pause significantly after the blessing. With gratitude, mirroring what Abram must have felt, communicate the concluding narrative line.

READING II — 1 Corinthians 11:23–26

A reading from the first Letter of Saint Paul to the Corinthians

Brothers and **sisters**:
I **received** from the **Lord** what I **also handed on** to **you**,
  that the **Lord Jesus**, on the night he was **handed over**,
  took bread, and, after he had given **thanks**,
  broke it and **said**, "**This** is my **body** that is for **you**.
Do this in **remembrance** of **me**."

Corinthians = kohr-IN-thee-uhnz

Emphasize the verbs in the actions of the Lord Jesus to help make the connection to the First Reading and the Gospel.
Differentiate in your tone between the declarative statements, "This is my body" and "This cup is" and Jesus' two commands to "Do this…"

READING I In the verses before the First Reading picks up, Abram has won a battle with a united army of kings from the east who have been menacing the communities in the Jordan Valley and who have taken captive his kinsman, Lot. The local leaders are grateful. Among them is Melchizedek, described as a king of Salem (Jerusalem) and a priest of God Most High. He declares Abram blessed by God the Most High, revealing that Abram is blessed because God worked through him to bring victory. The priest celebrates this moment by setting out a feast of bread and wine. The reading ends with Abram's gesture of gratitude—a tithe—the return of a tenth of the possessions he recovered after the battle.

READING II We heard the Second Reading previously this year on Holy Thursday because it is the oldest account of the institution of the Lord's Supper in the New Testament. It appears in 1 Corinthians as part of the section in which Paul addresses the divisions among the Corinthians caused because some members of the community are not

Communicate the command as a solemn instruction, not an overpowering order.

A confident statement of faith. This is what we do now. Keep a strong voice until the end. Make eye contact.

In the **same** way also the **cup**, after **supper**, saying,
      "This **cup** is the **new covenant** in my **blood**.
Do this, as **often** as you **drink** it, in **remembrance** of me."
For as **often** as you **eat** this **bread** and **drink** the **cup**,
      you **proclaim** the **death** of the **Lord** until he **comes**.

GOSPEL   Luke 9:11b–17

A reading from the holy Gospel according to Luke

Jesus spoke to the crowds about the **kingdom of God**,
      and he **healed** those who **needed** to be **cured**.
As the day was drawing to a **close**,

Let your voice express the concern that the Twelve feel for the people.

      the **Twelve** approached him and **said**,
      "**Dismiss** the **crowd**
      so that they can go to the surrounding **villages** and **farms**
      and find **lodging** and **provisions**;
      for we are in a **deserted** place here."

Communicate Jesus' order to the disciples as if it were addressed to the assembly.

The disciples are a bit overwhelmed with the task at hand and disappointed with the provisions they have.

Another order from Jesus. Convey this with authority.

He said to them, "**Give** them some **food yourselves**."
They replied, "Five **loaves** and two **fish** are **all** we **have**,
      unless we **ourselves** go and **buy** food for **all** these people."
Now the men there numbered about **five thousand**.
Then he said to his disciples,
      "Have them **sit down** in groups of about **fifty**."
They **did** so and made them **all sit** down.

---

able to participate in the common meal that accompanied the liturgy of the Eucharist. Those who participated in the meal may have arrived early. Most likely they were of high status and did not have to work the entire day, making it possible for them to arrive at the private house of the celebration when there was still enough room to enter. Those who came later either found the house filled to capacity or entered, but could not partake in the

meal because of their social status. Paul argues that the Lord's Supper is fundamentally related to how they live as Christ's body. Factions between the rich and poor deny the truth of the Eucharist: the truth that believers are one body in Christ.

To take the bread and break it and take the wine and drink it and do both in remembrance of the Lord Jesus, is to proclaim his salvific Death for many, not just for those who rank high enough in society to participate in the meal. For Paul, all are

welcome to the Lord's Supper. All are welcome to proclaim the Death through which the victory of the Resurrection came, that Death we proclaim in the Memorial Acclamation.

GOSPEL | In Luke's narrative prior to today's Gospel, Herod the tetrarch poses the question "Who then is this about whom I hear such things?" (Luke 9:9). Herod was hearing a variety of tales

Emphasize the verbs describing Jesus' actions.

Then taking the five **loaves** and the two **fish**,
    and looking up to **heaven**,
    he said the **blessing** over them, **broke** them,
    and **gave** them to the **disciples** to set before the **crowd**.
They all **ate** and were **satisfied**.
And when the leftover **fragments** were picked up,
    they filled **twelve** wicker **baskets**.

These lines reveal the miracle. Express contentment in your voice. Everyone has been fed and there are leftovers.

about Jesus. Some told him that Elijah had appeared, others that a prophet had arisen, and others that John the Baptist had been raised from the dead despite the fact that Herod himself had had John beheaded. Herod's question is one lens through which to view the feeding miracle you proclaim today.

We who celebrate the Solemnity of the Body and Blood of Christ believe that Jesus is the true, real, and substantial food we eat when we celebrate Eucharist. In our celebration of this miracle, we proclaim Jesus as the Savior of the world. This is his identity, the answer to the question Herod poses. But our proclamation of Jesus' identity comes with the same responsibility Jesus' disciples discovered they had.

Luke does not provide us with any details about the feeding miracle itself. All we know is that Jesus left it to his disciples to go and feed the crowds after he said the blessing over their limited provisions. We know the miracle happened because of the summary lines at the end of the Gospel. The disciples must have accepted the responsibility Jesus set before them to feed the crowds since we read that the crowds ate and were satisfied. Luke also leaves us wondering what should be done with the great amount of leftovers, an obvious testimony to the greatness of the miracle. Your task is to leave the assembly pondering this same question.

10TH SUNDAY IN ORDINARY TIME

Lectionary #90

READING I   1 Kings 17:17–24

A reading from the first Book of Kings

Elijah = ee-LĪ-juh
Zarephath = ZAYR-uh-fath
Sidon = SĪ-duhn

Elijah went to Zarephath of **Sidon** to the house of a **widow**.
The **son** of the mistress of the house fell **sick**,
    and his sickness grew more severe until he **stopped breathing**.
So she said to Elijah,

Ask the widow's questions in an accusatory tone.

    "**Why** have you done this to **me**, O man of **God**?
Have you come to me to call attention to my **guilt**
    and to kill my **son**?"
Elijah said to her, "**Give** me your son."
Taking him from her **lap**, he **carried** the son to the upper room
    where he was staying, and put him on his **bed**.

Elijah speaks kindly.

Elijah **called out** to the LORD:
    "O LORD, my **God**,
    will you afflict **even** the **widow** with whom I am staying
    by killing her son?"
Then he stretched himself out upon the child three times
    and **called out** to the LORD:

Elijah poses a serious question to God and then he presents a simple, but profound request.

    "O LORD, my **God**,
    let the **life breath** return to the **body** of this **child**."
The LORD **heard** the prayer of **Elijah**;
    the life breath returned to the child's body and he **revived**.
Taking the child, Elijah **brought** him down into the house
    from the upper room and **gave** him to his **mother**.

READING I The prophet Elijah, like Moses, acted as a mediator between the Lord and his people. In today's reading, Elijah is at the house of a widow in Sidon. In the verses preceding today's reading, she has sheltered him during a time of drought, and following the prophet's instructions, has fed him out of the little she had (1 Kings 17:7-16). In today's passage, the widow's son has become sick and stopped breathing. She is a Gentile, not a Jew; in her grief and guilt, presumably for not believing in the Lord, she blames the prophet Elijah. Elijah

responds, not with angry words, but with action that shows he is a man of God who intercedes for others.

The prophet's prayer begins with a question to the Lord, followed by his request that the breath of life return to the widow's son. His words reveal his firm understanding that the God of Israel, not Baal, the Canaanite fertility god, is the author of life.

The reading concludes with the woman's confession of Elijah's prophetic identity. It is God's Word, not merely a human word that Elijah speaks, for Elijah is a

prophet. And this word which you proclaim today is about the unbounded love of God, a love which extended beyond Israel's borders in Elijah's time and goes forth from the church doors in ours.

READING II For the next five Sundays, the Second Reading is from Paul's Letter to the Galatians. Paul wrote it around AD 54 or 55 to the churches of Galatia (around modern-day Ankara, Turkey). The people were Gentiles whom he had converted. Paul's tone is highly charged and defensive because he has

Let your voice be strong on both Elijah's final words to the widow and her reply. Both are affirmations of the life that comes from God and God's Word.

Elijah said to her, "**See!** Your son is **alive**."
The woman replied to Elijah,
      "Now **indeed** I know that **you** are a man of **God**.

READING II   Galatians 1:11–19

Galatians = guh-LAY-shuhnz

Proclaim the opening verses about the origin of the Gospel convincingly.

A reading from the Letter of Saint Paul to the Galatians

I want you to know, brothers and sisters,
      that the **gospel** preached by **me** is not of **human origin**.
For I did not **receive** it from a human being, nor was I **taught** it,
      but it **came** through a **revelation** of **Jesus Christ**.

Pace yourself during Paul's first person narrative. Use the punctuation and stanza breaks as a guide for pauses. Use an even, narrative tone throughout as you convey the facts that legitimize the Gospel Paul preaches and his apostolic authority.

zealot = ZEL-uht

For you heard of my **former** way of life in **Judaism**,
      how I **persecuted** the church of God beyond measure
      and tried to **destroy** it, and progressed in Judaism
      beyond many of my contemporaries among my race,
      since I was even more a **zealot** for my ancestral **traditions**.
But when **God**, who from my mother's womb had set me apart
      and **called** me through his **grace**,
      was **pleased** to **reveal** his Son to me,
      so that I might proclaim him to the **Gentiles**,
I did not **immediately** consult flesh and blood,
      nor did I go up to Jerusalem
      to those who were apostles before me;
      rather, I went into Arabia and then returned to Damascus.

Arabia = uh-RAY-bee-uh
Damascus = duh-MAS-kuhs

Cephas = SEE-fuhs

Then **after** three years I went up to Jerusalem
      to confer with Cephas and remained with him for fifteen days.
But I did not see any other of the **apostles**,
      only **James** the brother of the **Lord**.

---

received word during his mission in Ephesus that others, probably Jewish-Christian missionaries, were preaching a "different gospel" than the one he preached. This different Gospel, or teaching, required the Gentile Christians to follow Jewish laws such as circumcision. For Paul, making such legal demands a condition for accepting Christ perverted the Gospel. He was incensed that some were accepting the teaching of these "agitators" and abandoning the Gospel to which God originally called them by the grace of Christ.

In the reading you proclaim, Paul defends the Gospel he preached to the Galatians and his call to be an apostle of Christ. Paul stresses that the Gospel he proclaimed was not his invention; it came from God. Nor was his own authority and work as an apostle something he created for himself. God called him to be an apostle. Paul recounts his personal history from the onset of his call in his mother's womb through his journey to Arabia, Damascus, and then Jerusalem, where his meetings with Peter and James would link him to the Apostles.

Focus your proclamation of Paul's self-reflection, defensive as it is, on the truth of God's revelation in Jesus Christ. This is the Gospel of grace and freedom God calls you, like Paul, to proclaim to your assembly.

GOSPEL Today's Gospel is a striking parallel with the Old Testament reading from 1 Kings. Elijah journeys to Zarephath in Sidon and Jesus journeys to Nain (a city approximately 5.5 miles southeast of Nazareth). Like Elijah, who is concerned with a widow grieved by

Nain = nayn
Use a narrative tone to set the scene.

Speak Jesus' words to the widow with compassion. Return to a narrative tone as the scene moves forward.

Let Jesus' power of healing and new life be heard in your voice as you speak his command to the dead widow's son. Then return again to a narrative tone. Fill your voice with confidence and optimism as your sole voice proclaims the confession of the large crowd. Take your time with the two distinct statements. Return to a narrative tone at the conclusion of the reading.

GOSPEL Luke 7:11–17

A reading from the holy Gospel according to Luke

Jesus journeyed to a city called Nain,
and his disciples and a large crowd accompanied him.
As he drew near to the gate of the city,
a man who had **died** was being carried out,
the **only** son of his **mother**, and she was a **widow**.
A large crowd from the city was with her.
When the Lord saw her,
he was moved with **pity** for her and said to her,
"Do not **weep**."
He stepped forward and **touched** the coffin;
at this the bearers halted,
and he said, "Young **man**, I tell you, **arise**!"
The dead man sat up and began to speak,
and Jesus **gave** him to his **mother**.
Fear **seized** them all, and they **glorified** God, exclaiming,
"A great **prophet** has arisen in our midst,"
and "God has **visited** his people."
This report about him spread through the whole of Judea
and in all the surrounding region.

her son's apparent death, Jesus happens upon a funeral procession in which a widow mourns her dead son, as he approaches the city's entrance. Both stories involve a widow and end in a resuscitation that leads to a confession.

One key difference is that unlike Elijah, Jesus does not pray to the Lord to put the breath of life back in the widow's son; rather, Jesus himself is the power and life and breath of God. On the basis of Jesus' word, the dead man speaks. Another notable feature is that Luke often juxtaposes miracle stories in which the gender of the main character switches from male to female. Today's healing story follows upon another, in which a centurion, a Gentile man, asks for healing for his slave.

Both Elijah and Jesus hand the resuscitated sons to their mothers, entrusting the miracles to them. They now have a choice to make—to believe or not—and to live accordingly. In both stories, this action after the miracle leads to a confession. In 1 Kings, the confession is personal. In the Gospel, the confession is communal.

Surrounded from the outset by his disciples and a large crowd, this cohort praises Jesus as a great prophet in whom God has come.

Entrust this miracle story and the miracle of life through God in Jesus Christ to the assembly as you proclaim this Gospel. The life which exists in them and in you is nothing less than the life that comes from God. We confess this life when we publicly recite the Creed, when we offer the gifts of bread and wine to become Christ's Body and Blood, and when we go forth to live as Christ's body in the world.

11TH SUNDAY IN ORDINARY TIME

Lectionary #93

READING I   2 Samuel 12:7–10, 13

Samuel = SAM-yoo-uhl

Nathan = NAY-thuhn

Open the reading in a declarative tone of voice.

Pause noticeably after each statement about what the Lord has done for David. Show a little exasperation as you give the concluding statement.

Uriah = yoo-RĪ-uh
Hittite = HIT-tīt
Ammonites = AM-uh-nītz

Use a serious tone to communicate the consequence of David's actions.

David is contrite; mirror his sorrow in your voice.

Offer the words of forgiveness compassionately.

A reading from the second Book of Samuel

Nathan said to **David**:
"**Thus** says the LORD **God** of **Israel**:
    'I **anointed** you **king** of **Israel**.
I **rescued** you from the hand of **Saul**.
I **gave** you your lord's **house** and your lord's **wives** for your **own**.
I **gave** you the **house** of **Israel** and of **Judah**.
And if **this** were not **enough**, I could count up for you **still**
        more.
Why have you **spurned** the LORD and done **evil** in his sight?
You have **cut down Uriah** the **Hittite** with the **sword**;
    you **took his** wife as your **own**,
        and **him** you **killed** with the **sword** of the **Ammonites**.
Now, **therefore**, the **sword** shall **never depart** from your **house**,
    because **you** have **despised** me
    and have **taken** the **wife** of **Uriah** to be **your wife**.'"
Then **David** said to **Nathan**,
    "I have **sinned** against the LORD."
Nathan answered **David**:
    "The LORD on **his** part has **forgiven** your sin:
    you shall **not die**."

READING I   In today's First Reading, the prophet Nathan undertakes the daunting task of speaking truth to power as he meets face-to-face with King David, delivering words from God. The entire story of Nathan's confrontation spans verses 1–15a, beginning with Nathan telling David a parable about two men, one rich and one poor. The poor man had only one ewe, but he cared for her and fed her out of the little he had, and she became like a daughter to him. The rich man deceived the poor man and took his ewe. As the parable ends, David becomes indignant with the rich man, saying to Nathan that he deserves death for his action. Nathan then turns the table on David, rebuking him and saying "You are the man!" (1 Kings 12:7a).

This is the point at which today's reading begins—with the Lord's words, spoken by the prophet. We hear a litany of all the Lord has done for David, concluding with the general statement about how much more could be said concerning God's favors to him. The prophet's question is pivotal: "Why have you spurned the LORD . . . ?" It shines a glaring light on David's actions.

Now we hear how David has sinned, killing Uriah and then taking the dead man's wife as his own. Because of his actions, he deserves the same fate as the rich man in the parable. Finally, David sees clearly and responds to this opportunity for repentance: "I have sinned . . . ." He doesn't try to defend himself, and Nathan's absolution is immediate and brief. The prophet offers the Lord's compassion and forgiveness. Through the confrontation, David comes to understand that sin has

READING II   Galatians 2:16, 19–21

Galatians = guh-LAY-shuhnz

Make eye contact on the opening line. The believers before you know God justifies them through faith, not by works of the Law.

Emphasize the contrast between "died" and "live."

Stress the difference between Paul living in himself and Christ living in him.

Express hope, despite the negatives in the concluding verse. We know Christ did not die for nothing.

A reading from the Letter of Saint Paul to the Galatians

Brothers and **sisters:**
We who **know** that a person is **not justified** by **works** of the **law**
　　but through **faith** in **Jesus Christ,**
　　even **we** have **believed** in **Christ Jesus**
　　that **we** may be **justified** by **faith** in **Christ**
　　and **not** by **works** of the **law,**
　　because by **works** of the **law no one** will be **justified.**
For **through** the **law I died** to the **law,**
　　that I might **live** for **God.**
I have been **crucified** with **Christ;**
　　yet **I live,** no longer I, but **Christ lives in me;**
　　insofar as **I** now **live** in the **flesh,**
　　I live by **faith** in the **Son** of **God**
　　who has **loved me** and **given himself** up for **me.**
I do not **nullify** the **grace** of **God;**
　　for if **justification** comes through the **law,**
　　then Christ **died** for **nothing.**

consequences and that the Lord's mercy remains available to sinners.

READING II We can find the context for this reading in Paul's account of the Council of Jerusalem at the beginning of Galatians, Chapter 2, as well as in Acts 15. These descriptions of the Council relate that the Gospel Paul preached to the Gentiles, which did not require that they be circumcised in order to become Christians, received approval.

No longer would Gentile Christians be considered less than Jewish Christians. A handshake of partnership sealed the agreement that the same God was present in the Gospel preached by James, Cephas (Peter), and John, as that preached by Paul and Barnabas.

Yet when Cephas and Paul met up in Antioch, there was tension, not around circumcision, but concerning Jewish dietary laws. Apparently, Cephas had been eating with Gentiles until some sympathizers of

James appeared. (James advocated strict adherence to Jewish dietary laws.) In their presence, Cephas no longer ate with Gentiles. Paul interpreted his withdrawal as an abandonment of his belief and proclamation of the Gospel of justification by faith in Jesus Christ.

The reading you proclaim is Paul's restatement of this Gospel in plain terms: The Law does not set us right with God. Only faith in the crucified and resurrected One does this. And, just in case Cephas and the Galatians do not comprehend this

GOSPEL Luke 7:36—8:3

A reading from the holy Gospel according to Luke

A **Pharisee** invited **Jesus** to **dine** with him,
and he entered the **Pharisee's house** and reclined at **table**.
Now there was a **sinful woman** in the city
who **learned** that he was at table in the house of the **Pharisee**.
Bringing an alabaster flask of **ointment**,
she stood behind him at his feet **weeping**
and began to **bathe** his feet with her **tears**.
Then she **wiped** them with her **hair**,
kissed them, and **anointed** them with the **ointment**.
When the Pharisee who had invited him **saw** this
he said to himself,
"If **this man** were a **prophet**,
he would **know who** and **what sort** of **woman** this is
who is **touching** him,
that she is a **sinner**."
Jesus said to him in reply,
"**Simon**, I have something to **say** to **you**."
"**Tell me**, teacher," he said.
"Two people were in **debt** to a certain **creditor**;
one **owed five hundred** days' wages and the **other owed fifty**.
Since they were **unable** to **repay** the **debt**, he **forgave** it for **both**.
Which of them will **love** him **more**?"
Simon said in reply,
"The **one**, I suppose, whose **larger** debt was forgiven."
He said to him, "You have judged **rightly**."

Use a narrative tone of voice until the Pharisee's statement.

alabaster = AL-uh-bas-ter. Alabaster is a calcite, a carbonate of calcium used to make jars and other vessels in the early centuries.

The Pharisee is belittling Jesus. Use a slightly condescending tone.

Put a little uncertainty in your tone as you give Simon the Pharisee's answer.

Note the parallel structure between what Simon did not do and what the woman did. Pause noticeably between the parallel phrases all three times.

---

point, Paul repeats it no less than three times in the opening section. In the next section, as is often the case in his letters, Paul offers his own self-reflection. He personalizes the Gospel he preaches in order to draw others to reflect on their faith. Through your proclamation of Paul's words, you can enable those in the assembly to ponder how Paul's story is their story.

GOSPEL This story takes place in the context of an ordinary meal. Yet the ordinary becomes extraordinary as soon as we learn that it is a Pharisee who invites Jesus to dine with him. Pharisees advocated a strict interpretation of the Law and in this passage represent Jewish Christians who placed restrictions on those who could be a part of their communities. That the sinful woman touched Jesus makes her all the more "sinful." Yet she is the one who performs the expected hospitality rituals, welcoming Jesus as the guest by anointing him first with her tears and then with oil.

The Pharisee, not surprisingly, balks inwardly in response to her gestures of hospitality. Of course, Jesus knows his thoughts and presents him with a teaching by way of a very brief parable. Jesus does

Emphasize the present reality of the forgiveness of sins. Make eye contact.

Then he turned to the **woman** and said to **Simon**,
   "Do you **see** this woman?
When I **entered** your house, **you** did **not** give me **water** for my **feet**,
   but **she** has **bathed** them with her **tears**
   and **wiped** them with her **hair**.
You did **not** give me a **kiss**,
   but she has **not ceased kissing** my **feet** since the time I **entered**.
You did **not anoint** my head with **oil**,
   but **she anointed** my **feet** with ointment.
So I **tell** you, **her many sins** have been **forgiven**
   because **she** has shown **great love**.
But the one to whom **little** is forgiven, **loves little**."
He said to **her**, "**Your** sins are **forgiven**."
The **others** at table said to themselves,
   "**Who is this** who even forgives **sins**?"
But he said to the **woman**,
   "Your **faith** has **saved** you; go in **peace**."

Astonished and a bit suspicious.

Make eye contact. Begin Jesus' statement in a strong tone, then shift to a lighter, more gentle tone to reflect peace.

Return to the narrative voice used at the beginning of the reading.

Afterward he journeyed from **one town** and **village** to **another**,
   preaching and **proclaiming** the **good news** of the **kingdom**
      of **God**.
Accompanying him were the **Twelve**
   and some **women** who had been **cured** of **evil spirits**
      and **infirmities**,
   Mary, called **Magdalene**, from whom seven **demons**
      had gone out,
   Joanna, the wife of **Herod's** steward **Chuza**,
   Susanna, and many **others** who **provided** for them out
      of their **resources**.

not tell the Pharisee, named Simon, his point, but rather draws it out of him through the use of questions. Simon's answer is tentative, as we know by the words "I suppose." Jesus expands on the Pharisee's correct answer by explaining the generosity of the sinful woman's hospitality. It's not that little won't be forgiven, but great love yields forgiveness exponentially.

The narrative continues with the other table guests being drawn into the story. The question they ask is christological and based on the woman's experience of forgiveness, although Luke does not tell us whether Jesus forgave her sins before coming into the Pharisee's home or during the meal. Jesus' final words are personal, addressed only to the woman. What we don't know is whether the others at table

overheard the words and received the message that faith saves. What we do know is this: now Jesus begins to preach the Good News of the Kingdom of God throughout Galilee.

12TH SUNDAY IN ORDINARY TIME

Lectionary #96

READING I   Zechariah 12:10–11, 13:1

Zechariah = zek-uh-RĪ-uh

Begin in a strong voice, then soften your tone to reflect the spirit of grace and petition, as well as the sadness of mourning and grief.

Hadadrimmon = hay-dad-RIM-uhn
Megiddo = meh-GID-doh

Proclaim these last lines about opening the purifying fountain in a hopeful tone of voice.

A reading from the Book of the Prophet Zechariah

Thus says the LORD:
  I will **pour out** on the house of **David**
  and on the inhabitants of **Jerusalem**
  a **spirit** of **grace** and **petition**;
  and they shall **look** on him whom they have **pierced**,
  and they shall **mourn** for him as one mourns
    for an **only son**,
  and they shall **grieve** over him as one **grieves**
    over a **firstborn**.

On that **day** the mourning in **Jerusalem** shall be as **great**
  as the mourning of **Hadadrimmon** in the plain
    of **Megiddo**.

On **that** day there shall be **open** to the house of **David**
  and to the **inhabitants** of **Jerusalem**,
  a **fountain** to **purify** from **sin** and **uncleanness**.

READING I This reading is part of a longer oracle at the beginning of Zechariah 12 about future salvation through a suffering messiah figure. It foretells that Judah and Jerusalem will be delivered from their oppressors, but first there will be suffering and mourning that will purify them.

The opening proclaims that in the Jerusalem of the messianic vision, the Lord will pour out "a spirit of grace and petition." This spirit will empower God's

people to seek reconciliation and peace after a period of deep and profound mourning. The spirit will come through an unidentified victim, perhaps linked to the suffering servant of Isaiah 52:13—53:12 and whom the evangelist John indentifies with the crucified Christ (John 19:37). The mourning for the pierced one will be so great that it will be reminiscent of the people's grief for King Josiah, killed at Hadadrimmon, on the Megiddo plain, although there are other interpretations of this reference and the exact meaning is unclear. The reading ends on an optimistic note. The house of David

and the inhabitants of Jerusalem will indeed be purified. Just as the Lord takes the initiative to pour out the spirit of grace, the Lord will also open the fountain of living water to cleanse the people of their sins—the sin of internal strife and disunity and the sin of idol worship. In messianic Jerusalem, new life will come through the Lord, who is the purifying fountain.

Galatians = guh-LAY-shuhnz

Make eye contact.

Look around at different places in the assembly as you proclaim the abolition of distinctions in Christ Jesus. Take your time on the concluding line "you are all one in Christ Jesus," continuing the eye contact and panning around the assembly. Be careful not to move away from the microphone as you do so.

A solemn proclamation of our inheritance of the promise.

A reading from the Letter of Saint Paul to the Galatians

Brothers and sisters:
Through **faith** you are **all** children of **God** in **Christ Jesus.**
For **all** of you who were **baptized** into Christ
    have **clothed** yourselves with **Christ.**
There is neither **Jew** nor **Greek,**
    there is neither **slave** nor **free** person,
    there is not **male** and **female;**
    for you are **all one** in Christ **Jesus.**
And if you **belong** to **Christ,**
    then you are **Abraham's descendant,**
    heirs according to the **promise.**

READING II In the four verses that comprise today's Second Reading, Paul makes three main points. First, on the basis of their Baptism, the Galatians now participate in Christ's life. Second, having become sons and daughters of God through Baptism, the social distinctions that previously ordered their communal life no longer matter. In Baptism, Christ's gratuitous gift of himself does away with all advantage gained on the basis of one's ethnicity, economic status, or gender. All Galatians who profess their faith in Christ Jesus are children of God. Through Baptism, they are one in him. They need not perform any additional acts such as circumcision or follow any particular dietary laws in order to experience this unity.

Paul's third point links the unity of baptized believers to God's covenant with Abraham. Abraham is our father in faith. We who participate in Christ's life through Baptism are forever linked to Abraham as his descendants. We inherit the promise of the covenant solely on the basis of being children of God in Christ Jesus. Let your proclamation make palpable the unconditional nature of belonging to Christ, the freedom that is inherent in our participation in his life, and the responsibility that God's children bear for transforming communities.

GOSPEL   Luke 9:18–24

A reading from the holy Gospel according to Luke

Once when **Jesus** was praying in **solitude**,
   and the **disciples** were with him,
   he **asked** them, "Who do the **crowds** say that I **am**?"
They said in reply, "John the **Baptist**;
   others, **Elijah**;
   still **others**, 'One of the ancient **prophets** has **arisen**.'"
Then he said to them, "But who do **you** say that I am?"
Peter said in reply, "The **Christ** of **God**."
He **rebuked** them
   and **directed** them **not** to **tell** this to **anyone**.

He said, "The Son of **Man** must **suffer greatly**
   and be **rejected** by the **elders**, the chief **priests**,
     and the **scribes**,
   and be **killed** and on the **third** day be **raised**."
Then he said to **all**,
   "If **anyone** wishes to come **after me**,
     he must **deny** himself
   and take up his **cross daily** and **follow** me.
For whoever wishes to **save** his life will **lose** it,
   but whoever **loses** his life for **my** sake will **save** it."

Begin in a reserved tone of voice. Jesus is interested, curious.

State each of the responses clearly and distinctly, giving the assembly time to process them.

Emphasize "you," making eye contact with the assembly. Be firm and certain in proclaiming Peter's correct response.

In a serious tone.

Proclaim Jesus' instructions on discipleship slowly, to give the assembly time to process how demanding discipleship is.

GOSPEL | Today's Gospel begins with Jesus at prayer, a state in which Luke often portrays Jesus. Out of that prayer arises his question to the disciples about his identity. Jesus in interested in what others are thinking about him, but more importantly, he wants to teach his most devoted followers about discipleship.

The disciples respond to his question in a variety of ways. Then, Jesus shifts the question, personalizing it and addressing it directly to the disciples. Peter responds correctly, but Jesus' response is rebuke instead of affirmation. In the same grave tone, Jesus takes full advantage of the teachable moment to warn them of the suffering to come. The Evangelist does not indicate whether the disciples fully understand this first prediction of the Passion, and that Jesus himself is the Son of Man who must suffer (dei). But Jesus' words that follow the prediction provide the instructive link to those who choose to follow him.

To be a disciple, one must take up the cross (dei), not once a year, once a month, or whenever one chooses, but daily. The emphasis on daily acceptance of the cross is Luke's amendment to Mark's original verse. This change shifts the emphasis from Jesus' pending suffering and Death to the meaning of discipleship, while at the same time heightening the connection between the two. Through his Death and Resurrection, Jesus saves. By losing our lives for his sake, we accept the gift of salvation he gives.

13TH SUNDAY IN ORDINARY TIME

Lectionary #99

READING I   1 Kings 19:16b, 19–21

Elijah = ee-LĪ-juh

Elisha = ee-LĪ-shuh

Shaphat = SHAY-fat

Abel-meholah = AY-b*l muh-HOH-lah

Make this natural request kindly.

Use a firm tone of voice for Elijah's command and then switch to a lighter tone for his question. Elijah is not the one who places the demands on Elisha, the Lord is, but the Lord leaves him free to choose.

Pace yourself and use a narrative tone so as not to lose the meaning of Elisha's ritual and the fact that he did follow Elijah.

A reading from the first Book of Kings

The LORD said to Elijah:
    "You shall anoint Elisha, son of Shaphat of Abel-meholah,
    as prophet to succeed you."

Elijah set out and came upon Elisha, son of Shaphat,
    as he was plowing with twelve yoke of oxen;
    he was following the twelfth.
Elijah went over to him and threw his cloak over him.
Elisha left the oxen, ran after Elijah, and said,
    "Please, let me kiss my father and mother goodbye,
    and I will follow you."
Elijah answered, "Go back!
Have I done anything to you?"
Elisha left him, and taking the yoke of oxen, slaughtered them;
    he used the plowing equipment for fuel to boil their flesh,
    and gave it to his people to eat.
Then Elisha left and followed Elijah as his attendant.

READING I   Stories of God's call abound in Ordinary Time. Today's First Reading is the call of the prophet Elisha. But before this event, the prophet Elijah, wearied by Israel's infidelity to the covenant, attempted to walk out on his mission by fleeing to the desert. There, sitting under a broom tree, he complained to the Lord that he could not continue. An angel of the Lord guided Elijah to God's mountain, where Elijah encountered God at the entrance to a cave. The Lord listened to the prophet's frustration, then told him to reverse his journey on the desert road back to Damascus and carry out specific tasks. One was to anoint Elisha as his successor. The Lord's words instructing Elijah to anoint Elisha begin today's First Reading.

Elijah throws his cloak over Elisha as a symbolic ritual action of passing on the prophetic mantle. Elisha asks to say goodbye to his loved ones, for prophets must leave family behind to preach the Lord's word. Elijah then offers the final spoken words in the passage. He commands Elisha to return to say goodbye. His question, probably rhetorical, suggests that there is nothing holding Elisha back from bidding farewell to his parents.

The reading ends with a narrative section describing Elisha's ritual sacrifice of his economic well-being. He severs ties with his past life to follow Elijah, who meanwhile has continued on the journey. Yet Elisha did not forget to feed his people before he embraced his new life, a life in which he would feed people with the Lord's word.

READING II   Galatians 5:1, 13–18

A reading from the Letter of Saint Paul to the Galatians

Brothers and **sisters**:
For **freedom Christ** set us **free**;
    so stand **firm** and do not submit **again** to the yoke of **slavery**.

For **you** were called for **freedom**, brothers and sisters.
But do **not** use this **freedom**
    as an opportunity for the **flesh**;
    rather, **serve** one another through **love**.
For the **whole law** is fulfilled in **one statement**,
    namely, *You shall **love** your **neighbor** as **yourself**.*
But if you go on **biting** and **devouring** one another,
    beware that you are not **consumed** by one another.

I say, then: **live** by the **Spirit**
    and you will certainly not **gratify** the **desire** of the **flesh**.
For the **flesh** has **desires against** the Spirit,
    and the **Spirit** against the **flesh**;
    these are **opposed** to each other,
    so that you may **not do** what you **want**.
But if **you** are **guided** by the **Spirit**, you are **not** under the **law**.

Open strongly and boldly.

Make eye contact as you instruct the assembly that they were called for freedom.

Use an instructive, but not overly didactic tone.

Use a serious tone for Paul's warning.

An optimistic, lighter tone should color the concluding section. Be careful that your proclamation does not become sing-songy as you communicate the contrast between Spirit and flesh that occurs several times.

READING II | The Second Reading begins with the opening verse from Galatians 5 and then skips to the middle section of the same chapter. You will want to read all of Galatians 5 to understand better the context of the verses you proclaim.

The first words of the reading could easily be a rallying cry for the Apostle Paul's message. Christ set the Galatians free, and intends that they live in that freedom. The Galatians, however, are struggling with this freedom. Under the influence of other missionaries who told the people to adhere to the Mosaic Law, which Paul is calling a "yoke of slavery," some Galatians have been unable to stand firm in the freedom Christ offers.

Paul then instructs the Galatians on how to live in the freedom of Christ. The life of freedom entails following the great commandment to love your neighbor as yourself. It does not condone continuing to denigrate those who think, act, or live differently because of the desire to inflate your own ego; rather, as Paul tells the Galatians and us in the final section, this new life asks nothing short of living by the Spirit. The Spirit transforms the flesh so that we do not indulge its desires, which are in opposition to the Spirit. These desires include giving the Law more authority than the Spirit's power. Thus, you are proclaiming to the assembly that their freedom in Christ is freedom in the Spirit to live in love of one another.

GOSPEL   Luke 9:51–62

A reading from the holy Gospel according to Luke

Emphasize Jesus' unwavering determination to go to Jerusalem.

Samaritan = suh-MAYR-uh-tuhn

When the days for **Jesus'** being **taken up** were **fulfilled**,
    he **resolutely** determined to **journey** to **Jerusalem**,
    and he sent **messengers** ahead of him.
On the **way** they entered a **Samaritan** village
    to **prepare** for his **reception** there,
    but they would **not welcome** him
    because the **destination** of his **journey** was **Jerusalem**.
When the disciples **James** and **John** saw this they **asked**,
    "**Lord**, do you want us to call down **fire** from **heaven**
    to **consume** them?"
Jesus **turned** and **rebuked** them, and they journeyed
        to **another** village.

Let some desire for retaliation be heard in your voice as you ask the disciples' question.

Narrate Jesus' rebuke in a strong tone of voice and then shift the tone to a lighter one as you say that the journey continues.

As they were **proceeding** on their journey someone **said** to him,
    "I will **follow** you **wherever** you go."
Jesus **answered** him,
    "**Foxes** have **dens** and birds of the **sky** have **nests**,
    but the **Son** of **Man** has **nowhere** to rest his head."

Pause noticeably between each of the encounters with potential followers.

Let the serious and demanding nature of discipleship be heard in your voice each time you give Jesus' reply.

And to **another** he said, "**Follow** me."
But **he** replied, "**Lord**, let me go **first** and bury my **father**."
But he **answered** him, "Let the **dead** bury their **dead**.
But **you**, **go** and **proclaim** the **kingdom** of **God**."
And **another** said, "**I** will **follow** you, Lord,
    but **first** let **me** say **farewell** to my family at **home**."
To **him** Jesus said, "**No one** who sets a **hand** to the **plow**
    and **looks** to what was left **behind** is **fit** for the **kingdom**
        of **God**."

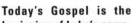

GOSPEL Today's Gospel is the beginning of Luke's narrative of Jesus' journey to Jerusalem. Its opening reference to Jesus being "taken up" includes Jesus' Death, Resurrection, and Ascension, and also refers back to the Transfiguration narrative earlier in Luke 9. We are told that Jesus was "resolutely determined to journey to Jerusalem." He will do God's will no matter what the journey entails.

A cloud of hardship and ambivalence seems to hang over this journey. The Samaritan villagers will not welcome Jesus. Ethnic and religious animosity between Samaritans and Jews hardens their hearts. Jesus, however, accepts the rejection quietly. In response to his disciples' offer to call down fire from heaven to destroy the Samaritans as the prophet Elijah had twice done (2 Kings 1:10, 12), Jesus censures them and simply continues the journey.

In the next section, Jesus encounters three potential followers. The first expresses unconditional willingness to follow Jesus. The second and third place conditions on their discipleship. The three proverbs with which Jesus responds are all exaggerations intended to signify the serious and demanding nature of discipleship, and are not to be taken literally. They are intended to instill in potential disciples a resoluteness that mirrors Jesus' own single-mindedness in the face of life's everyday distractions.

14TH SUNDAY IN ORDINARY TIME

Lectionary #102

Isaiah = ī-ZAY-uh

READING I   Isaiah 66:10–14c

A reading from the Book of the Prophet Isaiah

Use an emphatic tone on the opening declarative statement introducing the Lord's words.

Thus says the LORD:
Rejoice with **Jerusalem** and be **glad** because of her,
    all **you** who **love** her;
exult, **exult** with her,
    all **you** who were **mourning** over her!
Oh, that you may suck **fully**
    of the **milk** of her **comfort**,
that you may **nurse** with **delight**
    at her **abundant** breasts!
For **thus** says the LORD:

The introduction of the mother image. Hope should mark your tone. Don't shy from the physicality in this text.

The second declarative statement. Again be emphatic.

Speak of the motherly actions of Jerusalem and the Lord in a gentle tone.

Lo, I will spread **prosperity** over **Jerusalem** like a **river**,
    and the **wealth** of the **nations** like an **overflowing torrent**.
As **nurslings**, you shall be **carried** in her **arms**,
    and **fondled** in her **lap**;
as a **mother comforts** her **child**,
    so will **I comfort you**;
    in **Jerusalem** you shall **find** your **comfort**.

In a stronger, but not overpowering voice. The Lord's power is in his gentle strength.

When you **see** this, your heart shall **rejoice**
    and your bodies **flourish** like the **grass**;
the LORD's **power** shall be **known** to his **servants**.

READING I Today's First Reading comes from the final chapter of Isaiah, written by an author known as Third Isaiah. In this last section of the book, God's Chosen People, the Israelites, have returned to their homeland after exile in Babylon. The author presents visions for Israel's future life with the Lord, developing such themes as opening the Lord's house to all people who believe in him and gathering people from distant lands to proclaim the Lord's praises.

The beautiful poem you proclaim today seems misplaced, following directly upon Third Isaiah's rant against worship that emphasizes worldly, sacrificial offerings and does not draw people to an internal conversion of heart. In fact, this poem seems more in the optimistic, joyful style of Second Isaiah, who offered consolation to a people in exile in Babylon.

The author portrays Jerusalem as a mother giving birth to her children and nourishing them with the food of life from her breasts, the milk of comfort. Joy will

be so prevalent when Jerusalem gives birth to the new people of God that she will not experience any labor (66:7–9). This is so unrealistic that the author himself questions how it can happen!

In the end, Third Isaiah's theme is "rejoice," for the birth will happen, and continue to rejoice, because after the birth, Jerusalem and the Lord will comfort the newborn infants like a human mother comforts her own. As a result of this care, the young ones, the new inhabitants of

Galations = guh-LAY-shuhnz

Paul's prayer for himself. Use a reflective tone.

A summary reminder to the Galatians. Proclaim in a teacher-like fashion.

Express peace and mercy in your voice.

Cautionary, but with resolve, because Paul bears the marks of Jesus.

Offer the liturgical greeting to the assembly. Don't be flustered if they might join with you in the "Amen."

READING II Galatians 6:14–18

A reading from the Letter of Saint Paul to the Galatians

Brothers and **sisters**:
May I **never boast** except in the **cross** of our **Lord Jesus Christ**,
    through which the **world** has been **crucified** to me,
    and **I** to the **world**.
For **neither** does **circumcision** mean **anything**,
        nor does **uncircumcision**,
    but only a **new creation**.
Peace and **mercy** be to all who **follow** this **rule**
    and to the **Israel** of **God**.

From now **on**, let **no one** make **troubles** for me;
    for I **bear** the **marks** of **Jesus** on my **body**.

The **grace** of our **Lord Jesus Christ** be with your **spirit**,
    brothers and **sisters. Amen.**

the heavenly Jerusalem, will rejoice. The mother's care will also cause her children to grow physically. Their growth, like that of grass, will be visible to others, and through them, those from distant lands will see the Lord's power. This is indeed a new vision that Third Isaiah relates, in which the Lord's compassion, this maternal care and comfort, is presented as a sign of the Lord's power.

READING II This is the fifth and final Sunday in a row in which the Second Reading comes from Paul's Letter to the Galatians. Today's passage is the conclusion of Galatians. Having heard Paul's definitive statement about freedom in Christ last Sunday and its implications for living in Christian community according to the Spirit, today's postscript gives us Paul's final word. In a few short verses, Paul summarizes the main points he tried to communicate in the letter.

The freedom that comes through Jesus Christ is the purpose of his ministry; it is the Gospel he preaches and the one that the Galatians accepted. Salvation comes through the cross, not through any external works such as circumcision that the Galatians might perform. Neither external works nor worldly categories should divide believers. The Galatians must return to this truth if they are to live in freedom as the new creation of Christ that they are. In

GOSPEL   Luke 10:1–12, 17–20

A reading from the holy Gospel according to Luke

Narrate as if you are telling a story.

At **that** time the **Lord** appointed seventy-two **others**
    whom he sent **ahead** of him in **pairs**
    to every **town** and **place** he intended to **visit**.
He **said** to them,
    "The **harvest** is **abundant** but the **laborers** are **few**;
    so ask the **master** of the **harvest**
    to send out **laborers** for his **harvest**.
Go **on** your way;

Contrast lambs with wolves.

    behold, I am sending you like **lambs** among **wolves**.
Carry no **money bag**, no **sack**, no **sandals**;
    and greet **no one** along the **way**.
Into whatever **house** you enter, **first** say,
    '**Peace** to this **household**.'

Speak calmly.

If a peaceful person **lives** there,
    your **peace** will **rest** on him;
    but if **not**, it will **return** to you.
Stay in the **same house** and **eat** and **drink** what is **offered** to you,
    for the **laborer deserves** his **payment**.
Do **not** move **about** from **one** house to **another**.

---

other words, they must reject this false Gospel the other missionaries preach.

In contrast to the benevolent words of greeting Paul offers in his other letters, his concluding words in this letter merely exhort the Galatians not to cause him any trouble. They should not undermine his authority because he carries on himself enduring wounds from preaching the cross of Christ, and these physical scars forever mark him as belonging to Christ.

Paul is, however, not completely unsympathetic to the plight of the Galatians. He closes the letter with a liturgical greeting, which is the basis for liturgical greetings today. It indicates that he prays at the deepest level for the Lord's grace to permeate the hearts and souls of the Galatians so that they might be drawn back to the true Gospel and live in its freedom. And despite the tenuous relationship he has with the Galatians, he still calls them "brothers and sisters," an expression of reconciliation. Make this conclusion your

prayer for the assembly as you proclaim Paul's words.

GOSPEL | Today's Gospel is Luke's reflection on mission as he sends seventy-two "others," after having already sent the Twelve in the previous chapter (9:1–6). Scholars differ on whether the intended number is seventy or seventy-two. Regardless, Luke's intent is to emphasize the universal nature of mission, in other words, that Jesus' mission extends to all who follow him, whether Jew or Gentile.

Emphasize "for you." Make eye contact with the assembly.

Whatever **town** you **enter** and they **welcome** you,
    eat what is set **before** you,
    cure the **sick** in it and **say** to them,
    'The **kingdom** of **God** is **at hand** for **you**.'
Whatever town you **enter** and they do **not** receive you,
    go out into the **streets** and **say**,
    'The **dust** of your **town** that **clings** to our **feet**,
    even that we **shake off against** you.'
Yet know **this**: the **kingdom** of **God** is at **hand**.
I **tell** you,
    it will be **more** tolerable for **Sodom** on that day
        than for **that** town."

Use a serious tone on this warning.

Sodom = SOD-uhm

Switch to a confident tone.

The seventy-two returned **rejoicing**, and said,
    "**Lord**, even the **demons** are **subject** to us because
        of your **name**."
Jesus said, "I have observed **Satan** fall like **lightning**
        from the **sky**.
Behold, I have given you the **power** to '**tread** upon **serpents**'
        and **scorpions**
    and upon the **full force** of the **enemy**
        and **nothing** will **harm** you.
Nevertheless, do **not rejoice** because the **spirits** are **subject** to you,
    but **rejoice** because your **names** are **written** in **heaven**."

Take your time on the last line. It summarizes the reason for all that precedes it in the Gospel. Use an instructive tone.

[Shorter: Luke 10:1–9]

Luke offers few but intriguing details in his instructions about the mission. The missionaries are told to take nothing with them, just as the Twelve were told to travel without baggage. They are to offer words of peace and warning, depending on what the situation warrants. Luke tells us they are to eat and drink what they are offered. Then he repeats this instruction a verse later. One specific task assigned is to heal the sick and tell them the Kingdom of God is at hand for them. They are also told how to respond to rejection. As followers of Jesus, they will know both acceptance and rejection, just as he does.

The final section of the long form of the Gospel notes the return of the seventy and the success they enjoyed on their mission. They return elated. They sense the immensity of the Lord's power because even the demons and other evil forces acquiesced to it. Jesus does not deny the power they have experienced. His final words to them, however, reveal the main purpose of his teaching on mission. Power is not the goal of mission; rather, it is salvation. This is a striking reversal of the human desire for power, similar to the connection between power and compassion in today's First Reading. Be deliberate in your proclamation of the final verses to help people understand the true reason they are to rejoice in being Jesus' faithful disciples.

15TH SUNDAY IN ORDINARY TIME

Lectionary #105

READING I — Deuteronomy 30:10–14

Deuteronomy = d<u>oo</u>-ter-AH-nuh-mee or dy<u>oo</u>-ter-AH-nuh-mee

Moses' words are both pleading and hopeful. The opening stanza is all one sentence. Follow the given punctuation.

A reading from the Book of Deuteronomy

Moses said to the **people**:
"If **only** you would **heed** the **voice** of the LORD, your **God**,
    and keep his **commandments** and **statutes**
    that are **written** in this **book** of the **law**,
    when you **return** to the LORD, your **God**,
    with **all** your **heart** and **all** your **soul**.

"For this **command** that I **enjoin** on you **today**
    is **not** too **mysterious** and **remote** for you.
It is **not** up in the **sky**, that you should say,
    '**Who** will **go up** in the **sky** to **get** it for us
    and **tell** us of it, that we may **carry** it **out**?'
Nor is it across the **sea**, that you should say,
    '**Who** will **cross** the **sea** to **get** it for us
    and **tell** us of it, that we may **carry** it **out**?'
No, it is something **very near** to **you**,
    already in your **mouths** and in your **hearts**;
    you have **only** to **carry it out**."

Raise the tone of your voice slightly at the end of the question.

Slower to emphasize the broadness of the sea. The question is the same as the previous one except for the word "sea." Mirror your proclamation of the first question, but emphasize "sea."

The Lord's command is personal. Lower your tone of voice. Proceed a bit more slowly. Emphasize the personal responsibility the command carries. Make eye contact on the final phrase.

READING I   God's people, the Israelites, have wandered in the wilderness for forty years. Soon they will cross the Jordan River into the promised land. But Moses will die before this crossing, and today's reading is a small part of Moses' final instructions about returning to the Law. Fidelity to the Law will be the path of repentance for the people.

In this farewell address, Moses reminds the Israelites that the Law is not difficult and remote; it is close to them, and the responsibility for following the Law rests solely on them, for they already have it in their mouths and in their hearts. Living in harmony with the Law is theirs alone to do.

Strive to communicate the many highs and lows in the reading by the way you modulate your voice. Stress directional words such as "remote," "up," "across," and "near." By changing your modulation, you will help paint a picture for the assembly of where they can find the Lord's word.

READING II   For the next four Sundays, the Second Reading comes from Colossians. Although some scholars question whether Paul wrote this letter, it does reflect Paul's thought and language. The letter aims to present the correct teaching about Christ and his role in salvation to the church at Colossae. At the time, false teachers were suggesting that other principalities and powers played a role in salvation. The author felt a need to restate Christ's identity and role so as to help return Christians to correct belief and practice.

Today's reading is a well-known and much-loved liturgical hymn. The first part describes Christ's role in creation. He is

READING II Colossians 1:15–20

Colossians = kuh-LOSH-uhnz

Open with the confidence of faith in who Jesus Christ is.

Lower your tone of voice on the phrases that describe why Christ Jesus is the firstborn of all creation.

Note the parallel structure of "He is" which occurs three times. Pause noticeably at the conclusion of each sentence or phrase beginning with "He is."

Speak of the reconciliation offered by Christ with serenity.

A reading from the Letter of Saint Paul to the Colossians

Christ Jesus is the **image** of the **invisible God**,
  the **firstborn** of **all creation**.
For in **him** were **created** all things in **heaven** and on **earth**,
  the **visible** and the **invisible**,
  whether **thrones** or **dominions** or **principalities** or **powers**;
  all things were **created through him** and **for him**.
He is **before** all things,
  and in **him** all things **hold together**.
He is the **head** of the **body**, the **church**.
He is the **beginning**, the **firstborn** from the **dead**,
  that in **all** things he himself might be **preeminent**.
For in **him all** the **fullness** was pleased to **dwell**,
  and **through** him to **reconcile** all things for **him**,
  making **peace** by the **blood** of his **cross**
  through him, whether those on **earth** or those in **heaven**.

GOSPEL Luke 10:25–37

An inquisitive, but somewhat fussy question.

Jesus' question in reply is straightforward.

A confident recitation of the Law.

A reading from the holy Gospel according to Luke

There was a scholar of the **law** who stood up to **test** him and said,
  "**Teacher**, what must I **do** to inherit **eternal life**?"
Jesus **said** to him, "What is **written** in the **law**?
How do **you** read it?"
He said in reply,
  "You shall love the Lord, your God,
  with all your heart,

the firstborn of creation; everything in heaven and on earth was created in him. Thus, no question remains as to the ordering of the principalities and powers in relation to Christ, since the author includes them as part of all that was created in Christ and now oriented toward him. Christ himself has touched everything with his divinity, including the principalities to which false teachers were ascribing divine power apart from Christ.

The second part of the hymn details Christ's redemptive role. Phrases from the first part of the hymn are repeated to emphasize Christ's relationship to the created world. His relationship to the Church is also clarified for the first time in the New Testament: he is the head of the body. Church *(ekklēsia)* here refers to the universal Church, in contrast to Paul's use of the word in his earlier letters to denote local communities.

The second part of the Christ hymn also emphasizes the reconciliation Christ brings—reconciliation that comes through

him, in him, and is for him. The peace which is the fruit of reconciliation comes from Christ's sacrifice on the cross. For those in the churches in Colossae and the surrounding area, the hymn at this point is eminently practical. Believers need reconciliation in the face of false teachers. But, all must recognize that this reconciliation—the bringing together again of all people and powers—only comes in, for, and through Christ, not through any other astrological, cultic, or human powers.

with *all your being,*
with all your strength,
and with all your mind,
and your neighbor as yourself."
He **replied** to him, "You have answered **correctly**;
   do this and you will **live**."

But because he wished to **justify** himself, he said to **Jesus**,
   "And **who** is my **neighbor**?"
Jesus replied,
   "A **man** fell **victim** to **robbers**
   as he went down from **Jerusalem** to **Jericho**.
They **stripped** and **beat** him and went **off leaving** him **half-dead**.
A **priest** happened to be going down that road,
   but when he **saw** him, he **passed by** on the **opposite** side.
Likewise a **Levite** came to the place,
   and when **he saw** him, **he passed by** on the **opposite** side.
But a **Samaritan** traveler who came upon him
   was moved with **compassion** at the sight.
He **approached** the victim,
   poured oil and **wine** over his **wounds** and **bandaged** them.
Then he **lifted** him up on his own **animal**,
   took him to an **inn**, and **cared** for him.
The **next** day he took out **two** silver **coins**
   and **gave** them to the **innkeeper** with the instruction,
   'Take **care** of him.
If you **spend more** than what I have **given** you,
   I shall **repay** you on my way **back**.'
Which of these three, in **your** opinion,
   was **neighbor** to the robbers' victim?"
He answered, "The **one** who **treated** him with **mercy**."
Jesus said to him, "**Go** and **do likewise**."

Ask the follow-up question in a self-serving tone.

Use a storytelling voice for the beloved parable of the Good Samaritan.
Jericho = JAYR-ih-koh

Levite = LEE-vĭt

Samaritan = suh-MAYR-uh-tuhn
Proceed slowly as you detail the actions of the Samaritan.

Direct Jesus' final question of the legal scholar to the assembly. Give the scholar's answer in a tone of honest recognition.
Jesus' concluding statement is a command. Be directive, not overly authoritative, because the scholar realizes what he must do.

GOSPEL   The opening question in today's Gospel is one that people of faith often ponder: "what must I do to inherit eternal life?" This scholar of the Law is concerned about learning and performing whatever actions are required to merit heaven. When Jesus simply affirms the man's own answer to his question, the scholar presses further, intent on "justify[ing] himself," on acquiring a thorough understanding so as to guarantee his future. He needs to know who his neighbor is—whom he must love as himself.

In the parable with which Jesus answers, the first two passersby, the priest and the Levite, both follow the Law carefully, but do not assist the victim. It is the third traveler, the Samaritan, a person to whom law-abiding Jews would have been openly antagonistic, who stops and aids the half-dead man, caring for his wounds and making sure that he has a place to rest and heal. Compassion exudes from the Samaritan who even wants to make sure he justly remunerates the innkeeper.

The point of the parable is not that we earn salvation by our compassionate actions, nor that following the Law merits eternal life; rather, the point is that if we count ourselves as members of God's Chosen People by virtue of our Baptism, then we must follow the example of the Samaritan. His spontaneous love and compassion made human distinctions irrelevant. Everyone is a neighbor. Be strong and straightforward as you end the proclamation with Jesus' bold challenge to "Go and do likewise."

16TH SUNDAY IN ORDINARY TIME

Lectionary #108

READING I   Genesis 18:1–10a

A reading from the Book of Genesis

Genesis = JEN-uh-sis

terebinth = TAYR-uh-binth. A small, deciduous Mediterranean tree that is a source of turpentine.

Mamre = MAM-ree or MAHM-ray

Quicken your pace slightly.

The LORD appeared to **Abraham** by the **terebinth** of **Mamre**,
  as he sat in the **entrance** of his **tent**,
  while the day was growing **hot**.
Looking **up**, Abraham saw **three men standing** nearby.
When he **saw** them, he **ran** from the entrance of the tent
    to **greet** them;
  and **bowing** to the ground, he said:
  "**Sir**, if I may ask you this **favor**,
  please do not go on **past** your servant.

Slow the pace as Abraham details all the acts of hospitality he desires to perform.

Let some **water** be brought, that you may **bathe** your **feet**,
  and then **rest** yourselves under the **tree**.
Now that you have come this **close** to your **servant**,
  let me **bring** you a little **food**, that you may **refresh** yourselves;
  and **afterward** you may go on your **way**."

Speak in an agreeable tone.

The **men** replied, "**Very well**, **do** as you have **said**."

Quicken your pace slightly again. Use an instructive, but not commanding tone for Abraham's words to Sarah.

Abraham **hastened** into the tent and told **Sarah**,
  "**Quick**, three measures of fine **flour**! **Knead** it
    and **make rolls**."
He **ran** to the **herd**, picked out a **tender**, **choice steer**,
  and gave it to a **servant**, who quickly **prepared** it.

Slow the pace as Abraham offers the food to the men.

Then Abraham got some curds and **milk**,
  as well as the **steer** that had been prepared,

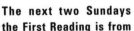 **The** next two Sundays the First Reading is from Genesis 18. The two stories we hear, that of the three visitors to Abraham and Sarah, and Abraham asking God to spare Sodom, are part of a single story. This one story also includes the narrative in Genesis 19 about the visitors' experience in Sodom and the city's destruction.

Today's reading has traditionally been seen as a story about hospitality. At the outset, notice that it is Abraham who takes the initiative to greet the visitors and request that they stop and visit. His invitation is quite urgent. Abraham obviously knows the requirements of hospitality as he lists all that he wants to do for his guests. Abraham is clearly eager to serve his visitors, yet at this point he does not recognize the Lord in them. Although God

is close to Abraham, he has difficulty recognizing the Lord's presence. After the meal, the visitors ask Sarah's whereabouts. After Abraham replies, only one of the three responds with the promise of a son to be born in a year. You will leave the assembly with this promise that your listeners, in faith, will recognize as the Lord's promise. Perhaps they, like Sarah, might initially laugh at the promise (Genesis 18:12) and then trust that the Lord will keep his word.

and **set** these before the three men;
and he **waited** on them under the **tree** while they **ate**.

They **asked** Abraham, "**Where** is your wife **Sarah**?"
He replied, "**There** in the **tent**."
One of them said, "I will **surely return** to you
about **this** time next **year**,
and **Sarah** will then have a **son**."

Speak in a polite, conversational tone.

Communicate the promise in confidence and hope.

READING II Colossians 1:24–28

A reading from the Letter of Saint Paul to the Colossians

Brothers and **sisters**:
Now I **rejoice** in my sufferings for **your** sake,
and in my **flesh** I am filling **up**
what is **lacking** in the **afflictions** of **Christ**
on behalf of his **body**, which is the **church**,
of which **I** am a **minister**
in accordance with God's **stewardship given** to me
to bring to **completion** for you the **word** of **God**,
the **mystery** hidden from **ages** and from generations **past**.
But **now** it has been **manifested** to his **holy ones**,
to whom **God** chose to make **known** the **riches** of the **glory**
of this **mystery** among the **Gentiles**;
it is **Christ** in **you**, the **hope** for **glory**.
It is **he** whom we **proclaim**,
admonishing everyone and **teaching everyone**
with **all wisdom**,
that we may **present everyone perfect** in **Christ**.

Begin confidently.

Make eye contact on "Christ in you."
Express even more confidence as you speak of proclaiming Christ and the reason you proclaim him, which is given in the last line ("that we may present . . .").
Differentiate between the stronger, corrective term "admonishing" and the word "teaching."

READING II Today's Second Reading, like last Sunday's, is from Colossians 1. Paul had neither founded the church at Colossae nor visited it (1:4), so this passage begins with a brief presentation of his apostleship. This legitimates Paul's authority to the congregation so that they might confront those who teach falsely about Christ Jesus and his role in creation and redemption. Paul founds his ministry entirely on his participation in the cross of Christ. His words might suggest

that something is missing in Christ's own suffering. However, this is not the case. The awkward phrase indicates that the proclamation of the Gospel is not yet finished. It continues through Paul, and, as the next stanza puts forward, in the holy ones in whom Christ now lives.

God revealed the mystery of the cross to the members of the church at Colossae. Christ was present in this community, including its Gentile members. Through faith and Baptism, Christ now lives in all believers. The consequence of this is that neither Paul nor any other apostolic

leader has to undertake the proclamation of the Gospel alone. The community has a responsibility to proclaim the Gospel side by side with its leaders. The proclamation of Christ involves the mutual correction of behavior and instruction given in the Spirit's wisdom. The goal is not just that some believers live with Christ forever, but that "everyone" (note the three repetitions of this word) experiences this perfect, abundant new life at the parousia, Christ's second coming.

Use a narrative voice to set the scene. Emphasize Martha's hospitality and Mary's listening.

The question comes out of Martha's frustration and is followed by Martha giving a command to the Lord.

Use a calm, instructive tone.

GOSPEL Luke 10:38–42

A reading from the holy Gospel according to Luke

Jesus entered a **village**
    where a **woman** whose name was **Martha welcomed** him.
She had a **sister** named **Mary**
    who sat **beside** the **Lord** at his feet **listening** to him speak.
Martha, **burdened** with much **serving**, came to him and **said**,
    "**Lord**, do you not **care**
    that my **sister** has left me by **myself** to do the serving?
Tell her to **help** me."
The Lord said to her in **reply**,
    "**Martha**, **Martha**, you are **anxious** and **worried**
        about **many** things.
There is need of **only one** thing.
Mary has chosen the **better** part
    and it will **not** be **taken** from her."

GOSPEL Today's Gospel follows directly upon last Sunday's parable of the Good Samaritan, in which Jesus taught the legal scholar to imitate the compassion of the Samaritan toward the dying man on the roadside. Recall that the scholar's initial question was about what he needed to do to inherit eternal life.

In today's Gospel, Martha is so much about "doing" that the Evangelist describes her as "burdened" by all the service she performs. The spoken lines in the passage belong only to Martha and Jesus. Martha's words disclose her obvious frustration with her sister, Mary, and her disappointment that the Lord does not seem to care that Mary remains unhelpful. Martha's disappointment is so great that in a reversal of roles, she tells the Lord what to do!

In the first sentence of his response, the Lord calmly acknowledges Martha's anxiety. In the second sentence, however, he seems to create a hierarchy in which Mary's way of being is preferred to Martha's frenzied service. One might wonder whether Martha, in her anxious state, would even have been able to hear what the Lord was saying. If your proclamation gets the assembly to wonder this, then you have performed your ministry of proclamation well. For this is exactly the point: listening to the Word of the Lord leads to acts of service, but when the Lord speaks, we must first, like Mary, open ourselves to hear.

17TH SUNDAY IN ORDINARY TIME

Lectionary #111

READING I   Genesis 18:20–32

Genesis = JEN-uh-sis

Sodom = SOD-uhm

Gomorrah = guh-MOHR-ah

A reading from the Book of Genesis

In **those** days, the LORD said:
"The **outcry** against **Sodom** and **Gomorrah** is so **great**,
    and their **sin** so **grave**,
    that I must go **down** and **see** whether or not their **actions**
    fully **correspond** to the **cry** against them that **comes** to me.
I mean to find **out**."

While **Abraham's visitors** walked on **farther** toward **Sodom**,
    the LORD remained **standing** before **Abraham**.
Then **Abraham** drew **nearer** and said:

The second question marks the beginning of Abraham's persistence. Reflect this in your voice.

"Will you sweep away the **innocent** with the **guilty**?
Suppose there were fifty **innocent** people in the city;
    would you **wipe out** the place, **rather** than **spare** it
    for the **sake** of the **fifty innocent people** within it?

Abraham's other words are presumptuous.

Far be it from **you** to do such a thing,
    to make the **innocent** die with the **guilty**
    so that the **innocent** and the **guilty** would be treated **alike**!
Should not the **judge** of all the **world** act with **justice**?"
The LORD **replied**,

Give the Lord's responses in the same measured tone each time.

"If I find **fifty** innocent people in the city of Sodom,
    I will **spare** the **whole place** for **their** sake."

READING I   Humans love to negotiate, and Abraham is no exception. In this reading, he confidently engages in a lengthy process of bargaining with the Lord. The reading follows upon last Sunday's story of Abraham providing hospitality to the three men who stood near his tent, resting from their journey. During their visit, Abraham hears the Lord's implausible promise to Sarah, that she will bear a son.

In the verses between last week's reading and this week's, Abraham joins the three men as they continue their journey to Sodom and Gomorrah. On the way, the Lord ponders whether or not Abraham should be privy to news of the impending destruction of the two cities. Today's reading begins with the Lord telling Abraham that indeed the reports of grave sin in these locales require investigation. There are different accounts of the sin found in the Old Testament. Genesis 19 understands the sin as sodomy, whereas the prophet Isaiah presents the sin as neglecting justice and care for one's neighbors in favor of numerous sacrifices (Isaiah 1:9; 3:9). The

prophet Ezekiel describes Sodom's sin as giving no help to the poor and needy as well as other "abominable crimes" (Ezekiel 16:49–50). Jeremiah indicates the outcry against Sodom stems from adultery, lying, and a conscious choice to live in a state of evil.

While the other two visitors walked on toward Sodom, the Lord stood before Abraham, seemingly poised for an encounter. Abraham begins with a general question about the Lord's stance toward the innocent. He doesn't allow the Lord a chance to answer, but continues with the

Express this almost arrogantly.

Abraham spoke up **again**:
 "**See** how **I** am **presuming** to speak to my Lord,
 though I am but **dust** and **ashes**!
What if there are five **less** than **fifty** innocent people?

Ask the question as if it were meant to induce guilt.

Will you destroy the **whole city** because of those **five**?"
He answered, "I will **not** destroy it, if I find **forty-five** there."

Increase the persistence in your tone of voice.

But Abraham **persisted**, saying "What if only **forty** are
 found there?"
He replied, "I will **forbear** doing it for the **sake** of the **forty**."
Then Abraham said, "Let **not** my Lord grow **impatient** if I go on.

Become even more persistent in your delivery.

What if only **thirty** are found there?"
He replied, "I will **forbear doing** it if I can find but **thirty** there."
Still Abraham went **on**,

Again heighten the degree of persistence, not volume, in your tone of voice.

 "Since I have thus **dared** to speak to my **Lord**,
 what if there are no more than **twenty**?"
The LORD answered, "I will **not destroy** it, for the **sake**
 of the **twenty**."
But he **still** persisted:

Plead in preparation for the final inquiry.

 "**Please**, let **not** my Lord grow **angry** if I **speak** up this **last** time.
What if there are at **least ten** there?"

Slightly slower, but reflect the same mercy that is in the Lord's previous statements.

He replied, "For the **sake** of those **ten**, I will **not destroy** it."

---

first of his six specific questions, intended to test the boundaries of the Lord's mercy and patience. Abraham, knowing his incessant questioning would test any human person, employs his psychological skills by naming the emotions which might surface and thereby seeking to diffuse them. It seems surprising, however, that Abraham speaks as if bargaining with a human, rather than petitioning God. Has he failed to fully recognize the Lord's presence, as he did when he entertained the visitors?

Nowhere in the passage does the author indicate that the tenor of the Lord's voice changes. This leads us to believe that the Lord would spare Sodom and Gomorrah even if the cities included only one innocent person between them. Knowing the Lord would spare ten innocent people finally led Abraham to get the point: the Lord's mercy is available for all who seek and ask, even for one.

READING II The brief Second Reading is the culmination of the author's argument about the sovereignty of

Christ, about his reign over creation. The first verse testifies to the Colossians' experience of Christ's reign by virtue of their Baptism. Through Baptism, they participate in Christ's Death and Resurrection. This union with Christ grows from God's power and their faith in it. God raised Christ, and now raises them in Christ.

Next the author speaks of the Colossians' state before Baptism. When they were mired in sin and had not overcome the impurities of the flesh, God still brought them to life in Christ. How did God do this? He brought the Colossians to life

READING II   Colossians 2:12–14

Colossians = kuh-LOSH-uhnz

Contrast "buried" and "raised" by changing the inflection in your voice from heavier to lighter.

There is similar contrast between "dead" and "life."

"Obliterating" provides onomatopoeia. When all the consonants are audible, the word sounds like the action of obliterating or destroying.

Slightly extend the first syllable of the word "nailing" so it reflects the finality of Christ's act of forgiveness.

A reading from the Letter of Saint Paul to the Colossians

Brothers and **sisters:**
You were **buried** with him in **baptism,**
  in which you were also **raised** with him
  through **faith** in the **power** of **God,**
  who **raised** him from the **dead.**
And even when you were **dead**
  in **transgressions** and the **uncircumcision** of your **flesh,**
  he **brought** you to **life** along **with** him,
  having **forgiven** us all our **transgressions;**
  obliterating the bond **against** us, with its **legal** claims,
  which was **opposed** to us,
  he also **removed** it from our midst, **nailing** it to the **cross.**

GOSPEL   Luke 11:1–13

A sincere and profound request. Speak it slowly, so that people in the assembly can make it their own.

Take your time with each petition.

A reading from the holy Gospel according to Luke

Jesus was **praying** in a certain **place,** and when he had **finished,**
  one of his **disciples** said to him,
  "**Lord, teach** us to **pray** just as **John** taught **his** disciples."
He said to them, "When you **pray,** say:
  Father, hallowed be your **name,**
    your kingdom come.
    Give us each day our **daily bread**
    and **forgive** us **our sins**

by canceling the bond (*cheirographon,* literally, "handwritten note") of sin that carried legal claims against them. Once for all, in his Death, Christ cancelled all debts that humankind owed. The act of nailing the bond to the Cross signifies the finality of Christ's act of forgiveness. Allow the concluding line to create a visual image in your mind. This will leave no doubt about the irrevocability of the act. Those who once lived in the morass of fleshly sin need no longer suffer shame or disgrace for their previous life. They are now alive in Christ Jesus.

GOSPEL   Today's Gospel comes from the beginning of chapter 11 and follows immediately after the passage about Martha and Mary. Jesus, having just described Mary's contemplative listening as the better part in comparison with Martha's busyness, is himself at prayer, communicating with the Father. One of the disciples asks Jesus to teach them how to pray. It was customary for disciples to learn how to pray from their leader. While many might have treated the disciples' request as an interruption to their own

prayer, Jesus responds simply by inviting the disciples to learn and share in the prayer we traditionally know as the Our Father.

Luke's form of the Our Father has five petitions. It is earthy from the start. God is addressed with the unmodified term "Father," a reference to a loving and kind parent who is present with his children. Given Luke's emphasis on human divisions ceasing in the Kingdom of God, the petition, "your kingdom come" encourages disciples to herald the Kingdom's coming in their actions in this world. "Daily bread"

for **we ourselves** forgive **everyone** in **debt** to **us**,
and do **not subject** us to the **final test**."

Tell the parable in a storytelling voice.

And he said to them, "Suppose one of you has a **friend**
to whom he goes at **midnight** and says,
'**Friend, lend** me three loaves of **bread**,
for a **friend** of mine has **arrived** at my **house** from a **journey**
and I have **nothing** to **offer** him,'
and he says in reply from **within**,
'Do **not bother** me; the door has **already** been **locked**
and my **children** and **I** are already in **bed**.
I **cannot** get **up** to give you **anything**.'
I **tell** you,

Be insistent.

if he does **not** get up to give the visitor the loaves
because of their **friendship**,
he **will** get up to give him **whatever** he needs
because of his **persistence**.

Use an instructive tone on Jesus' interpretation of the parable. Pace your proclamation so the repeated parallel structure stands out.

"And I **tell** you, **ask** and you will **receive**;
seek and you will **find**;
knock and the door will be **opened** to you.
For **everyone** who **asks, receives**;
and the one who **seeks, finds**;
and to the one who **knocks**, the **door** will be **opened**.

These questions are tinged with irony.

What **father among** you would hand his **son** a **snake**
when he **asks** for a **fish**?
Or **hand** him a **scorpion** when he **asks** for an **egg**?
If **you** then, who are **wicked**,
know **how** to give **good** gifts to your **children**,

Raise your voice slightly at the end of the question, even though it's rhetorical. Pause significantly after the question and before beginning "The Word of the Lord."

how much more will the **Father** in **heaven**
give the **Holy Spirit** to those who **ask** him?"

---

includes both physical and spiritual sustenance, not just for certain people in the community, but for all. This is a corporate, not an individual petition, just as the petition about forgiveness is in the first person plural. This petition also recognizes that the disciples need to forgive not just those whom they choose to forgive, but every person who has harmed them. The final petition asks that God spare the disciples from the time of final trial before the end of this age.

Following the prayer itself is Jesus' teaching to his disciples about prayer. A parable about a friend in need emphasizes persistence and provides a direct link with Abraham's persistent questioning of God in the First Reading.

The interpretation of the parable follows, including two verses with parallel structure: ask/receive, seek/find, knock/open. Notice that in the first verse of the interpretation, Jesus speaks directly to the

disciples. In the following verse, he generalizes his teaching to everyone. The passage concludes with two overstated rhetorical questions which heighten Jesus' teaching, and Luke names the Holy Spirit as the gift the Father will give everyone who asks. Jesus is teaching that God universally provides in this world and the next.

18TH SUNDAY IN ORDINARY TIME

Lectionary #114

READING I   Ecclesiastes 1:2; 2:21–23

Ecclesiastes = ih-klee-zee-AS-teez

Qoheleth = koh-HEL-uhth

This is a discouraging reality.

Raise your voice slightly at the end of the question.

Use a rueful tone to express sorrow and grief.

A reading from the Book of Ecclesiastes

Vanity of **vanities**, says **Qoheleth**,
   vanity of **vanities**! **All** things are **vanity**!

Here is one who has **labored** with **wisdom** and **knowledge**
      and **skill**,
   and **yet** to **another** who has **not labored** over it,
   he must **leave property**.
This **also** is vanity and a **great misfortune**.
For **what profit comes** to **man** from all the **toil** and **anxiety**
      of **heart**
   with which he has **labored** under the **sun**?
All his days **sorrow** and **grief** are his occupation;
   even at **night** his mind is **not** at **rest**.
This **also** is **vanity**.

READING I   How often we feel the same way as the author of Ecclesiastes in today's First Reading! (Qoheleth is Greek for the Hebrew name meaning "one who convokes an assembly.") All our hard work is for naught. Today's opening is perhaps the most well-known verse of this book, which we hear from only once in the three-year Lectionary cycle. Its wisdom sounds a pessimistic

tone, which will continue throughout. The verses from chapter 2 that follow the reading's first verse describe a real-life situation which some in your assembly will have experienced. The hard work a person expends to maintain property is not enough. The property must be turned over to someone who has not toiled over it. Qoheleth's question is a natural one: What do we stand to gain from our work? To him, it seems that work produces only sorrow, grief, and a restless mind.

This, however, is not the whole story. As you prepare to proclaim this reading, read the final three verses of Ecclesiastes 2. In them, you will see that Qoheleth regards work positively because it comes from God. Although we must toil during life, when we do so recognizing God's gifts of wisdom and knowledge, we will find joy in the ordinary, everyday course of life. Knowing this, don't proclaim the reading with complete despair. This is the set-up for illuminations that will come in the readings that follow.

READING II Colossians 3:1–5, 9–11

Colossians = kuh-LOSH-uhnz

Offer Paul's reminders about being raised with Christ in a positive tone.

A reading from the Letter of Saint Paul to the Colossians

Brothers and **sisters**:
If you were **raised** with **Christ**, **seek** what is **above**,
    where **Christ** is **seated** at the **right hand** of God.
Think of what is **above**, **not** of what is on **earth**.
For **you** have **died**,
    and your **life** is **hidden** with **Christ** in **God**.
When **Christ** your **life appears**,
    then **you too** will **appear** with him in **glory**.

Communicate the command to "Put to death" in a serious tone. Take your time with the list of vices.

Emphasize "stop lying to one another." Make eye contact.

Put to **death**, then, the **parts** of you that are **earthly**:
    immorality, **impurity**, **passion**, **evil desire**,
    and the **greed** that is **idolatry**.
Stop **lying** to one another,
    since you have taken off the **old** self with its **practices**
    and have put on the **new** self,
    which is being **renewed**, for **knowledge**,
    in the **image** of its **creator**.

Conclude positively, but also in an instructive tone, because the message of unity in Christ is both encouraging and challenging.

Scythian = SITH-ee-uhn

Here there is not **Greek** and **Jew**,
    circumcision and **uncircumcision**,
    barbarian, **Scythian**, **slave**, **free**;
    but **Christ** is **all** and **in all**.

READING II We proclaim the first part of today's Second Reading every year on Easter Sunday. Since the reading speaks of our sharing in Christ's Resurrection, it is an obvious choice for Easter. But why proclaim the reading in the middle of Ordinary Time? Paul needed to remind the Colossians that through their Baptism they now live with Christ. They died to the earthly ways of life, although they continued to be attracted to them through the preaching of false teachers. We are also in need of Paul's reminder.

Paul's words become highly practical as he provides a list of five earthly vices the Colossians should avoid. Another list of five vices follows a few verses later, but is not a part of today's reading (Colossians 3:8). Paul also exhorts the Colossians to stop lying and to remember that in the Christian community divisions based on religion, ethnicity, and social status cease to exist. All are one in Christ through faith affirmed in Baptism.

Colossians 3:11 is similar to Galatians 3:28: human divisions cease to exist in the Christian community. Faith in the risen Christ requires believers to act in a particular way, recognizing that all people are created in the image of God. We must be an Easter people in Ordinary Time!

 GOSPEL The next three Sundays, the Gospel comes from Luke 12. In this chapter, Luke shows us the twofold opposition Jesus and his disciples face. First, they face a general human

GOSPEL Luke 12:13–21

A reading from the holy Gospel according to Luke

Someone in the **crowd** said to **Jesus**,
　"**Teacher**, tell my **brother** to **share** the **inheritance** with me."
He **replied** to him,
　"**Friend**, **who** appointed **me** as your **judge** and **arbitrator**?"
Then he said to the **crowd**,
　"Take **care** to **guard against all greed**,
　for though **one** may be **rich**,
　one's **life** does not consist of **possessions**."

Then he told them a **parable**.
"There was a **rich** man whose **land** produced a **bountiful harvest**.
He **asked** himself, '**What** shall I **do**,
　for I do **not** have **space** to **store** my **harvest**?'
And he said, '**This** is what I shall do:
　I shall **tear down** my **barns** and build **larger** ones.
There I shall **store all** my grain and **other goods**
　and I shall **say** to myself, "**Now** as for **you**,
　you have so **many** good things stored up for **many years**,
　rest, eat, drink, be merry!" '
But **God** said to him,
　'You **fool**, **this night** your **life** will be **demanded** of you;
　and the things you have **prepared**, to **whom** will they **belong**?'
Thus will it be for **all** who store up treasure for **themselves**
　but are **not rich** in **what matters** to **God**."

Communicate the command strongly, emphasizing inheritance so as to orient the assembly to the theme of material possessions.
Ask Jesus' question in a conversational tone, without frustration.
Use an instructive tone.

Speak the parable in a narrative tone, shifting as appropriate to communicate the selfish nature of the man's greed.

Emphasize the transitional phrase "But God said to him."
Pause after the question and before God's summary statement that concludes the Gospel.

resistance to placing sufficient, but not excessive, importance on material possessions, and second, a specific, in-house resistance coming from religious leaders whom Luke often characterizes as greedy.

Today's Gospel has two sections. The first opens with an exchange between Jesus and a member of the crowd who asks Jesus to use his didactic authority to tell his brother to share an inheritance. Jesus replies with a question that intentionally draws a boundary. His role is not

to interfere in family disputes, but rather to teach family members how to mutually discern the best course of action. The principle for discerning how to act is simple: greed is unacceptable and life is not defined by possessions.

Jesus continues with a parable which illustrates this principle. The prosperous farmer in the parable decides to rest on his laurels, enjoying the goods his land produced. In the meaningful twist particular to this parable, God speaks to the man, informing him of his foolish choice. God demands

more of a disciple than self-centered greed. God demands that the disciple's life be oriented toward God. A disciple's life is focused on belonging to God; it is not attached to the world's goods. Although a disciple might be reasonably concerned about how practical needs will be met, utter dependence on God eases this human worry. It allows us who are disciples to be rich in and with God, so that we can live for God in the world.

19TH SUNDAY IN ORDINARY TIME

Lectionary #117

READING I   Wisdom 18:6–9

A reading from the Book of Wisdom

The reading opens with a solemn remembrance. Use the commas as a guide for pausing in the opening sentence.

> The **night** of the **passover** was known **beforehand** to our **fathers**,
>   that, with **sure knowledge** of the **oaths** in which they
>   put their **faith**,
>   they might have **courage**.
> Your people **awaited** the **salvation** of the **just**
>   and the **destruction** of their **foes**.
> For when you **punished** our **adversaries**,
>   in this you **glorified** us whom you had **summoned**.
> For in **secret** the **holy children** of the **good**
>   were offering **sacrifice**
>   and putting into **effect** with one **accord** the **divine institution**.

Contrast "punished" with "glorifed."
adversaries = AD-ver-sayr-eez
Express the courageous actions of the Chosen People in a bold, confident tone, even though they carried out the actions in secret.

READING II   Hebrews 11:1–2, 8–19

A reading from the Letter to the Hebrews

Brothers and **sisters**:
Faith is the **realization** of what is **hoped** for
    and **evidence** of things **not seen**.
Because of it the **ancients** were well **attested**.

By **faith** Abraham **obeyed** when he was **called** to go **out** to a place
        that he was to **receive** as an **inheritance**;
    he **went out**, **not knowing where** he was to go.

Read these lines about faith boldly, with the certainty of your own faith.

Emphasize "By faith" each of the four times the phrase occurs.

READING I — Today's First Reading attests to the steady, covenant faith of the Israelites through the centuries, a faith in God's love that prepared them to endure hardship, confident that they would be delivered. It is in this sense, through the long practice of trusting in the covenant, that the "fathers" knew "beforehand" of the Passover.

The author of Wisdom also meditates on the strange dynamic in which Israel was strengthened by the same events that caused her enemies suffering. From chapter 11 on, the author has developed the explanation in five examples, known as diptychs, because one act provides the hinge or connection from which both the blessing of the Israelites and the punishment of the Egyptians takes place. Those examples include water coming from the rock contrasted with the first plague of the Nile's water turning into blood; God providing quail to nourish his people instead of the plagues of frogs, gnats, and flies; nature raining manna instead of hail, thunder, and lightning that punish; God's presence in the pillar of fire instead of the plague of darkness; and the saving of Israel's sons during the Passover when the tenth plague put to death the Egyptians' sons. The final diptych starts one verse before the beginning of today's three-verse reading.

Mysterious and intricate as God's actions are, the people know that they must steadfastly trust in God's love for them.

READING II — For the next four Sundays, the Second Reading comes from Hebrews, a late first-century composition by an unknown author who probably had connections to Paul. Hebrews has two main themes: the high priesthood of Jesus

sojourned = SOH-jernd

By **faith** he sojourned in the **promised** land as
        in a foreign **country**,
    dwelling in **tents** with **Isaac** and **Jacob**,
        heirs of the **same promise**;
    for he was looking **forward** to the city with **foundations**,
    whose **architect** and **maker** is **God**.
By **faith** he received **power** to **generate**,
    even though he was **past** the **normal** age
    —and Sarah **herself** was **sterile**—
    for he thought that the one who had **made** the promise
        was **trustworthy**.
So it was that there came **forth** from **one** man,
    himself as **good** as **dead**,
        descendants as **numerous** as the **stars** in the **sky**
    and as **countless** as the **sands** on the **seashore**.

Broaden your tone and slow down slightly as you speak of Abraham's descendants being as "numerous as the stars."

Emphasize "faith." Pause after the sentence.
Proclaim this section in a neutral, explanatory tone.

All these **died** in **faith**.
They did **not receive** what had been **promised**
    but **saw** it and **greeted** it from **afar**
    and **acknowledged** themselves to be **strangers** and **aliens**
        on **earth**,
    for those who **speak thus show** that they are **seeking**
        a **homeland**.
If they had been **thinking** of the land from which they had **come**,
    they would have had **opportunity** to **return**.
But **now** they desire a **better** homeland, a **heavenly** one.
Therefore, God is **not ashamed** to be called their **God**,
    for he has **prepared** a **city** for them.

The last time "By faith" occurs.

By **faith** Abraham, when put to the **test**, offered up **Isaac**,
    and he who had **received** the **promises** was ready
        to **offer** his **only son**,
    of whom it was said,

and the journey of God's people to their heavenly homeland.

Today's reading begins with a frequently quoted definition of faith, although the author does not intend it as a definition. Faith for the Hebrews involved both "what" they hoped for and God's assurance that what they hoped for would become reality. Faith is also a personal act centered in hope in God through Jesus Christ. Evidence of all that faith is found not in this world, but in the spiritual world that cannot be seen through human eyes.

The passage then describes how Abraham embodies this understanding of faith, using four repetitions of the phrase "By faith" to emphasize that God calls the Hebrews and us today to live in faith, following our patriarch's example. Abraham's faith in God's promises of land, progeny, and prosperity is the basis for his descendants' journey to the heavenly homeland. The final stanza, which begins "By faith," speaks of the great test Abraham faced: God asking Abraham to sacrifice his only son, Isaac.

The author of Hebrews concludes the passage by interpreting Abraham's faith in light of Christ's Resurrection. He sees God's gift of returning Isaac to Abraham as a prefiguring of God raising Jesus from the dead. The author's point is this: we Christians should be all the more hopeful of our resurrection to the heavenly city of Jerusalem since we have both the faith of Abraham and the knowledge of Christ's Resurrection to sustain us in our commitment to the journey!

"Through **Isaac** descendants shall **bear** your **name**."
He reasoned that **God** was able to **raise** even from the **dead**,
   and he received **Isaac back** as a **symbol**.

[Shorter: Hebrews 11:1–2, 8–12]

GOSPEL   Luke 12:32–48

A reading from the holy Gospel according to Luke

Jesus said to his **disciples**:
   "Do not be **afraid** any **longer**, little **flock**,
   for your **Father** is **pleased** to give you the **kingdom**.
Sell your belongings and give **alms**.
Provide **money** bags for yourselves that do **not** wear **out**,
   an **inexhaustible treasure** in **heaven**
   that no **thief** can reach nor **moth destroy**.
For where your **treasure** is, **there also** will your **heart** be.

"**Gird** your **loins** and **light** your **lamps**
   and be like **servants** who await their master's return
     from a **wedding**,
   ready to open **immediately** when he **comes** and **knocks**.
Blessed are those **servants**
   whom the master finds **vigilant** on his arrival.
Amen, I say to you, he will **gird** himself,
   have them **recline** at **table**, and **proceed** to **wait** on **them**.
And should he **come** in the **second** or **third** watch
   and find them **prepared** in this way,
   blessed are those servants.
Be **sure** of **this**:
   if the **master** of the house had **known** the hour
   when the **thief** was coming,
   he would **not** have let his house be broken **into**.

Proclaim the final sentence straightforwardly, using a stronger tone than you used for the previous narrative section.

The opening words of Jesus are reassuring.

Give Jesus' two directives to his disciples in an instructive tone.

Emphasize "treasure" and "heart." Express the statement peacefully.
gird = gerd
The tone of Jesus' words becomes stronger and more serious. It now also includes a sense of urgency.

Set off the "Amen" which introduces Jesus' solemn teaching by pausing at the comma.

Make eye contact with the assembly on "I say to you."

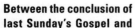

Between the conclusion of last Sunday's Gospel and the beginning of this Sunday's, Jesus elaborates on the theme of dependence on God. He advises the disciples not to worry about their physical needs, but rather to seek first the Kingdom of God. Today's Gospel begins with Jesus gently reinforcing his point that they need not fear for their well-being. He gives his disciples three instructions: sell everything they have, give alms, and provide themselves with lasting money bags. He then uses the image of a treasure as he did in last Sunday's Gospel. The disciples' treasure must be God and their heart must be in God. When this is the case, they will be rich in what is important.

The longer form of today's Gospel continues with the servant parable and its interpretation. The shorter form includes only the parable's interpretation. In its emphasis on vigilance, the parable seems more fitting for Advent than Ordinary Time.

Yet disciples must always be prepared to serve the Master, the Son of Man.

Peter wants to find out if all must be vigilant servants, or if this only applies to church leaders. Jesus responds with a question, which he immediately answers. The disciples may have expected Jesus to identify exactly who among the servants the master would name as the faithful and prudent steward, the one who would give service to all the other servants and the master.

Emphasize "You" and make eye contact. Jesus' words are a serious directive.

You also must be prepared, for at an **hour** you do **not expect**,
  the **Son** of **Man** will **come**."

Then **Peter** said,
  "**Lord**, is this parable meant for **us** or for **everyone**?"
And the Lord **replied**,
  "**Who**, **then**, is the **faithful** and **prudent steward**
  whom the **master** will put in **charge** of his **servants**
  to distribute the **food allowance** at the **proper time**?
Blessed is that servant whom his **master** on **arrival** finds **doing** so.
Truly, I **say** to you, the **master** will put the servant
  in charge of **all** his property.

Again set off the "Truly" which introduces Jesus' solemn teaching by pausing at the comma.

But if **that servant** says to himself,
  'My master is **delayed** in coming,'
  and begins to **beat** the menservants and the maidservants,
  to **eat** and **drink** and get **drunk**,
  then that servant's **master** will **come**
  on an **unexpected day** and at an **unknown hour**
  and will **punish** the servant **severely**
  and assign him a **place** with the **unfaithful**.
That servant who **knew** his master's will
  but did **not** make **preparations nor act** in **accord** with his **will**
  shall be beaten **severely**;
  and the **servant** who was **ignorant** of his master's will
  but **acted** in a way **deserving** of a **severe** beating
  shall be beaten **only lightly**.

Proclaim the concluding interpretation of the parable slowly and seriously. Emphasize it as a personal requirement of discipleship by making eye contact.

Much will be **required** of the **person entrusted** with much,
  and still **more** will be demanded of the person **entrusted**
    with **more**."

[Shorter: Luke 12:35–40]

But as often happens in the interpretation of parables, Jesus' answer provides an unexpected twist. The steward will be the servant who is already doing the service that needs to be done. The steward is one who does not need to be told what to do, but is constantly engaged in God's work.

The parable's interpretation also includes Jesus' explanation of the severe consequences for the servant's brutality and debauchery, should the master's coming be delayed. Lines about beating are difficult to proclaim in a day when we decry such violence. Remember that these lines are not to be taken literally. They underscore the importance of serving faithfully, and, along with the final lines, they distinguish between levels of expectation. In the end, however, we all follow Jesus the Servant.

THE ASSUMPTION OF THE BLESSED VIRGIN MARY: VIGIL

Lectionary #621

READING I   1 Chronicles 15:3–4, 15–16; 16:1–2

Chronicles = KRAH-nih-k*ls

Emphasize David's actions: "David assembled," "David called together," "David commanded," and so on.

Aaron = AYR-uhn
Levites = LEE-vīts

A reading from the first Book of Chronicles

David **assembled** all **Israel** in **Jerusalem** to bring the **ark**
      of the LORD
   to the **place** that he had **prepared** for it.
David also called together the **sons** of **Aaron** and the **Levites**.

The Levites bore the **ark** of **God** on their **shoulders** with **poles**,
      as **Moses** had **ordained** according to the **word** of the LORD.

David commanded the **chiefs** of the **Levites**
   to appoint their **kinsmen** as **chanters**,
   to play on **musical instruments**, **harps**, **lyres**, and **cymbals**,
   to make a loud **sound** of **rejoicing**.

Use a warm and reverent tone of voice for the ritual of the presentation of the ark and David's blessing of the people. Make eye contact with the assembly as you speak of David blessing the people in the Lord's name.

They **brought** in the **ark** of **God** and set it within the **tent**
   which **David** had **pitched** for it.
Then they offered up **burnt offerings** and **peace offerings** to **God**.
When **David** had **finished** offering up the burnt offerings
      and peace offerings,
   he **blessed** the people in the **name** of the LORD.

READING I This reading may seem a puzzling choice for the Vigil of the Assumption, but the reference to the ark of the LORD provides the connection to this solemnity. For the Israelite people, the ark represented God's presence with them. It was the ornate, rectangular box the Israelites carried with them from the time of the exodus until the building of the Temple. Some traditions suggest that the ark contained the written word of the Law (1 Kings 8:9). What the ark held was so holy that only an authorized person

could come in contact with it. Once the Temple of Solomon was built, the ark was placed in the Holy of Holies, a site only the high priest could enter. Prior to Solomon's reign, the ark was kept safe in a tent or tabernacle set up at each location where the Israelites stopped on their journey.

In the Scriptures, there is a clear parallel between Mary and the ark. The story of David bringing the original ark into Jerusalem in 2 Samuel 6:4–16 is similar to Mary's visitation of Elizabeth in Luke 1:39–56, the Gospel proclaimed tomorrow for tomorrow's celebration of the Solemnity of

the Assumption. Just as David journeys to Jerusalem with the ark, Mary, pregnant with Jesus, journeys to Elizabeth. This similarity provides the basis on which the tradition of the Church understands Mary as the ark, the bearer of God's presence.

Through your proclamation, lead the assembly to reflect on how they carry Jesus with them on their journeys, both short and long, and how they reverence him at each town, place of work, and home they visit.

READING II   1 Corinthians 15:54b–57

A reading from the first Letter of Saint Paul to the Corinthians

Brothers and **sisters**:
When that which is **mortal** clothes itself with **immortality**,
     then the **word** that is **written** shall come **about**:

Death is swallowed up in victory.
Where, O death, is your victory?
Where, O death, is your sting?

The **sting** of *death* is **sin**,
     and the **power** of **sin** is the **law**.
But thanks be to **God** who gives us the **victory**
     through our **Lord Jesus Christ**.

Corinthians = kohr-IN-thee-unz

Pause slightly before and after the lines quoting Isaiah 25:8 and Hosea 13:14: "Death is swallowed up . . . ." Remember to raise your voice slightly as you near the end of the questions.

Proclaim the victory joyfully, with obvious gratitude, because you and the assembly know this victory and desire to share it with others.

READING II This short passage from the First Letter to the Corinthians is part of Paul's response to questions raised earlier in chapter 15 about the nature of the risen body and how the dead are restored to life (15:35). Drawing on Isaiah 25:8 and Hosea 13:14, Paul makes the case that death does not last; rather, God through Jesus Christ gives victory over death. The sting of death— sin—no longer has power over us.

Just as Paul taught the Corinthians that through Christ's Resurrection they will become a transformed body, bearing the image of the risen body of Christ, so too, "the Assumption of the Blessed Virgin is a singular participation in her Son's Resurrection and an anticipation of the resurrection of other Christians" (*Catechism of the Catholic Church*, 966). Your proclamation of Paul's words on the eve of the Assumption can lead those in the assembly to understand that Mary's

participation in Christ's Resurrection exemplifies the transformation that awaits all Christians at the end of our earthly life. What a joyful proclamation this is!

GOSPEL The two verses that compose the Gospel on the Vigil of the Assumption are found in the section of Luke that narrates the journey of Jesus and his disciples into Jerusalem (9:51—19:27). Prior to these verses, Jesus

GOSPEL Luke 11:27–28

State the opening announcement ("A reading from . . .") clearly and strongly. Pause after the announcement, gaining the assembly's attention for the very brief Gospel that follows.

Pause slightly at the comma after "he replied." Proclaim his reply directly to the assembly, inviting them to follow Mary's example of hearing the word of God.

A reading from the holy Gospel according to Luke

While **Jesus** was **speaking**,
    a **woman** from the crowd **called out** and **said** to him,
    "**Blessed** is the **womb** that **carried** you
    and the **breasts** at which you **nursed**."
He **replied**,
    "**Rather**, **blessed** are those
    who **hear** the **word** of **God** and **observe** it."

casts out a demon (11:14), speaks about Satan (11:18–19), and teaches about the effects of unclean spirits (11:24–26). In the midst of Jesus' teaching, an unidentified woman in the crowd interrupts him, raises her voice, and says, "Blessed is the womb . . . ." Jesus responds, neither rebuking her nor denying her words, but rather by completing her statement. The woman praises and honors Mary for her role as Jesus' mother. Jesus affirms that Mary is blessed because she heard the word of God and responded obediently to it. She is a model of holiness for us.

THE ASSUMPTION OF THE BLESSED VIRGIN MARY: DAY

Lectionary #622

READING I   Revelation 11:19a; 12:1–6a, 10ab

A reading from the Book of Revelation

God's temple in heaven was **opened**,
   and the **ark** of his **covenant** could be **seen** in the temple.

A great **sign** appeared in the **sky**, a **woman clothed** with the **sun**,
   with the **moon** beneath her **feet**,
   and on her **head** a **crown** of **twelve stars**.
She was with **child** and **wailed aloud** in **pain** as she **labored**
     to give **birth**.
Then **another sign** appeared in the **sky**;
   it was a **huge red dragon**, with **seven heads** and **ten horns**,
   and on its heads were **seven diadems**.
Its **tail swept away** a **third** of the **stars** in the **sky**
   and **hurled** them down to the **earth**.
Then the **dragon** stood before the **woman** about to give **birth**,
   to **devour** her **child** when she gave **birth**.
She gave **birth** to a **son**, a **male child**,
   destined to **rule** all the **nations** with an **iron rod**.
Her **child** was caught up to **God** and his **throne**.
The woman **herself fled** into the **desert**
   where she had a **place prepared** by **God**.

Then I heard a **loud voice** in **heaven** say:
   "**Now** have **salvation** and **power** come,
     and the **Kingdom** of our **God**
     and the **authority** of his **Anointed One**."

Revelation = rev-uh-LAY-shuhn

Be clear in your announcement of the reading from "the Book of Revelation," not Revelations.

Let beauty and wonder be heard in your voice as you narrate the words "A great sign appeared . . . ." Take your time painting the vision of the woman, giving people time to engage their imaginations and make the connection to Mary and the child, Jesus.

Pause before the introduction of the dragon. Refrain from being overly dramatic in this scene.

Fill your voice with trust and faith as you narrate how the child and the woman experienced union with God.

Boldly proclaim the concluding verse. Keep strength throughout the verse.

READING I   The Book of Revelation is from the genre of literature known as apocalyptic. It was probably written between AD 92 and 96 at the end of the reign of the Emperor Domitian. Through a dramatic vision given by Christ to a man named John, the author expresses the belief that the world is corrupt and therefore will be destroyed. In the end, the unrighteous will suffer death with the world's destruction and the righteous will experience life in union with God.

The author of Revelation wrote for people who faced persecution by Roman leaders. The vision contained in his work urged the people to stand up for their faith, for in doing so God would rescue them—if not in this life, then in the next.

Apocalyptic literature is usually replete with symbolism, as in today's First Reading. This symbolism is not meant to be taken literally; the nature of a symbol means that it stands for or represents something beyond itself. For example, in the first section of the reading, the Catholic tradition has historically interpreted the "woman clothed with the sun" as Mary and the child the woman bore as Jesus. Yet the woman also symbolizes the heavenly Israel, the bringing together of God's Chosen People in the Old Testament with the new Israel, the Church, of the New Testament.

In the reading's second section, the sign of the "great red dragon" represents the power of the devil and the many forces of evil in the world that oppose the goodness of God and God's people, the Church.

Corinthians = kohr-IN-thee-unz

Make eye contact with the assembly.

Pause before the words "For just as in Adam." On the next phrase "so too in Christ," shift to a more hopeful tone of voice.

Build in intensity from "then, at his coming."

READING II   1 Corinthians 15:20–27

A reading from the first Letter of Saint Paul to the Corinthians

Brothers and **sisters:**
Christ has been **raised** from the **dead,**
    the **firstfruits** of those who have **fallen asleep.**
For since **death** came through **man,**
    the **resurrection** of the **dead** came **also** through **man.**
For just as in **Adam** all **die,**
    so too in **Christ** shall all be **brought** to **life,**
    but **each one** in **proper order:**
    Christ the **firstfruits;**
    then, at his **coming,** those who **belong** to Christ;
    then comes the **end,**
    when he **hands over** the **Kingdom** to his **God** and **Father,**
    when he has **destroyed every sovereignty**
    and e**very authority** and **power.**
For he must **reign** until he has put **all** his **enemies** under his **feet.**
The **last enemy** to be **destroyed** is **death,**
    for "he subjected **everything** under his **feet.**"

The author of Revelation most likely intended the dragon to symbolize the Roman leaders who were putting down the fledgling Church (see Revelation 12:13–18).

The third and final section of the reading shows that God protects the child to whom the woman gives birth. The child arrives at God's throne, a reference to the belief that Christ reigns forever with God through his Resurrection and Ascension. The woman, too, resides in a special place in the desert where God protects and nourishes her.

We understand the woman in the vision to be Mary, the Mother of Christ and the Mother of the Church. Therefore, this vision also symbolizes that the Church will last throughout all time, a fundamental conviction held by the Christian community since its earliest days. Our belief that Jesus, the Son of God and the son of Mary, is Lord for all time is the basis for the eternal nature of the Church.

READING II Like the Second Reading for the Assumption Vigil, the Second Reading for today comes from

chapter 15 of Paul's First Letter to the Corinthians. The focus of that chapter is Paul's teaching about the Resurrection of Christ and what it means for our resurrection. Paul develops his theology of resurrection around two main points in today's reading. First, Paul uses the agricultural image of the "firstfruits" to show that Christ's Resurrection anticipates the resurrection of Christians at the end of time. The "firstfruits" were the part of the harvest offered in thanksgiving to God in anticipation of the whole harvest that was to come.

GOSPEL   Luke 1:39–56

A reading from the holy Gospel according to Luke

Narrate the opening lines with a sense of urgency.

Zechariah = zek-uh-Rī-uh

Mary set **out**
   and traveled to the **hill** country in **haste**
   to a town of **Judah**,
   where she entered the house of **Zechariah**
   and greeted **Elizabeth**.
When **Elizabeth heard Mary's greeting**,
   the **infant leaped** in her **womb**,
   and **Elizabeth**, filled with the **Holy Spirit**,
   cried out in a loud **voice** and said,
   "**Blessed** are **you** among **women**,
   and **blessed** is the **fruit** of your **womb**.

Fill your voice with praise.

Pause after Elizabeth's acclamation of Mary and before her question. Ask Elizabeth's question with humility by lightening the tone of your voice and lowering the volume slightly.

Return again to the tone of praise— though use a more reserved tone than that used for the first acclamation.

And **how** does this **happen** to me,
   that the **mother** of my **Lord** should **come** to me?
For at the **moment** the **sound** of your **greeting** reached my **ears**,
   the **infant** in my **womb leaped** for **joy**.
Blessed are you who **believed**
   that what was **spoken** to you by the **Lord**
   would be **fulfilled**."

Second, Paul develops an Adam-Christ typology in which he identifies Christ as a human being like Adam. Paul argues that since death (sin) came through Adam, life also must come through a person like Adam. Thus, since we all have inherited the human condition of sinfulness from Adam, so at the second coming of Christ—the risen one who has destroyed sin—we, too, will be raised.

Why proclaim this reading on the Assumption? Through Mary's Assumption into heavenly glory, she participates in a unique way in her son's Resurrection, and in doing so, anticipates our own resurrection (*Catechism of the Catholic Church,* 966). From the Annunciation to the Cross, Mary's role as Mother of God never ceased. Because of her closeness to Christ and to us, she intercedes for all Christians as we look forward to the gift of eternal life in union with God.

GOSPEL   In today's Gospel, the beloved, familial narrative of the Visitation, Elizabeth praises Mary twice. Her first words ("Blessed are you among women") draw attention to Mary's election from among all other women to be the Mother of the Lord. These words are a statement of faith regarding the child Mary carries in her womb. They are reminiscent of Jael's and Judith's liberation of their people in Judges 5:24 and Judith 13:18, respectively, and as such, show how Mary will contribute to the freedom believers experience when she gives birth to the Savior, Jesus Christ. Together with words of the angel Gabriel, "Hail, full of grace! The Lord is with you" (Luke 1:28), they form the basis for the first half of the traditional prayer, the Hail Mary.

Proclaim the canticle of Mary (the Magnificat) with joy. You are praising God through Mary's words and calling the assembly to do the same.

And **Mary** said:
"My **soul proclaims** the **greatness** of the **Lord;**
    my **spirit rejoices** in **God** my **Savior**
    for he has **looked** with favor on his **lowly servant**.
From **this day all generations** will call me **blessed:**
    the **Almighty** has done **great** things for me,
    and **holy** is his **Name**.
    He has **mercy** on those who **fear** him
    in **every** generation.

He has shown the **strength** of his **arm**,
    and has **scattered** the **proud** in their **conceit**.
He has **cast down** the **mighty** from their **thrones**,
    and has **lifted up** the **lowly**.
He has **filled** the **hungry** with **good things**,
    and the **rich** he has sent away **empty**.
He has **come** to the **help** of his **servant Israel**
    for he has **remembered** his **promise** of **mercy**,
    the **promise** he **made** to our **fathers**,
    to **Abraham** and his **children** for **ever**."

Mary remained with her about three months
    and **then** returned to her home.

Pause at the conclusion of the canticle and before offering the concluding summary slowly, in a narrative tone.

At the conclusion of Elizabeth's response to Mary's greeting, she again praises her cousin. Her words, "Blessed are you who believed that what was spoken to you by the Lord would be fulfilled," set Mary apart as a model believer whose act of listening to the Lord's word stands before us to emulate.

The Gospel concludes with Mary's hymn of praise to God, the Magnificat. Luke places the hymn at this point in his narrative to show how Mary's experience of the

Lord's presence in her life extends to all. In the first stanza of the Magnifcat, Mary praises God for what God has done specifically for her. In the second stanza, Mary generalizes her experience and speaks of God's presence to all people, particularly the lowly, the hungry, and the servant Israel.

Mary's praise of God, which follows upon Elizabeth's praise of her, shows us that our own praise of Mary draws us to a deeper praise and worship of God. As the popular devotional phrase attests, our faith goes "to Jesus through Mary." Mary's

Assumption, body and soul into heavenly glory, places her forever as our mother in the order of grace. She now intercedes on our behalf, leading us closer to Jesus and to union with the Father through the Holy Spirit. Thus, any celebration of Mary is first and foremost a celebration of her son, Jesus Christ, the Savior of the world.

20TH SUNDAY IN ORDINARY TIME

Lectionary #120

READING I   Jeremiah 38:4–6, 8–10

Jeremiah = jayr-uh-MĪ-uh

State the princes' words matter-of-factly as a report to the king, though with a hint of their displeasure at the prophet.

Zedekiah = zed-uh-KĪ-uh

cistern = SIS-tern
Malchiah = mal-KĪ-uh

Slow your pace slightly and increase the heaviness in your tone as you describe Jeremiah sinking into the mud.
Ebed-melech = ee-bid-MEE-lik
Cast blame on the princes as you proclaim Ebed-melech's words. Then switch to a tone of concern as you speak of Jeremiah's fate.

A reading from the book of the prophet Jeremiah

In those days, the **princes** said to the **king**:
"**Jeremiah** ought to be put to **death**;
   he is **demoralizing** the **soldiers** who are **left** in this **city**,
   and all the **people**, by **speaking** such things to them;
   he is **not interested** in the **welfare** of our **people**,
   but in their **ruin**."
King **Zedekiah** answered: "**He** is in **your** power";
   for the **king** could do **nothing** with them.
And so they **took Jeremiah**
   and **threw** him into the **cistern** of Prince **Malchiah**,
   which was in the **quarters** of the **guard**,
   letting him down with ropes.
There was **no water** in the **cistern**, only **mud**,
   and **Jeremiah sank** into the **mud**.

Ebed-melech, a court official,
   went there from the **palace** and said to him:
   "**My lord king**,
   these **men** have been at **fault**
   in all they have **done** to the **prophet Jeremiah**,
   casting him into the cistern.
He will **die** of **famine** on the **spot**,
   for there is **no more food** in the **city**."

READING I   In today's reading, we hear the fate of a prophet who calls God's people back to fidelity. The princes desired Jeremiah's death because his message demoralized them, or understood literally, it weakened the soldier's hands. But the prophet's word remained constant: fighting the Babylonian powers was futile because the Lord had given Jerusalem over to them, and Jeremiah counseled surrender (see Jeremiah 21:10 and 38:1–3). The princes saw this message as unsupportive of the people. King Zedekiah's response reflected reality. The princes held the true power in the city.

Jeremiah's situation in the miry cistern seems hopeless. He will certainly perish. But at this point the tone of the reading shifts. Just when we think the princes have sealed Jeremiah's fate, a court attendant appears before the king and speaks for Jeremiah. The man's words do not so much defend the prophet's message as pronounce judgment on the princes for their disregard of the prophet's life. The king seems ready to endorse this support of Jeremiah, and orders his rescue.

Of course there is much more to the story. As you prepare this reading, continue to read in chapter 38, so you know the conclusion of the narrative. Jeremiah is indeed raised from the cistern. He remains imprisoned in the guard's quarters, still speaking the Lord's dire message to the heedless king as the city is about to fall.

Cushite = KOOSH-ĭt

Speak in a lighter tone. The king's order resolves the situation for now.

Then the **king** ordered **Ebed-melech** the **Cushite**
  to take three men along with him,
  and **draw** the **prophet Jeremiah** out of the **cistern**
  before he should **die.**

READING II   Hebrews 12:1–4

A reading from the letter to the Hebrews

Brothers and **sisters:**

Confidently.

Since we are **surrounded** by so great a **cloud** of **witnesses,**
  let us **rid** ourselves of **every burden** and **sin** that **clings** to us
  and **persevere** in running the **race** that lies **before** us
  while keeping our **eyes fixed** on Jesus,
  the **leader** and **perfecter** of **faith.**
For the **sake** of the **joy** that lay **before** him
  he **endured** the **cross,** despising its **shame,**
  and has taken his **seat** at the **right** of the **throne** of **God.**

Summarily.

Consider how he **endured** such **opposition** from **sinners,**
  in order that you may not **grow weary** and **lose heart.**
In **your struggle** against **sin**

Close in a thoughtful tone that calls the assembly to reflect on their own struggle against sin.

  you have not yet **resisted** to the **point** of **shedding blood.**

READING II Everyone in the assembly will be able to relate to this passage from Hebrews! Opposition and struggle are part of life. The author of Hebrews suggests that perseverance is the antidote to the fatalism that often pulls humans off the path into sin.

The perseverance the author describes is possible because our ancestors in faith (the "cloud of witnesses") accompany us on life's journey. Noah, Abraham, Moses, and Jacob, among others described in

Hebrews 11, which immediately precedes the beginning of today's reading, provide a model of faithfulness for us. We must focus our eyes on Jesus. In him lies the example par excellence of what it means to persevere. He "endured" the pain and shame of the Cross, trusting in the joy that was to come.

Your proclamation must rally energy and hope in the assembly, so that in spite of obstacles in their lives, and even in the face of their own sin, they will persist in their own faith journey. Prepare yourself to

proclaim both the realism and the optimism of this passage.

GOSPEL The fervor in Jesus' dynamic opening words in today's Gospel sets the stage for the question that follows. Jesus' characterization of his mission as "set[ting] the earth on fire" reveals that he is engaged in purifying and refining. So necessary and urgent is his mission that he wishes the fire were already burning. Yet Jesus will not fully accomplish his

GOSPEL Luke 12:49–53

A reading from the holy Gospel according to Luke

Jesus said to his **disciples**:
  "I have **come** to set the **earth** on **fire**,
    and how I **wish** it were **already blazing**!
There is a **baptism** with which I **must** be **baptized**,
    and how **great** is my **anguish** until it is **accomplished**!
Do you **think** that I have **come** to establish **peace** on the **earth**?
No, I tell you, but rather **division**.
From now **on** a **household** of **five** will be **divided**,
    three against **two** and **two** against **three**;
    a **father** will be **divided** against his **son**
    and a **son** against his **father**,
    a **mother** against her **daughter**
    and a **daughter** against her **mother**,
    a **mother-in-law** against her **daughter-in-law**
    and a **daughter-in-law** against her **mother-in-law**."

In a serious and strong tone

Ask the rhetorical question of the assembly. Take your time with the response; it is the opposite of what we expect from Jesus.

Pace yourself as you list those who will be divided among themselves so the assembly understands that the list excludes no one who believes in Jesus from the reality of divisiveness.

work of refining until his Death. This is the meaning of the allusion to the baptism which he must undergo.

The question which follows upon Jesus' opening words, he himself answers. The disciples and we who follow Jesus today would likely want to answer "yes" and believe that Jesus has definitely come only to bring peace. But Jesus' response

appears to say that he has come to bring the opposite of peace—division, even in family relationships.

The idea of Jesus bringing division is surprising since peace is such an important theme in Luke's gospel account. But consider the context. Jesus and the disciples are journeying toward Jerusalem, which helps us understand that the peace Jesus brings comes with a cost. It is upon the Cross of hope and forgiveness that the

refining of the world and relationships among peoples takes place. This is the hope you proclaim to the assembly as you speak Jesus' words about conflict and division. These words communicate the demands of taking up the Cross of forgiveness and peace.

21ST SUNDAY IN ORDINARY TIME

Lectionary #123

READING I Isaiah 66:18–21

Isaiah = ī-ZAY-uh

Begin confidently and serenely. Keep this tone throughout the reading.

Tarshish = TAHR-shish
Put = poot
Lud = luhd
Mosoch = MOH-sok
Tubal = TOO-buhl
Javan = JAY-vuhn

Pause noticeably before the concluding verse to help make the connection that the Lord calls people to priestly service out of those he gathers as his people.
Levites = LEE-vīts

A reading from the Book of the Prophet Isaiah

Thus says the LORD:
I know their **works** and their **thoughts**,
and I **come** to gather **nations** of **every language**;
    they shall **come** and **see** my **glory**.
I will set a **sign** among them;
    from **them** I will send **fugitives** to the **nations**:
    to **Tarshish**, **Put** and **Lud**, **Mosoch**, **Tubal** and **Javan**,
    to the **distant coastlands**
    that have never **heard** of my **fame**, or **seen** my **glory**;
    and they shall **proclaim** my **glory** among the **nations**.
They shall bring **all** your **brothers** and **sisters** from all the **nations**
    as an **offering** to the **LORD**,
    on **horses** and in **chariots**, in **carts**, upon **mules**
        and **dromedaries**,
    to **Jerusalem**, my **holy mountain**, says the **LORD**,
    just as the **Israelites** bring **their offering**
    to the **house** of the **LORD** in **clean vessels**.
Some of these I will take as **priests** and **Levites**, says the **LORD**.

READING I Today's First Reading comes from the concluding chapter of Isaiah. Most scholars believe three authors wrote three different parts of Isaiah. Chapters 56–66 are the work of the third author, called Third Isaiah. He wrote during a period when those exiled in Babylon had returned home, and he struggled with returnees who wanted to maintain a narrow vision of who belonged to God's people. Today's reading shows the prophet proposing a different vision. However, this idea of bringing all peoples together to see the Lord's glory is not something he created; it comes directly from the Lord.

The "fugitives" the Lord will send as a sign are the Lord's messengers who speak, not simply of the importance of gathering all people together, but of the reason for gathering the peoples: that all may see God's glory. The foreigners come from all directions. Nations named in the reading were located in southern Spain, Africa, near the Black Sea, and Greece. The different types of transport by which the fugitives will bring new followers (horses, chariots, carts, mules, and dromedaries), shows that people come to the Lord in diverse ways.

The final sentence shows just how expansive the Lord's vision is. Not only will many new and diverse peoples come to worship the Lord, but from among them the Lord will take priestly leaders. The word "some" many scholars believe points to Gentiles (non-Israelites) to whom the priesthood would now be opened.

READING II Hebrews 12:5–7, 11–13

A reading from the Letter to the Hebrews

Sternly, but with noticeable compassion.

Brothers and **sisters**,
You have **forgotten** the **exhortation** addressed to you as **children:**
"My **son**, do not **disdain** the **discipline** of the **Lord**
        or lose **heart** when **reproved** by him;
    for whom the **Lord loves**, he **disciplines**;
        he **scourges** every **son** he **acknowledges**."
Endure your **trials** as "**discipline**";
    God treats you as **sons**.

Pause after the rhetorical question and before continuing on.

For what "**son**" is there whom his **father** does **not discipline**?
At the time,

In an explanatory tone.

    all discipline seems a **cause** not for **joy** but for **pain**,
    yet **later** it brings the **peaceful fruit** of **righteousness**
    to those who are **trained** by it.

Encouraging and hopeful.

So **strengthen** your **drooping hands** and your **weak knees**.
Make **straight paths** for your **feet**,
    that what is **lame** may **not** be **disjointed** but **healed**.

READING II   The passage from Hebrews, much of which is a restatement of Proverbs 3, is not a reprimand; it is more akin to a reminder to those who are struggling to remain faithful. Any parent knows that love and discipline go together. While the reading refers only to the relationship between father and son, mothers are often the ones responsible for the discipline of their sons and daughters. Be conscious to address your proclamation to all in the assembly.

The use of the father-son terminology shows the intimacy of the Lord's relationship with those who believe in him. Since he himself endured the greatest trial of all, the trial of the Cross, his followers have a model of perseveramce through trials. Staying the course is part of the discipline involved in being a disciple.

The author of Hebrews is realistic as he acknowledges the pain of life's trials. Yet for those who remain faithful, he says, the "peaceful fruit of righteousness" comes. The Lord's justice is the peaceable

gift for believers staying the course of righteousness.

The passage concludes with strong encouragement, which you will offer to the assembly. Your proclamation will be authentic when you offer the encouragement based on your own faith in the Lord. Through love and discipline, he strengthens his sons and daughters and makes straight our paths.

GOSPEL   Luke 13:22–30

A reading from the holy Gospel according to Luke

Jesus passed through **towns** and **villages**,
  teaching as he went and **making** his **way** to **Jerusalem**.
Someone **asked** him,
  "**Lord**, will **only** a **few people** be **saved**?"
He **answered** them,
"**Strive** to **enter** through the **narrow** gate,
  for **many**, I tell you, will **attempt** to **enter**
  but will not be **strong** enough.
After the **master** of the **house** has **arisen** and **locked** the door,
  then will you stand **outside knocking** and **saying**,
  'Lord, **open** the **door** for us.'
He will **say** to you in **reply**,
  'I do **not know where** you are **from**.'
And **you** will **say**,
  'We **ate** and **drank** in your **company** and you **taught**
    in our **streets**.'
Then **he** will **say** to you,
  'I do **not know where** you are **from**.
Depart from me, **all** you **evildoers**!'
And there will be **wailing** and **grinding** of **teeth**
  when you see **Abraham**, **Isaac**, **and Jacob**
  and **all** the **prophets** in the **kingdom of God**
  and **you yourselves** cast **out**.
And people will come from the **east** and the **west**
  and from the **north** and the **south**
  and will **recline** at **table** in the **kingdom** of **God**.
For **behold**, some are **last** who will be **first**,
  and some are **first** who will be **last**."

Ask the opening question clearly. Pause after it, allowing time for it to resonate with the assembly. It continues to be a question on the hearts and in the minds of many believers and nonbelievers today.

Jesus' words are instructional.

Switch from a teacher-like tone to your storytelling tone. Build in intensity to the exclamatory words "Depart from me . . . ."

The consequence of not knowing Jesus is severe. Proclaim in an ominous tone. Lighten your tone as you describe the gathering of peoples from all corners of the world at the Kingdom's table.

Pause after the introductory words "For behold," to gain people's attention for the Gospel's main point.

GOSPEL   The question posed by the onlooker at the beginning of today's Gospel is one that many still ask today. Jesus' response, the short parable about the narrow gate, seems restrictive. Yet read in the context of the rest of the Gospel, the message is not about exclusivity, but rather about hard work and due diligence—virtues that do not come easily to us. Yet the issue is not the hard work of earning salvation, but rather the hard work of remaining faithful to the gift of salvation we receive from the Lord. Observe that it is the Lord who has control of opening the door of salvation, not us.

A sense of urgency fills this Gospel and should fill your proclamation as well. Will we accept Jesus' message sooner rather than later? The acceptance Jesus desires contrasts with the rejection that he faced, especially from Jewish leaders. Many did indeed eat and drink in his company, but some failed to believe in him and live his message.

The consequence Jesus says they face is surprising. Their places in the kingdom will be taken by people who come from all corners of the earth. These people, many of whom the world considers last, will be among the first to feast at the kingdom's eternal banquet. The imagery of people approaching the table of the kingdom from all directions is a fitting parallel to the gathering of nations in the First Reading. Taken together, they strengthen the main theme: salvation is offered to all, (if only they will accept it). The vastness and beauty of this eternal gift of Christ is the word you proclaim today. The warning you also proclaim is clear. Some who have not lived into this image of salvation now might be denied entrance into the kingdom.

22ND SUNDAY IN ORDINARY TIME

Lectionary #126

READING I   Sirach 3:17–18, 20, 28–29

A reading from the Book of Sirach

My **child**, conduct your affairs with **humility**,
   and you will be **loved more** than a **giver** of **gifts**.
Humble yourself the **more**, the **greater** you **are**,
   and you will find **favor** with **God**.
What is **too sublime** for you, **seek not**,
   into **things** beyond your **strength search not**.
The **mind** of a **sage** appreciates **proverbs**,
   and an **attentive ear** is the **joy** of the **wise**.
Water quenches a **flaming fire**,
   and **alms atone** for **sins**.

Sirach = SEER-ak

Let the assembly hear humility in your voice as you speak about this virtue.

Proclaim each of the individual proverbs slowly so the assembly hears the uniqueness of each.

READING II   Hebrews 12:18–19, 22–24a

A reading from the Letter to the Hebrews

Brothers and **sisters**:
You have **not** approached that which could be **touched**
   and a **blazing fire** and **gloomy darkness**
   and **storm** and a **trumpet** blast
   and a **voice speaking words** such that **those** who **heard**
   begged that **no message** be further **addressed** to them.

Emphasize "not."

READING I | Ben Sira, the author of the Book of Sirach, lived during the late third and early second centuries BC, probably in Jerusalem. He spent much of his life studying and teaching the Torah, and wrote the Book of Sirach to instruct people in the advantages of the Jewish over the Greek way of life. The book is a collection of proverbs, intertwined in places with Israel's history. Today you proclaim a passage on humility.

The opening sentences teach us that humility is an important virtue for everyone. The greater one's station in life, however, the more one needs humility. Sirach 3:19, the verse not included in the reading, provides the reason for embracing humility. It is to the humble, rather than the proud, that God grants understanding. When we act humbly, we bring glory to God. In other words, our humility is not a technique we should use to advance ourselves; rather, we practice humility to point ourselves and others toward God. In fact, to pursue

things beyond our grasp or strength is counterproductive. We come closer to God through humility than through greatness.

The final stanza of the reading tells us that wise people appreciate proverbs and are always alert for wisdom. Finally, the author tells us an obvious fact—water puts out a blazing fire—and concludes with a spiritual application. As water put out fire, and prevents damage, we can prevent the damage caused by our sins; we can atone, by giving alms.

Zion = ZĪ-uhn or ZĪ-ahn

Build in enthusiasm and confidence as you make your way through the second stanza. The high point of the stanza is "Jesus." Lower your tone as you describe the blood that speaks eloquently.

Abel = AY-b*l

No, you have **approached Mount Zion**
    and the **city** of the **living God**, the **heavenly Jerusalem**,
    and countless **angels** in festal **gathering**,
    and the **assembly** of the **firstborn enrolled** in **heaven**,
    and **God** the **judge** of **all**,
    and the **spirits** of the **just** made **perfect**,
    and **Jesus**, the **mediator** of a new **covenant**,
    and the **sprinkled blood** that speaks more **eloquently**
        than that of **Abel**.

GOSPEL   Luke 14:1, 7–14

A reading from the holy Gospel according to Luke

Use a narrative tone to set the scene and introduce the parable.

On a **sabbath Jesus** went to **dine**
    at the home of one of the leading **Pharisees**,
    and the **people** there were **observing** him **carefully**.

He told a **parable** to those who had been **invited**,
    noticing how they were choosing the **places** of **honor**
        at the **table**.
"When you are **invited** by someone to a **wedding banquet**,
    do not **recline** at table in the **place** of **honor**.

Humility should be heard in your voice as you speak of not taking the place of honor.

A more **distinguished** guest than you may have been
        invited by him,
    and the **host** who invited **both** of you may **approach you**
        and **say**,
    'Give your **place** to **this man**,'
    and then you would **proceed** with **embarrassment**
    to take the **lowest** place.

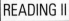 **READING II** | This reading presents us with two assemblies. The first stanza describes the gathering of the Israelites at Mount Sinai for the sealing of their covenant and the giving of the Law. The second stanza paints the picture of Jesus' followers gathered together in the heavenly Jerusalem to receive the new covenant sealed in his blood.

Take your time with the description of each assembly. Let the repetitions of the word "and" guide your proclamation. The word "No" marks the contrast between the text which comes before and after. Make sure to emphasize "No" and pause after it, to gain the assembly's attention. They are part of the assembly of Jesus' followers you will describe. These descriptions are striking and beautiful. Give them their due. Although the reading suggests clearly that the second assembly is superior to the first, maintain a tone of awe and solemnity rather than triumphalism.

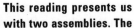 **GOSPEL** | By noting that Jesus is dining at the home of one of the leading Pharisees on a Sabbath, the opening sentence of today's Gospel reminds us of the continuing controversy between Jesus and the Pharisees, a controversy which began at the end of Luke 13.

The lines setting the context for Jesus' parable of the wedding banquet tell how Jesus observed the guests taking places of honor. His observations echo the people's close watching of him, described

Emphasize "Rather," the word that introduces how guests are to act. Highlight the proverb, which contains the main point of the Gospel, in a teacher-like tone.

Rather, when you are **invited**,
　　go and **take** the **lowest place**
　　so that when the **host comes** to **you** he may say,
　　'My **friend**, **move up** to a **higher** position.'
Then you will **enjoy** the **esteem** of your **companions** at the **table**.
For **every one** who **exalts** himself will be **humbled**,
　　but the one who **humbles** himself will be **exalted**."
Then he **said** to the **host** who **invited** him,
　　"When you hold a **lunch** or a **dinner**,
　　do **not** invite your **friends** or your **brothers**
　　or your **relatives** or your **wealthy neighbors**,
　　in case they may **invite** you **back** and you have **repayment**.
Rather, when you hold a **banquet**,
　　invite the **poor**, the **crippled**, the **lame**, the **blind**;
　　blessed indeed will you be because of **their inability**
　　　　to **repay you**.
For **you** will be **repaid** at the **resurrection** of the **righteous**."

Emphasize "Rather," once again, used as a word of contrast to introduce Jesus' instruction to the host. Take your time with the list of people the host should invite.

Allow the alliteration in the phrase "resurrection of the righteous" to stand out.

in the reading's opening sentence. Jesus, as any good teacher would, does not let a teachable moment pass. He proceeds to tell a parable about humility, which ties this reading directly to today's First Reading from Sirach.

Jesus extends the teaching on humility beyond the mere exchange of places of honor for lower places at the table. In this uniquely Lucan parable, Jesus points out that humility involves not only how we behave as guests at others' banquets, but

whom we invite when we host a gathering. It is not about simply hosting a banquet with our friends and relatives so that in the future they will invite us to another lavish meal. Although this way of thinking was common in Greco-Roman society and still is today, Jesus' way of thinking was much different. He calls his followers to invite people that his society would consider least desirable: the poor, the crippled, the lame, the blind—outcasts. The poor, a special concern of Luke, are added to the list.

These are the people Jesus invites to the eternal banquet and the ones we should invite to the Eucharistic feast now. Repayment does not matter. All that we need God will provide now and at the "resurrection of the righteous."

23RD SUNDAY IN ORDINARY TIME

Lectionary #129

READING I   Wisdom 9:13–18b

A reading from the Book of Wisdom

Raise the tone of your voice slightly at the end of the opening question.

The statement answers the question. Emphasize "mortals."

> **Who** can **know** God's **counsel**,
>   or who can **conceive** what the LORD **intends**?
> For the **deliberations** of **mortals** are **timid**,
>   and **unsure** are our **plans**.
> For the **corruptible body burdens** the **soul**
>   and the **earthen shelter** weighs down the **mind**
>   that has **many concerns**.
> And **scarce** do we **guess** the things on **earth**,
>   and what is within our **grasp** we find with **difficulty**;
>   but when **things** are in **heaven**, **who** can **search** them out?
> Or **who** ever **knew** your **counsel**, except **you** had given **wisdom**
>   and **sent** your **holy spirit** from on **high**?
> And **thus** were the **paths** of those on **earth** made **straight**.

Use a slightly heavier tone here to reflect the weightiness of the earthly body.

Raise your voice slightly again as you come to the end of the question.

Slow down on the phrase "except you had given wisdom" for it hints at the answer to the question.

End declaratively.

 READING I Today's reading comprises the last six verses of Solomon's prayer for divine Wisdom, characterized in the prayer and other wisdom literature as a female person. In the earlier part of the prayer, Solomon has called upon the God of his Hebrew ancestors to give him the wisdom he lacks to properly serve as king. Solomon attests that Wisdom resides with God and was present at creation. Now he asks God directly to send Wisdom forth from the heavenly throne to work with him so that he might judge justly.

The part of the prayer you proclaim today consists of Solomon's reflection on the human person's inability to know God's wisdom unless God sends Wisdom. God must send divine Wisdom to reside within the human person. Wisdom herself will then enable mortals to know what God intends. God's intention for Solomon and for us is God's counsel. This counsel (*boulē* in Greek) is not God's preordained plan, but rather God's unfolding will for us as we live in the world. Solomon desired to rule with Wisdom, not apart from her.

Your proclamation of the reading calls people to recognize that when they open themselves to Wisdom and collaborate with her, she will make their paths straight. This is good news!

READING II Today is the only Sunday in the three-year Lectionary cycle of readings when the Second Reading comes from Paul's brief letter to Philemon. Paul addressed this letter to three individuals: Philemon, a co-worker with Paul and Timothy; Apphia, whom Paul refers to as our sister and who perhaps was Philemon's

24TH SUNDAY IN ORDINARY TIME

Lectionary #132

READING I   Exodus 32:7–11, 13–14

Exodus = EK-suh-duhs

A reading from the Book of Exodus

The LORD said to **Moses**,
"Go down at **once** to your **people**,
    whom you brought **out** of the land of **Egypt**,
    for they have become **depraved**.
They have soon turned **aside** from the way I pointed **out** to them,
    making for themselves a **molten calf** and **worshiping** it,
    sacrificing to it and crying out,
    '**This** is your God, O **Israel**,
    who brought you **out** of the land of **Egypt**!'
I see how **stiff-necked** this people is," continued the LORD
    to Moses.
"Let me **alone**, then,
    that my **wrath** may blaze up **against** them to **consume** them.
Then I will make of you a **great nation**."

But Moses **implored** the LORD, his God, saying,
"**Why**, O LORD, should your **wrath** blaze up
        against your **own people**,
    whom **you** brought out of the land of Egypt
    with such **great power** and with so **strong** a **hand**?
Remember your **servants Abraham**, **Isaac**, and **Israel**,
    and how you **swore** to them by your **own self**, saying,
    'I will make your **descendants** as **numerous** as the **stars**
        in the **sky**;

Speak the Lord's words in a commanding tone tinged with disappointment for the people's infidelity.

molten = MOHL-t*n

Note the repetition of the line "who brought you out of the land." This time it's addressed to the wrong god.
The LORD is frustrated.

Pleading.

Communicate the promise in a lighter tone of voice. Pause after it.

READING I   The First Reading picks up part way through an important story from the history of God's Chosen People. The Israelites had grown impatient with the LORD. Moses, their leader, appeared to them to be spending an inordinate amount of time on Mount Sinai, receiving the commandments. The Israelites' impatience led them to make a poor choice. In their frustration, they impulsively called upon Aaron, one of the men Moses appointed to hear complaints in his absence, to make a new god to be their leader.

Aaron was not the strongest of leaders, and he implemented a plan to fulfill the Israelite's desire. All members of the Israelite community would donate their gold earrings. Once melted, Aaron would fashion a molten calf which the people would worship and identify as Israel's god. Aaron would go so far as to build an altar in front of the calf, on which the people would present sacrificial offerings. After the offerings, the Israelites would feast, eating and drinking around the idol. The meal ritual signified their acceptance of

the idol as their new god and their rejection of the Lord.

Today's reading begins with the LORD commanding Moses to return to his people, the people he has brought out of Egypt, because they have gone astray. Moses' people have violated the most fundamental of the commandments—to worship only the LORD and no other gods. To their new god, the Israelites even attributed their freedom from the land of Egypt. This is the second time in the reading the phrase "who brought you out of the land of Egypt" occurs.

and **all** this **land** that I **promised,**
I will **give** your **descendants** as their **perpetual heritage.**'"
So the LORD **relented** in the **punishment**
he had **threatened** to **inflict** on his **people.**

Express relief that the Lord relented.

READING II   1 Timothy 1:12–17

A reading from the first Letter of Saint Paul to Timothy

Beloved:
I am **grateful** to him who has **strengthened** me, **Christ Jesus**
    our **Lord,**
    because he **considered** me **trustworthy**
    in **appointing** me to the **ministry.**
I was once a **blasphemer** and a **persecutor** and **arrogant,**
    but I have been **mercifully treated**
    because I **acted** out of **ignorance** in my **unbelief.**
Indeed, the **grace** of our **Lord** has been **abundant,**
    along with the **faith** and **love** that are in **Christ Jesus.**
This saying is **trustworthy** and deserves **full acceptance:**
    Christ Jesus came into the **world** to **save sinners.**
Of these I am the **foremost.**
But for **that reason** I was **mercifully treated,**
    so that in **me,** as the **foremost,**
    Christ Jesus might **display** all his **patience** as an **example**
    for those who would come to **believe** in him for **everlasting life.**
To the **king** of **ages, incorruptible, invisible,** the **only God,**
    honor and **glory forever** and **ever. Amen.**

Open the reading in a reflective tone.

Honor the pause after "abundant" to draw attention to that generosity.

Pause after "acceptance" and make eye contact with the assembly to prepare them to hear the saying that follows: "Christ Jesus came into the world . . . ." Take time with the saying.

End boldly. Keep the boldness through the "Amen." Once again, be prepared to have some in the assembly spontaneously respond "Amen" with you.

The LORD is furious. He points out the people's stubbornness, and says he will "consume them" with his wrath. He will not, however, harm Moses, who has been faithful. The LORD promises to make him a great nation.

But Moses stands up for the Israelites. In the third and final repetition of the phrase "who brought you out of the land of Egypt," Moses turns the tables back on the Lord. A true leader of faith, Moses recognizes that the people do not belong to him. They belong to the Lord. Their liberation from Egypt was a result of the Lord's power,

not his. And now, if Israelites are to return to the LORD, it will be the power of the Lord's own mercy that brings them back.

Moses reminds the LORD of his own promises to the patriarchs and the weight his vow holds. On the basis of Moses' reminder, the LORD relents on the Israelites' punishment. This would not be the last time the LORD forgives the Israelite's for their apostasy. Their unfaithfulness was a consistent sin that tested the breadth and depth of God's mercy.

Many of us today have consistent sinful habits that we just seem to repeat and repeat. The good news of this reading is that God's mercy prevails. And the message of today's Gospel is that God will always rejoice at finding us when we're lost and at bringing us back home. God's mercy is a joyful mercy.

READING II   Over the course of the next seven Sundays, the Second Reading comes from 1 and 2 Timothy, two of the three pastoral letters in the New

GOSPEL Luke 15:1–32

A reading from the holy Gospel according to Luke

Tax collectors and **sinners** were all drawing **near** to **listen**
    to **Jesus**,
  but the **Pharisees** and **scribes** began to **complain**, saying,
  "**This** man **welcomes sinners** and **eats** with them."
So to **them** he addressed this **parable**.
"**What man** among you having a **hundred** sheep
    and losing **one** of them
  would not **leave** the **ninety-nine** in the desert
  and go after the **lost one** until he **finds** it?
And when he **does** find it,
  he **sets** it on his **shoulders** with **great joy**
  and, upon his arrival **home**,
  he **calls** together his **friends** and **neighbors** and **says** to them,
  '**Rejoice** with me because I have **found** my **lost sheep**.'
I tell you, in **just** the **same way**
  there will be **more joy** in **heaven** over **one sinner** who **repents**
  than over **ninety-nine righteous people**
  who have **no need** of **repentance**.

"Or **what woman** having **ten coins** and **losing one**
  would not **light** a **lamp** and **sweep** the **house**,
  searching carefully until she **finds** it?
And when she **does** find it,
  she **calls** together her **friends** and **neighbors**
  and **says** to them,
  '**Rejoice** with me because I have **found** the **coin** that I **lost**.'

Side notes (left margin):

Grumbling.

Pause slightly after the rhetorical question.

Communicate the man's invitation to rejoice with him happily, in a lighter tone.

The second parable begins. Pause again after the rhetorical question.

Use the same lighter tone as in the first parable to communicate the woman's invitation to rejoice with her.

Testament. (Titus is the third.) These letters are "pastoral" in the sense that they address practical aspects of the Church's life together in its early, formative years and provide direction for community leaders. They are "pseudonymous" epistles or letters written by an unidentified follower of Paul who wishes to continue Paul's work, carrying it forward to a new generation.

The two letters to Timothy seem particularly aimed at church leaders. They encourage faithfulness to the Gospel in the face of philosophical opponents who deviate from the true Gospel and church order

and who emphasize only right knowledge *(gnōsis)*. These opponents were wreaking havoc within Christian households and causing division within the community.

Today's Second Reading comes from the opening chapter of 1 Timothy. It follows immediately upon the author's description of the false teachers (1 Timothy 1:3–11). Written as if Paul himself were the author, these verses recount Paul's own conversion to the Gospel of Christ Jesus in a self-reflective manner. He himself was

once a false teacher and nonbeliever, but Christ Jesus called him to the ministry of apostleship.

The reference to how Paul was "mercifully treated" appears twice, once in the opening stanza and again near the conclusion of the reading. Neither right thinking nor right action will merit salvation, the author reminds us The Lord's grace is freely and abundantly given. Through it, Christ Jesus saves and he saves even the biggest of sinners such as Paul. If Christ Jesus saved Paul and waited patiently for

The third and longest parable begins.

In **just** the **same way**, **I tell you**,
 there will be **rejoicing** among the **angels** of **God**
 over **one sinner** who **repents**."

Then he said,
 "A man had **two sons**, and the **younger** son said to his **father**,
 '**Father give** me the **share** of your **estate** that should **come**
 to me.'
So the **father divided** the **property between** them.
After a few **days**, the younger son **collected** all his **belongings**
 and **set** off to a **distant country**
 where he **squandered** his inheritance on a **life** of **dissipation**.
When he had **freely** spent **everything**,
 a **severe famine** struck that **country**,
 and he **found** himself in dire **need**.
So he **hired** himself **out** to one of the local **citizens**
 who sent him to his **farm** to tend the **swine**.
And he **longed** to **eat** his **fill** of the **pods** on which the **swine** fed,
 but **nobody gave** him any.
Coming to his **senses** he **thought**,
 'How **many** of my father's hired **workers**
 have **more** than **enough** food to eat,
 but here am **I**, **dying** from **hunger**.
I shall **get up** and **go** to my **father** and I shall **say** to him,
 "**Father**, I have **sinned** against **heaven** and **against you**.
I no longer **deserve** to be **called your son**;
 treat me as you would **treat one** of your **hired workers**."'"

Try a range of tones for the son's words of confession, from somewhat sincere to lacking all sincerity. Which feels right to you?

him to know the Gospel, surely, the supposed reflection by Paul suggests, his grace will save us.

Let the optimism in your proclamation of this saving grace build to the doxology which concludes the reading. After the teaching you proclaim, how could there be an ending more fitting than one that praises the only God!

GOSPEL The Evangelist, Luke, often depicts Jesus welcoming sinners and sharing table fellowship with them. From the beginning of today's gospel

passage, we are called to see ourselves belonging to the group of sinners whom Jesus embraces and with whom he dines. The opening verse also challenges us to see whether we would dine with those whom Jesus welcomes. The Pharisees and scribes won't, but would we?

The long form of the Gospel includes three parables with the same theme: God's loving forgiveness in response to the repentance of one sinner. The first parable is about the shepherd with a hundred sheep who rejoices at finding the one that was

lost. The second parable recounts a woman's joy at finding one of her ten lost coins. The third parable is the much-loved story of the prodigal son. The father rejoices at the return of his son who had left home only to squander his inheritance through selfish, dishonest, and immoral living. In the first two parables, the man and woman diligently search for the lost sheep and the lost coin. In the third parable, the son comes to his own senses and returns to the father.

The prodigal son's internal motives for returning might have been selfish: he

The son follows through on his confession.

Increase the momentum as you read about the preparations for the feast.

Slow your pace as you begin to narrate the older son's return.

So he **got up** and **went back** to his **father**.
While he was **still** a **long way off**,
    his **father** caught **sight** of him,
    and was **filled** with **compassion**.
He **ran** to his son, **embraced** him and **kissed** him.
His son **said** to him,
    '**Father**, I have **sinned** against **heaven** and **against you**;
    I no longer **deserve** to be called **your son**.'
But his **father** ordered his **servants**,
    '**Quickly** bring the **finest robe** and put it **on** him;
    put a **ring** on his **finger** and **sandals** on his **feet**.
Take the **fattened calf** and **slaughter** it.
Then let us **celebrate** with a **feast**,
    because this **son** of **mine** was **dead**, and has **come** to **life** again;
    he was **lost**, and has been **found**.'
Then the **celebration began**.
Now the **older** son had been **out** in the **field**
    and, on his way **back**, as he **neared** the **house**,
    he heard the **sound** of **music** and **dancing**.
He **called** one of the **servants** and **asked** what this might **mean**.
The servant said to him,
    '**Your brother** has **returned**
    and your **father** has **slaughtered** the **fattened calf**
    because he has him **back safe** and **sound**.'
He became **angry**,
    and when he **refused** to enter the house,
    his **father came out** and **pleaded** with him.

was starving and his father's hired workers had "more than enough food to eat." A more positive read of the son's thoughts could find a little humility ("treat me as one of your hired workers"). The words he would speak directly to his father recognize a severed relationship ("I no longer deserve to be called your son").

The father's forgiveness is unconditional. It is God's grace in action. Even before the son speaks his penitent words, the father embraces him in compassion.

The father never questions his son's motives for returning, but simply orders a celebration to begin immediately. He even orders the servants to prepare a fattened calf for everyone to enjoy. This truly is a special occasion.

The older son, however, does not understand the lavish celebration for his brother's return. He is hurt and angry with his father. He speaks of his own faithfulness, which hints at his perfectionism ("not once did I disobey your orders"). He is unaware of his own need for his father's mercy. The father loves both sons.

As in the parable, God's love for us is unconditional, unmerited, free, spontaneous, compassionate, forgiving, merciful, constant, personal, relational, participatory ("everything I have is yours"), life-giving. This love we call grace, and the feast that celebrates this love is the Eucharist. In this love and in this meal, we rejoice, for God finds us in Christ Jesus and nourishes us to welcome others home.

Express deep disappointment and frustration as you speak the older son's words to his father.

He said to his father in reply,
  '**Look, all** these **years I served you**
  and not **once** did I disobey **your orders**;
  yet you **never** gave me **even** a **young goat** to **feast** on
      with **my friends**.
But when **your** son **returns**,
  who **swallowed** up **your property** with **prostitutes**,
  for **him** you **slaughter** the fattened **calf**.'
He **said** to him,
  '**My son**, **you** are here with me **always**;
  everything I have is **yours**.
But **now** we **must celebrate** and **rejoice**,
  because your **brother** was **dead** and has **come** to **life** again;
  he was **lost** and has been **found**.'"

The father's words don't scold. The first line is a gentle, loving reminder of the Father's care. Offer the rest of the conclusion as an invitation for the older brother to join the celebration.

[Shorter: Luke 15:1–10]

GOSPEL   Luke 16:1–13

A reading from the holy Gospel according to Luke

Jesus said to his **disciples,**
  "A **rich** man had a **steward**
  who was **reported** to him for **squandering** his **property.**
He **summoned** him and said,
  'What is this I **hear** about you?
Prepare a full **account** of your **stewardship,**
  because you can **no longer** be my **steward.'**
The **steward** said to himself, '**What** shall I **do,**
  now that my **master** is taking the **position** of **steward**
    away from me?
I am **not strong** enough to **dig** and I am **ashamed** to beg.
I **know** what I shall **do so** that,
  when I am **removed** from the **stewardship,**
  they may **welcome** me into their **homes.'**
He called in his master's **debtors one** by **one.**
To the **first** he said,
  '**How much** do you **owe** my master?'
He replied, '**One hundred measures** of **olive** oil.'
He said to him, '**Here** is your **promissory** note.
Sit down and quickly **write** one for **fifty.'**
Then to **another** the steward said, 'And **you,**
    how much do **you** owe?'
He replied, '**One hundred kors** of **wheat.'**
The steward **said** to him, '**Here** is **your** promissory note;
  write one for **eighty.'**

A brief soliloquy by the steward... his thoughts reflectively and deli...

The amounts are significant. Emphasize each of them.

ity. Paul would not lie about Christ Jesus' testimony because God appointed him to preach the Good News of salvation to Jews and Gentiles. The wording is similar to Romans 9:1. In the final section, the apostle hopes for the day when people will pray everywhere without dissension. The false teachers encouraged disputation, a form of argumentative discourse, which often resulted in division within the community. But Christians prayed liturgically with hands outstretched and palms turned upward in the traditional orans position,

signifying openness to God and God's activity through Christ Jesus in the world and all its peoples.

GOSPEL   In this parable, more appropriately called an "example story," Jesus makes a dishonest steward an example of discipleship. We know that God works through people in unexpected ways. However, God working through a dishonest steward seems a bit far-fetched, or is it? Consider that it is not the dishonesty of the fired steward that Jesus extols, but rather the steward's wisdom.

The steward acted "prudently." His practical wisdom led him to forge deals with his master's debtors that eliminated the profit originally figured into the transaction. Usually when a debt was calculated, the profit was included in the lump sum a debtor owed. When the steward reduced the amount the debtors owed, he was eliminating either his own or the master's usurious profit. In the first case, the steward would lose money but gain support from the debtors. In the second, the master would probably only break even.

Express satisfaction at how the dishonest steward acted.

And the master **commended** that dishonest steward
for acting **prudently**.

"For the **children** of **this world**
are more **prudent** in **dealing** with their **own generation**
than are the **children** of **light**.

Address Jesus' words to the assembly.

I **tell** you, make **friends** for **yourselves** with **dishonest wealth**,
so that when it **fails**, you will be **welcomed**
into **eternal dwellings**.
The **person** who is **trustworthy** in **very small** matters
is also **trustworthy** in **great ones**;
and the **person** who is **dishonest** in **very small** matters
is also **dishonest** in **great ones**.
If, therefore, you are **not trustworthy** with **dishonest wealth**,
who will **trust** you with **true** wealth?

Pause after each of the questions, giving the assembly time to answer them.

If you are **not trustworthy** with what **belongs** to **another**,
who will **give** you what is **yours**?
No servant can serve **two** masters.
He will **either hate** one and **love** the **other**,
or be **devoted** to one and **despise** the other.
You cannot serve both God and mammon."

State the concluding fact slowly and strongly.

[Shorter: Luke 16:10–13]

Yet the master commends the steward for his clever action. Why?

The interpretation of the example story which follows suggests that the wisdom of the steward and his ability to act decisively, not his dishonesty, are what Jesus' disciples should imitate. At this point in Jesus' journey to Jerusalem, the disciples are half-hearted and often clueless about what it truly means to follow the Master. Jesus is trying to teach them what it means to make prudent decisions daily

and to herald the Kingdom of God resolutely through their actions.

In the telling of the parable, Jesus also offers three statements about the proper use of money. First, "make friends for yourselves with dishonest wealth," teaches the disciples that they are to use all worldly possessions prudently, with the objective of sharing with the poor. Second, "If, therefore, you are not trustworthy with dishonest wealth," instructs the disciples that if they do not share their material possessions, they will not see the heavenly reality, the treasure of God's Kingdom.

Third, "You cannot serve God and mammon," means that disciples must dedicate themselves solely to God.

From God comes the gift of prudence, the gift of the Spirit upon the disciples. This is the same Spirit that was upon Jesus and anointed him to bring glad tidings to the poor, that enables us to live out our discipleship single-mindedly, and that gave wisdom to the steward.

When the **poor man died**,
  he was carried away by **angels** to the **bosom** of **Abraham**.
The **rich man also died** and was **buried**,
  and from the **netherworld**, where he was in **torment**,
  he **raised** his **eyes** and saw **Abraham** far **off**
  and **Lazarus** at his **side**.
And he **cried** out, 'Father Abraham**, have **pity** on me.
Send Lazarus to **dip** the tip of his **finger** in **water** and **cool**
    my **tongue**,
  for I am **suffering torment** in these **flames**.'
Abraham replied,
  '**My child**, **remember** that you received
  what was **good** during your **lifetime**
  while **Lazarus** likewise **received** what was **bad**;
  but **now he** is **comforted** here, whereas **you** are **tormented**.
Moreover, between **us** and **you** a **great chasm** is established
  to **prevent anyone** from **crossing** who might **wish** to go
  from **our side** to **yours** or from **your side** to **ours**.'
He said, 'Then I **beg** you, **father**,
  send him to my **father's house**, for I have **five brothers**,
  so that he may **warn** them,
  lest they **too come** to this **place** of **torment**.'
But **Abraham replied**, 'They have **Moses** and the **prophets**.
Let them **listen** to **them**.'
He said, 'Oh **no**, father **Abraham**,
  but if **someone** from the **dead** goes to them, they will **repent**.'
Then **Abraham** said, 'If they will **not** listen to **Moses**
    and the **prophets**,
  neither will they be **persuaded** if someone should **rise**
    from the **dead**.'"

Speak longingly the words the rich man speaks from the netherworld. He now sees where he could be.

Abraham's words are explanatory. Emphasize the contrasts.

Intensify the pleading in your voice as the rich man now begs that his brothers be spared his fate.

Strengthen the pleading in your tone one last time.

Speak Abraham's final words realistically and with resignation to this fact.

eaten the scraps that fell from the table highlights his status: his poverty makes him as lowly as a dog scavenging for falling table food.

The second section narrates the fate of the rich man and Lazarus. We hear that the rich man recognizes where Lazarus now resides and we listen in on the ensuing conversation between the rich man and Abraham. The ironic twist of the conversation is that the rich man, who in his life of luxury had no regard for Lazarus,

now asks Lazarus to come to his aid as he suffers from the heat of the netherworld's flames. Abraham doesn't even address the rich man's paradoxical request, except to state that their prior lives have determined their present state.

In the Gospel's third section, the rich man doesn't argue with Abraham about his own fate; rather, he seems to have accepted the consequence of his former inaction. Now he asks on behalf of his brothers that Abraham send the dead Lazarus to give warning to them. In a preview of how some will refuse to repent even with

knowledge of Jesus' Resurrection, Abraham denies the rich man's request, noting that Moses and the prophets went unheard. Abraham's remark draws a direct parallel to the First Reading, in which the leaders refuse to heed the prophet's call to renounce their opulence.

27TH SUNDAY IN ORDINARY TIME

Lectionary #141

READING I   Habakkuk 1:2–3; 2:2–4

Habakkuk = huh-BAK-kuhk or
HAB-uh-kuhk

Convey frustration as you speak the
prophet's complaints. Maintain,
even slightly increase, the intensity
throughout the prophet's words.
"Cry out" as the text states.

Pause significantly between the
prophet's words and the LORD's response.

Lighten the tone and lower the volume of
your voice on the LORD's words. Proceed
slowly as you speak of waiting for
the vision.

End confidently, expressing hope for
the faithful.

A reading from the Book of the Prophet Habakkuk

How long, O LORD? I cry for **help**
     but you do not **listen**!
I cry out to you, "**Violence!**"
     but you do **not intervene**.
Why do you let me see **ruin**;
     why must I look at **misery**?
Destruction and **violence** are before me;
     there is **strife**, and **clamorous discord**.
Then the LORD **answered** me and said:
     Write down the **vision clearly** upon the **tablets**,
     so that one can **read** it **readily**.
For the **vision** still has its **time**,
     presses **on** to **fulfillment**, and will **not disappoint**;
if it **delays**, **wait** for it,
     it will **surely come**, it will **not** be **late**.
The **rash one** has **no integrity**;
     but the **just one**, because of his **faith**, shall **live**.

READING I   We proclaim from the Book of the Prophet Habakkuk only once in the entire three-year Lectionary cycle. This prophet wrote in the late seventh and early sixth centuries BC, a time when the Chaldeans, whose seat of power was in Babylon, ruled the ancient Near East. The book is a short three chapters, the first two of which are a conversation between God and the prophet.

Today's reading comes from the beginning of both the first and second chapters of Habakkuk. Overcome with misfortune, the prophet makes his complaint to the Lord in a classic question: "How long, O Lord?" The prophet gives voice to a basic human situation.

In Habakkuk's time, chaos and lawlessness were rampant. The people suffered violence and social injustice at the hands of the Babylonians regularly. The prophet seeks answers from God in a personal way. Notice the use of the first person pronoun throughout most of the passage. Even the Lord's response to Habakkuk is personal, though he does not intend the vision to remain solely with the prophet.

By writing the vision down, Habakkuk will ensure that everyone will be able to read it and begin to have confidence that their oppressors will not win the day. The Lord uses six different phrases to communicate to Habakkuk that the vision will take shape. It will come to fruition, but patience—holy waiting—will be a mark of the just one who will live.

Take your time as you proclaim the encouraging lines at the end of the reading that speak of waiting. In our fast-paced, multitasking societies, we can often feel

READING II   2 Timothy 1:6–8, 13–14

A reading from the second Letter of Saint Paul to Timothy

Beloved:
I **remind** you to **stir** into **flame**
    the **gift** of **God** that you have through the **imposition**
      of my **hands**.
For **God** did not give us a **spirit** of **cowardice**
    but rather of **power** and **love** and **self-control**.
So do **not** be **ashamed** of your **testimony** to our **Lord**,
    nor of me, a **prisoner** for **his sake**;
    but **bear your** share of **hardship** for the **gospel**
    with the **strength** that comes from **God**.

Take as your **norm** the **sound words** that you **heard** from **me**,
    in the **faith** and **love** that are in **Christ Jesus**.
Guard this **rich trust** with the **help** of the **Holy Spirit**
    that **dwells within** us.

Address the opening instruction to the assembly.

State the second instruction, not to be ashamed, in an encouraging manner.

A third dire

The fourth instruction. Speak reverently, valuing the worth of the Gospel.

more like the rash one who doesn't practice the virtue of waiting for the fulfillment of the Lord's vision. Some would prefer to see their own vision, but the faithful wait patiently for the Lord's.

READING II Today is the first of four Sundays on which the Second Reading comes from 2 Timothy, the second of the three pastoral epistles. This passage comes from the first chapter of four

in this brief letter. 2 Timothy is more personal in character than 1 Timothy, and the verses you proclaim today are an example.

Paul counsels Timothy, his younger companion on his second and third missionary journeys, to remain faithful to the grace of God he received through Christ Jesus. Paul bases his advice, not on theory, but on his own experience of apostleship, knowing full well that preaching the Gospel brings hardship, and even for him, imprisonment.

Pay careful attention to the active verbs in this passage. They provide the flow between the verses. In the conclusion, the verbs provide Paul's prescription. Timothy will be able to stir into flame the grace of God which comes from the laying on of hands and be faithful to the Gospel despite hardship, because of the rich trust of the words Paul himself has spoken. We see here continuity between generations of believers in the Gospel we preach and

GOSPEL   Luke 17:5–10

A reading from the holy Gospel according to Luke

Speak the Apostles' request genuinely.

The **apostles** said to the **Lord**, "**Increase** our **faith**."
The **Lord replied**,
  "If you have **faith** the size of a **mustard seed**,
    you would **say** to this **mulberry** tree,
    'Be **uprooted** and **planted** in the **sea**,' and it would **obey** you.

A series of three rhetorical questions. Raise your voice slightly as you come to the end of each. Pause slightly, allowing the assembly time to quickly think about the response.

"**Who** among you would **say** to your **servant**
    who has **just** come in from **plowing** or **tending sheep**
      in the field,
    '**Come here immediately** and **take** your **place** at **table**'?
Would he **not rather say** to him,
    '**Prepare** something for **me** to **eat**.
Put on your **apron** and **wait** on me while I **eat** and **drink**.
You may **eat** and **drink** when I am **finished**'?
Is he **grateful** to that **servant** because he **did** what
      was **commanded**?
So should it **be** with **you**.
When you have **done all** you have been **commanded**,
    say, 'We are **unprofitable servants**;
    we have **done** what we were **obliged** to do.'"

Let a sense of relief be heard in your proclamation in the final words, for it is God's grace not the servant's works that brings salvation.

live. No believer carries the truth of the Gospel alone. Through the Holy Spirit, the rich trust of the Gospel lives on in the communion of believers.

GOSPEL | The Apostles ask the Lord to "increase our faith." To their credit, they recognize that only Jesus can build up their faith; they cannot achieve this on their own. Many of us have sought a renewal of faith. The Lord's reply to the disciples teaches a mystery that every disciple must ponder: even the smallest

amount of faith can cause great things to happen.

The second teaching in today's Gospel is unique to the Evangelist, Luke, and helps substantiate the Gospel's main point: God's grace is freely given; there is nothing we can do to earn it. Yet this saying, a short parable in itself, stresses the disciple's obligation in response to God's free gift. That obligation entails living out one's call to discipleship responsibly. Acknowledging that "We are unprofitable servants" is not self-deprecating, but rather an affirmation of the firmness of the faith

on which they stand. This faith allows the disciples to see that all they have done has been a response to God's graciousness in Jesus, the gift that will increase their faith and ours, and carry us through a disciple's journey. Who knows, then, how many mulberry trees will move because of our response to God's gift of faith!

28TH SUNDAY IN ORDINARY TIME

Lectionary #144

READING I   2 Kings 5:14–17

Naaman = NAY-uh-muhn

Elisha = ee-LĪ-shuh

A retinue is the group of attendants that accompany a high-ranking official from place to place.

Proclaim Naaman's statement of faith confidently and his offer of a gift graciously.

Speak Elisha's words refusing the gift instructively, not negatively.

Communicate Naaman's response in a courteous manner. Slow in tempo as you conclude strongly with a restatement of his faith.

A reading from the second Book of Kings

Naaman went down and **plunged** into the **Jordan seven times**
    at the **word** of **Elisha**, the **man** of **God**.
His **flesh** became **again** like the **flesh** of a little **child**,
    and he was **clean** of his **leprosy**.

Naaman returned with his whole **retinue** to the **man** of **God**.
On his **arrival** he **stood** before **Elisha** and **said**,
    "**Now** I **know** that there is **no God** in **all** the **earth**,
    except in **Israel**.
Please **accept** a **gift** from your **servant**."

Elisha replied, "**As** the LORD **lives** whom I **serve**, I will **not**
    take it,"
    and **despite Naaman's urging**, he **still refused**.
Naaman said: "If you will **not accept**,
    please let me, your **servant**, have **two mule-loads** of **earth**,
    for I will **no longer** offer **holocaust** or **sacrifice**
    to **any other god** except to the LORD."

READING I The passage about Naaman's cure from leprosy begins in verses earlier than those we read today. Starting at 2 Kings 5:1 we learn that Naaman is a highly esteemed and respected commander of the king of Aram. A new servant in his household, a girl whom the Arameans had captured from Israel's land, wanted Naaman to present himself to the prophet in Samaria, who would cure him of his leprosy. Upon hearing this wish, Naaman speaks to the king of Aram, who sends him on his way with a letter for the king of Israel, attesting to the desire for a cure.

The king of Israel, however, responds derisively, tearing his garments and exclaiming that Naaman is only there to start an argument. The prophet Elisha somehow finds out about the encounter between the two and sends word to the king to send Naaman to him. Naaman, along with his cohort, arrives at the door of Elisha's house. At the doorstep, Naaman receives the message from the prophet to go and wash seven times in the Jordan and his flesh will be healed. But Naaman balks, disappointed that the prophet himself did not come out to greet him, invoke the Lord's name, and lay hands over his body's diseased spots. Naaman's anger leads him to turn away from Elisha's home. He concludes that Elisha's God, the God of Israel, is no better than any other god.

Naaman's disappointment, however, is not the end of the story. His servants intervene and help him to think logically about the situation, ultimately convincing him to follow through on the simple act of washing in the Jordan. This is the point

READING II   2 Timothy 2:8–13

A reading from the second Letter of Saint Paul to Timothy

Beloved:
Remember Jesus Christ, raised from the **dead,**
    a **descendant** of **David:**
    such is my **gospel,** for which I am **suffering,**
    even to the point of **chains,** like a **criminal.**
But the **word** of **God** is **not chained.**
Therefore, I bear with **everything** for the **sake** of **those**
    who are **chosen,**
    so that **they too** may **obtain** the **salvation** that is
        in **Christ Jesus,**
    together with **eternal glory.**
This **saying** is **trustworthy:**
    If we have **died** with him
        we shall also **live** with him;
    if we **persevere**
        we shall also **reign** with him.
    But if **we deny him**
        he will deny us.
    If **we** are **unfaithful**
        he remains **faithful,**
        for he **cannot deny himself**.

Invite the assembly to recall that the risen Jesus is the Gospel they proclaim.

Separate the four conditional statements in the one saying, by pausing noticeably after each one. Contrast words such as "died" and "live" and "unfaithful" and "faithful."

at which today's First Reading begins. The focus of the reading is not so much Naaman's cure, but his confession of faith. Elisha's refusal of Naaman's gift in thanksgiving for the cure is also a confession of faith. It shows that those who serve the Lord are not in need of material gifts, because their life comes from the Lord God, and is true gift itself.

At the end of the reading, Naaman requests two mule-loads of earth so that he can continue to worship God in his homeland.

READING II Written in a deeply personal style, this passage begins with Paul urging Timothy to remember the Gospel of Jesus Christ, the same Gospel for which Paul is enduring suffering and imprisonment. The Word of God stands in stark contrast to this imprisonment. Chains never limit the Gospel. The freedom of God's Word allows Paul to bear with his own suffering for the sake of those whom God chooses.

The reading concludes with verses that probably come from a hymn used in first-century house churches. The sayings in the hymn are parallel in structure, the first two stated in the positive, the second two in the negative. They are hopeful and encouraging.

The last verse, which speaks of Christ's faithfulness, seems to contrast with the previous statement that Christ will deny us if we deny him. Christ indeed will remain faithful to God—the God who always calls his people back from their infidelity to receive his love in Christ.

GOSPEL Luke 17:11–19

A reading from the holy Gospel according to Luke

As **Jesus** continued his **journey** to **Jerusalem**,
 he traveled through **Samaria** and **Galilee**.
As he was entering a **village**, **ten lepers** met him.
They **stood** at a **distance** from him and **raised** their **voices**, saying,
 "**Jesus**, **Master**! Have **pity** on us!"
And when he **saw** them, he said,
 "**Go show** yourselves to the **priests**."
As they were **going** they were **cleansed**.
And one of them, **realizing** he had been **healed**,
 returned, **glorifying God** in a loud **voice**;
 and he **fell** at the **feet** of **Jesus** and **thanked** him.
He was a **Samaritan**.
Jesus **said** in **reply**,
 "**Ten** were **cleansed**, were they **not**?
Where are the **other nine**?
Has **none** but this **foreigner** returned to give **thanks** to **God**?"
Then he **said** to him, "**Stand up** and **go**;
 your **faith** has **saved** you."

Samaria = suh-MAYR-ee-uh

Speak with eagerness.

A simple instruction which followed the Law.

Increase the momentum as you speak of the one leper who returns. Pause after narrating his return and before identifying him as a Samaritan.

A series of three questions. Leave more time for the assembly to ponder the second question. We don't know why the other nine did not return. There is no negative judgment about the Samaritan's identity in the third question.

Speak Jesus' final words with the assurance that faith in him saves.

GOSPEL Today's Gospel is the familiar story of the cleansing of the ten lepers. Jesus encounters the lepers as he travels through Samaria and Galilee, coming near the end of his journey to Jerusalem. The Lectionary fittingly pairs this Gospel reading with Naaman's cure from leprosy in the First Reading. In both, a healed leper's confession of faith teaches us that faith saves.

In neither case does religious or ethnic background pose obstacles to salvation. Both foreigners, Naaman and the Samaritan leper, are examples of faith to us all. The reading includes a mere statement of fact that gives the returning leper's identity: "He was a Samaritan." Make sure to take your time with this statement, for although the assembly might be suspicious about the leper's identity from the beginning, they will not know until you disclose it. The third of Jesus' trio of questions connects the Samaritan's identity to being a foreigner. Leave time for the assembly to respond internally to the questions.

Jesus' command concluding this uniquely Lucan passage sends the healed Samaritan on his way knowing that his faith brings him salvation's wholeness. Like Naaman, he goes forward in life differently now: a grateful and saved foreigner who speaks of new life. Leave the assembly wondering how they, too, can be unexpected messengers of salvation, and also open themselves to "foreigners" who will lead them to faith.

29TH SUNDAY IN ORDINARY TIME

Lectionary #147

READING I   Exodus 17:8–13

Exodus = EK-suh-duhs

Amalek = AM-uh-lek

A reading from the Book of Exodus

In those days, **Amalek** came and waged **war** against **Israel**.
Moses, therefore, said to **Joshua**,
    "Pick out certain **men**,
    and **tomorrow** go out and **engage Amalek** in **battle**.
I will be standing on top of the **hill**
    with the **staff** of **God** in my **hand**."
So **Joshua did** as **Moses told** him:
    he **engaged Amalek** in battle
    after **Moses** had **climbed** to the top of the hill
        with **Aaron** and **Hur**.
As long as **Moses** kept his **hands** raised **up**,
    Israel had the **better** of the fight,
    but when he let his **hands rest**,
    Amalek had the **better** of the fight.
Moses' hands, however, grew **tired**;
    so they put a **rock** in **place** for him to **sit** on.
Meanwhile Aaron and **Hur supported** his **hands**,
    one on **one** side and **one** on the **other**,
    so that his **hands** remained **steady** till **sunset**.
And **Joshua mowed** down **Amalek** and his **people**
    with the **edge** of the **sword**.

Hur = her

Take your time with the narration so as to paint a picture of Moses' hands going up and down.

Wearily and in a slower pace.

Conclude with the confidence of faith. God prevails.

 Moses' uplifted hands are a prayer gesture familiar to us from the liturgy. They are a sign, not that Moses gives up his own strength and ability to lead his people in battle, but rather that this great leader recognizes the source of his power and skill.

Some in the assembly will find it difficult to hear about the Lord taking sides in war. Focus your proclamation on Moses' prayer gesture by emphasizing the phrases that point out God's staff. It is the same staff God commanded Moses to lift up and, with his outstretched arms, to split the Red Sea in two so that the Israelites could pass through it on dry land and the Egyptians suffer demise as the waters reunited.

Moses' fatigue shows us his humanity. No leader, however physically powerful, could hold that pose for days. The situation demonstrates that humans are nothing without the Lord. We do not learn who put the rock in place to support Moses, but their gesture, pragmatic as it is, is one of faith.

Aaron and Hur, mentioned again in Exodus 24:14 (along with the elders as those who will adjudicate disputes within the Israelite camp) also respond pragmatically to Moses' fatigue, supporting his hands in the uplifted position. Their personal assistance is also an act of faith that shows the need for community in the living out of faith. God's people—including community leaders—do not have to be faithful alone. With God as the One who leads his people and whose Spirit resides in them, calling them to action both individually and corporately, the outcome can only be the victorious one you proclaim at the end of the reading!

READING II   2 Timothy 3:14—4:2

A reading from the second Letter of Saint Paul to Timothy

Beloved:

Remain **faithful** to what you have **learned** and **believed**,
   because you **know** from **whom** you **learned** it,
   and that from **infancy** you have known the **sacred Scriptures**,
   which are **capable** of giving you **wisdom** for **salvation**
   through **faith** in **Christ Jesus**.
All Scripture is **inspired** by **God**
   and is **useful** for **teaching**, for **refutation**, for **correction**,
   and for **training** in **righteousness**,
   so that **one** who **belongs** to **God** may be **competent**,
   equipped for **every good work**.

I **charge** you in the presence of **God** and of **Christ Jesus**,
   who will **judge** the **living** and the **dead**,
   and by his **appearing** and his kingly **power**:
   proclaim the **word**;
   be **persistent** whether it is **convenient** or **inconvenient**;
   convince, **reprimand**, **encourage** through **all patience**
      and **teaching**.

Open in an encouraging, teacher-like manner.

In an explanatory tone.

Reflect the stronger verb "charge" in your tone of voice.

Make eye contact with the assembly on the succinct command: "Proclaim the word."
Emphasize each verb by pausing noticeably at the commas. Contrast "encourage" with the stronger verbs that precede it.

READING II In the earlier part of chapter 3, preceding the verses from 2 Timothy that are today's Second Reading, Paul is warning about false teachings and immoral behavior that will mark the last days. Indeed, the false teachings and dangers are already present. People are self-centered, they love money, they are proud, haughty, abusive, disobedient to their parents, ungrateful; they love pleasure rather than loving God (2 Timothy 3:2–4). Paul's advice to Timothy in the face of all these is straightforward: "Reject them" (2 Timothy 3:5).

In the passage you proclaim, Paul proposes an alternative to the rampant falsehoods: God's Word as found in the inspired Sacred Scriptures. This is a passage on which we base our belief in the divine inspiration of the Scriptures. The divine inspiration of the Scriptures is why Paul tells Timothy they can be useful to him in all areas of his pastoral work: teaching, refutation, correction, and training in righteousness. Formation in the Word of God makes a leader competent to carry out his or her call.

In the final paragraph, Paul states his charge to Timothy as straightforwardly as he gave his command to reject false teachings. The apostle's words, "Proclaim the word," communicate the essence of the work of a pastoral leader. Like Moses, who with the help of his colleagues Aaron and Hur, persisted in holding his hands up in prayer, so Paul admonishes Timothy to persevere in the proclamation of the Word. No matter how untimely or irrelevant the Word might seem, the concluding list of Timothy's tasks, which parallels the list in the previous paragraph, describes how he

GOSPEL   Luke 18:1–8

A reading from the holy Gospel according to Luke

Open in a narrative tone. Watch your pace so the opening line doesn't go by too quickly. It contains the purpose of the parable.

Jesus told his **disciples** a **parable**
　　about the **necessity** for them to **pray always**
　　　　without becoming **weary**.
He **said**, "There was a **judge** in a certain **town**
　　who **neither feared God** nor **respected** any **human being**.
And a **widow** in that town used to **come** to him and **say**,
　　'**Render** a **just decision** for me against my **adversary**.'
For a **long time** the judge was **unwilling**, but **eventually**
　　　　he thought,
　　'While it is **true** that I neither **fear God** nor **respect**
　　　　any **human being**,
　　because this **widow** keeps **bothering** me
　　I shall **deliver** a just **decision** for her
　　lest she finally **come** and **strike** me.'"

Express the judge's words with resignation. His words are self-centered and clearly present the motive for his decision to grant the widow justice.

The **Lord** said, "**Pay attention** to what the **dishonest judge says**.
Will not **God** then secure the **rights** of his **chosen** ones
　　who **call out** to him **day** and **night**?
Will he be **slow** to **answer** them?
I **tell** you, he will **see to it** that **justice** is **done** for them **speedily**.
But when the **Son** of **Man comes**, will he find **faith** on **earth**?"

Pose the final question to the assembly.

---

must continue to proclaim the Word and use it to help believers remain faithful.

GOSPEL   This Sunday's Gospel is the first of two parables on prayer found in Luke 18. The second parable is next Sunday's Gospel. All of the readings today offer perspectives on persistence. If you look ahead to the concluding line of the Gospel, you will see that persisting in prayer does not simply mean praying continuously. When the Son of Man comes, he will be looking for faith.

The faith of a disciple contrasts with that of the Pharisees who sought the strict observance of legal works to showcase their faith. But the faith Jesus seeks is that which trusts in God's gracious love.

The two rhetorical questions offer an interpretation of the parable. Make sure to pause noticeably after each one to give the assembly a chance to ponder them. In contrast to the deceitful judge who, out of his own fatigue, selfishly responds to the persistent widow so she will stop bothering him, God responds constantly to the disciple's own constant prayer. God's justice, in

contrast to that of the judge, will not be slow in coming, but will come speedily.

The final question is the climax of the Gospel and provides the connection between prayer and faith. Give significant time for silence after you ask the question and before you conclude with "The Gospel of the Lord." Doing so will indicate both the serious nature of the question and the fact that we cannot easily answer it.

30TH SUNDAY IN ORDINARY TIME

Lectionary #150

READING I Sirach 35:12–14, 16–18

Sirach = SEER-ak

Use a strong voice to speak of the Lord's justice.

Switch to a compassionate tone when speaking of the weak and oppressed.

Use a warm and inviting tone when describing the Lord listening to the orphan and widow.

Increase the pace in the second half of the reading. Speak with confidence in the power of prayer.

Slow the tempo on the concluding line. Proclaim "the LORD will not delay" with confidence.

A reading from the Book of Sirach

The LORD is a **God** of **justice**,
    who knows **no favorites**.
Though not **unduly partial** toward the **weak**,
    yet he **hears** the **cry** of the **oppressed**.
The LORD is **not deaf** to the **wail** of the **orphan**,
    nor to the **widow** when she **pours** out her **complaint**.
The **one** who **serves God willingly** is **heard**;
    his **petition** reaches the **heavens**.
The **prayer** of the **lowly pierces** the clouds;
    it does **not rest** till it **reaches** its **goal**,
nor will it **withdraw** till the **Most High responds**,
    judges justly and **affirms** the **right**,
and the LORD will **not delay**.

READING I | The First Reading from Sirach, a book belonging to the collection of books known as Wisdom literature, draws our attention in the opening paragraph to the God of justice who hears the "cry of the oppressed" and the "wail of the orphan." This God listens to the complaining widow, unlike the dishonest judge from last Sunday's Gospel who only selfishly responded to the widow so she would no longer bother him.

The second paragraph continues to describe the people whose prayers the Lord hears. Notice the sentence structure shifts. Instead of the Lord being the subject of the sentence, the person who serves God is the subject of the opening sentence. The second sentence takes as its subject the "prayer of the lowly." The content of both of these sentences is very similar to the opening paragraph: God hears the prayer of those who come to him. Yet the first paragraph examines God's point of view and the second focuses on the petitioner's.

The conclusion of the reading illustrates God's response to prayer: it will be just, right, and timely. God will not delay in hearing prayers. Your call to the assembly to pray may find its greatest spur in this description of God's faithful response.

READING II | Taken from 2 Timothy's fourth and final chapter, the reading begins with Paul's recognition that his martyrdom is close at hand. Paul uses athletic imagery to express his perseverance in living a life of faith in Christ Jesus. In the face of persecution, he has stayed the course of an apostle. Just as victorious athletes and warriors received laurel wreaths as a sign of their triumph,

READING II 2 Timothy 4:6–8, 16–18

A reading from the second Letter of Saint Paul to Timothy

Beloved:
I am **already** being **poured out** like a **libation**,
    and the time of my **departure** is at **hand**.
I have **competed well**; I have **finished** the **race**;
    I have **kept** the **faith**.
From now on the **crown** of **righteousness** awaits me,
    which the **Lord**, the **just judge**,
    will **award** to me on that day, and **not only** to **me**,
    but to all who have **longed** for his **appearance**.

At my **first** defense **no one appeared** on my **behalf**,
    but **everyone deserted** me.
May it **not** be held **against** them!
But the **Lord stood by** me and **gave** me **strength**,
    so that **through** me the **proclamation** might be **completed**
    and all the **Gentiles** might **hear** it.
And I was **rescued** from the **lion's mouth**.
The **Lord** will **rescue** me from **every evil threat**
    and will bring me **safe** to his **heavenly kingdom**.
To him be **glory forever** and **ever**. **Amen**.

Slowly, with a sense that Paul has crossed the finish line.

Convey the apostle's confidence in his destiny in the Lord.

Let the apostle's cry for mercy be heard in your voice.

In praise of what the Lord has done for the apostle.

Build in strength as you move through the final lines, so as to convey our hope in the Lord.

so Paul will receive a "crown of righteousness." The Lord will present this crown to him and to others who have remained faithful.

There are eight verses from this farewell section of 2 Timothy. They begin with the crown of righteousness verse and continue beyond today's reading. In those additional verses, Paul remembers those who were helpful to him in his ministry and

those who deserted him. Yet in every circumstance, the Lord provided Paul with the strength to continue his witness to the Gospel so that it would be made available to all, including Gentiles.

The reading concludes on the strong and hopeful note of faith. The Lord defended and saved Paul in his first trial, and he will do so again and again, bringing Paul safely to the heavenly Kingdom. In this hope we live and boldly give glory to God!

GOSPEL Today's Gospel examines two attitudes of prayer: humility and righteousness. We are invited to ponder whether we resemble the tax collector or the Pharisee, and to choose a course for the future. The righteousness of the Pharisee, which is self-righteousness, not the righteousness of God, is not the attitude that belongs to a follower of Jesus. The outward signs of fasting and paying tithes that the Pharisee uses to set himself apart from the rest of humanity are sanctimonious and only show his arrogance. In

GOSPEL Luke 18:9–14

A reading from the holy Gospel according to Luke

Jesus addressed this **parable**
   to those who were **convinced** of their **own righteousness**
   and **despised everyone else**.
"Two **people** went up to the **temple** area to **pray**;
   one was a **Pharisee** and the **other** was a **tax collector**.
The **Pharisee** took up his position and spoke this prayer
      to himself,
   'O God, I thank you that I am not like the rest of humanity—
   greedy, dishonest, adulterous—or even like this tax collector.
I fast twice a week, and I pay tithes on my whole income.'
But the tax collector stood off at a distance
   and would not even raise his eyes to heaven
   but beat his breast and prayed,
   'O God, be merciful to me a sinner.'
I tell you, the latter went home justified, not the former;
   for whoever exalts himself will be humbled,
   and the one who humbles himself will be exalted."

Open in a moderate pace so that the assembly can see themselves as people who are occasionally convinced of their own righteousness.

Speak the Pharisee's words self-righteously, but don't overdramatize.

In a lower tone of voice, communicate the tax collector's humility.

Emphasize the contrasts in the explanation of the parable. Practice beforehand so as not to get tongue-tied at liturgy.

proclaiming them, he seems to express that he has no need for God and God's mercy, and therefore, no need for God's justification. He has justified himself according to Pharisaic legal standards.

The tax collector, on the other hand, knows he is a sinner and in humility asks for God's mercy. Like the widow of last Sunday's Gospel, who taught us that prayer requires a certain resolve, the tax collector shows us that humility must mark our prayer's determination.

One of the challenges you face in proclaiming today's Gospel is that most in the assembly will know that the tax collector's humility is preferable. You will want to make the Pharisee someone to whom people can relate. We all can be self-righteous at times and fail to see our need for God. Not overdrawing the contrast between the two characters will help. We need to recognize that we are probably somewhere between the Pharisee and the tax collector in our own prayer lives.

ALL SAINTS

Lectionary #667

READING I   Revelation 7:2–4, 9–14

Revelation = rev-uh-LAY-shun

Enunciate the opening words ("I, John"), which identify the first-person narrator, clearly, observing the pauses at the commas.
Maintain the strength in your voice and a moderate pace throughout this lengthy sentence.

Pause before the words "After this." Build excitement from the beginning of this section through to "They cried out . . . ."

Pause at the semicolon after "They cried out in a loud voice" and then proclaim the words "Salvation comes . . ." boldly and confidently, increasing the volume in your voice and making eye contact with the assembly.
Pause after the words of the multitude and before the words "All the angels . . . ." Then lower your voice to the usual tone you use for proclamation.

A reading from the Book of Revelation

I, **John**, saw another **angel** come up from the **East**,
   holding the **seal** of the **living God**.
He **cried out** in a loud **voice** to the four **angels**
   who were given **power** to damage the **land** and the **sea**,
   "Do **not** damage the **land** or the **sea** or the **trees**
   until we put the **seal** on the **foreheads** of the **servants**
      of our **God**."
I heard the **number** of those who had been **marked**
      with the **seal**,
   one **hundred** and forty-four **thousand** marked
   from **every** tribe of the **children** of Israel.

After **this** I had a **vision** of a great **multitude**,
   which no one could **count**,
   from every **nation**, **race**, **people**, and **tongue**.
They stood before the **throne** and before the **Lamb**,
   wearing **white robes** and holding **palm branches** in their **hands**.
They **cried out** in a loud **voice**:

   "**Salvation** comes from our **God**, who is **seated** on the **throne**,
   and from the **Lamb**."

All the angels stood around the **throne**
   and around the **elders** and the four living **creatures**.
They **prostrated** themselves before the throne,
   worshiped **God**, and exclaimed:

READING I This passage from Revelation can be difficult to understand because it is apocalyptic and highly symbolic. The two visions that comprise the reading announce the salvation of the faithful people chosen by the Lord. The first vision uses the number 144,000, or twelve squared, which represents the twelve tribes of Israel of the Old Testament; it symbolizes the new Israel, the People of God, the Church, sealed as the new community of God's chosen ones.

Whereas the first vision symbolically embraces a limited number of people who belong among God's chosen ones, the second vision ("After this . . . before the Lamb") expands the group to those of every nation, race, people, and language. Like the saints, these are people who profess that salvation comes from God and from the Lamb, Jesus, who gave his life in the blood of the Cross.

The Lord's description to John explains that the people of this multitude experienced suffering, even persecution. Through their faithfulness to God and to the Lamb, Jesus' own suffering made them pure. They have participated in his Death, and the Cross has transformed them. The white robes symbolize their transformation for a new way of life in Christ.

As you paint John's apocalyptic visions for the assembly, differentiate between the narrative lines and the spoken words of the various angels, elders, and John himself. These words reveal that God sets apart his servants for salvation. To the God of salvation, all glory is due. Focus on how you will lead the assembly to praise the Lamb on this All Saints Day.

Shift your tone again to the exclamatory tone previously used for the words of the multitude as you proclaim the words "Amen. Blessing . . . ."

Pause before "Then one . . . ." Lower your tone of voice back down to your usual tone for proclamation.

Communicate the elder's words that conclude the reading in a softer tone that is not a whisper, but that gets across the relief and contentment of those who survived distress and have been made new in the Lamb.

"**Amen. Blessing** and **glory, wisdom** and **thanksgiving,**
    honor, power, and **might**
        be to our **God forever** and **ever. Amen.**"

Then one of the **elders** spoke up and said to me,
    "**Who** are these wearing **white robes,**
        and **where** did they **come from?**"
I said to him, "My **lord, you** are the one who **knows.**"
He said to me,
    "**These** are the ones who have **survived** the time
        of great **distress;**
    they have **washed** their **robes**
        and made them **white** in the **Blood** of the **Lamb.**"

READING II   1 John 3:1–3

A reading from the first Letter of Saint John

Beloved:
See what **love** the **Father** has bestowed on **us**
    that **we** may be **called** the **children** of **God.**
Yet so we **are.**
The reason the **world** does not **know us**
    is that it did not **know him.**
Beloved, **we** are God's children **now;**
    what we **shall be** has not yet been **revealed.**
We **do know** that when it is revealed we shall be **like him,**
    for we shall **see him** as **he is.**
Everyone who has **this** hope based on **him** makes himself **pure,**
    as he is **pure.**

As you proclaim this reading, take each line as it comes, being conscious not to rush from sentence to sentence. All the lines are in the first person plural ("we" and "us") except for the final line, so making eye contact with the assembly for as much of the reading as you can do so with ease, will enhance your proclamation of the close bond between the Father and his children.

READING II   The emphasis of this passage from 1 John is the identity of faithful Christians as the "children of God." Because Christians believe and accept the sign of God's love in the gift of his Son (John 3:16), they are God's children.

At the time 1 John was written, the Christian community was divided about Jesus' identity. Some believed Jesus was not fully human; others suggested he was not fully divine. The author recounts that some members left the community on account of this dispute. In an earlier passage, he identifies those people as the antichrist (2:18–23). In contrast, those faithful, then, now, and in the future, who profess that Jesus is the Christ, belong to the family of God's children. They live in the hope that they will be like God, and this hope makes them holy now, just as God is holy.

GOSPEL   There are two versions of the Beatitudes, Matthew's account proclaimed today and Luke's account (Luke 6:20–26). Whereas in Matthew, the Beatitudes are part of the "Sermon on the Mount" and addressed to his disciples as well as the crowds, in Luke, the Beatitudes are found in the "Sermon on the Plain" and addressed only to Jesus' disciples. The first, second, fourth, and ninth Beatitudes in Matthew's account are echoed in Luke, although with slight modifications, in Luke 6:20, 21b, 21a, and 22–23, respectively.

Because Matthew adds the words "in spirit" to the first Beatitude, some scripture scholars suggest that he "spiritualizes" its teaching. Often this interpretation

A reading from the holy Gospel according to Matthew

When **Jesus** saw the **crowds**, he went **up** the **mountain**,
    and after he had sat **down**, his disciples **came** to him.
He began to **teach** them, saying:

"**Blessed** are the poor in **spirit**,
    for **theirs** is the **Kingdom** of **heaven**.
Blessed are they who **mourn**,
    for they will be **comforted**.
Blessed are the **meek**,
    for they will **inherit** the **land**.
Blessed are they who **hunger** and **thirst** for **righteousness**,
    for they will be **satisfied**.
Blessed are the **merciful**,
    for they will be **shown** mercy.
Blessed are the **clean** of **heart**,
    for they will **see God**.
Blessed are the **peacemakers**,
    for they will be called **children** of **God**.
Blessed are they who are **persecuted** for the sake
        of **righteousness**,
    for **theirs** is the **Kingdom** of **heaven**.
Blessed are **you** when they **insult** you and **persecute** you
    and utter every kind of **evil** against you **falsely**
        because of **me**.
Rejoice and be **glad**,
    for **your reward** will be **great** in **heaven**."

Proclaim the opening lines in a narrative tone of voice.

Pause after the words "began . . ." and before the beginning of the list of Beatitudes. Because the Beatitudes are parallel in structure, you will want to be careful to practice your proclamation so it does not sound "sing-song," that is, containing the same rise and fall in inflection for each Beatitude. Try pausing after each Beatitude and matching your tone of voice to the descriptive words in each one. For example, on "poor in spirit" use a slightly lighter tone of voice and on "inherit the land" use a tone that is fuller and firmer.

As you proclaim the final Beatitude, make eye contact with the assembly to emphasize the change in the pronoun from "they" to "you." Maintain eye contact through "Rejoice and be glad." Let joy be heard in your voice and a smile be seen on your face to express the happiness of the great reward in heaven!

comes with a negative connotation, suggesting that Matthew did not recognize those who were materially poor. Certainly it is true that Matthew's version of the Beatitudes is less concrete than Luke's. (In 6:21, Luke adds a Beatitude for those who are hungry now, and also includes three "woes.") Matthew's version, however, with the addition of "in spirit" might mean simply that those, no matter their economic state, rich or poor, who believe in God's presence in Jesus, belong to the Kingdom of heaven.

In writing for a predominantly Jewish Christian audience around AD 80 to 90, one of Matthew's goals was to show how the Kingdom of Heaven is open to all, Gentiles included, who acknowledge Jesus as the Son of God. Matthew's version of the Beatitudes, and especially the particular Beatitude "Blessed are the poor in spirit," serves this purpose.

The future passive tense of all but two of the Beatitudes reveals Matthew's eschatological emphasis. Happiness, which comes from living out the Beatitudes (*beatitude* in Latin means "happy"), is a reward that God will give in the future to all the faithful.

The first and tenth Beatitudes tell us that the Kingdom of Heaven is also available now to those who dedicate themselves to following Jesus and living his teachings (the crowds), even if they are not part of the inner circle of disciples, or are not canonized saints. The multitude of the faithful can draw strength and inspiration from these Beatitudes and thus grow closer to Christ (See the *Catechism of the Catholic Church*, 956).

COMMEMORATION OF ALL THE FAITHFUL DEPARTED

Lectionary #668

READING I   Wisdom 3:1–9

A reading from the Book of Wisdom

Proclaim the opening line in a confident tone of voice. Then lower the intensity as you continue.

The **souls** of the **just** are in the **hand** of **God**,
  and **no torment** shall **touch** them.
They **seemed**, in the **view** of the **foolish**, to be **dead**;
  and their **passing away** was thought an **affliction**
  and their **going forth** from us, utter **destruction**.
But **they** are in **peace**.

Communicate the line "but they are at peace" in a deliberate pace and with a gentle tone, slightly lower in volume than that used in the previous section.

For if before **men**, indeed, they be **punished**,
  yet is their **hope** full of **immortality**;
chastised a **little**, they shall be **greatly blessed**,
  because **God tried** them
  and found them **worthy** of himself.

Gradually build in intensity and confidence as you proceed through this section so that when you proclaim the concluding line of the reading the tone of your voice matches the opening line.

As **gold** in the **furnace**, he **proved** them,
  and as **sacrificial offerings** he **took** them to **himself**.
In the **time** of their **visitation** they shall **shine**,
  and shall **dart** about as **sparks** through **stubble**;
they shall **judge nations** and **rule** over **peoples**,
  and the LORD shall be their **King forever**.
Those who **trust** in him shall **understand truth**,
  and the **faithful** shall **abide** with him in **love**:
because **grace** and **mercy** are with his **holy ones**,
  and his **care** is with his **elect**.

READING I This passage from Wisdom provides four references to God's love and care for the souls of those who have died. First, the opening lines convey the belief that "the wise"—those who trust in God—can be confident that the souls of the just are now with God. "The foolish," on the other hand, who simply believe that physical death is the end of all life, do not understand the peace in which the souls of the faithful reside.

Second, while the author states that the souls of the just are at peace, the words "For though in the sight . . ." suggest some ambiguity about their state immediately after they die. Some scholars see a reference to a final purification of the elect in the slight chastisement that the souls undergo before they enter fully into the joy of life with God. However, this is not necessarily the intention of the author (see *Catechism of the Catholic Church*, 1030–1032).

The third reference is the phrase "In the time of their visitation," an allusion to God's judgment that is experienced at some point after death. Whereas the souls of the just will live with God forever, those of the wicked will never be released from the snares of suffering and death (Wisdom 2:24; 3.10–12).

Fourth and finally, the reading concludes with a statement reiterating that the Lord's constant care is always with his chosen. The statement's purpose is two-fold: it comforts those concerned for their deceased loved ones and it provides hope for those who remain on earth.

Address the assembly with the words "Brothers and sisters" by looking up and making eye contact. Continue your eye contact as you slowly and optimistically proclaim "Hope does not disappoint." Be careful not to drop your inflection too much as you proceed with the clause after the comma ("because the love of God . . . ").

"How much more then" can sound like a question, but it is a statement. Proclaim it emphatically. Do not raise the pitch of your voice when you come to the end of the statement. Do the same as you come to the second statement, "How much more, once reconciled."

READING II   Romans 5:5–11

A reading from the Letter of Saint Paul to the Romans

Brothers and **sisters:**
Hope does **not disappoint,**
    because the **love** of **God** has been **poured out** into our **hearts**
    through the **Holy Spirit** that has been **given** to us.
For **Christ,** while we were **still helpless,**
    died at the appointed time for the **ungodly.**
Indeed, only with **difficulty** does one **die** for a **just person,**
    though **perhaps** for a **good person**
    one might **even find courage** to **die.**
But **God proves** his **love** for us
    in that while we were **still sinners Christ died** for us.
How much more then, since we are **now justified** by his **Blood,**
    will we be **saved** through **him** from the **wrath.**
Indeed, if, while we were **enemies,**
    we were **reconciled** to God through the **death** of his **Son,**
    how much more, once **reconciled,**
    will we be **saved** by his **life.**
Not only **that,**
    but we **also boast** of **God** through our **Lord Jesus Christ,**
    through **whom** we have now **received reconciliation.**

Or:

 ROMANS 5. Christian hope is genuine because it comes through the Cross. Through Christ's Death on the Cross while we were still unjustified sinners, God poured out his love on us. In Christ's own sacrifice, we see God sharing his very self with us so that we might share in divine life.

Paul sees Christ's death on the Cross as the example par excellence of God's love. For Paul it is proof of God's tremendous love for us because it occurred while we were still "ungodly." Paul makes his argument in steps by first explaining that it would be hard to die, even for a just and righteous person. For a good person, it would still not be easy, but one could perhaps find the strength to do so. The climax of Paul's argument is his statement about the totally free and gratuitous nature of Christ's death. Christ died, not on behalf of a just person or a good person, but on behalf of his enemies, those who were still sinful. Through his Death, Christ offered reconciliation, a reunification of sinners with God. According to Paul, by reconciling us to himself, Christ saved those who were God's enemies.

On this day when we commemorate the souls of all the faithful departed, we rejoice and boast in the reconciliation Christ offers. We joyfully profess that one day we will all meet together in Christ, and live reconciled with our brothers and sisters for ever. (See *Order of Christian Funerals,* 175.)

READING II   Romans 6:3–9

A reading from the Letter of Saint Paul to the Romans

Brothers and **sisters:**
Are you **unaware** that **we** who were **baptized** into **Christ Jesus**
    were **baptized** into his **death?**
We were indeed **buried** with him through **baptism** into **death,**
    so **that,** just as **Christ** was **raised** from the **dead**
    by the **glory** of the **Father,**
    we **too** might **live** in **newness of life.**

For if we have **grown** into **union** with him through a **death**
    like his,
    we shall also be **united** with him in the **resurrection.**
We know that our **old** self was **crucified** with him,
    so that our **sinful body** might be **done away** with,
    that we might **no longer** be in **slavery** to **sin.**
For a **dead** person has been **absolved** from sin.
If, then, we have **died** with **Christ,**
    we **believe** that we shall also **live** with him.
We know that **Christ, raised** from the **dead, dies** no **more;**
    death no longer has **power** over **him.**

Address the opening greeting directly to the members of the assembly by looking up and making eye contact with them. Because the reading is entirely in the first person plural ("we"), strive to make as much eye contact with the assembly as you can without disrupting the flow of your proclamation.

Let the confidence of faith be heard in your proclamation of the conditional statement ("If, then, we have died . . .") through to the end of the reading. Keep your tone strong through the final word. Then pause before saying, "The Word of the Lord."

ROMANS 6. Paul wrote this passage from Romans as a response to a question posed by those who thought the Gospel promoted moral leniency (Romans 3:5–8, 23–24). The question was this: Why not do evil if God's gift of justification comes to those who sin? In his response, Paul shows the foundation Baptism gives for a new relationship with Christ.

In Baptism, Christians are baptized "into Christ" (eis Christon). This phrase denotes that in Baptism Christ incorporates us into his person so that we participate in his Death and Resurrection.

Because Christ's Death was death to sin, our unity with him in his Death means that our old, sinful body is washed clean. Our unity with Christ in his Resurrection, means that we experience new life in him.

Being freed from sin, then, the baptized person participates in the new life brought through Christ's Resurrection. It is this life in Christ that now has power and control. Paul believes this new life impels the Christian to live uprightly in relation to God and neighbor. Thus, moral laxity ceases to be an option. While ethical behavior for the old self might not have

any qualifiers, for the new self it does. Christians must see to it that sin, which causes them to give in to destructive human desires, does not rule their bodies.

Paul concludes today's passage with a statement of belief in our future life with Christ. For him, our life on earth as persons baptized into Christ's Death and Resurrection prepares us for the future. If our future life in Christ interests us, we must do our best now to live according to our new selves—baptized members of the Body of Christ.

A reading from the holy Gospel according to John

Jesus said to the crowds:
"Everything that the Father gives me will come to me,
    and I will not reject anyone who comes to me,
    because I came down from heaven not to do my own will
    but the will of the one who sent me.
And this is the will of the one who sent me,
    that I should not lose anything of what he gave me,
    but that I should raise it on the last day.
For this is the will of my Father,
    that everyone who sees the Son and believes in him
    may have eternal life,
    and I shall raise him on the last day."

The first sentence is lengthy. Pausing at the commas, and adding a minor pause after the words "own will," will help make for a smooth and understandable proclamation.

Communicate the reassuring line, "that I should not lose . . ." with hope in your voice, making eye contact with the assembly to convey that Jesus will not lose them.

Proclaim this climactic line of the Gospel with unwavering strength.

GOSPEL As today's passage begins, we see Jesus teaching the crowds that he will not turn away anyone who approaches him. Earlier in John's account, "the Jews" had cast out from the synagogue those who believed in Jesus (9:34–35). Jesus, however, welcomes them, not simply of his own accord, but on behalf of the Father. Jesus recognizes that just as the Father sent him, all who come to him also come from the Father. On the last day, then, Jesus will raise them up to be one with the Father so that they might share in eternal life.

The Eucharist in which the faithful departed have participated anticipates the gift of eternal life. Through their reception of the bread of life, they professed their belief in Jesus. At their death, their "soul goes to meet God, while awaiting its reunion with its glorified body" on "the last day" when Christ comes again and those who died in Christ will rise (*Catechism of the Catholic Church,* 997, 1001). The last verse of the Gospel explains the hope of believers for themselves and their faithful departed loved ones. As you prepare to proclaim this Gospel during the week, reflect on how your own life gives evidence of this hope. A confident, faith-filled proclamation will help strengthen the faith of others and lead them to greater hope. We are all living in the hope of the Father's will for our eternal life through his Son's Resurrection.

31ST SUNDAY IN ORDINARY TIME

Lectionary #153

READING I   Wisdom 11:22—12:2

A reading from the Book of Wisdom

In a compassionate tone befitting the Lord's mercy.

Contrast "love" and "loathe" in your tone of voice.

Emphasize the Lord's authorship of life. Allow the assembly a few seconds to come to the answer of the rhetorical question: a thing could not remain without the Lord having called it forth.

The emphasis is not on the Lord's rebuke, but on his compassionate reminder of the people's sins.

End with a bold call to believe in the Lord.

Before the LORD the whole **universe** is as a **grain**
     from a **balance**
  or a **drop** of morning **dew** come down upon the **earth.**
But **you** have **mercy** on **all,** because you can **do all things;**
  and you **overlook** people's **sins** that they may **repent.**
For you **love all** things that **are**
  and **loathe nothing** that you have **made;**
  for what you **hated,** you would not have **fashioned.**
And how could a thing **remain,** unless **you willed** it;
  or be **preserved,** had it not been **called forth** by **you?**
But you **spare** all things, because they are **yours,**
     O LORD and **lover** of **souls,**
  for your **imperishable spirit** is in **all** things!
Therefore you **rebuke offenders little** by **little,**
     warn them and **remind** them of the **sins**
        they are **committing,**
     that they may **abandon** their **wickedness** and **believe**
        in **you, O** LORD!

READING I Even the smallness of the universe compared to God's expansive power does not prevent God from loving all things. This simple message stands at the heart of today's First Reading. Such generous love is difficult for human beings to imagine, since we love within the limits of humanity. In our best attempts at love, sin still creeps in and often makes human love conditional, rather than unconditional.

The message of Wisdom's author couldn't be clearer in today's passage. God's love, exemplified by God's constant mercy,

will never cease. God hates nothing he has made. Everything that is, belongs to God—willed by God from the beginning. God shows mercy to all because God's "imperishable spirit" is in everything. The spirit referred to here is either God's life breathed into creatures at creation or divine Wisdom, representative of God's presence in all that God created. Through this spirit, God gently calls sinners back to faith.

The many ways in which this reading asserts God's merciful love provide you with excellent opportunities to communicate that love to the assembly. There is

great power in God's love, but it is not strength you are after in the proclamation of this reading. Emphasize the beauty and constancy of God's love by keeping an even pace throughout your proclamation and using a tempered, reassuring tone throughout.

READING II For the next three Sundays, the Second Reading comes from 2 Thessalonians. In this letter, Paul writes to encourage the Thessalonians to resist false prophecy regarding the parousia, or second coming of Christ, and

Thessalonians = thes-uh-LOH-nee-uhnz

Clearly communicate the two prayer intentions (that God make you worthy of his call and that the name of our Lord Jesus may be glorified in you).

Put Paul's request in the second half of the reading directly to the assembly. Do so confidently as you tell your brothers and sisters not to be disturbed.

READING II 2 Thessalonians 1:11—2:2

A reading from the second Letter of Saint Paul to the Thessalonians

Brothers and sisters:
We **always pray** for you,
    that our **God** may make you **worthy** of his **calling**
    and powerfully bring to **fulfillment every** good **purpose**
    and **every effort** of **faith**,
    that the **name** of our **Lord Jesus** may be **glorified** in **you**,
    and **you** in **him**,
    in accord with the **grace** of our **God** and **Lord Jesus Christ**.

We **ask** you, **brothers** and **sisters**,
    with regard to the **coming** of our **Lord Jesus Christ**
    and our **assembling** with him,
    not to be **shaken** out of your **minds** suddenly, or to be **alarmed**
    either by a "**spirit**," or by an **oral statement**,
    or by a **letter allegedly** from **us**
    to the **effect** that the **day** of the **Lord** is at **hand**.

to endure patiently until the day of the Lord arrives.

Today's passage begins with Paul's prayer for the Thessalonian community found at the end of the letter's first chapter. In this heartfelt prayer, Paul emphasizes God's grace now working in the Thessalonians so that the Lord Jesus is glorified in them and they are glorified in him. This shared glorification occurs because of the grace of God active in Jesus Christ.

The second paragraph of the reading focuses on the parousia. Paul asks the

Thessalonians not to panic because of news, received either from false teachings, spoken words, or a letter falsely attributed to him, predicting that the day of the Lord is imminent. "Remain calm" is Paul's message to his brothers and sisters in faith. Christ's Second Coming will occur in the future at a time known only to the Father, and for Paul's audience, thought to be imminent. It will complete the life of faith when Christ will assemble with those judged to be faithful.

With patience and hope, communicate to the assembly Paul's message of

calm, so that they can find ways to live faithfully in this interim of unknown duration until Christ comes again. Even now, living by the Gospel constitutes a life with and in God's grace.

GOSPEL The opening paragraph sets the scene for this well-known gospel passage. Zacchaeus, whose name literally means "clean," was not highly regarded because of his status as a tax collector, yet he was rich. The story will not disparage him for his wealth, but rather will show how followers of

GOSPEL Luke 19:1–10

A reading from the holy Gospel according to Luke

At that **time**, **Jesus** came to **Jericho** and intended
     to pass **through** the town.
Now a **man** there named **Zacchaeus**,
     who was a chief **tax** collector and also a **wealthy** man,
     was seeking to **see who Jesus was**;
     but he could **not see** him because of the **crowd**,
     for he was **short** in **stature**.
So he **ran** ahead and **climbed** a **sycamore** tree in order to **see Jesus**,
     who was about to **pass** that **way**.
When he **reached** the place, **Jesus looked** up and said,
     "**Zacchaeus**, come down **quickly**,
     for **today** I **must stay** at your **house**."
And he **came** down **quickly** and received him with **joy**.
When they **all saw** this, they began to **grumble**, saying,
     "He has **gone** to **stay** at the **house** of a **sinner**."
But **Zacchaeus stood** there and said to the **Lord**,
     "**Behold**, **half** of my **possessions, Lord**, I shall **give** to the **poor**,
     and if I have **extorted anything** from **anyone**
     I shall **repay** it **four times over**."
And **Jesus** said to him,
     "**Today salvation** has come to this **house**
     because **this** man **too** is a **descendant** of **Abraham**.
For the **Son** of **Man** has come to **seek**
     and to **save** what was **lost**."

Jericho = JAYR-ih-koh

Zacchaeus = zuh-KEE-uhs
Take your time as you set the scene of this beloved narrative.

Emphasize the words that are so important to Luke: "today" and "must."

Complaining.

Proclaim Zacchaeus's generosity in an expansive, broad tone. He is changed and commits himself to a new way of life.

Emphasize "Today" again. Proclaim both sentences of Jesus' words with the same conviction and volume. Keep the momentum through both lines.

Jesus can correctly manage money and possessions by sharing them with the poor.

As the story progresses, so does its energy and momentum. Zacchaeus puts forth energetic efforts to see Jesus—running ahead and climbing a tree. Jesus matches Zacchaeus' enthusiasm by instructing him to descend just as quickly as he ascended. The use of the word "today" in Jesus' command, as well as at the end of the passage, discloses the present reality of salvation offered in the person of Jesus and available now to those who come to him.

Zacchaeus's joy as he receives Jesus into his home continues the momentum of the passage. The crowds' grumbling because Jesus has gone to eat at the home of one whom they believe to be a sinner does not deter the pace of the story. Whether Zacchaeus thought himself to be or sinner or not is immaterial as the story continues with his decision to give half of his possessions to the poor and return fourfold anything he has extorted. His words express a commitment to a new life, a life changed because he has found Jesus. Named now as a descendant of

Abraham, Zacchaeus is a sign that salvation will come through Israel. The Son of Man who sought him also saved him, whether or not he knew he was a lost sinner. Perhaps Zacchaeus did know, since he did seek Jesus. In Zacchaeus's seeking, he opened himself to a new way of life. In Jesus' seeking, Zacchaeus found the wholeness of a new life. Both contain the possibilities of seeking and saving that you proclaim to the assembly today.

32ND SUNDAY IN ORDINARY TIME

Lectionary #156

READING I 2 Maccabees 7:1–2, 9–14

Maccabees = MAK-uh-beez

A reading from the second Book of Maccabees

It **happened** that **seven brothers** with their **mother** were **arrested**
and **tortured** with **whips** and **scourges** by the **king**,
to **force** them to eat **pork** in **violation** of **God's law**.
One of the brothers, **speaking** for the **others**, said:

Speak the brother's words resolutely.

"**What** do you **expect** to **achieve** by **questioning** us?
We are **ready** to **die** rather than **transgress** the **laws**
of our **ancestors**."

At the point of **death** he said:

fiend = feend

Begin in an accusatory tone, then switch to a confident tone. "He" refers to the second brother.

"You **accursed fiend**, you are **depriving** us of this **present life**,
but the **King** of the **world** will **raise** us up to **live again forever**.
It is for **his** laws that we are **dying**."

After him the **third** suffered their cruel **sport**.
He put out his tongue **at once** when told to do so,
and **bravely** held out his **hands**, as he spoke these noble **words**:

Courageously, with the same conviction as the second brother spoke.

"It was from **Heaven** that I received these;
for the **sake** of his **laws** I **disdain** them;
from **him** I **hope** to **receive** them **again**."
Even the **king** and his **attendants marveled**
at the young man's **courage**,
because he regarded his **sufferings** as **nothing**.

With astonishment.

After he had **died**,
they **tortured** and **maltreated** the **fourth** brother
in the **same** way.

READING I This is the only time in the three-year Lectionary cycle that the First Reading comes from 2 Maccabees. We hear this passage as the liturgical year draws to a close because of its emphasis on resurrection. Today's passage describes the martyrdom of four brothers whom the king tortured, along with their mother, for refusing to disobey God's Law and eat pork.

As you prepare to proclaim this passage, read the entire account of the seven brothers and the mother. The reading only speaks about four of the brothers, but all seven and the mother eventually die at the hands of the king. Having witnessed the deaths of her seven sons all in one day, she speaks words that reflect her hope in the Lord. She recognizes that the Lord gave the breath of life to her sons and will mercifully give it back to them because they remained faithful to God's Law.

Emphasize the different, but interrelated, themes of the brothers' words when you proclaim them. The second brother speaks of the King of the world raising them to eternal life. Belief in the resurrection was not widespread, even at the time of Jesus. This is one of the few places in the Old Testament where we find a clear reference. The second brother reiterates the first brother's point that faithfulness to God's Law is what is at issue. For that, he, too, will die.

The third brother tells his torturers that he received his hands from God. He willingly gives them up, because he trusts that God will return them to him. Notice that the words of the third brother stress not what he is doing (giving up his hands), but what God will do in return for his suffering.

Proclaim the fourth brother's words confidently. They are the basis of our faith, too. End seriously and sternly as you convey the consequence the king faces.

When **he** was **near death**, he said,
  "It is my **choice** to **die** at the **hands** of **men**
   with the **hope God** gives of being **raised up** by him;
   but for **you**, there will be **no resurrection** to **life**."

READING II 2 Thessalonians 2:16—3:5

Thessalonians = thes-uh-LOH-nee-uhnz

**A reading from the second Letter of Saint Paul
  to the Thessalonians**

Brothers and **sisters**:
May our **Lord Jesus Christ himself** and **God** our **Father**,
  who has **loved** us and **given** us **everlasting encouragement**
  and **good hope** through his **grace**,
  encourage your **hearts** and **strengthen** them
    in every **good deed** and **word**.

Proclaim prayerfully, in an encouraging manner.

Finally, **brothers** and **sisters**, **pray** for us,
  so that the **word** of the **Lord** may speed **forward** and be **glorified**,
  as it did among **you**,
  and that we may be **delivered** from **perverse** and **wicked people**,
  for **not all** have **faith**.

Direct the instruction to pray to the assembly. Lower your tone as you express the reality that not all people have faith.

But the Lord **is faithful**;
  he will **strengthen** you and **guard** you from the **evil one**.

Switch to a confident tone as you proclaim the Lord's faithfulness.

We are **confident** of **you** in the **Lord** that what **we instruct you**,
  you are **doing** and will **continue** to do.
May the **Lord direct your hearts** to the **love** of **God**
  and to the **endurance** of **Christ**.

Offer Paul's concluding prayer with warmth in your voice.

The fourth brother confidently expresses his hope that God will raise him up, and he also names the consequence of the king's failure to follow God's Law. The king will not be eligible for resurrection.

READING II Paul's words to the Thessalonians that you proclaim today affirm and encourage them in the most powerful form: prayer. In this beautiful benediction, Paul uses the phrase "good hope" to evoke Christ's second coming. Paul's prayer, then, is for the Thessalonians to remain true to their faith

until the Lord comes again. When confronted with those who do not believe, they are to be strengthened by the "good hope" of grace that Jesus Christ will once again be with them and they with him.

Paul knows that he and his partners who preach the Gospel are also in need of prayer. Since the Thessalonians are already living the Gospel, he uses their example as the basis for the prayer he requests of them. The Thessalonians are to pray that Paul and his coworkers keep their distance from those who do not have faith and would draw them away from their

work. With this request, Paul is also reminding the Thessalonians of the danger they face in their own midst.

The final section of the reading emphasizes the Lord's fidelity to his people. Under the Lord's direction, their hearts will know the love of God. Faced with the wickedness around them, they will endure as Christ did—and endure confidently together in God's love until the parousia.

GOSPEL Jesus has just entered Jerusalem and is teaching in the temple area when the Sadducees

GOSPEL Luke 20:27–38

A reading from the holy Gospel according to Luke

Sadducees = SAD-yoo-seez

Some **Sadducees**, those who **deny** that there is a **resurrection**,
    came **forward** and put this **question** to Jesus, saying,
    "**Teacher**, **Moses** wrote for us,
    *If someone's **brother** dies leaving a **wife** but **no child**,*
    *his **brother** must **take** the wife*
    *and raise up **descendants** for his brother.*
Now there were **seven** brothers;
    the **first** married a **woman** but **died childless**.
Then the **second** and the **third** married her,
    and likewise all the **seven died childless**.
Finally the **woman also** died.
Now at the **resurrection** whose **wife** will **that woman be**?
For **all seven** had been **married** to her."
Jesus said to them,
    "The **children** of **this age marry** and **remarry**;
    but those who are **deemed worthy** to **attain** to the **coming age**
    and to the **resurrection** of the **dead**
    neither marry nor are **given** in **marriage**.
They can no longer **die**,
    for they are **like angels**;
    and they are the **children** of **God**
    because **they** are the **ones** who will **rise**.
That the **dead will rise**
    even **Moses** made known in the **passage** about the **bush**,
    when he called out '**Lord**,'
    the **God** of **Abraham**, the **God** of **Isaac**, and the **God** of **Jacob**;
    and he is not **God** of the **dead**, but of the **living**,
    for to **him all** are **alive**."

[Shorter: Luke 20:27, 34–38]

Take your time asking the Sadducees' question so the assembly will have time to realize how off-base it is.

Use a lighter tone to convey the beautiful images of the ones who no longer die.

Take your time proclaiming Jesus' words about God which conclude the reading. Express them strongly to convey hope.

question him. The question the Sadducees pose to Jesus in this reading is the third in a series of three. By asking whose wife a childless widow will be at the resurrection, they intend to show Jesus that belief in the resurrection is false. The basis of the Sadducees' question, the Law of levirate marriage found in Deuteronomy 25:5–10, is logical for this group of people who only believe in the authority of the Pentateuch (Torah), but it makes a mockery of belief in the resurrection of the dead.

Jesus' reply to the Sadducees' question turns the tables on the very foundation upon which they ask the question. Referring to Exodus 3:2, 6, verses with which the Sadducees would be familiar, Jesus explains that rising to life is not about whether one has married or remarried or had children in this world; rather it is about the children of God believing in the living God of Abraham, Isaac, and Jacob. In this God who created us, we are all alive!

Confidently proclaim our hope in the living God to the assembly as we draw ever closer to the end of the liturgical year. Emphasize the references to the "resurrection of the dead." This will help remind the assembly that as Christians, we proclaim our belief in the resurrection every time we celebrate the liturgy.

33RD SUNDAY IN ORDINARY TIME

Lectionary #159

READING I   Malachi 3:19–20a

Malachi = MAL-uh-kī

Seriously and ominously, in a dark tone of voice.

A reading from the Book of the Prophet Malachi

> **Lo**, the day is **coming**, **blazing** like an **oven**,
>   when all the **proud** and all **evildoers** will be **stubble**,
> and the **day** that is **coming** will set them on **fire**,
>   leaving them **neither root nor branch**,
>   says the LORD of **hosts**.
> But for **you** who **fear** my **name**, there will **arise**
>   the **sun** of **justice** with its **healing rays**.

Lighten your tone of voice to convey the hope of the Lord's promise.

READING II   2 Thessalonians 3:7–12

Thessalonians = thes-uh-LOH-nee-uhnz

**A reading from the second Letter of Saint Paul
    to the Thessalonians**

Brothers and **sisters:**
You **know** how one must **imitate** us.
For we did **not act** in a **disorderly** way **among** you,
    nor did we eat **food** received **free** from **anyone**.
On the **contrary**, in **toil** and **drudgery**, **night** and **day**
    we **worked**, so as not to **burden any** of you.

Make eye contact on the opening line.

Proclaim as a fact, not in a defensive tone.

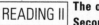 In the time of Malachi, there were people who did evil to get ahead of others in society. People were pessimistic because the evildoers prospered from the bad choices they made. From the perspective of the people who were doing good and following God's Law, the world's order appeared upside down. The prophet realizes this and speaks God's word of assurance to them. He also warns the evildoers that no matter how hard they dig in their heels or extend their arms in greed, the fire will scorch their roots and branches, the means by which wickedness takes hold of all that is around them.

A different destiny, however, awaits those who remain faithful to God. The "sun of justice" will heal the oppression they have experienced. Christians might well see this phrase in relation to Jesus, through whom redemption's healing comes. Yet this modest reference simply reminds us of the warmth of the sun's rays extending from the sky to reach creation. These natural healing rays symbolize God's affection and love for his people who, having survived oppression by remaining faithful, now bask in the light of divine justice.

READING II The obvious theme of the Second Reading is our imitation of Paul and his colleagues who have worked tirelessly to preach the Gospel among the Thessalonians. Through their own labor, Paul and his coworkers supported themselves as they preached the

Emphasize "imitate us." The phrase repeats the point in the opening line.

Not that we do not **have** the **right**.
Rather, we wanted to **present** ourselves as a **model** for you,
   so that you might **imitate** us.
In **fact**, when we were **with** you,
   we **instructed** you that if **anyone** was **unwilling** to work,
   neither should that one **eat**.
We hear that some **are conducting** themselves among you
      in a **disorderly** way,
   by not keeping **busy** but **minding** the **business** of **others**.
Such people we **instruct** and **urge** in the **Lord Jesus Christ**
      to **work quietly**
   and to **eat** their **own food**.

Speak clearly and at a slower pace to get across the play on words. Conclude in a serious tone.

GOSPEL Luke 21:5–19

A reading from the holy Gospel according to Luke

While **some** people were speaking about
   how the **temple** was adorned with **costly stones**
      and **votive offerings**,
   Jesus said, "**All** that you **see** here—
   the days will **come** when there will **not** be **left**
   a **stone** upon **another stone** that will not be **thrown down**."

Try looking around the physical space of the church as you speak Jesus' line, "All that you see here—."

Then they **asked** him,
"**Teacher**, **when** will this **happen**?
And what **sign** will there be when **all** these things
      are **about** to **happen**?"

Allow a bit of anxiety to be heard as you ask the people's questions.

Gospel. They did not even eat free food, which, Paul acknowledges, they surely could have. Paul tells the Thessalonians straightforwardly that they are to imitate his example as they await the return of the Lord Jesus Christ. We are to do the same.

Paul 's statement that he and his colleagues did not act in a "disorderly way" contrasts their behavior with that of others in the community who were acting "disorderly." The Greek word for "disorderly," *ataktoi,* points to Paul's criticism of idle behavior, but is also more expansive in

its meaning. In the context of this letter, it refers to any behavior that would disrupt the proclamation and living out of the Gospel, particularly falsely prophesying that the day of the Lord is actually at hand. (See 2 Thessalonians 2:1–4.) Those who taught this in Paul's name caused alarm in the community, and the apostle is now trying to help the community reorder itself.

The passage concludes with what we today would call advice for the "busybody." They should find solitary work and eat their own food. In this, they will be following Paul's example.

GOSPEL   Today's reading is part of Jesus' eschatological discourse in the Gospel according to Luke. The passage begins with Jesus' ruminations on the destruction of Jerusalem. (Recall that the Evangelist, Luke, wrote after the destruction of the Temple in AD 70.) In response to Jesus' prediction of the Temple's destruction, the disciples want to know when this will happen. They request a sign that the destruction is imminent, perhaps so they can prepare themselves in advance.

He **answered**,
"**See** that you not be **deceived**,
    for **many** will come in my **name**, saying,
    '**I** am **he**,' and 'The **time** has **come**.'
Do **not follow** them!
When you hear of **wars** and **insurrections**,
    do **not** be **terrified**; for such things **must** happen **first**,
    but it will not **immediately** be the **end**."
Then he said to them,
"**Nation** will **rise** against **nation**, and **kingdom** against **kingdom**.
There will be **powerful earthquakes**, **famines**, and **plagues**
    from **place** to **place**;
    and **awesome sights** and **mighty signs** will come from **the sky**.

"**Before** all this **happens**, **however**,
    they will **seize** and **persecute** you,
    they will **hand you over** to the **synagogues** and to **prisons**,
    and they will have you **led** before **kings** and **governors**
    because of **my name**.
It will **lead** to your giving **testimony**.
Remember, you are **not** to **prepare** your defense **beforehand**,
    for I **myself** shall **give** you a **wisdom** in **speaking**
    that **all** your **adversaries** will be **powerless** to **resist** or **refute**.
You will even be **handed over** by **parents**, **brothers**,
        relatives and **friends**,
    and they will put **some** of you to **death**.
You will be **hated** by **all** because of my **name**,
    but not a **hair** on your **head** will be **destroyed**.
By your **perseverance** you will **secure** your **lives**."

Emphatically state, "Do not follow them!"

Emphasize the reason for the people being led before the rulers.

Deliver as a teacher instructing his students. The lesson is trust. Let it be heard in your voice.

The strong emotion of "hate" should be overcome by an even stronger proclamation of the security found in Jesus and his care for his followers.

Jesus' response gives them more than they ask for! He lists not just one sign of the end times, but many. From wars to insurrections to nations and kingdoms turning against each other to cosmic disasters, "awesome sights" and "mighty signs" that will come from the sky, disciples of Jesus will witness many events as the prelude to the eschaton.

The prelude to the prelude, Jesus tells his disciples, will be their own persecution, imprisonment, and trial before kings and governors. Having warned the disciples that the rulers will require their testimony, Jesus knows they will want to prepare it ahead of time. But he preempts their question about what they should say at trial, and assures the disciples that when the time comes, he will give them wisdom to speak the appropriate words. The power of his divine wisdom will render the persecutors powerless.

The final paragraph describes the extent of the persecution disciples will experience: immediate family members and relatives will participate, even to the point of putting disciples to death. The fate of the disciples for testifying to their faith in Jesus parallels his own impending fate. That they will not experience even the slightest harm is a look forward at their life through the lens of Jesus' Resurrection. This hopeful conclusion carries us through to the celebration of the solemnity of Christ the King, which draws the liturgical year to a close next Sunday.

OUR LORD JESUS CHRIST, KING OF THE UNIVERSE

Lectionary #162

READING I   2 Samuel 5:1–3

A reading from the second Book of Samuel

In those days, **all** the **tribes** of **Israel** came to **David**
      in **Hebron** and said:
   "**Here** we **are**, **your bone** and **your flesh**.
In days **past**, when **Saul** was our **king**,
   it was **you** who led the **Israelites out** and brought them **back**.
And the LORD said to you,
   '**You** shall **shepherd** my **people Israel**
   and shall be **commander** of **Israel**.'"
When all the **elders** of **Israel came** to **David** in **Hebron**,
   King David made an **agreement** with them there
      before the LORD,
   and they **anointed** him **king** of **Israel**.

Hebron = HEB-ruhn

Saul = sawl

Proclaim David's accomplishment and the fact that the Lord called him to shepherd Israel with confidence.

Use a solemn tone as you proclaim David's agreement with the elders and his anointing.

READING I In this reading, the tribes of Israel gather at Hebron and recall that the Lord appointed David to care for the people pastorally and to be their commander. By enumerating the ways he guided the Israelite community in the past, the tribes affirmed to David his leadership capability. Now as the reading continues, the elders approach the king at the same spot, Hebron. That David made an agreement with them seems to imply that some negotiation took place. Observe that the writer gives David the title "King"

even before mentioning his anointing by the elders.

As you prepare this reading, it would be helpful to read through 2 Samuel 7:8–16. These verses contain the Lord's vision to David communicated by the prophet Nathan. The vision culminates in the Lord's promise to raise up an heir to David from his own lineage when he rests with his ancestors. The Lord will be like a father to this heir and he will be like a son to the Lord. Christians see Jesus as the fulfillment of this messianic prophecy. In David,

we have a pastoral leader who foreshadows Christ's own leadership.

READING II Today's Second Reading is the Christ hymn, perhaps the best-known passage from Colossians. This hymn also served as the Second Reading back on the Fifteenth Sunday in Ordinary Time. Today, three additional verses introduce the hymn. They speak of the redemption brought by the Father, who has led us into his beloved Son's Kingdom where we live as God's redeemed and forgiven people.

READING II   Colossians 1:12–20

Colossians = kuh-LOSH-uhnz

Open strongly and boldly.

Lower your tone of voice as you summarize what the Father has done.

Use the parallel openings of the verses ("He is") as a guide to your proclamation.

Slow your pace and speak with contentment in your voice as you draw the hymn to a conclusion.

A reading from the Letter of Saint Paul to the Colossians

Brothers and **sisters:**
Let us give **thanks** to the **Father,**
   who has made you **fit** to **share**
   in the **inheritance** of the **holy ones** in **light.**
He **delivered us** from the **power** of **darkness**
   and **transferred us** to the **kingdom** of his **beloved Son,**
   in whom we have **redemption**, the **forgiveness** of **sins.**

> He is the **image** of the **invisible God,**
>   the **firstborn** of **all creation.**
> For in **him** were **created** all things in **heaven** and on **earth,**
>   the **visible** and the **invisible,**
>   whether **thrones** or **dominions** or **principalities** or **powers;**
>   **all** things were **created through him** and **for him.**
> He is **before all** things,
>   and **in him all things** hold **together.**
> **He** is the **head** of the **body,** the **church.**
> **He** is the **beginning,** the **firstborn** from the **dead,**
>   that in **all** things he **himself** might be **preeminent.**
> For in **him all** the **fullness** was **pleased** to **dwell,**
>   and **through** him to **reconcile** all **things** for him,
>   making **peace** by the **blood** of his **cross**
>   through him, whether those on **earth** or those in **heaven.**

The liturgical hymn itself has two sections. The first describes Christ's role in creation. He is the firstborn of creation on the basis of his Resurrection from the dead. Everything in heaven and on earth was created in him. Since the author includes the principalities and powers as part of all that was created in Christ and now oriented toward him, there remains no question as to their ordering in relation to Christ. Christ himself has touched everything with his divinity, including the principalities to which false teachers were ascribing divine power apart from Christ.

The second part of the hymn details Christ's redemptive role. Phrases from the first part are repeated in order to emphasize Christ's relationship to the created world. There is also a statement of Christ's relationship to the Church which, for the first time in the New Testament, identifies him as the head of the body. Church *(ekklēsia)* here refers to the universal Church, in contrast to Paul's use of the word in earlier letters to denote local communities.

The reconciliation Christ brings is also a major theme of the second section of the hymn. Reconciliation comes through him, in him, and is for him. The peace which is the result of reconciliation comes from Christ's sacrifice on the Cross. For those in the churches in Colossae and the surrounding area, the hymn at this point is eminently practical. Believers need reconciliation in the face of false teachers. Through the Cross, Christ truly is the forgiving and reconciling Lord of all on earth and in heaven. Christ is not King for himself, but for us, for the sake of our redemption. This is the King we celebrate with contentment and joy today. To God we give thanks for the kingship of his Son!

GOSPEL Luke 23:35–43

A reading from the holy Gospel according to Luke

The rulers **sneered** at Jesus and said,
   "He **saved others**, let him **save himself**
   if he is the **chosen** one, the **Christ** of **God**."
Even the **soldiers** jeered at him.
As they **approached** to offer him **wine** they called out,
   "If **you** are **King** of the Jews, **save** yourself."
Above him there was an **inscription** that read,
   "**This** is the **King** of the Jews."

Now **one** of the **criminals** hanging there **reviled** Jesus, saying,
   "Are **you** not the **Christ**?
Save yourself and **us**."
The **other**, however, **rebuking** him, said in **reply**,
   "Have **you** no **fear** of **God**,
   for you are **subject** to the **same condemnation**?
And **indeed**, **we** have been **condemned justly**,
   for the **sentence** we **received corresponds** to our **crimes**,
   but **this** man has done **nothing** criminal."
Then he said,
   "**Jesus**, **remember** me when you **come** into your **kingdom**."
He **replied** to him,
   "**Amen**, I **say** to **you**,
   today you will be with **me** in **Paradise**."

Use a mocking tone.

The question is disparaging. Let this be heard in your voice.

Contrast the words of the second criminal with those of the first. Start with an admonishing tone and then switch to a teacher-like tone as he explains their just condemnation. Finally, switch to a tone of humility as you speak his words to Jesus. It is a polite request, a prayer.

Speak Jesus' words of reply solemnly and with confidence, expressing the present reality of the Kingdom.

GOSPEL "The people stood by and watched." This Lucan observation occurs in the first half of verse 35, but the Lectionary passage omits the line. Its importance lies in the fact that it contrasts the people's reaction to that of the rulers, soldiers, and the "bad" criminal, all of whom scoff at and mock Jesus. The people's contemplative silence stands in marked contrast to the ironic sarcasm of those with decreasing levels of societal authority. The people (laos) have yet to voice a judgment about Jesus' identity, while the negative statements of those who jeer at Jesus all paradoxically contain a true christological confession. Jesus is "the Christ of God," "the King of the Jews," and "the Christ."

Yet it is one of the criminals, the one often referred to as the "good" criminal, who offers the Gospel's final confession when he begins his request by calling Jesus by his name. The crucifixion scene with the good criminal is uniquely Lucan and consistent with his emphasis on Jesus as the forgiving Savior who reaches out and embraces sinners.

The Gospel closes with Jesus solemnly responding to the good criminal. The use of the word "today" speaks of the present reality—the good criminal now resides in Paradise. Paradise for the good criminal and for us is neither a reality apart from Jesus nor completely in the future. In Paradise—in the Kingdom of God—we will live forever with Jesus, united with our compassionate King. Our Paradise begins today.